Social Sciences in Sport

Joseph Maguire, PhD

Loughborough University, United Kingdom

Editor

Human Kinetics

Library of Congress Cataloging-in-Publication Data

Maguire, Joseph A., 1956-
  Social sciences in sport / Joseph Maguire, PhD.
    pages cm
  Includes bibliographical references and index.
  1. Sports--Sociological aspects. 2. Sports--Anthropological aspects. 3. Sports--Psychological aspects. 4. Social sciences. I. Title.
  GV706.5M342 2014
  306.4'83--dc23
                               2013004170
  ISBN-10: 0-7360-8958-6
  ISBN-13: 978-0-7360-8958-6

Acquisitions Editor: Myles Schrag; **Developmental Editor:** Christine M. Drews; **Assistant Editors:** Amy Akin, Casey A. Gentis, Melissa J. Zavala, and Anne Mrozek; **Copyeditor:** Tom Tiller; **Indexer:** Nancy Ball; **Permissions Manager:** Dalene Reeder; **Graphic Designer:** Fred Starbird; **Graphic Artist:** Kathleen Boudreau-Fuoss; **Cover Designer:** Keith Blomberg; **Photo Production Manager:** Jason Allen; **Art Manager:** Kelly Hendren; **Associate Art Manager:** Alan L. Wilborn; **Illustrations:** © Human Kinetics; **Printer:** Sheridan Books

Printed in the United States of America   10   9   8   7   6   5   4   3   2   1

The paper in this book is certified under a sustainable forestry program.

Human Kinetics
Website: www.HumanKinetics.com

United States: Human Kinetics
P.O. Box 5076
Champaign, IL 61825-5076
800-747-4457
e-mail: humank@hkusa.com

Canada: Human Kinetics
475 Devonshire Road Unit 100
Windsor, ON N8Y 2L5
800-465-7301 (in Canada only)
e-mail: info@hkcanada.com

Europe: Human Kinetics
107 Bradford Road
Stanningley
Leeds LS28 6AT, United Kingdom
+44 (0) 113 255 5665
e-mail: hk@hkeurope.com

Australia: Human Kinetics
57A Price Avenue
Lower Mitcham, South Australia 5062
08 8372 0999
e-mail: info@hkaustralia.com

New Zealand: Human Kinetics
P.O. Box 80
Torrens Park, South Australia 5062
0800 222 062
e-mail: info@hknewzealand.com

E5027

To my wife, Jennifer,
and my sons,
Thomas, Ruaidhri, and Tiernan

Contents

Part III	Capital: Wealth, Power, and Resources	163

Part IV	Governance: Regulation, Organization, and Implementation	247

Contributors

Aaron Beacom, PhD
University of St. Mark & St. John
Plymouth, UK

Christopher Gaffney, PhD
Universidade Federal Fluminense
Niterói, Brazil

Jonathan Grix, PhD
University of Birmingham
Birmingham, UK

Deborah Healey, LLB, LLM (Hons)
University of New South Wales
Sydney, Australia

Alan Klein, PhD
Northeastern University
Boston, Massachusetts

John Kremer, PhD
Queen's University Belfast
Northern Ireland, UK

David Lavallee, PhD
University of Stirling
Stirling, Scotland, UK

Roger Levermore, PhD
University of Liverpool
Liverpool, UK

Sigmund Loland, PhD
Norwegian School of Sport Sciences
Oslo, Norway

Joseph Maguire, PhD
Loughborough University
Loughborough, UK

University of the Western Cape
Cape Town, South Africa

Michael McNamee, PhD
Swansea University
Swansea, Wales, UK

Aidan Moran, PhD
University College Dublin
Dublin, Ireland

University of Waikato
Hamilton, New Zealand

Dawn Penney, PhD
University of Waikato
Hamilton, New Zealand

David Rowe, PhD
University of Western Sydney
Sydney, Australia

Ramón Spaaij, PhD
La Trobe University
Melbourne, Australia

University of Amsterdam
Amsterdam, Netherlands

Stefan Szymanski, PhD
University of Michigan
Ann Arbor, Michigan

Lucie Thibault, PhD
Brock University
St. Catharines, Ontario, Canada

Wray Vamplew, PhD
University of Stirling
Stirling, Scotland, UK

Preface

This book is timely and necessary. Over the past 50 years, our stock of social science knowledge about sport and physical activity has expanded considerably in range and depth. Each discipline and subject area has developed unique expertise, and this type of specialization has become a feature of the study of sport. Students invariably have to consult specialist journals, textbooks, or monographs. While that is valuable in itself, our intention here is both to draw on this specialization and to enable students and practitioners to see the collective contribution that a social science approach can make. Indeed, given the problems, challenges, and dilemmas that mark contemporary sport, the need for a collective social science understanding is arguably more pressing than ever.

Social Sciences in Sport is designed to achieve two main goals: first, to provide in-depth coverage of current knowledge in a range of disciplines; and second, to draw connections between these disciplines to help illuminate key issues and concerns regarding sport and thereby to hold out the possibility of change. The text provides teachers and students with both a comprehensive account of discipline-specific knowledge in the social sciences and an overview of how social science knowledge as a whole contributes to understanding the problems and potentialities of contemporary sport practices and experiences. Written by leading figures in the social sciences, the book synthesizes theory and research in social science and sport while giving special attention to four distinct aspects:

- Identity: definitions, development, and the individual
- Community: place, space, image, and the social
- Capital: wealth, power, and resources
- Governance: regulation, organization, and implementation

These aspects, which correspond to the four main sections of the book, provide a framework with which to orient thinking and coordinate actions derived from a social science perspective. In keeping with the premise of the book, the individual chapters can be read separately, but they can also be read in such a way as to highlight links between disciplines, both within a specific part and across the four parts. Indeed, each expert has sought both to make such links where appropriate and to hold in mind questions of identity, community, social capital, and governance. Each chapter provides a comprehensive account that focuses on four key elements: a historical overview of the discipline or subject area; core concepts and main theoretical perspectives in that area of expertise; key critical findings; and contemporary debates that characterize sport. In taking this approach, the authors—and the text as a whole—make the case for the importance, relevance, and utility of a social science perspective on sport and physical activity. That, indeed, is the promise of this book.

Part I considers **identity**. In society and in sport, individuals are faced with questions of who they are, where they have come from, and how they address the ethical concerns they encounter on a daily basis. In seeking to make sense of these questions of identity, individuals can benefit from using knowledge—concepts and data—produced in the disciplines of history, philosophy, and psychology. Yet individuals also encounter sport as part of social groups. Thus part II focuses on questions of **community** and how they are contoured by issues of place, space, image, and society. The extent to which local or national communities fragment or share a sense of togetherness, and the question of whether such processes of emotional and communal identification extend across societies, also characterize discussion of sport subcultures and sport worlds more generally. Evidence regarding the role that sport plays in providing a sense of identification, belonging, and community is provided by research in anthropology, sociology, geography, and media studies.

The role of local and global sport in shaping identities and communities is contingent on various forms of capital—status, wealth, power, and resources. Thus part III examines **capital**, drawing on research in the disciplines of economics, political science, and international relations. Finally, part IV focuses on questions of **governance**. Individuals and communities, both in sport and in society more generally, are faced with what has been described as a runaway world and a sense of "future shock," and in such a context questions of governance arise. How can individuals and communities order their lives, regulate wider sporting and societal processes, and organize and implement more effective policies regarding sport and physical activity that enhance well-being, human performance, and social development? These concerns are addressed by drawing on expertise in the study of sport law, social policy, management, and education.

This collection of work represents some, though not all, of the contributions that a social science perspective can make to the study of sport and physical culture. Additional questions—concerning, for instance, the role of the environment, religion, bioethics, political economy, social change, and development—could merit separate attention. Some, though again not all, of such issues could and should have a more prominent place in the text, and aspects of them are indeed surfaced in specific chapters. Yet any collection of this nature is a selection; indeed, given the dynamic nature of contemporary sport worlds, new problems, questions, concerns, and even whole new emerging areas of inquiry continue to develop. My contention is that, equipped with the social science knowledge and orientation that this book represents, students and practitioners will be better able to navigate their way through old, current, and newly emerging problems and challenges. With this social science compass, they will be better able to determine what we already know, what we still need to know, and, on that basis, how best to develop body cultures that are less wasteful of lives and resources, of habitus and habitat. This is my hope.

eBook
available at
HumanKinetics.com

Acknowledgments

A book of this nature would not be possible without the patience and expertise of those who have contributed. I thank them all and hope that the journey, though longer than expected, has been worthwhile. My own personal journey began before this project, and in reflecting on whatever I have learned along the way, thanks are also due to my undergraduate teacher Bob Pearton and my PhD advisor Eric Dunning. I am fortunate to count them as friends. Likewise, students past and present reaffirm the belief that education can empower and that social science has a part to play in this regard. The students at Loughborough University and other universities in Europe, North America, Africa, Asia, and Australia have played a part in shaping my thinking and the sentiments that underpin this book. Likewise, as I have traveled to different parts of the world, I have found colleagues who have been supportive, willing to listen and offer advice, and provide friendship along the way. They are too numerous to mention, but I have been lucky to escape to their universities and their warm reception. For those who I have encountered on my travels, I have really appreciated your company, advice, and friendship. Thank you.

Finally, I would like to thank Christine Drews and Myles Schrag at Human Kinetics. The initial idea for a book of this nature started with a conversation Myles and I had while waiting for a plane. Flight delays have some benefits. His support in the early stages of this book and Christine's expert editorial eye ensured that we got here in the end, with much appreciation on my part.

Introduction:

Making the Case for the Social Sciences of Sport, Exercise, and Health

The importance of taking a social science perspective on sport and physical activity increases as a range of social problems, issues, and concerns merge within and affect sport worlds. As a result, though a natural science approach to the study of sport and physical activity is necessary to a comprehensive analysis, it is not sufficient. Indeed, a social science perspective is needed not only as a complement to natural science; in some ways, social science is better equipped to make sense of a range of phenomena evident in global sport and physical cultures today. Yet, too often, a natural science explanation is used in isolation, without recourse to a social science analysis, in several manifestations—for example, in the teaching of sport, exercise, and health science students; in the views of politicians and senior officials in the world of sport; and in the folklore of people who seek to explain various aspects of sport. Thus, this text remakes the case for taking a social science perspective on sport that Gunther Luschen and George Sage (1981) made more than 30 years ago (see also Coakley & Dunning, 2000).

This collection shares both with Luschen and Sage and with Coakley and Dunning a belief that a social science perspective adds to our knowledge and understanding of individuals, communities, and societies. Social science seeks to explore what we think, how we feel, the ways in which we live, and how we cope with the problems of interdependence with each other and the world as a whole. Hence this volume engages disciplines and fields of study that explore some or all of these features of human life—in the wider society and in various sporting and physical cultures. While the genesis of a social science perspective is a more recent development than a natural science perspective in human knowledge, the endeavor of seeking to explain human behavior, social groups, and societal relations in a systematic way represents a decisive breakthrough in our understanding of ourselves. Connected in part to humanity's transition to "modern" societies, the social science perspective has sought not only to explain this transition but also to use such knowledge to improve the human condition. Such sentiments also underpin the advocacy of a human development model in sport, exercise, and health sciences as outlined later in this introduction.

Since Luschen and Sage's publication, various issues, problems, and concerns have intensified within sport, arguably making their case far more pressing. Indeed, as noted, this perspective can provide a necessary corrective to mythologies, political ideologies, and wishful thinking held by a range of people, including politicians and practitioners. In particular, a social science perspective better equips us to address the following:

1. The function and meaning of sport in the lives of people, the identities they form, and the communities they create together

2. The role that sport does and could play in dealing with societal and global problems, issues, and concerns and the resources consumed by those involved in the sport-industrial complex.

3. Local and global questions of inequality, power, governance, democracy, transparency, and accountability in sport and in society more broadly

Equipping ourselves in this way involves not simply gaining knowledge of social science but also developing an intellectual approach that emphasizes certain qualities in the teaching and research agenda of sport, exercise, and health sciences. Sadly, some of those in authority are content to pursue research income, academic rankings, and "impact" in terms of improving performance or hosting events—mega or otherwise. The approach advocated here takes a different tack: We need to reorient our thinking away from a model that emphasizes uncritical appreciation of performance efficiency or bioscience understanding of health and physical activity and focus instead on the potential of a model that highlights human development. Let me briefly spell this out.

Various disciplines have become established features of, or outsiders in relation to, the development of sport, exercise, and health sciences. For example, biomechanics and exercise physiology remain part of the established group, whereas the social sciences of sport have been at the margins since the development of the subject. In one sense, this was a deliberate step by natural scientists. In the shift from physical education, the quest for respectability seemed to lie in adhering to a specific view of science and statistical accuracy, which sports medicine advocates and sport and exercise scientists hoped would make them more likely to be accepted by established scientists in the academy. One consequence, however, is that the philosophy of sport and the history of physical education have been actively marginalized. Increasingly, pedagogy is under threat as an essential part of the curricula within sport and exercise science degree programs, and thus the case for the social sciences of sport has to be made anew.

The Sport Ethic and the Natural Sciences

What counts in sport, exercise, and health sciences is related to what matters in the "sport ethic," which reinforces the marginalization of the social sciences. The sport ethic reflects the actual practice of sport. Also, the practices of sport science teaching and research are embedded in the assumptions of the sport ethic. Several features of the sport ethic can be identified (Coakley, 2003), including the following: a willingness to make sacrifices, a striving for distinction, an acceptance of risk and the possibility or probability of participating while enduring pain, and a tacit acceptance that there is no limit to the pursuit of the ultimate performance. The practice of this sport ethic is learned early on, and it becomes normalized and taken for granted—it is part of the body of the performer and the agenda of the teacher and researcher.

Social scientists have documented the logical consequences of this sport ethic—cheating, drug abuse, and disordered eating. Debate about drugs and sport indicates that it is difficult to maintain binary dichotomies between what counts as natural and what counts as synthetic, between diet supplementation and drug taking, and between restorative and enhancing treatments. The next frontier in achievement sport is genetic engineering. Such features of global sport are reinforced by and reflected in the assumptions and practices of the sport-industrial complex, which has several dimensions—structural, institutional, ideological, and cultural. This complex is composed of several key groups, including state agencies, transnational corporations, nongovernmental agencies, and sport associations. The institutional framework of this complex involves at least four main elements: sports medicine, sport science, sport science support programs, and regional and national centers of excellence. The emergence of this complex—initially in Western or developed nations less restricted by the legacy of a play- and player-oriented amateur attitude toward sporting success—is not surprising. Eager to compete on a global stage, governments fund research and departments that focus on talent identification, production, and performance; it also recruits advocates of coaching science, sport science, and sports medicine to help deliver "success."

As a result of these broader processes, sport and exercise scientists gear their research and teaching toward a performance efficiency model. Exercise physiologists, for example, examine the most advantageous biological conditions for training and competing, and biomechanists trace the most rational way to use specific forces and angles to meet the demands of competitive tasks. These natural scientists have been joined by sports medicine experts and geneticists who seek to divide the human population into specific categories, sometimes with a presumed racial component, or contribute to the gene transfer revolution, ostensibly with health in mind—but with performance goals also motivating the research. Nutrition and related sports medicine specialists are also involved in reinforcing the performance efficiency model or a bioscience interpretation of health and well-being. If, however, advocates of sport, exercise, and health sciences are serious about contributing to development *through* sport, and not just development *of* sport, what must change?

Proposing a Human Development Model

The performance efficiency and bioscience model encourages a type of academic practice in which the researcher becomes a technocrat who thinks and speaks in performance terms and reflects the concerns of the sport-industrial complex and the bioscience health nexus. This type of logic was vividly captured by C. Wright Mills (1956), who wrote about the hierarchies of state, corporation, and military (the military-industrial complex). Arguably, such themes are echoed in the development of sport, exercise and health sciences, sport science support programs, and centers of excellence. Academic practice is guided and shaped by a technological discourse that focuses attention on talent identification, optimal training regimens, masking agents, goal setting, attention styles, and health regimes. Yet not all natural scientists embrace this focus; the humanistic intellectual still survives in the study of physical culture. At one point, the humanist tradition was an integral part of physical education and found expression in areas such as history, philosophy, and pedagogy. At its best, as the chapters in this volume clearly demonstrate, it was concerned with themes and issues such as morality, equity, participation, learning, cooperation, and the intrinsic properties of play and games. Like folk body cultures, however, humanists—at least in the context of sport, exercise, and health science departments—are in danger of becoming extinct.

A reconfiguration of sport, exercise, and health sciences would not only liberate the natural scientist from this technocratic model but also promote the mission of the humanistic intellectual. This approach would counter the continuing drift toward a restrictive scientization of physical education discourses and the consolidation of technocratic physical education. The alternative proposed here is underpinned by a belief that science has the potential to be a mode of enlightenment and emancipation—but that left in the hands of the power elite of the sport-industrial complex and the bioscience health nexus, this potential will be diminished. As currently configured, the field of sport, exercise, and health sciences thus *takes* rather than *makes* the problems it examines. That is, academics should exercise greater autonomy in selecting what constitutes a problem, how this problem can be interpreted and explained, and what solutions can be offered. Failure to do so stems from being too closely tied to the here and now and from seeking to provide solutions to short-term, performance-based problems; furthermore, "short-termism" and pandering to vested interests potentially lead to loss of the critical and skeptical character of sport science, and questions of power become neglected. Failing to challenge the trend toward short-termism in departments, universities, and associations also carries its own danger, namely that of further accelerating the decline of those aspects of physical education, sport, exercise, and health promoted by the humanities and social sciences. As a result, sport and exercise scientists are increasingly involved in the production of high-performance sport and embedded in the agenda of the bioscience health complex. In turn, the development of knowledge concerning the pressing needs of humanity as a whole are neglected.

Research funds and academic posts are thus targeted toward those who deliver short-term results in terms of performance or narrow definitions of health., Students in turn recognize whose knowledge counts and how that knowledge is used in the sport-health-industrial complex. That is, students learn "that technical, market-driven science and professionalism . . . [are] more advanced and esteemed than [the] social-trustee, civic science and professionalism [approach]" (Ingham & Lawson, 1999, np). Here, then, questions arise regarding the scale and sources of funding for teaching and research, curriculum design and development, and the status and esteem given to various forms of knowledge and modes of communication within the sport, exercise, and health sciences. Reviewing the field, it is clear that technical, market-driven science and professionalism hold sway, and this tendency may be increasing in Europe, North America, and elsewhere. Technical, market-driven scientists command attention, attract funds, claim key academic positions, and set the teaching and research agenda. This is the new orthodoxy of the subject area.

In contrast, the social-trustee, civic science, and professionalism approach requires that sport, exercise, and health scientists and professionals "integrate their formal roles with that of their own citizenship" (Ingham & Lawson, 1999, np). We must become sensitive to the production, dissemination, curricular use, and application of the knowledge we generate no matter whom we are providing it for: students, athletes, coaches, administrators, the media, or governmental agencies. We must also address a series of questions including the following: How wasteful is the present system? Who are the winners and the losers in global sport—both on and off the field of play, at different levels of sport, and in different modes of movement culture? What are the costs, as well as the health benefits, of the system being constructed—for the individual, the community, and society as a whole?

The shift to a human development model would not only provide emancipatory knowledge for sport communities and societies; it would also release the sport, exercise, and health sciences community from the tentacles of achievement sport. We need to engage in involved advocacy (Ingham & Lawson, 1999, np) of a human development model with emphasis on justice, citizenship, and equity. Social-trustee, civic science professionals must act "as stewards of the just society" and "protect and support free spheres of action and public social spaces" (Ingham & Lawson, 1999, np). These observations need to be extended to consideration of environmental concerns ("green" issues) and notions of sustainable sport. In so doing, sport, exercise, and health scientists would be engaging in forms of committed service (Ingham & Lawson, 1999) similar to what some physical educationists were traditionally involved in. Now that would be real impact.

Despite the new orthodoxy outlined, how can such sentiments and practices be nurtured? One way is to develop coalitions of advocates for such an approach within sport, exercise, and health sciences, involving natural and social scientists. In the context of sport and physical activity, such an approach could help address questions about injury, pain, violence, and drugs. Another step forward would be to ask whose body culture counts. Modern achievement sport could continue to be promoted in our universities and schools as the dominant, even exclusive form of body culture. In this scenario, sport education replaces physical education, coaches replace teachers, and talent identification schemes channel young people's early experiences of movement along narrow, prescribed lines. Alternatively, we could formulate sport, exercise, and health science degree programs underpinned by a model of human development that promoted diversity and recognized the richness of diverse body cultures. Furthermore, by developing sustainable sport and the teaching of environmental ethics, we could encourage stewardship of both habitat and habitus. These changes would be parts of an attempt to move global sport toward being a more democratic endeavor characterized by more transparent decision making and more accountable decision makers. Natural and social scientists of sport can, if they choose, serve a humanistic role and thus contribute to development through sport—or they can continue to serve the sport-industrial and bioscience health complex.

My hope is that this collection's comprehensive coverage of various social science disciplines and subject areas not only reaffirms the case for a social science explanation of sport and physical activity but also opens up intellectual space for natural and social scientists to discuss, debate, and come together in a teaching and research agenda focused on how the subject area can help development both of and through sport and physical cultures.

References

Coakley, J. (2003). *Sport in society* (8th ed.). New York: McGraw-Hill.

Coakley, J., & Dunning, E. (Eds.). (2000). *Handbook of sport studies*. London: Sage.

Ingham, A., & Lawson, H. (1999, September). *Prolympism and globalization: Knowledge for whom, by whom?* Paper presented at the meeting of the German Association of Sport Science, Heidelberg, Germany.

Luschen, G., & Sage, G. (Eds.). (1981). *Handbook of social science of sport*. Champaign, IL: Stipes.

Mills, C. Wright. (1956). *The power elite*. Oxford, UK: Penguin.

PART

I

Identity: Definitions, Development, and the Individual

Part I focuses on questions of identity. In society and in sport subcultures, individuals are faced with questions about who they are, where they have come from, and how they address the ethical concerns they encounter on a daily basis. In making sense of these questions, it is helpful to draw on knowledge—concepts and data—from the disciplines of history, philosophy, and psychology.

At the same time, individuals encounter sport as part of social groups, and in chapter 1 Wray Vamplew offers a historical perspective on the economic, societal, cultural, and political elements that contour and shape sport on national and individual levels. For Vamplew, this historical sensitivity allows us to set benchmarks and analyze both continuities and changes. A study of the sporting past helps us understand how that past has shaped the present sport world, as well as its implications for the future of sport. Rather than focusing on the deeds and results of past sporting encounters, Vamplew's persuasive sport history focuses mainly on the social matters of ethnicity, gender, and class—fault lines of society that, in both the past and the present, have structured and shaped sport experiences.

Chapter 2, where Sigmund Loland and Michael McNamee address the philosophy of sport, is also concerned with questions of identity and with individual understanding and experience of sport and physical activity. For them, it is crucial to define what characterizes sport and what are the actual and possible meanings of sport in people's lives. They also explore questions about the actual and possible values of sport in and to society, as well as the lived experience of sport and physical activity: How can human embodiment and movement be understood? Loland and McNamee brilliantly demonstrate that a philosophical perspective is crucial to clarifying these issues; indeed, without such a perspective, any explanation would be not only less systematic but also lacking in critical reasoning.

In chapter 3, David Lavallee, John Kremer, and Aidan Moran provide a masterful historical overview of the psychology of sport, especially its development in the 20th century, and its key focuses. For them, the subdiscipline is concerned with both basic and applied aspects of psychology; as a result, the way in which the psychology of sport is defined—what it is—depends on which aspect is emphasized. Attention has been paid in the field to theory development relating to personality, motor learning, and cognition, usually with reference to a performer's thoughts, mental images, and concentration processes. This latter work has led to increasing consideration of performance enhancement, testing, and counseling interventions, thus highlighting the applied nature of the subdiscipline. More recently, however, attention has also been given to questions of health, well-being, and human development that draw on more basic aspects of psychology.

Each of these chapters, then, highlights questions of identity, meaning, and the roles that individuals have played and do play in the development of sport and body cultures. Taken together, they provide a cogent account of, and an overall structure for, understanding how we define and experience sport over time and in the contemporary world.

CHAPTER 1

History of Sport

Wray Vamplew, PhD

Sport history is more than the results of sport competitions. It can offer a perspective on the economic, social, cultural, and political behavior of both nations and individuals. Its major contribution to the study of sport is its time dimension, which allows us to set benchmarks and analyze change.

Development of the Discipline

Once winners started to be recorded, sport history began. Academic sport history, however, was much longer in coming. There were isolated pioneers, such as Seymour (1960) in North America and McIntosh (1952, 1963) in England, but no concerted productivity in the field until the 1970s. Two strands developed: one out of physical education, whose practitioners mainly saw sport history as facts and stories about past performances, and the other started by historians moving into a new field after being stimulated by the growing interest in social history, particularly "history from below." Although there has been some exploration of economic and political aspects of sport history, this focus on the social—matters of gender, ethnicity, identity, and especially class—has continued to dominate sport history publication.

The role of the sport historian is to set straight the sporting record: not just the basic "sportifacts" confirming who won what, where, and by how many, but, more important, offering an explanation of why and when sport has changed and how it has arrived at a particular situation. No fully informed debate on sport can take place without reference to the historical dimension. We cannot properly study contemporary sport without a sense of history, for the sporting past helped shape the sporting present and, by implication, the sporting future. All sports have some "inheritance from the past" (Polley, 2007, p. 12), be it rules, governing bodies, styles of play, competitions, or equipment, none of which are totally "reinvented on a daily basis" (Polley,

I am grateful for debate over the years with many colleagues in the broad church that is, and should be, sport history.

2003, p. 49). However, good sport history looks at more than the ludic; it also contextualizes events by placing them in a wider social, political, economic, or cultural environment. Using cricket as an example, the outrage of Australians at England's body-line tactics in 1932 and 1933—in which the bowlers deliberately directed the ball at the bodies of the batsmen—becomes more explicable when it is noted that Australia was gripped by economic depression and that England was reluctant to increase imperial preference in its trading relationships. Similarly, the severing of cricketing ties between England and South Africa in the 1960s—when Basil D'Oliveira, classified as "coloured" by the apartheid regime, was chosen to tour South Africa—is fully understandable only in light of the latter's apartheid policies, from which D'Oliveira had fled to establish himself as a cricketer in Britain.

Sport history does not appear only in academic books and articles. Looking back at sport has become an industry in its own right, as nostalgia, catered to both individual and collective memory, has become an earner. Sport marketers offer merchandise and memories to sport fans via heritage kits and seniors events; auction houses employ sport historians to advise them on memorabilia sales; and museums, at the club level often linked to a stadium tour, encourage worshippers to pay (for) homage to past sporting heroes. Public sport history itself takes three major forms. The first, populist sport history, uses media outlets, particularly television, film, and the Internet. The latter is often the resort of amateur historians who amass facts about their favorite team or player. The others are often criticized by academic historians for sacrificing historical accuracy in the interest of a story line, but this is what attracts viewers, and far more people watch a sport history film or program than ever read history books. Second, sport museums serve as what has been called "the public face of sport history" (Vamplew, 1998, p. 279). These institutions can be the best places to replicate the performance, drama, romance, passion, and emotion of sport, and they have done much to educate through entertainment. Unfortunately, too often they have also catered to the nostalgia market and, in doing so, perpetuated myths, lacked historical objectivity and subtlety of argument, failed to contextualize artifacts, eschewed the controversial, and been prone to obsession with winners and winning. They have also tended to concentrate on sport that is competitive, adult, and male dominated (Hill, Moore, & Wood, 2012; Phillips 2012). A third form of public sport history is the "official" history, authorized or commissioned by a governing body or the like. Here, the criticism focuses on both omission and commission: Funders are told what they want to hear, and a positive spin is often put on controversial issues. For example, Celtic Football Club's approved histories make much of the club being founded in 1887 to raise money to feed poor Catholics in the east end of Glasgow, but they never mention that within a decade Celtic had become a limited liability company and no longer made charitable donations (Kay & Vamplew, 2010).

Relationships With Other Disciplines

It might be assumed that the more present-based sport disciplines would have little time for history. To the contrary, sport scientists take care to cite pioneering works in their areas of research, sport law is full of (historical) precedence, and most disciplines make use of a literature review that draws on the history of the subject under scrutiny. But the use of history can go beyond the confines of discipline-specific citations. It can also be used to set benchmarks: All surveys are taken at a point in time. If we want to know where sport is heading, it is useful to know where it has been. Indeed, any mention of process implies change over time, and history can provide us with the evidence to set events and incidents in their proper context and aid in explanation by giving us an awareness of underlying forces. Often, short- or medium-term history (perhaps a decade at most) is applied, but some disciplines have gone much further back in time.

Sport historians and sociologists have much to offer each other in the historical study of class, status, and power in sport. Indeed, sociologists have used historical evidence to contribute to an understanding of sport development, sport violence over time, and football hooliganism in particular (Dunning, Malcolm, & Waddington, 2004). However, as a generalization, each discipline still harbors suspicion of the other's methodology: Sociologists claim that historians lack conceptual frameworks for their research, and in retaliation historians maintain that sociologists dispense with empirical verification of their theories.

Nonetheless, cross-disciplinarity offers considerable benefits particularly in economics where, for example, Szymanski (2010) has argued that, via choice theory, economics could help sport historians explain the development of the sport club, and Vamplew (2012) suggests that the application of basic economic concepts of supply (natural resources, the labor force, monetary resources, entrepreneurship, and technology) and demand (income and wealth, prices, population, time, and taste) offers an explanatory toolkit for the development of commercialized sport. Porter (2010) advocates that business history and sport history could profitably come together to trace the history of clubs as operating enterprises—paying wages, renting or buying premises, promoting their product, and generating revenue—and to say more about the retailing of sporting goods. Economic theory could also contribute to historical explanations of the dark side of sport, including corruption, discrimination, and drug taking (Andreff & Szymanski, 2006).

Regarding other disciplines, geography brings a sense of space and place (Bale, 1994); media researchers have examined the historical relationship between press, radio, television, and sport (Whannel, 1992; Boyle and Haynes, 2010); and the application of cultural studies theory to historical sources is providing a way to explore what sport has meant to players, officials, and fans (Oriard, 2006).

Core Concepts

Historians often borrow concepts from other disciplines, especially when investigating a historical topic in light of modern developments in social science theory. At the same time, history—including sport history—can also lay claim to key concepts that it has made its own, in particular the duality of continuity and change. Sport historians are interested in explaining why some sports of the preindustrial period (e.g., folk football) continue to be played in the 21st century (Hornby, 2008), while others (e.g., stowball, pall mall, and hawkey) have disappeared from the scene (Collins, Martin, & Vamplew, 2005). They want to trace the process by which some sports have changed in character and structure so that, while maintaining their basic theme, they have been accepted by a modern audience, as with cricket's limited overs and Twenty20 versions. They also wish to explain the development of new sports, often associated with technological change, such as the coming of bicycle racing, speedway, and skydiving, as well as the long residuals associated with sport—the unholy trinity of sex, alcohol, and gambling.

Another historical concept is that of heritage, which can cover a wide spectrum of visual and material culture, including defunct and nostalgic sport sites, statues and other effigies, streets and stadiums named after sporting celebrities, photographs and films, ephemera, and memorabilia. Some statue erections and renamings of venues commemorate recently deceased sporting heroes, whereas others reflect "a new sensibility for the past," in which acts of reparation are made to "past generations" in a public appreciation of sporting heritage (Russell, 2006, p. 9). Sport heritage can also become part of our daily speech when sporting terminology enters the vernacular, as it has, for example, in the phrases "throwing in the towel" (from prizefighting), "the rub of the green" (from golf), and "stickler for the rules" (from early wrestling, in which judges used sticks to assess whether a competitor's shoulders were pinned to the floor).

Another concept seen as the cultural property of sport history is that of sporting tradition; indeed, *Sporting Traditions* even serves as the title of the journal of the Australian Society for Sports History. In essence, this concept combines heritage and continuity, thus enabling, for example, the English racing community to boast that the St. Leger Stakes, first run in 1776, is the oldest classic race in the world; it also explains why the terminology of fencing is largely French and why that of judo is Japanese. There is, however, a dark side of "invented tradition," in which a false continuity with the past is claimed and evidence to the contrary is ignored or willfully misinterpreted. As a result, so-called traditional sports have been created for commercial or nostalgic reasons or, the reverse, attempts have been made in rugby and baseball to invent the origins of those sports so as to separate rugby from working-class folk football and baseball from an English game for girls (Collins, 2005b).

History might also claim that memory lies within its province, both that in living recollection (as pursued by oral historians) and, more generally, a collective cultural belief, usefully defined by Mewett (2000, p. 2) as "an imaging [or even imagining] of prior happenings that is pertinent to the construction of the social situation in which the remembering takes place."

Main Theoretical Perspectives

Sport historians adopt a variety of approaches to their work, and some are more inclined than others to use theoretical concepts and statistical analysis. All, however, are concerned with applying evidence to a historical situation, for sport history is an empirically based, interpretive social science.

Approaches and Methodology

In terms of methodology, dichotomies occur between those who opt for quantification and those who prefer a qualitative approach; between those who seek information at the aggregate level (often the quantifiers) and those who look at the individual (mainly the nonstatistical historians); between those who apply theory and theoretical concepts and those who are more empirically focused; and between those who pose modern questions in a historical setting and those who try to understand what mattered to those in the past.

Statistics provide a quantified basis for historical assertions. Sport is full of statistics, but beyond the likes of batting averages and record times we should add such things as the proportion of players from a particular ethnic background and the gender balance of sport club membership. As elsewhere in the social sciences, argument by example is no substitute for the use of hard, quantified data, and measurement can allow historians to be more precise in their answers (Cronin, 2009). To postulate that a relationship is positive or negative is not enough; we need to know not only the direction of the relationship but also its strength. The great contribution of the quantifiers is to help determine what is typical. For example, a biography of Harry Vardon, the Tiger Woods of his day, contributes to the understanding of a champion golfer troubled by tuberculosis and marital difficulties (A. Howell, 1991). This is interesting but would be more useful as sport history if contextualized into asking whether tuberculosis was an industrial disease of professional golfers and whether the marriage problems emanated from Vardon's time away from home making a living as an elite professional who designed courses and played in championships. To put it another way, if you study 3,000 professional golfers, you are able to say something about the average age at appointment to a club position and retirement, length of career, degree of mobility between clubs, and the modal level of earnings (Vamplew, 2008b). Yet this strength might be seen as a weakness by researchers more concerned with the experience of the individual. In seeking to generalize, then, aggregation can marginalize those who do not fit the standard pattern, those who are statistical outliers.

In his seminal work, Booth (2005) takes sport historians to task for failing to engage more extensively with theory and criticizes those who simply gather facts to tell a story. Yet Booth can be too harshly judgmental and appears unwilling to accept that approaches other than his own can be useful. Although (very) few sport historians discuss theoretical issues, many implicitly do use theory, or, more precisely, theoretical concepts, to help them frame questions. Booth (2010) acknowledges that theoretical frameworks such as modernization, materialism, hegemony, structuration, feminism, discourse, and textualism have been embraced in this way. Yet some sport historians worry that these concepts are being applied uncritically. The concept of the "body," for example, pervades a corpus of writing by sport historians, but how many of them are clearly aware of the subtleties and complexities of Michel Foucault's work on the knowledge–body–power trilogy? For his part, Booth plays down the possibility that the theory being applied could be erroneous. However, no theory is immutable. If the facts do not fit the theory, then the historian should check the facts again, and, if he or she is still convinced they are correct, the theory should be modified. Historians must be prepared not only to use theory but also to adapt it. Indeed, until substantiated by evidence, theories are just competing hypotheses. As such, they might aid our understanding, but they do not explain a situation completely; empirical support is a necessary concomitant for accepting any hypothesis.

Generally, sport historians have applied theories from other disciplines to historical material rather than develop theories of their own. Two notable exceptions can be found in the overarching theories used to explain the development of sport put forward by Guttmann and Szymanski. Guttmann (1978, 2004) postulated sport history's own version of "modernization," in which he argued that seven features of modernization could be used to measure how near a sport was to being modern at any time in its history. He saw such modernization as a cultural expression of an increasingly scientific world. First, modern sport was secular, with no religious reasons for participation. Second, it should demonstrate equality: Theoretically, everyone should have an opportunity to compete, and conditions of competition should be the same for all contestants. Third, it introduced the idea of specialization; for example, everyone who wanted to could join in folk football, a sport with no sharply defined roles, but the emphasis on achievement in modern sport brought in specialization both within a sport and between sports. Fourth came rationalization, in particular the development of rules, which in primitive societies were often considered divine instructions for God-given rituals that were not to be tampered with by mere humans; in contrast, secular modern sports have been invented and provided with written rules. Even more rationalization came via the development of coaching and sport science. Guttmann's fifth feature was bureaucratization. Almost every major modern sport has its national and international organizations, which have developed extensive bureaucracies to establish and oversee implementation of universal rules for the sport. These organizations were not needed, of course, when there were no written rules. The sixth feature was quantification, by which modern sports transform every athletic feat into statistics. Following on from quantification was Guttmann's seventh point—the modern emphasis on records. Like many models, Guttmann's was an ideal-type postulation, which may never have all its conditions fully satisfied. It has, however, stood the test of time, if not in its entirety then as a basis on which others have built. Modifications have been made that suggest his model required more input on press publicity, commercialization, and professionalization, and a recent major criticism has been made of his use of Weberian concepts (Adelman, 1986; Vamplew & Kay, 2003; Tomlinson & Young, 2010).

In the early 18th century, a movement began in Britain that involved the formation of clubs for many purposes—not least, for sports such as cricket, golf, pugilism, and horse racing. They enabled people with a common purpose to come together, provided a basis for agreeing on common rules and regulations, created a framework for competitive interaction, and secured a location for participation and sociability. Szymanski (2008a, 2008b) has argued that modern British sport emerged from these new forms of associativity, which developed autonomously in Britain following the retreat of the state from the control of associative activities. This process contrasted, he contends, with the situation in countries, such as France and Germany, where club formation continued to require the explicit or implicit approval of the state. In those cases, modern sport developed in ways consistent with, or even in the service of, the objectives of the state, most notably the need to maintain military preparedness. Szymanski's critics (Riess, 2008; Krüger, 2008; MacLean, 2008; Nathaus, 2009) acknowledge the ambition of the analysis but suggest missing elements and alternative causal factors. They argue that more evidence is required to support the hypothesis, that Szymanski should have looked further back in time for his European material, that he failed to adequately address the issue of class, and that he understated the role of commercialization. More recently, researchers in a major project on European sport history have suggested that other models of development can be identified, including within Europe alone, Soviet, German, and Scandinavian (Tomlinson & Young, 2011).

Sport historians can approach the content of their research in two main ways. One way is to engage issues of current interest and ask whether they applied in the past. Historians might, for example, consider body performance in 19th-century sport or how sport coped in the past with economic recession. Here, applied history may be used to offer advice to the present. The other approach is to ask what sport meant and what aspects of sport mattered during the time period being studied. For example, topics might include the Scottish Football Association's worries about disguised professionalism in the early 1890s or U.S. President Theodore Roosevelt's concern with violence in American college football. Here, the past is being understood on its own terms; nevertheless, it can still be analyzed using modern concepts or theories.

Veracity of Evidence

Without evidence from the past, there can be no sport history. Booth (2005, pp. 210, 81) maintains that sport history generally remains "very firmly anchored to a bedrock of empiricism" and criticizes sport historians' "slavish devotion to sources and evidence." In itself, this is not a bad thing, but a totally empirical approach does run the risk of building up so much detail that no patterns or explanations can be advanced. This is sometimes the case with the enthusiastic, nonacademic historian, but even then it can provide information with which to test ideas and hypotheses. Readers also need to be aware that some researchers employ what could be termed "reverse research," in which the search is made solely for evidence that will justify predetermined views. Many writers offer "history by example," in which statements are illustrated by pertinent examples, but the reader should query whether the examples are representative or the most interesting ones available. When evidence is not provided and justified, there is a danger that history will lapse into myth, which, as nostalgia clouds memory over time, becomes engrained as conventional wisdom.

History is an empirically based, interpretive social science. What historians do is use evidence in such a way as to create "cumulative plausibility" so that readers are increasingly convinced by the argument (Holt, 2000, p. 50). History thus depends on evidence, though sport historians must interrogate their sources so as to assess their authenticity and validity. As Holt (2000, p. 49) has noted, "finding a reliable way to collect data does not ensure that such data is worth collecting." Historians should be aware that archives are sites of power that privilege some information above other information; which evidence is collected and which is saved can be functions of power in both past and present society. Hence subordinate groups—usually people who do not keep diaries, are not interviewed, and are too often nameless—do not always get their voice "heard" in historical documents. A case in point is an inquiry by the Agenda Club (1912) into the welfare of golf caddies in Edwardian Britain, which took evidence from golf club secretaries but not from a single caddie. Booth (2006, p. 97) has shown that all references to the alleged misconduct of Australian swimming icon Dawn Fraser during the 1964 Olympics in Tokyo were physically cut from the archives of the Australian Swimming Union. Similarly, photographs can be doctored, newspapers can be beholden to the political views of their proprietors, oral testimony may be affected by false memory, and committee minutes can hide the intensity of a debate.

Sport historians have also placed undue reliance on newspapers, which were, prior to television, perhaps "the great instrument of popular communication" (Hill, 2006a, p. 121), as a source for reconstructing the history of sport by dint of match reports, details of annual general meetings, and interviews with players. Hill (2006a) for one has stressed that the press should be seen as a text to be interpreted rather than as a factual source to be merely accepted. Indeed, some aspects of reportage are on a par with inventing tradition: Adding anecdotes, selecting facts, and forwarding opinion can help sell newspapers but tarnish their value as providers of reliable, straightforward source material. As American sportswriter Leonard Koppett has pointed out, journalists write tomorrow's news—not history (Booth, 2005).

Historians should always ask three major questions of any primary source material: When was it produced? What was the authority of the person producing it? Why was it produced? It is important to know whether a document was contemporary to the event being investigated or produced some time later with the benefit of hindsight. It also matters whether the author wielded expert knowledge or insider information and whether he or she carried value judgments in his or her cultural baggage. And it is important to know whether any hidden agendas lie behind the overt reasons for producing the document. Where possible, historians should make use of triangulation and seek alternative sources against which to check "evidence," as did Kay (2009) in her study of the origins of the Glasgow Charity Cup.

Traditionally, sport historians, like other historians, have relied on written sources for their evidence—among them not only newspapers but also minute books, letters, diary entries, and official reports. In recent years, however, these sources have been supplemented by new ones: oral and e-mail interviews, visual sources (e.g., photographs, films, and other works of art), ethnographic sources in which sport history is explored by means of site visits, and other sources where material culture is subjected to historical examination.

Oral history can provide a personal perception of events and what they meant to particular people, but it can go back only as far as living memory.

Moreover, it runs the risk of falling into pitfalls such as false and selective memory, the random survival of those involved, and the interjection of hindsight. However, in producing material not available from other sources, oral recollection can give life to dry historical evidence.

Huggins (2008, p. 327) has appealed for sport historians to more effectively exploit visual material on the basis that "to exclude the visual is to reject a key area of human [sporting] experience." Such material enables us to appreciate what the past looked like. Huggins' plea has been echoed by Phillips and his colleagues with respect to photographs, film, and monuments (Phillips, O'Neill, & Osmond, 2007), and Oriard (1993) has explored the use of illustration in "creating football" as a spectacle in the U.S. popular press. Sport historians have often used photographs to illustrate key points, but they can also become the focus of the research itself, as in Osmond's (2010) sociopolitical interpretation of the iconic picture of the 1968 Black Power salute at the Mexico Olympics, in which he gave due credence to the white Australian athlete, Peter Norman, who shared the podium with black Americans Tommie Smith and John Carlos. Osmond points out that the picture's captioning, positioning, and accompanying text all play an explanatory or interpretive role. Earlier, Terret (2006) looked at representations of race and gender via illustrations in a French sport magazine, and Bale (2006) analyzed colonial race discourse around an image of a Rwandan jumper.

Both film and photograph confirm the very existence of the past, and film offers the added dimension of movement, of the body in action, as a central feature of sport. Baker (2006) has explored the socially constructed identities of sportspersons in American cinematic representations, though this approach has similar problems to that of using written fiction as a source. In other examples, early documentary film from Edwardian Britain has allowed historians to see how sport was actually played and has shown the overt composition of the crowd (Toulmin, 2006); Huggins (2007) has looked at how interwar newsreels showed women's sport through the male gaze; and Headon (1999) has studied how Australian sport was presented in silent movies.

As with all other forms, visual evidence must be interrogated. For example, when researching their book on the relationship between sport and alcohol, Collins and Vamplew (2002, pp. 6–7) found that not all inns with signs that apparently depicted sport actually had a sporting heritage. To the contrary, many bears, bulls, falcons, and greyhounds represented not sport but the coats of arms of local nobility.

In Bale's (1994, p. 121) application of the notion of topophilia—love of place—he has shown that sites where sport was played can still matter in the present by creating "fond memories, or possibly a sense of place." Visits to such sites can emphasize this phenomenon by a physical engagement with the sporting territory. Polley (2010) has gone further—literally and historically—by first identifying and then walking the route of the 1908 Olympic marathon, though he argues that such self-immersed journeys should not be simply antiquarian fact-finding exercises; rather, they should be engaged in critically so that fresh perspectives might be gained.

Some postmodernists have suggested that fiction could be a valuable source as a cultural force that has shaped how people understand the world around them (Hill 2006b). Yet sport historians have been reluctant to use such sources, viewing them as unreliable and subjective. Nevertheless, novels, particularly those written in the period being studied, can cast light on the context in which sport took place (Johnes, 2007b). Literary texts can add color and give insights into matters on which conventional sources are opaque, in particular the role of sport in everyday life. They can also bring in the passion and emotion of sport, which are lacking in most academic histories.

Occupying the middle ground between the fiction of the novel and overtly factual accounts are autobiographies, which often contain fictive elements and thus, despite being "probably the most substantial body of published material on the history of sport" (Taylor, 2008, p. 470), have been regarded by most sport historians as an imperfect source of information. Nevertheless, these self-narratives do purport to relate to real experiences, and they are not written in cultural isolation. Hence, at a minimum, they can provide atmosphere, but often they can also act as vehicles of subjective identity and self-representation, which enable historians to give meaning to a sporting career. The sum of the parts may also allow something to be said about the sporting culture in which the players operated.

The material culture of sport is huge, but Hardy, Loy, and Booth (2009) have suggested a typology of nine categories: playing equipment, venues, training equipment and sports medicine technology, sportswear, prizes, symbolic artifacts, performance measurement technology, ephemera and detritus, and memorabilia. They argue that these categories could be analyzed according to six residuals that, though sometimes changing in character, generally exhibit long-term continuity of belief and practice: agon (the core contest between opposing individuals or teams); craft (the skills, practices, and technology required to achieve in the competition); community (the ways in which both athletes and spectators create bonds and bridges that simultaneously link and separate groups through shared sporting passions); gambling (the wagering on the outcome of competition that drives much of the passion surrounding sport); eros (the sexual attraction of agonal bodies); and framing (the tendency to surround the agon with frames of spectacle and festival). Hardy and colleagues believe that analysis along these lines would provide a vehicle for developing a better understanding of sporting practices.

Postmodern sport historians argue that all sources are biased, all of them distort or filter the truth (whatever that might be), and all of them need interpretation. Indeed, Booth (2005, p. 30) believes that all "facts are propositional statements about the nature of reality." At its extreme, postmodern sport history is almost a nihilistic rejection of a subject in which no information can be trusted. A more moderate version would suggest two lessons for all sport historians, both of which are already enacted by the better practitioners. First, they should continually interrogate the archive so as to assess their sources carefully and certainly defend any privileging of material (Johnes, 2007a). Second, they should accept that there exist differing versions of events depending on whose perspective the narrative is constructed from; indeed, historical perspective is contested terrain with a plurality of meanings. To illustrate by example, an account of the previously mentioned body-line cricket test series in Australia would present different pictures if based on official reports, press reportage, or players' diaries; it would also vary depending on whether one used Australian or English sources.

Although historians deal in facts, quite often these facts turn out to consist of percentage of likelihood, reasoned speculations, or even personal bias—sometimes consciously so, more often a subconscious product of the historian's background. Evidence is indeed an issue, but so is the historian who, it is often forgotten, creates a personal relationship with the subject that can be influenced by factors such as upbringing, education, and politics. Booth (2005, p. 211) has called for greater reflexivity in the discipline—"an awareness that historians play creative roles in the production and presentation of history." Historians should be more open with their value judgments and acknowledge how subjectivity affects their approaches and narratives.

Critical Findings

We know a good deal about the chronological development (though less about some time periods) of many sports, sometimes contextualized in their political, social, and economic circumstances, though more often not. Significant findings made in some areas of research have become the prevailing conventional wisdom on the subject. For summaries of the "state of play" in a variety of countries, see the relevant chapters in Pope and Nauright (2010).

In an Anglo-Saxon context, we accept that gambling played a major role in the development of sport, particularly among the wealthier members of society—that is, the men who owned the racehorses and fighting cocks, patronized the pugilists and wrestlers, organized the cricket teams, and put up their servants as competitors in footraces. Much of their involvement was associated with gambling, which can be seen as an aspect of conspicuous consumption—spending to show others that they had the money to spend. At the time, few consumer goods or investment opportunities were on offer,

Case Study

DONALD MACKINTOSH

Sport historians often play the part of offering correctives to conventional wisdom by demonstrating that the reality of a situation was not what has been customarily believed. Sometimes, however, their role is simply to set straight the sporting record by correcting sins of omission rather than commission.

Until the 1980s, the official list of Olympic gold medalists was one shy of being complete: The records did not include Donald Mackintosh's victory in shooting at the Paris Olympic Games of 1900. Fortunately, diligent research by Reet and Max Howell (1988) for their study of Australian Olympians brought Mackintosh his rightful place in Olympic history. They showed that he had finished first in one event and third in another. Their findings were accepted by the International Olympic Committee, and in 1987 Mackintosh was posthumously awarded his medals. He was also inducted into the Australian Sport Hall of Fame.

One reason for Mackintosh's win being forgotten was his event: live pigeon shooting. Over time, the killing of birds for competitive sport (rather than for sport as hunting) fell into disfavor, and success at such an event was no longer applauded (or remembered). Indeed, it disappeared from the Olympic program until it was revived in the more humane form of clay pigeon shooting. Moreover, Australia did not take the early Olympic Games seriously. Only one Australian competed at Athens in 1896, three at Paris in 1900, and two at St. Louis in 1904. No official team was sent until 1908, and that was an Australasian one in which Australia and New Zealand combined forces. Nor did Mackintosh receive any medals at the time, since such awards were not introduced until 1904.

Perhaps the main reason for Mackintosh's disappearance from sporting history is the fact that the Paris Olympics were, for financial reasons, held in conjunction with a trade fair, the Paris Exposition Universelle. Indeed, there has been much confusion as to which events were Olympic ones and which were associated with the exposition. The events in which Mackintosh participated were the Prix Centenaire de Paris, which he won, and the Grand Prix de l'Exposition, in which he finished third, neither of which was obviously an Olympic shooting match.

so gambling offered an expenditure outlet, and some gamblers developed sport as a means to wager. Sport and gambling proved to be symbiotic as betting added to the excitement of the event.

Although commercialized and professionalized sport underwent a step change in late 19th-century Britain, it existed well before this time. Cricket, pedestrianism (professional athletics), prizefighting, rowing, and especially horseracing had "a long history of mass spectating, profit-seeking promoters, paid performers, stake-money contests and gambling" (Tranter, 1998, pp. 14–15). Much of the commercialization of the time was associated with the sport (e.g., beer and food stalls, itinerant entertainers) rather than being of the sport itself. Later, in all countries, industrialization and associated urbanization created the conditions in which organized, commercial, gate-money sport could flourish. Although the clubs that adopted limited liability company status in late 19th-century Britain were still not defining themselves primarily as businesses, this was not the case in the United States, where profit maximization came to the fore.

Modern sport fit well into the new urban, industrial environment, since it emphasized just those features that employers wanted: discipline, loyalty, fitness, and obeying of orders. But the link with industrialization should not be exaggerated. Sport, or that version that emanated from the British public schools, encompassed the idea of chivalry (fair play) rather than that of ruthless industrial capitalism. Sport, as can be seen from Sir Henry John Newbolt's famous 1892 poem "Vitaï Lampada" ("The Torch of Life"), taught the virtues of war, not of commerce.

We are also aware that sport has always had its dark side: corruption stemming from sport's involvement with gambling or simply from the desire to win; discrimination on the grounds of gender, race, or ethnicity; and violence, that distinctive contribution that men have brought to sport. Some of these elements may have reflected the societies in which sport was played. Certainly, the harshness of existence in preindustrial society flowed into the recreational sector, which often exhibited high levels of violence in the activities pursued, reaching its extreme in public hangings and the burning of witches. Human blood sports (e.g., cudgeling, clogging, pugilism) abounded, and, in societies where human life was cheap, scant regard was paid to cruelty to animals as practiced in the baiting sports and cockfighting.

Sport, at least in Britain, was often also associated with the abuse of alcohol, which, of course, is part of British sporting tradition; consider, for example, why cups were given as trophies. The drinking of alcohol by both participants and spectators was socially sanctioned. Where there was a crowd watching sport, there was alcohol being drunk; hence landlords and brewers were at the forefront of sport promotion. At times, this led to crowd disorder, and there is also considerable evidence that alcohol took its toll on sportspersons as well, due in part to the nature of their careers. Professional athletes—the people who provide sports entertainment—have very different career structures and working lives as compared with those of most of the population. They retire earlier, face greater public appraisal of their work performance, have more erratic income flows, and must often change their place of work on a regular basis. This was as true historically as it is now (Vamplew, 2005).

However, no topic in sport history will ever be exhaustively researched, partly because as the cultural climate changes, new ways of looking at historical issues are formulated. As Polley (2007, p. 4) puts it, the past is continually being rewritten "in the light of . . . current needs and interests." For instance, the historical relationship between sport and charity can be revisited by applying the modern business concept of corporate social responsibility (Kay & Vamplew, 2010). This approach might show that sport was indeed a ready vehicle for charity and that, in turn, charity has been a positive image maker for sport. Such a study would contribute to the economic theory of the nonprofit sector and demonstrate social capital formation via associational philanthropy.

Key Debates

The key ongoing debates about content (as opposed to approach) in sport history revolve around sport violence and the "civilizing process" theories of Norbert Elias and his disciples, the diffusion of sport, and the already-discussed role of associativity in developing sport.

One main thrust of the sociological thought emanating from Elias' work is that, since the Middle Ages, Western Europe has seen an observable decline in people's propensity to obtain pleasure from participating in or witnessing acts of physical violence. The "threshold of repugnance" was lowered partly because the state became more effective in curbing violence; as a social activity, sport was not immune from such change, and, with the assistance of the sport authorities (acting, in effect, as the state for a particular sport), violence was reduced. Indeed, Dunning and Sheard, two followers of Elias, have emphasized the lower level of violence as a conspicuous difference between traditional folk games and modern sport. However, two other leading sport historians have contested the application of the civilizing thesis to sport. Collins has focused his criticisms on the historical method and the associated problems of hindsight, progress, and perspective, whereas Vamplew has focused on the use of historical evidence (Collins, 2005a; Curry, Dunning, & Sheard, 2006; Vamplew, 2007a; Malcolm, 2008). As regards football hooliganism, the main area of sociological historical research in the civilizing debate, Lewis (1996) has argued that, in attempting to show the extent of the problem in British football before 1914, Elias adherents double-counted incidents and used a loose definition of "hooliganism" that included verbal abuse and pitch invasion.

Historians are rarely concerned with pinpointing when a sport started; indeed, a precise date cannot usually be found. Much more important is when the sport became popular and how it was diffused. Although some work has been done on the diffusion of sport within national boundaries and the international transfer of technology (Bale, 1989; Vamplew, 2004), much remains to be done on the historical diffusion and cultural transmission of sport between nations. In Britain, imperialism has long been a major concern of sport historians, who have focused mainly on how Britain exported its sports and games to the colonies and how the recipient countries adopted and adapted them. In recent years, growing interest has been shown in postcolonial analysis (Bale & Cronin, 2003), and MacLean (2010) has applied the subaltern aspect of this approach to West Indian cricket to consider how black West Indians themselves perceived the imported English sport and its social nuances. This tack opens up new queries about traditional sources in which subalterns have responded to imperial representatives with "shy civility," giving the reply that was wanted rather than what was believed. Elsewhere, a recent project has examined the spread of both sport and specific sports in Europe with a focus on the various responses to the appearance of foreign sports, including aversion, resistance, adoption, adaptation, and reinterpretation (Tomlinson & Young, 2011). Work is also emerging on America's sporting empire.

Identity

Identity can be viewed both collectively and individually. National identity can be seen in the way that a sport is played; the laws of the game may be the same, but the meanings of playing and watching may be different in different historical cultures. What rugby means to New Zealanders or to the Welsh could be significantly different from what the French or English take from it. At the opposite end of the identity spectrum, sporting biographies can be used to discover how an individual sportsperson identified himself or herself. Collectively, such microstudies can reveal information about sportspersons at the macrolevel. Both types of study have contributed to an awareness that people can have multiple identities. Billy Meredith, for example, was simultaneously a professional soccer player for Manchester City, a Welsh international, a union activist, a charity promoter, a family man, and a player guilty of corrupt practices (Harding, 1985).

Identities can hinge on gender and ethnicity. Modern sport was established as a male province from its conception and has done much to construct masculinity in many societies. As a site of much male voluntary activity, sport has been a major method of gender fixing, and the football (soccer) codes in particular have been markers of masculinity. For a set of studies looking at identity as a geographic, community, gender, religious, and racial concept, see Hill and Williams (1996). Racial and ethnic identities can be self-ascribed or imposed by others. For an illustrative study of how the construction of memory can be influenced by differing cultural viewpoints, see O'Neill

(2006) on the identity of 19th-century Aboriginal cricketer Unaarrimin (Johnny Mullagh).

Community

That so many sport teams have historically borne community-associated names suggests a major social role for sport. Toulmin's (2006) work on Edwardian film has shown how tiny vignettes of everyday life brought together local sporting activity and the local crowd, revealing strong links between sport and the community. This work reminds us that "what we call history or the past was the present for other people" (Polley, 2007, p. 6). As early as 1900 in Britain, few towns had resisted the appeal of a professional soccer team bearing their name as an exemplar of civic pride. Indeed, from the late 19th century onward, soccer in Europe and baseball in the United States were perhaps the primary means by which working-class males expressed civic patriotism. In an earlier period, as Underdown (2000) has shown, cricket was a major aspect of the fabric of popular festive practices in Britain, and throughout Europe the same applied to traditional sports and games.

There is unfortunately a downside, in that local derby matches could produce friction that spilled over into violence, and within Glasgow the rivalry between the Celtic and Rangers football clubs has become a focus for sectarianism. In New Zealand and Australia, late-20th-century soccer became the site for the re-creation of traditional homeland feuds between teams representing European immigrants (Vamplew, 2007c).

Wealth and Power

The history of virtually all sports suggests that the ability to access resources has always influenced who played. In Britain, mass participation in folk football was cheap; not so the costs of owning polo ponies or oceangoing yachts challenging for the America's Cup. Expensive add-ons have enabled those with wealth to promote social segregation in sport. The rich could afford subscriptions to golf clubs whose luxurious surroundings and employment of servants replicated the domestic situation of their members. The working-class golfer was relegated to the club's artisan section, where he was expected to work on maintaining the course as payback for access to it, or to one of the few municipal courses that offered pay-and-play facilities (Vamplew, 2010).

Thus wealth can bring power in sport, though such power may also be a function of class, gender, or race—aspects often associated with wealth but not exclusively so. One major feature of such power has been the ability to prevent others from participating. For most of the 19th century, and well beyond in many countries, half of the population faced restrictions on playing sport simply because they were female. Depending on the sport and the nation involved, the mechanisms used have included social disapproval from men *and* women, supposedly expert scientific and medical opinion, and the ancillary and regulatory rules imposed by clubs, organizations, and competitions. However, little work has been done on other factors, such as the time demands of employment, child rearing, and preference for other leisure activities (Bandy, 2010). Nor has much work been done on women as spectators, despite photographic evidence of their involvement.

Race, too, has been a significant long-term discriminatory tool wielded by those in power. Nauright and Wiggins (2010) outlined the historical stages of recognition in white sporting circles of black athletes, which have involved novelty value, exclusion, segregation, discrimination, and eventually acceptance, though often still carrying stereotyping based on conceptions of black physical ability. Nevertheless, regarding both gender and race, sport historians using new source material—often produced within the sector discriminated against—have shown that the barriers to participation were not as absolute as was previously believed.

Governance

Sports need rules—competitive sports in order to decide a winner, ritual sports in order to show participants how to play their part. Where sports were religious and ritualistic, the rules were often considered God given and inviolate (Guttmann, 2004); even folk games of the preindustrial period were often run by customary rules that were part of an oral tradition handed down through the generations (Collins et al., 2005). Those of modern sport, in contrast, are human made, written down, and rendered fit for the purpose by constant change. Sport has become a rule-governed practice: Constitutive rules, both prescriptive and proscriptive, define required equipment and facilities and set the formal rules of play; auxiliary rules specify and control eligibility; and regulatory rules place restraints on behavior independent of the sport itself.

Vamplew (2007b) has postulated a schema for the development of constitutive rules. He posits a seven-stage process for regulation: one-off rules for head-to-head contests individually negotiated; rules for head-to-head and all-comers contests using common features; rules for contests using standardized rules; codification of rules by national authorities; rules developed to ensure acceptance of the nationally codified rules; codification of rules by international authorities; and rules developed to ensure acceptance of the internationally codified rules. Vamplew suggests that primacy (but not exclusivity) in the formation and development of rules can be attributed to gambling, though, at later stages, economic factors became more important and, at times, fair play ideology also played a role. Standing outside this schema are the field sports of hunting, shooting, and fishing, which operate around a set of conventions and rituals rather than on the basis of formalized rules (Vamplew, 2009). Most country sports did not require formal, written rules because either they were not competitive (in the sense of having acknowledged winners and losers) or they were not associated with gambling. Where these factors were involved, written rules did emerge, as in coursing and cockfighting.

Although rules are vital to the playing of a sport, significant for those included or excluded from participation, and of relevance for the construction of social convention, the composition of rule-making bodies and the associated power structures await their historians. When the local populace involved themselves in petty betting on animal endurance sports at the alehouse or backing their champion at the annual fair, they accepted the rules as laid down, whether by custom, by the landlord, or by the promoter. They had no influence on the formulation of the rules. This was not the case with the wealthier members of society, who, though using gambling as a form of conspicuous consumption in which they demonstrated that they could afford to stake large sums, still wished to set the rules by which their money was at risk. Possibly, some of these men helped form or became members of private sport clubs that created rules for their own organizations. In turn, these regulations were adopted by others who, in a desire to rationalize their activities, turned to those to whom they deferred. These socially influential groups thus began to rule by common consent. The ruling bodies to which they belonged were not democratic institutions—as private clubs, they were at liberty to determine who could be members—so the rules of sport in the 18th and early 19th centuries were generally being developed by the aristocracy and gentry. Over time, however, the social context changed. The middle classes were enfranchised, both in politics and in sport. Meritocracy became more influential than social position, and democracy, in the form of club or association representation, was enshrined in the constitutions of new rule-making bodies.

Issues for the Sport History Research Agenda

The field of sport history encompasses many subjects not yet studied in detail, just a few of which are considered here. A decade ago, Tranter (1998, p. 96) suggested that too much attention had been paid to the "prestigious institutions, proprietors and performers," leaving "a history of the more mundane and obscure still waiting to be satisfactorily uncovered." Sport still needs its own version of "history from below," which should include the vast range of informal and unorganized sport practices. Moreover, sport history, like much other history, is generally written from the perspective of the winners. However, to be really representative of participation, sport history ought to be more cognizant of losers, for losing is the most typical of sporting experiences; after all, there can be only one champion, only one cup winner. Thus there is a place for the history of the also-rans: the jockeys who failed to keep their weight down, the runners who came in fourth in the Olympic marathon, and the golfers who couldn't break par.

Another failure by historians of sport is to fully grasp the emotion and physicality of sport. It has not been shown what is was like to be a passionate supporter of the Boston Red Sox in the early 20th century or a "manly" English batsman facing up to the hostile Australian fast bowling of Fred "The Demon Bowler" Spofforth. It would be poor history simply to transpose the modern experience of being a fan or a player into the past. Sport historians must search for new source material in match programs, the local press, diaries, and even novels of the time. Somehow, we need to hear the voices of the period.

Another little-researched area is that of children in sport. Huggins (2000) has argued that more needs to be done on the role of the family, and even that other major socializing agency, the school, has not been adequately explored. In Britain, most work has looked at the Victorian public schools, though it remains unclear whether their practice matched their rhetoric and how effective the socialization process was. State schools are practically virgin territory, though it is from the pupils of such educational institutions that most professional sportspersons emerged. Some children were even employed in professional sport. The boy jockey is untouched, but some work has been done on the child caddie in Edwardian golf (Vamplew, 2008a). Here, then, is an opportunity to explore the concepts of child labor (exploitative) versus child work (positive) and the dichotomy between work activities that are socializing and those that are instrumental.

More generally, on the economic side our knowledge is deficient regarding the production of, and trade in, sporting goods. We know something about the racehorse, whose genealogy dates back to the 1600s, but where did the early cricket bats and tennis rackets come from? The demand for a particular sporting good can be volatile, and there is a need here to look at fads and fashions in sporting gear. We also know very little about early sport sponsorship and advertising, by which business firms tried to make potential customers aware of their products. Historically, it existed in the form both of sportsmen endorsing cigarettes, cherry brandy, and various liniments and of brewers and others plastering their names across grandstand roofs, but there have been no studies on either its extent or its effectiveness. There is also a great gap in our historical knowledge of sport promoters and entrepreneurs. As yet, few have followed the pioneering path charted by Hardy (2010) more than 20 years ago, though a stimulating recent contribution by Porter (2010) may provide a way forward.

Finally, but incompletely, there is the issue of sport history tending to be conducted within the parameters of the nation-state and a reluctance (or inability) to cross national boundaries. Language can pose a barrier, but collaborative work could circumvent this hindrance, as in a current major project (Tomlinson & Young, 2001). aimed at developing ways of researching a sport history of Europe. Various themes could lend themselves to cross-cultural comparisons, including associativity, gender relations, children in sport, and racial and ethnic factors in participation.

Summary

Sport history, correctly practiced, provides a way to counter nostalgia, myth, and invented tradition. It can be considered as the sport memory of a nation: Without sport history, there is sporting amnesia. Sport history can indeed set straight the sporting record, but it can also explain why some things changed and why continuities also occurred. History's great contribution to sport studies is the time dimension. It provides the benchmarks for measuring progress and change (or the lack of it). It can help us appreciate the difference between trend and fluctuation; it can also help us realize that not everything seen as important in sport need have a permanent influence, and that not everything in modern sport is new.

Sport history offers an interpretation of the past. The sport historian attempts to make sense of the past by finding evidence, interpreting it, and using it to come to a plausible conclusion—not that many definite conclusions can be drawn. As Oriard has noted (2006, p. 79), "sport history at its best can only be an art of approximation, a fact requiring no apology or defense . . . just careful consideration." Apart from "sportifacts," there is no absolute truth in sport history.

Increasingly, it has been recognized that we can approach history from various perspectives, involving diverse interrogations and interpretations of the source material. Sport history is a contested terrain where it is possible to take different views of the same situation. Even the discipline's path forward is itself a bone of contention, as can be seen in a series of "Presidential Reflections" published in the *Journal of Sport History* between 2007 and 2009, in which the heads of several sport history organizations expressed their views about the subject's future.

Collins (2007, p. 399) has tasked sport historians with demonstrating "why and how sport and leisure mattered to society"—and, it should be added, to individuals and groups in a given society. This program might be advanced by connecting with histories of taste, leisure, and consumption and by drawing more on comparisons, not just over time but also over space. Sport history cannot exist in a ludic vacuum: What commonality of technique, social participation, or economic imperative is shared between deer stalking on a Scottish moor and cheese rolling in Gloucestershire? Such happenings need to be analyzed "in their own particular social contexts, as activities and manifestations of meaning for particular social groups, rather than as part of the continuum of sport" (Collins, 2007, p. 399). And any findings should be made with caution rather than with certainty, respecting the point that historical knowledge is always provisional.

References

Adelman, M.L. (1986). *A sporting time: New York City and the rise of modern athletics, 1820–70.* Champaign: University of Illinois Press.

Agenda Club. (1912). *The rough or the fairway: An enquiry by the Agenda Club into the problem of the golf caddie.* London: Heinemann.

Andreff, W., & Szymanski, S. (2006). *Handbook on the economics of sport.* Cheltenham, UK: Elgar.

Baker, A. (2006). *Contesting identities: Sports in American film.* Champaign: University of Illinois Press.

Bale, J. (1989). *Sports geography.* London: Spon.

Bale, J. (1994). *Landscapes of modern sport.* Leicester, UK: Leicester University Press.

Bale, J. (2006). Partial knowledge: Photographic mystifications and constructions of "the African athlete." In M. Phillips (Ed.), *Deconstructing sport history* (pp. 95–116). Albany: State University of New York Press.

Bale, J., & Cronin, M. (2003). *Sport and postcolonialism.* Oxford, UK: Berg.

Bandy, S.J. (2010). Gender. In S.W. Pope & J. Nauright (Eds.), *Routledge companion to sports history* (pp. 129–147). Abingdon: Routledge.

Booth, D. (2005). *The field: Truth and fiction in sport history.* Abingdon: Routledge.

Booth, D. (2006). Sites of truth or metaphors of power? Refiguring the archive. *Sport in History, 26,* 91–109.

Booth, D. (2010). Theory. In S.W. Pope & J. Nauright (Eds.), *Routledge companion to sports history* (pp. 12–33). Abingdon: Routledge.

Boyle, R., & Haynes, R. (2010). *Power play.* Essex: Longman.

Collins, T. (2005a). History, theory, and the "civilizing process." *Sport in History, 25,* 289–306.

Collins, T. (2005b). Invented traditions. In T. Collins, J. Martin, & W. Vamplew (Eds.), *Encyclopedia of British traditional rural sports* (pp. 171–173). London: Routledge.

Collins, T. (2007). Work, rest, and play: Recent trends in the history of sport and leisure. *Journal of Contemporary History, 42,* 397–410.

Collins, T., Martin J., & Vamplew, W. (Eds.). (2005). *Encyclopedia of British traditional rural sports.* London: Routledge.

Collins, T., & Vamplew, W. (2002). *Mud, sweat, and beers.* Oxford, UK: Berg.

Cronin, M. (2009). What went wrong with counting? Thinking about sport and class in Britain and Ireland. *Sport in History, 29,* 392–404.

Curry, G., Dunning, E., & Sheard, K. (2006). Sociological versus empiricist history: Some comments on Tony Collins's "History, theory, and the civilizing process." *Sport in History, 26,* 110–123.

Dunning, E., Malcolm, D., & Waddington, I. (2004). *Sport histories.* London: Routledge.

Guttmann, A. (1978). *From ritual to record*. New York: Columbia University Press.

Guttmann, A. (2004). *From ritual to record* (updated). New York: Columbia University Press.

Harding, J. (1985). *Football wizard*. Derby: Breedon Books.

Hardy, S. (1986). Entrepreneurs, organizations, and the sport marketplace: Subjects in search of historians, *Journal of Sport History, 13*(1), 14–33.

Hardy, S., Loy, J., & Booth, D. (2009). The material culture of sport: Towards a typology. *Journal of Sport History, 36*, 129–152.

Headon, D. (1999). Significant silents: Sporting Australia on film, 1896–1930. *Journal of Popular Culture, 33*, 115–127.

Hill, J. (2006a). Anecdotal evidence: Sport, the newspaper press, and history. In M. Phillips (Ed.), *Deconstructing sport history* (pp. 117–130). Albany: State University of New York Press.

Hill, J. (2006b). *Sport and the literary imagination*. Oxford, UK: Lang.

Hill, J., Moore, K., & Wood, J. (Eds.). (2012). *Sport, history, and heritage: Studies in public representation*. Woodbridge: Boydell Press.

Hill, J., & Williams, J. (1996). *Sport and identity in the north of England*. Keele, UK: Keele University Press.

Holt, R. (2000). The uses of history in comparative physical education. In J. Tollener & R. Renson (Eds.), *Old borders, new borders, no borders* (pp. 45–57). Oxford, UK: Meyer and Meyer.

Hornby, H. (2008). *Uppies and downies*. Swindon: English Heritage.

Howell, A. (1991). *Harry Vardon*. London: Stanley Paul.

Howell, R., & Howell, M. (1988). *Aussie gold: The Story of Australia at the Olympics*. Albion, Queensland: Brooks Waterloo.

Huggins, M. (2000). Second-class citizens? English middle-class culture and sport, 1850–1910: A reconsideration. *International Journal of the History of Sport, 17*, 1–35.

Huggins, M. (2007). And now, something for the ladies: Representations of women's sport in the newsreels between the wars. *Women's History Review, 16*, 681–700.

Huggins, M. (2008). The sporting gaze: Towards a visual turn in sports history—Documenting art and sport. *Journal of Sport History, 35*, 311–329.

Johnes, M. (2007a). Archives, truths, and the historian at work: A reply to Douglas Booth's "Refiguring the archive." *Sport in History, 27*, 127–135.

Johnes, M. (2007b). Texts, audiences, and postmodernism: The novel as a source in sports history. *Journal of Sport History, 34*, 121–133.

Kay, J. (2009). The archive, the press, and Victorian football: The case of the Glasgow Charity Cup. *Sport in History, 29*, 577–600.

Kay, J., & Vamplew, W. (2010). Beyond altruism: British football and charity, 1877–1914. *Soccer and Society, 11*, 181–197.

Krüger, A. (2008). Which associativity? A German answer to Szymanski's theory of the evolution of modern sport. *Journal of Sport History, 35*, 39–48.

Lewis, R.W. (1996). Football hooliganism in England before 1914: A critique of the Dunning thesis. *International Journal of the History of Sport, 13*, 310–339.

MacLean, M. (2008). Evolving modern sport. *Journal of Sport History, 35,* 49–55.

MacLean, M. (2010). Ambiguity within the boundary: Re-reading C.L.R. James's *Beyond a boundary. Journal of Sport History, 37,* 99–117.

Malcolm, D. (2008). A response to Vamplew and some comments on the relationship between sports historians and sociologists of sport. *Sport in History, 28,* 259–279.

McIntosh, P.C. (1952). *Physical education in England since 1800.* London: Bell.

McIntosh, P.C. (1963). *Sport in society.* London: Watts.

Mewett, P.G. (2000). History in the making and the making of history: Stories and the social construction of a sport. *Sporting Traditions, 17,* 1–18.

Nathaus, K. (2009). The role of associativity in the evolution of modern sport: A comment on Stefan Szymanski's theory. *Journal of Sport History, 36,* 115–122.

Nauright, J., & Wiggins, D.K. (2010). In S.W. Pope & J. Nauright (Eds.), *Routledge companion to sports history* (pp. 148–181). Abingdon: Routledge.

O'Neill, M. (2006). Remembering Johnny Mullagh: Australia's history wars and shifting memories of an Aboriginal cricketer. In R. Hess (Ed.), *Making histories, making memories* (pp. 1–21). Melbourne: Australian Society for Sports History.

Oriard, M. (1993). *Reading football.* Chapel Hill: University of North Carolina Press.

Oriard, M. (2006). A linguistic turn into sports history. In M. Phillips (Ed.), *Deconstructing sport history* (pp. 75–91). Albany: State University of New York Press.

Osmond, G. (2010). Photographs, materiality, and sport history: Peter Norman and the 1968 Mexico City black power salute. *Journal of Sport History, 37,* 119–137.

Phillips, M. (Ed.). (2012). *Representing the sporting past in museums and halls of fame.* Abingdon: Routledge.

Phillips, M., O'Neill, M.E., & Osmond, G. (2007). Broadening horizons in sport history: Films, photographs, and monuments. *Journal of Sport History, 34,* 271–293.

Polley, M. (2003). History of sport. In B. Houlihan (Ed.), *Sport and society* (pp. 49–61). London: Sage.

Polley, M. (2007). *Sports history: A practical guide.* Basingstoke: Palgrave.

Polley, M. (2010). "The archive of the feet": Field walking in sports history. *Journal of Sport History, 37,* 139–153.

Pope, S.W., & Nauright, J. (2010). *Routledge companion to sports history.* Abingdon: Routledge.

Porter, D. (2010). Entrepreneurship. In S.W. Pope & J. Nauright (Eds.), *Routledge companion to sports history* (pp. 197–215). Abingdon: Routledge.

Riess, S.A. (2008). Associativity and the evolution of modern sport. *Journal of Sport History, 35,* 33–38.

Russell, D. (2006). "We all agree, name the stand after Shankly": Cultures of commemoration in late twentieth-century English football culture. *Sport in History, 26,* 1–25.

Seymour, H. (1960). *Baseball: The early years.* New York: Oxford University Press.

Szymanski, S. (2008a). A theory of the evolution of modern sport. *Journal of Sport History, 35,* 1–32.

Szymanski, S. (2008b). A theory of the evolution of modern sport: Response to comments. *Journal of Sport History, 35*, 57–64.

Szymanski, S. (2010). Economists and sport history. *Journal of Sport History, 37,* 71–82.

Taylor, M. (2008). From source to subject: Sport, history, and autobiography. *Journal of Sport History, 35*, 469–491.

Terret, T. (2006). Race and gender in the French sporting press at the end of the 1950s: The example of *Sport & Vie. Sporting Traditions, 23*, 103–122.

Tomlinson, A., & Young, C. (2010). Sport in history: Challenging the *communis opinion. Journal of Sport History, 37*, 5–17.

Tomlinson, A., & Young, C. (2011). Towards a new history of European sport. *European Review, 19*, 487–507.

Toulmin, V. (2006). "Vivid and realistic": Edwardian sport on film. *Sport in History, 26*, 124–149.

Tranter, N. (1998). *Sport, economy, and society in Britain, 1750–1914.* Cambridge: Cambridge University Press.

Underdown, D. (2000). *Start of play.* London: Penguin.

Vamplew, W. (1998). Facts and artefacts: Sports historians and sports museums. *Journal of Sport History, 25*, 268–292.

Vamplew, W. (2004). Sporting innovation: The American invasion of the British turf and links, 1895–1905. *Sport History Review, 35*, 122–137.

Vamplew, W. (2005). Alcohol and the sportsperson: An anomalous alliance. *Sport in History, 25*, 390–411.

Vamplew, W. (2007a). Empiricist versus sociological history: Some comments on the "civilizing process." *Sport in History, 27*, 161–171.

Vamplew, W. (2007b). Playing with the rules: Influences on the development of regulation in sport. *International Journal of the History of Sport, 24*, 843–871.

Vamplew, W. (2007c). Success for all? Australia's (un)sporting record. In H. Hassam (Ed.), *Australian studies now* (pp. 361–374). New Delhi: Indialog.

Vamplew, W. (2008a, April 23). Childwork or child labour? The caddie question in Edwardian golf. idrottsforum. http://www.idrottsforum.org/articles/vamplew/vamplew080423.html.

Vamplew, W. (2008b). Exploited labour or successful workingmen: Golf professionals and professional golfers in Britain before 1914. *Economic History Review, 61*, 54–79.

Vamplew, W. (2009). Sports without rules: Hunting, shooting, and fishing in Edwardian Britain. *European Studies in Sport History, 1*, 34–51.

Vamplew, W. (2010). Sharing space: Inclusion, exclusion, and accommodation at the British golf club before 1914. *Sport and Social Issues, 34*, 359–375.

Vamplew, W. (2012). Economic approaches to sports (and cultural) history. In A. Gestrich & C. Eisenberg (Eds.), *Cultural industries in Britain and Germany* (pp. 110–123). Augsburg: Wißner-Verlag.

Vamplew, W., & Kay, J. (2003). A modern sport? "From ritual to record" in British horseracing. *Ludica, 9*, 125–139.

Whannel, G. (1992). *Fields of vision.* London: Routledge.

CHAPTER 2

Philosophy of Sport

Sigmund Loland, PhD,
and Michael McNamee, PhD

What characterizes sport? What are the actual and possible meanings of sport in people's lives? What are the actual and possible values of sport in and to society? What is fair play? Is competition compatible with play? Is it possible to distinguish, on rational grounds, between acceptable and unacceptable performance-enhancing means and methods? Can judged sports be objectively evaluated? How can human embodiment and movement be understood? Does prosthetic technology threaten our understanding of athleticism? What do we know when we say we know how to play a game?

These questions are widely asked in sport studies, and they can be answered, though only partly, by reference to empirical facts. The social sciences can critically describe and explain the various characteristics of sport and the effect of sport in individual lives and in society. Studies of sport cultures can inform us about ideas of fairness and aesthetic qualities. Sociologists, psychologists, and physiologists provide very different versions of the moving body in sport.

Nevertheless, such discussions form only part of a full-fledged response to these questions. Inquiries into the characteristics and potential values and meanings of sport and associated activities always require conceptual clarification and reflection and thus invite philosophical responses that are characterized by systematic and critical reasoning.

Philosophical activities are not limited by empirical facts or investigations, or even critical descriptions of the world as it is constructed. Rather, philosophy opens up considerations of possible views—of both normative and more descriptive kinds—about how sport is to be understood, conceived, and enacted. Sometimes, philosophical writings even go against common sense and empirical findings. The fact that a clear majority in society opposes doping practices does not necessarily make such practices morally wrong. The fact that 9 out of 10 referees in gymnastics may agree on the rationality of the grading system does not necessarily make it fair and just. The fact that a particular competitive sport, such as soccer, enjoys immense popularity does not necessarily make it the best sport practice for the individual or for society more generally if it brings in its wake homophobia, racism, and sexism.

What, then, are the significance and the relevance of philosophical examination of and for sport? One response is to point to the large number of people engaged in these practices. Most, though not all, children meet sport in the contexts of physical education in school. In Western societies, various studies suggest that more than half of the population engages in some kind of exercise at least once a week. Public interest in elite sport is immense, and sport is one of the most popular products on the international entertainment market, occupying a highly significant place in general media outlets with print or electronic outputs. Sport blogs abound the world over. Yet the ubiquity of Westernized competitive sport forms does not go unchallenged, whether in the social sciences or in the humanistic study of sport. There is a Socratic saying that "the unexamined life is not worth living." If this is true, then reflective knowledge of sport is of value in itself. From a more instrumental point of view, we need philosophical knowledge in order to be able to evaluate the possibilities and limitations of sport as a conceptual basis for sport studies and for sound sport policy and practice.

In this chapter, we take a brief look at the historical development of the philosophy of sport, its key concepts and theoretical perspectives, its critical findings, and its key debates. Our discussions are limited primarily to the Anglophone literature and do not cover the rather extensive literature in French, German, Japanese, and Chinese that relate to the philosophy of sport. We conclude with some reflections on the future development and possibilities of the discipline.

Historical Overview of the Discipline

Philosophizing over sport is by no means a new idea. The worlds of philosophy and sport have collided at least since Plato's early foray into wrestling at the Isthmian Games (Miller, 2004) and his recommendations for gymnastics in the early education of the philosopher-kings in *The Republic*. Indeed, ideas concerning the meaning and value of embodied capacities have been preeminent throughout history in most cultures of the world. More often than not, such ideas have been connected to military force and the development and maintenance of masculine identities. Examples range from the Spartan ethos of bodily discipline and toughness via the European knight ethos of the Middle Ages to the rise of modern sport in Victorian Britain—"the land of sport" (Holt, 1989).

In more recent times, although early works of high quality do exist on sport, play, and games—for example, Eugen Herrigel's *Zen and the Art of Archery* (1953) and Johan Huizinga's (1934) classic *Homo Ludens: A Study of the Play Element in Culture*—the development of the philosophy of sport as a systematic and critical academic field belongs to the general expansion and differentiation of academia in the postwar period. Works in Europe and the United States by Hans Lenk (1969), Howard S. Slusher (1967), Eleanor Metheny (1965), and Paul Weiss (1969) provided the ground for a development of the philosophy of sport as a subdiscipline of philosophy more formally. In institutional terms, the philosophy of sport might be said to have come into existence at a meeting of the American Philosophical Association in Boston on December 28, 1972, when the Philosophic Society for the Study of Sport (PSSS) was founded, thanks principally to the efforts of Professor Warren Fraleigh of the State University of New York at Brockport. The PSSS staged annual meetings across the world beginning in 1973. In the nascent studies of sport, and the many academic subject areas that grew out of it, philosophy of sport can rightly claim to be among the earliest formed. In 1999, the PSSS renamed itself the International Association for the Philosophy of Sport in order to indicate, among other things, the growing regional diversity of its membership. It has published the *Journal of the Philosophy of Sport* at least annually since 1974 (biannually since 2001). Many of its best early articles were collected in two editions by former editors Bill Morgan and Klaus Meier (1988, 1995).

While the subject enjoyed a strong basis in the United States and Canada, its development in the global context was somewhat uneven. Until recently, the only two formally organized national associations for the philosophy of sport, both formed in the 1970s, were the Japan Society for the Philosophy of Sport and Physical Education and the philosophy of sport section in the German Society of Sport Science (Deutsche Vereinigung für Sportwissenschaft). In 2002, the British Philosophy of Sport Association (BPSA) was formed, and it has generated only the second international journal in the field—*Sport, Ethics, and Philosophy*, which was published first three and now four times per year. Though the United Kingdom had sufficient critical mass to form a national association, BPSA also served as a focus for European scholarship, and a working group of that organization then established the European Association for the Philosophy of Sport in 2008. In 2012, the Czech Association for Sport Philosophy and Kinanthropology was instituted.

Main Theoretical Perspectives

In the introduction, we referred to the philosophical study of sport as one of systematic reflection. At its most general level, it is concerned with articulating the nature, as well as the possible meanings and values, of sport. Its more applied side deals with practical issues, such as how to draw lines and frame acceptable or admirable sporting conduct, how to understand ideas such as the most valuable player on a team, and how to allocate scarce coaching resources equitably.

The philosophy of sport has not crystallized; its methods require of practitioners an inherently self-critical conception of intellectual activity, one that
is continuously challenging its own preconceptions and guiding principles
of the nature and purposes of philosophy and of sport. Therefore, it draws
upon and develops many of the diverse branches of its parent discipline—
philosophy—and reflects a broad church of theoretical positions and styles.
It has most specifically interrogated substantive issues in the following
subfields (in parentheses, we offer an indicative question of relevance to
sport for each field):

- Aesthetics (Can some sports be considered art forms?)
- Epistemology (Do we know skills if we cannot describe them?)
- Ethics (Ought talent development include genetic screening?)
- Logic (Are auxiliary, constitutive, and regulative rules conceptually distinct?)
- Metaphysics (Are humans naturally game-playing animals?)
- Philosophy of education (Can dominant models of skill learning account for phenomenological insights?)
- Philosophy of law (Are sports rules legally enforceable?)
- Philosophy of mind (How can the moving body in sport be conceptualized and understood?)
- Philosophy of rules (Can rule following be distinguished from acts performed merely in accordance with rules?)
- Philosophy of science (How can we reach relevant and valid knowledge of sport, and how can this knowledge be organized?)
- Social and political philosophy (Is hypercommodification the necessary child of sport in neoliberal societies?)

In these areas of examination, the field is home to a variety of theoretical
and methodological approaches. To a certain extent, approaches carry geographical connotations. In Japan, as in Britain, a certain amount of philosophical scholarship in relation to sport has been generated in the philosophy of
education, where philosophical thinking in physical education has found a
more genial academic home. Britain has also seen very strong scholarship
in the fledgling fields of human movement studies and leisure studies, and,
later, sport and exercise sciences, where philosophers have played a prominent role in the very shaping of the fields themselves.

In the West (and therefore in the *Journal of the Philosophy of Sport*), there
has been a tendency for one philosophical tradition to dominate—analytical
philosophy, which emerged as an essentially conceptual inquiry whose aim
was foundational. It is often captured in Locke's famous remark about philo-

sophical scholarship being akin to an underlaborer working in the garden of knowledge. As a second-order activity, its central aim was to provide secure foundations for other disciplines by articulating their conceptual geography with rigor and precision. Of course, other social and humanistic disciplines have at times objected to the preeminence claimed by philosophy and have argued that it is also intrinsic to their scholarship and science so that they did not await philosophers' input in order to raise fundamental questions regarding their nature and purposes. In the philosophy of sport, for example, the earliest efforts to define the field were made in terms of clarifying key concepts in the field, such as play, games, and sport, as well as their possible interrelations (Suits, 1978).

The contested claim to preeminence of analytic philosophy was captured by the insistence that conceptual work precedes all proper empirical inquiry. Its exponents were equipped with the analytical tools of dissecting concepts for constituent criteria, drawing distinctions by their logical grammar, and seeking fine-grained differences in their employment. The discipline of philosophy was reduced in some quarters to the detailing of ordinary linguistic usages and necessary and sufficient conditions in order to detect the proper meaning of concepts that others had to operate with and between. Despite this "new" direction, there remained a strong sense of continuity with the ancient past. Philosophers such as Plato and Aristotle were also concerned with marking distinctions, bringing clarity where before there was puzzlement or, worse, commonsensical acquiescence.

In continental Europe, a significant body of disparate literature has emerged in native languages, notably in the Czech Republic, Germany, Hungary, Poland, and, more recently, Slovenia. One term in fairly common currency in Eastern Europe is "philosophy of physical culture"; others are "philosophy of movement culture" and "philosophical kinanthropology." In contrast to analytic philosophy, philosophers working in the continental tradition have largely developed research in the fields of existentialism, hermeneutics, ontology, and phenomenology (Martinkova & Parry, 2012). The differences of philosophical engagement reveal themselves clearly, though not sharply. The analytic philosopher looks at sport at a distance and aims at clear-cut distinctions and categories, whereas the phenomenologist engages in a reflective embrace of the phenomenon. A phenomenological perspective on the nature of sport would not be so concerned with conceptual line drawing but more with examining sport as a socioculturally contextualized expression of the human spirit and human embodiment and our possibilities as embodied beings in the world (Hyland, 1974; Eichberg, 2010). Phenomenologists favor interpretation over verification. In Hyland's work, for instance, play is defined as a particular stance taken toward the world. In an early classic from Kretchmar (1982), a phenomenological approach is used to better understand a skilled basketball player's movement on the court.

Key Debates

To a certain extent, key debates in the philosophy of sport have varied among the traditions we have just sketched. Some key themes, however, are shared: first and foremost, the nature and possible definitions or conceptualizations and interpretations of sport and related human practices; and second, ethical issues in sport, in particular competitive ethics and the use of performance-enhancing means and methods (e.g., doping). Let us briefly review the main debates in these two themes.

What is commonly called sport in the West draws upon a rich history of Greek and Roman athletics carried through to the modern incarnation of educational sport in Victorian Britain and finally to the rebirthing of the Olympic Games by Baron Pierre de Coubertin and others (McNamee & Parry, 2012). While the paradigmatic sports we recognize as Olympic ones were practiced and promoted across Europe, so too were alternative movement cultures, including fitness- and health-related activity groups and sport-for-all organizations, which bore only a "family resemblance" (Wittgenstein, 1958) to the rule-governed and competitive activities that are typically thought of and classified as being sports by the media, international event organizers, sport educators, and so on.

This approach certainly dominated the first 20 years of scholarship in the *Journal of the Philosophy of Sport*. Much of it revolved around conceptual relationships related to "the tricky triad" of play, games, and sport (Meier, 1988; Suits, 1988). One notable exception was Scott Kretchmar's work on the nature of the test–contest relationship, which sought to outline conceptual and phenomenological parameters of games and sports and the playing thereof (Kretchmar, 1975). Work on play had taken its lead not only from classic sources such as Plato but also from more modern scholarship, notably that of Johan Huizinga (Hyland, 1974, 1984).

The concept of "game," of course, had been no stranger to mainstream philosophical debates. In Wittgenstein's *Philosophical Investigations*, the concept was used as a foil set against an earlier pictorial theory of language and its relation to the world. The example could be taken as a hinge of an ancient philosophical debate: Could all games have nothing in common other than the fact that they are called games, or is some essence shared by them all? The latter, realist position was attacked by Wittgenstein, as is well known. Less well known, outside the philosophy of sport anyway, was Bernard Suits' challenge to Wittgenstein's thesis that all that games had in common were family resemblances in the class of activities called games. Suits' earliest statement of his position was an article titled "What Is a Game?" that was published in 1967 by the mainstream philosophical journal *Philosophy of Science*; he later developed it into a classic book-length essay titled *The Grasshopper: Games, Life, and Utopia* (1978).

In brief, Suits defined game playing as "the voluntary attempt to overcome unnecessary obstacles" (1978/2005). For example, soccer includes a rule against outfield players touching the ball with their hands; in hurdle races, physical obstacles are placed in the lanes; and alpine skiers must make turns through gates rather than going straight down the hill. Competitors cannot ignore these rules without violating the very idea of the sport. Suits contrasted game playing with everyday, instrumental (means–ends) activities as having no purpose outside itself. A game, with its unnecessary obstacles, exists in principle for no other reason than the game itself. This, according to Suits, is an expression of what he called "a lusory (i.e., playful) attitude."

As is evident in a 2008 special issue of the *Journal of the Philosophy of Sport* devoted to Suits' work, his position elicited many and varied critical responses and seemed to occupy a vast portion of the philosophy of sport in the 1980s and 1990s. Indeed, its enduring sophistication and relevance ensure that it is still extracted in edited collections in the philosophy of sport and sport ethics (Morgan, 2007; McNamee, 2010).

This openness regarding the classification of sport is extended to the divergent branches of philosophy itself. Just as more established branches of philosophy are not immune from fashion, neither is the philosophy of sport. If analytical investigations dominated the literature at one time, so too aesthetics and social philosophy have been well represented in the literature, as exemplified, respectively, by the work of Best (1978) and Morgan (1994). In the 1990s, however, ethics—and thus the ethics of sport—came to a position of dominance in research and scholarship in the philosophy of sport, and it has remained there ever since. The most common examples of ethics in sport that spring up in casual conversations, as well as in the academic literature, are matters of fair play and sportspersonship, equity in terms of social and financial justice, children's and women's rights in sport, and deviant subcultures and practices (e.g., doping, hooliganism). Given this dominance, we turn now to an account of the nature and purposes of sport ethics.

Typically, some degree of confusion surrounds the nature and scope of the very concept of sport ethics. For one thing, the words *ethics* and *morality* are used interchangeably in everyday language. Many mainstream philosophers have come to question the concept of morality as a peculiarly Western convention associated with an overly ambitious desire to universalize guides to right conduct. Along with the project of modernity, philosophers had been looking to universalize ethics along the lines that scientists had so powerfully done in discovering natural laws and thereby "mastering" the world. A number of traditions of moral thinking emerged that shared certain features in their development of systems of thought intended to guide the conduct of citizens of the globe wherever they existed.

In this modern philosophical vein, then, *ethics* was used to refer to the systematic study of morals—that is, universal codes or principles of right conduct. It is still worth observing a distinction between, on the one hand, rules, guidelines, mores, and principles of living (i.e., morality) that exist in time and space and, on the other hand, systematic reflection upon them (ethics). The idea that morality refers to that to which all reasonable persons ought to conform requires much more careful attention.

Having suggested a distinction between morality and ethics, we must also state that the very concept of ethics itself is hotly contested. The relevant theoretical positions is too numerous to list here beyond noting that it includes contractarianism, emotivism, intuitionism, and rights theory in the West, as well as a host of religioethical systems such as Confucianism in the East.

In philosophical scholarship in the ethics of sport (as opposed to sociological or historical studies), three families of theoretical and methodological approaches have been adopted—two modern and one ancient. Modern moral philosophy was dominated for much of that last 200 years by the universalistic ethics of either consequentialism or deontology. The last 20 years or so (a relatively short time in philosophical thought) have seen a revival of virtue theory work in mainstream ethics and in the ethics of sport. Some introductory remarks and references to indicative sources in the literature must suffice here.

Deontology (from the Greek word *deon*, translated roughly as duty) is the classical theory of right action. Deontologists argue (the writings of the German philosopher Immanuel Kant form the locus classicus here) that before we act, we must consider those duties (usually in the form of principles or rights) that we owe to others in our transactions with them. The ensuing system of principles is usually thought to have its foundation in a super-rule (often called the Golden Rule and enshrined in Christian thought, among other traditions) that one ought always to treat others with respect that acknowledges their inherent moral status. To cheat, deceive, harm, or lie to people is to disrespect them as persons. An elegant statement of the deontological ethic in sport can be found in Warren Fraleigh's classic *Right Actions in Sport* (1984), which attempts to cash out a system of guides to right conduct for participants and coaches engaged in sport. Sigmund Loland's *Fair Play in Sport* (2002) is an updated example of a deontological approach building on Rawlsian social contract theory, which models sport contests as attempts to establish the athletically superior contestant or team under reasonable conditions of fairness and with acceptance of certain unpredictable elements of chance and luck.

Of course, deontological ethicists still face philosophically troubling questions such as the following: What is meant by respect? Does respect always trump other moral values? Does respect entail not harming others even when they consent to it? Fraleigh (1984), for example, argued that boxing is immoral since it involves the intentional harming of another, even though he or she has consented to that harm. While deontology (whether focused on rights or duties) remains a commonsense ethic for many people, others think it simply starts from the wrong place.

In apparent contrast, consequentialism is a teleological theory (from the Greek word *telos*, translated roughly as nature or purpose). It is in fact a family of theories of the good, which justify actions according to their yielding the most favorable and least unfavorable consequences. The dominant strand of thinking here is utilitarianism, which comes in a variety of shapes and sizes but is generally based on maximizing utility or good. In distinguishing good from bad, we merely need to add up the potential consequences of different courses of action and take the one that maximizes good outcomes for all parties involved.

Unlike related branches of applied ethics (e.g., health care, medical ethics, and military ethics), the philosophy and ethics of sport have seen very few sustained efforts at utilitarian thinking. The clearest examples of systematic consequentialism in the field are Claudio Tamburrini's (2000) defense of Diego Maradona's infamous "Hand of God" incident in the 1986 soccer World Cup and related works. Tamburrini also attempts to argue, from a utilitarian perspective, for controversial conclusions to the doping issue (specifically, in favor of abolishing current anti-doping policy) and gender equity (in favor of non-sex-segregated sport).

Though deontology and consequentialism build on opposing foundations for justifying moral action (in sport, as in life), they also share certain important conceptual features. First, they are universal in scope: Moral rules apply in all places and times—it's just that they focus on different moral principles (respect versus utility). Equally important is their enshrinement of impartiality. In both theoretical traditions, no one person or group must be favored over another. Finally, they share the idea that moral rules have force: Once you understand them, you must act in a manner that brings the conclusion of moral consideration to life in your actions, for failure to do so would be not only immoral but also irrational.

The recent revival of virtue theory has usually taken the form of a resuscitation of Aristotle's work. Here, ethics is based on good character, and the good life will be lived by those who are in possession of a range of virtues (e.g., courage, cooperativeness, sympathy, honesty, justice, reliability) and who are free from vices (e.g., cowardice, egoism, dishonesty). Inspired by Alasdair MacIntyre's (1984) writings in *After Virtue*, many philosophers came to conceive of sport as consisting of social practices and moved away from ahistorical and asocial analytical accounts of the elements of games and sports. They often moved away also from the deontological accounts of sport ethics—especially in terms of the constructions of theories of fair play—into virtue theory accounts of sport and therefore of sport ethics. As often happens, shifts in mainstream studies (here, moral philosophy) affected related fields, in this case scholarship in the ethics and philosophy of sport. Since that time, Feezell (2006), McNamee (2008), Dombrowski (2009), and Reid (2010) have each presented sustained accounts of virtue ethics and sport that are inspired by ancient Greek ethics in contemporary contexts. This has meant detailing character traits and identities—as opposed to act-based thinking—that characterize good and bad sports and sportspersons. Such discussions focus on the subjects of everyday reflections of sport—for example, hubris or humility, courage or cowardice, empathy versus schaden-freude, and patriotism versus nationalism.

Future Directions

This sketch of philosophical themes and perspectives regarding sport is not merely suggestive; it is also a rather traditional one, and a series of other themes has emerged in the literature. What, then, are the future directions of the discipline?

Given the competitiveness, the strong and widespread emotional involvement, and the significance of sport in modern life, applied ethics will continue to play a predominant part in the philosophy of sport. One indicator of important emerging themes can be found in an unfolding 25-volume book series titled *Ethics and Sport* and edited by Mike McNamee and Jim Parry. Its topics include, among others, explorations of the hyper-commodification of sport; investigations of injury, pain, and risk; eating disorders; exploitation and sexual harassment; genetic ethics; and research ethics in relation to sport (for more information, see www.routledge.com/books/series/EANDS/page_1).

Another development is to be found in the epistemology of sport. Works here include Ziff's (1974) thesis, with an example from tennis, that there are no particularly interesting epistemological questions in sport, Scott Kretchmar's analysis of basketball (1982), Tamboer's (1992) account of motor actions, and Loland's (1992) discussion of alpine skiing, as well as recent articles deriving from Norway by Moe (2007), Breivik (2008), and Birch (2009) that apply ideas and insights from the philosophy of mind and neuroscience in sport. More work of this kind will certainly be stimulated by paradigms of mind build-ing that are emerging from the confluence of the biological (brain) sciences and humanistic interpretations.

A third, and growing, interest involves alternative sport cultures and their development. For example, increased interest in the relationship between sporting practices and the environment can be seen in works by Loland (1996) and Anderson (2001). We also see increased analysis of alternative move-ment cultures (e.g., snowboarding) and of risk cultures related to activities such as BASE jumping (Breivik, 2007) that place less emphasis on formalized competition and stronger emphasis on creativity and aesthetic qualities. Aesthetics has long been an interest of sport philosophers, who have a long history of addressing questions about the nature of beauty in sport and whether sport can be considered an art form (Kupfer, 2001; Cordner, 1984, 1988; Roberts, 1986; Best, 2009; Lacerda, 2011). This interest has found new expression in regard to alternative sport cultures that emphasize aesthetic qualities and individual artistic expression. Among all of sport's academic disciplines, the philosophy of sport should represent a frontier here thanks to its ambition to study not only dominant sport forms but also marginal and alternative movement forms, including those in the contexts of disability and Paralympic sport (Jespersen & McNamee, 2009).

A fourth noteworthy development is the increase in articles on sport policy. Dominant among these have been criticisms of anti-doping efforts, but other topics are emerging with greater frequency, including legislation addressing athletes' rights, intercollegiate sport, match fixing and corruption, Paralympic classification, and coaching education frameworks. These publications betoken a development toward more applied work for philosophers of sport.

Summary

One concern about the future of the philosophy of sport is shared by many of the humanistic disciplines in the study of sport—namely, the increasingly strong hegemony of the natural or biosciences of sport, which has led to the marginalization of minority sport subjects such as history, philosophy, and theology. Yet due to rapid cultural and technological development, the need for the work of philosophers of sport is stronger than ever. It may well be the case that philosophers of sport must work not only in their traditional disciplinary boundaries but also in tandem with those in other humanistic and social science fields to celebrate sport as a fundamentally human endeavor—and one not to be dominated by science and technology. Despite the scientization and technologization of sport and sport studies, the philosophy of sport appears to be in stronger health now than it has been for many decades.

References

Anderson, D. (2001). Recovering humanity: Movement, sport, and nature. *Journal of the Philosophy of Sport, 28*(2), 140–150.

Best, D.N. (1978). *Philosophy and human movement*. London: Allen and Unwin.

Birch, J.E. (2009). A phenomenal case for sport. *Sport, Ethics, and Philosophy, 3*(1), 30–48.

Breivik, G. (2007). Can BASEjumping be morally defended? In McNamee, M. J. (Ed.). Philosophy, risk and adventure sports. Abingdon: Routledge.168-185.

Breivik, G. (2008). Bodily movement—The fundamental dimensions. *Sport, Ethics, and Philosophy, 2*(3), 337–352.

Cordner, C. (1984). Grace and functionality. *British Journal of Aesthetics, 24*, 301–313.

Cordner, C. (1988). Differences between sport and art. *Journal of the Philosophy of Sport, 15*(1), 31–47.

Dombrowski, D.A. (2009). *Contemporary athletics and ancient Greek ideals.* Chicago: University of Chicago Press.

Eichberg, H. (2010). *Bodily democracy: Towards a philosophy of sports for all.* London: Routledge.

Feezell, R. (2006). *Sport, play, and ethical reflection.* Champaign, IL: University of Illinois Press.

Fraleigh, W.P. (1984). *Right actions in sport: Ethics for contestants.* Champaign, IL: Human Kinetics.

Herrigel, E. (1953). *Zen and the art of archery.* London: Routledge & Kegan Paul.

Holowchack, M.A., & Barkasi, M. (Eds.). *Journal of the Philosophy of Sport 35*(2),111-92.

Holt, R. (1989). *Sport and the British.* Oxford, UK: Oxford University Press.

Huizinga, J. (1934). *Homo ludens: A study of the play element in culture.* London: Paladin.

Hyland, D. (1974). *Philosophy of sport.* Lanham, MD: University Press of America.

Hyland, D. A. (1984). The question of play. Lanham, MD: University Press of America.

Jespersen, E., & McNamee, M.J. (2009). *Ethics, dis/ability, and sports.* Abingdon: Routledge.

Kretchmar, R.S. (1975). From test to contest. *Journal of the Philosophy of Sport, 2,* 23–30.

Kretchmar, R. S. (1982). Distancing: An essay on abstract thinking in sport performances. *Journal of the Philosophy of Sport, (9)*1, 6-18.

Kupfer, J. (2001). Perfection as negation in the aesthetics of sport. *Journal of the Philosophy of Sport, 28*(1), 18–31.

Lacerda, T. (2011). From ode to sport to contemporary aesthetic categories of sport: Strength considered as an aesthetic category. *Sport, Ethics, and Philosophy, 5*(4), 447–456.

Lenk, H. (1969). *Social philosophy of athletics.* Champaign, IL: Stipes.

Loland, S. (1992). The mechanics and meaning of alpine skiing: Methodological and epistemological notes on the study of sport technique. *Journal of the Philosophy of Sport, 19*(1), 55–77.

Loland, S. (1996). Outline of an ecosophy of sport. *Journal of the Philosophy of Sport, 23*(1), 50–70.

Loland, S. (2002). *Fair play in sport: A moral norm system.* London: Routledge.

MacIntyre, A.C. (1984). *After virtue* (2nd ed.). Abingdon: Routledge.

Martinkova, I., & Parry, S.J. (Eds.). (2012). *Phenomenological approaches to sport.* Abingdon: Routledge.

McNamee, M.J. (2008). *Sports, virtues, and vices: Morality plays.* Abingdon: Routledge.

McNamee, M.J. (Ed.). (2010). *The ethics of sport: A reader.* Abingdon: Routledge.

McNamee, M.J., & Parry, S.J. (Eds.). (2012). *Olympic ethics and philosophy.* Abingdon: Routledge.

Meier, K.V. (1988). Triad trickery: Playing with sport and games. *Journal of the Philosophy of Sport, 15,* 11–30.

Metheny, E. (1965). *Connotations of movement in sport and dance.* Dubuque, IA: Brown.

Miller, S. G. (2012). Arete: Greek sports from ancient sources. University of California Press.

Moe, V.F. (2007). Understanding the background conditions of skilled movement in sport: A study of Searle's "background capacities." *Sport, Ethics, and Philosophy, 1*(3), 299–324.

Morgan, W.J. (Ed.). (1994). *Leftist theories of sport: A critique and a reconstruction.* Champaign, IL: University of Illinois Press.

Morgan, W.J. (Ed.). (2007). *Ethics in sport* (2nd ed.). Champaign, IL: Human Kinetics.

Reid, H. L. (2010). Athletic virtue: Between east and west. *Sport, Ethics and Philosophy, (4)*1, 16-26.

Roberts, T.J. (1986). Sport, art, and particularity: The best equivocation. *Journal of the Philosophy of Sport, 13*(1), 49–63.

Slusher, H.S. (1967). *Man, sport, and existence: A critical analysis.* Philadelphia: Lea & Febiger.

Suits, B. (1967). What is a game? *Philosophy of Science, 34*(2), 148–156.

Suits, B. (1978/2005). *The grasshopper: Games, life, and utopia* (2nd ed.). Toronto: University of Toronto/Broadview Press.

Suits, B. (1988). Tricky triad: Games, play, and sport. *Journal of the Philosophy of Sport, 15*, 1–29.

Tamboer, J.W.I. (1992). Sport and motor actions. *Journal of the Philosophy of Sport, 19*, 82–90.

Tamburrini, C. (2000). *The "Hand of God": Essays in the philosophy of sports.* Gothenburg: University of Gothenburg Press.

Weiss, P. (1969). *Sport: A philosophic inquiry.* Carbondale: Southern Illinois University Press.

Wittgenstein, L. (1958). Philosophical investigations. Oxford: Blackwell.

Ziff, P. (1974). A fine forehand. *Journal of the Philosophy of Sport, 1*, 92–109.

CHAPTER 3

Psychology of Sport

**David Lavallee, PhD, John Kremer, PhD,
and Aidan Moran, PhD**

The history of the psychology of sport as a distinct and defined discipline is very brief, spanning only a few decades (Kremer & Moran, 2008), yet from the very earliest descriptions of sport the possible associations between the physical and the psychological have never been far from people's thoughts. From Homer onward, Greek literature includes references not only to the significance of sport but also to the psychology of sport. Greek historians vividly illustrate how training methods of ancient Greek athletes owed as much to psychology as to any other science—and how organized and professional that training became over time (Gardiner, 1930; Sweet, 1987). Even as early as the 4th century BC, Aristotle was able to write the following in the *Nicomachean Ethics*: "We argue more about the navigation of ships than about the training of athletes, because it has been less well organized as a science." Six hundred years later, in *Gymnasticus*, Philostratus challenged this "traditional" science by arguing against the rigidity of what had become the gold standard of athletic training—the tetrad or four-day system, which was guided by psychological as well as physiological principles (day 1, preparation; day 2, concentration; day 3, moderation; day 4, relaxation). These writings make clear that trainers were acting in some capacity as sport psychologists.

To both the ancient Greek and the later Roman civilizations, sport and physical prowess occupied a pivotal role. Psychologists today constantly extol the motto *mens sana in corpore sano* (a healthy mind in a healthy body). The phrase derives from the Roman author Juvenal's tenth satire, written in the 1st century AD. This work ponders a number of topics, most especially the onset of old age, which was the focus of the original quotation: *Orandum est ut sit mens sana in corpore sano* (your prayer must be that you may have a sound mind in a sound body).

Though it is difficult to chart a history of work from these early days of sport psychology to the beginning of the 20th century (Benjamin & Green, 2009), it is fair to say that sport in its many guises has always provided fertile opportunities for both participants and spectators to reflect on psychological issues. However, despite this long-standing preoccupation with the psychology of sport, it was only in the 1960s that people began to describe themselves as "sport psychologists." Before that time, a number of pioneers could legitimately be labeled as sport psychologists, but their endeavors were rarely supported by the dedicated infrastructures typically associated with academia and scientific discovery. For example, from the 1890s, various psychology departments included staff who were interested in the psychology of sport, but they rarely fostered structures that withstood the test of time.

Across the discipline as a whole, psychological research with a sporting dimension began to appear around the turn of the 19th century. The most famous early example of a research program was Norman Triplett's (1898) archival and experimental work on "dynamogenic factors" in the United States. Triplett was a teacher and an amateur cyclist who returned to Indiana University to work on a master's thesis titled *The Dynamogenic Factors in Pacemaking and Competition*. When Triplett examined official cycling records, he consistently found that the average times of paced race cyclists (1:55.5 per mile [1.6 km]) and competition cyclists (1:50.35 per mile) were faster than those of unpaced race cyclists (2:29 per mile). This archival research provided the impetus for a follow-up study involving an experiment in which children wound a length of silk onto a reel, either working alongside a coactor performing an identical task or working alone (see also S.F. Davis, Huss, & Becker, 2009). Those winding the line alongside another who was also reeling recorded significantly faster times than did those reeling alone. This result led Triplett to suggest that the presence of others serves as a stimulus to arouse the competitive instinct, which, in turn, frees nervous energy that cannot be released when competing alone.

This pioneering research has come to be recognized as the oldest experimental paradigm in social psychology. The study was also the first to look at what we now perceive as a sport psychology phenomenon, and some texts (e.g., Weinberg & Gould, 2007, pp. 525-526) even credit Triplett's research as the beginning of sport psychology in North America. What is more—and this predates the extensive literature on competitive anxiety in sport—Triplett acknowledged that individuals, whether professional cyclists or children, often responded very differently to the rigors of competition. Some rose to the challenge and performed better (Triplett noted "the arousal of their competitive instincts and the idea of a faster movement") while others were overstimulated by the prospect and performed worse in the presence of others ("going to pieces"). Indeed, the complex relationship between arousal and performance remains a problem that sport psychologists wrestle with more than 100 years later.

Other writers in this period were offering less systematic and less empirical appraisals of sporting behavior than Triplett's. For example, at roughly the same time that Sigmund Freud was describing the psychodynamics of crowd behavior in general, articles were beginning to appear on the topic of spectator psychology. These efforts included papers by Patrick (1903) on the psychology of American football and Howard (1912) on the cathartic effects associated with watching sport. However, calls for further spectator research went unheeded, at least until the 1950s (Hastorf & Cantril, 1954).

Leaving these early contributions aside, the psychology of sport experienced an important period in the 1920s due to the work of Coleman Roberts Griffith (Green, 2009). Griffith's interest in sport psychology began informally during his time as a PhD student at the University of Illinois and continued following his appointment to the teaching staff at the same university. An educational psychologist by training, Griffith taught in both the psychology and the physical welfare departments. In 1923, he introduced a course titled *Psychology and Athletics*, and in 1925 he established and subsequently directed the Athletic Research Laboratory. His research interests were wide ranging and included motor skills, motor learning, perception, personality, and individual differences, but he always placed primary emphasis on practical application. This orientation is reflected in the content of two books, *The Psychology of Coaching* (Griffith, 1926) and *Psychology and Athletics* (Griffith, 1928).

In North America, the decades that followed, between the 1930s and the 1960s, can be characterized as a period of stagnation, with the exception of motor learning research that flourished in the postwar years. This period was also relatively quiet in Eastern Europe, though as early as 1926 Griffith had visited two newly established sport psychology laboratories in Berlin; in addition, other European universities, such as Leipzig, included some sport psychology in their curricula. Evidence also suggests that Soviet sport scientists looked at the psychological benefits of physical activity dating back to the early part of the 20th century. Although the historical evidence is incomplete, it would appear that these initiatives survived in some form through World War II, but it was the period between 1945 and 1957 that marked the true emergence of sport psychology in the former Soviet Union (Hanin & Martens, 1978). Some of this work ran parallel with the Soviet space program; for example, self-regulation skills were used to train cosmonauts and, later, to help Eastern bloc athletes prepare for the 1976 Olympics (Garfield & Bennett, 1984).

By the time of the 1960 Olympics in Melbourne, sport psychologists were accompanying Eastern European teams, though at that time more likely as passive observers than as active consultants. From the 1970s onward, Olympic competitors from East Germany and the Soviet Union used sport psychologists as a matter of routine (Roberts & Kiiecik, 1989), and Eastern bloc countries in general had come to accept the benefits of psychological interventions such as mental practice and imagery. Even as early as the 1968 Mexico Olympics, Miroslav Vanek had put in place a large-scale psychological screening and interview program involving the Czechoslovakian athletes at the Games in an intervention that met with mixed success (Vanek & Cratty, 1970).

The stage was now set for the discipline to develop the structures normally associated with any academic discipline. The First World Congress of Sport Psychology, held in 1965 in Rome, led to the formation of the International Society of Sport Psychology, and preliminary meetings held in the same year would lead, by 1968, to the development of the European Federation of Sport Psychology, as well as the official recognition of the North American Society for the Psychology of Sport and Physical Activity as an entity distinct from its parent body, then called the American Association for Health, Physical Education and Recreation. Developments in other countries followed; for example, in 1977, the Canadian Society for Psychomotor Learning and Sport Psychology became independent from its parent body, the Canadian Association for Health, Physical Education and Recreation. Throughout these stages of growth, the parent discipline of psychology maintained a discreet distance. It was not until 1986 that the American Psychological Association finally and formally recognized sport psychology with the formation of a new section, Division 47, concerned with exercise and sport psychology. In 1998, Richard Suinn, an applied psychologist noted for his work with Olympic skiers, was elected president of the American Psychological Association, which by then included more than 150,000 members. Around the same time, entire issues devoted to sport psychology were published in the flagship journals of the American Psychological Association ("Role," 1996), the Australian Psychological Society ("Sport," 1995), and the British Psychological Society ("Sport," 2002).

In recent years, applied issues have become a focus in sport psychology, and this development has led to the introduction of specialized training programs with a focus on professional practice (Andersen, Van Raalte, & Brewer, 2001), as well as the establishment of professional organizations more devoted to applied issues, including the Association for the Advancement of Applied Sport Psychology in 1985. Also during this time, publications focusing predominantly on applied work were launched, including *The Sport Psychologist* in 1987, the *Journal of Applied Sport Psychology* in 1989, and several key textbooks (e.g., Murphy, 1995; Van Raalte & Brewer, 1996; J.M. Williams, 1986). As a result of these developments, applied sport psychology came to be considered part of the larger subdiscipline that focuses on identifying and understanding psychological theories and techniques to be applied in sport settings in order to enhance the performance and personal growth of athletes and in exercise contexts with physical activity participants (J.M. Williams, 2010).

Core Concepts

The psychology of sport employs numerous concepts that have been developed in a somewhat piecemeal fashion as the discipline has progressed. In the 1960s and 1970s, when the field lacked an agreed-upon knowledge base, research topics varied widely and were targeted toward many different populations. These topics ranged from personality theory development to experimental testing of motor learning and performance theories (Gill, 1997). Later, as sport psychology developed a cognitive focus, attention was directed to athletes' thoughts, mental images, and concentration processes (for a review, see Moran, 2009). The influence of cognitive theories led to an increase in field research and the ensuing development of specific models of practice in the 1980s and 1990s. Today, sport psychologists rely on these models to work across the broad areas of performance enhancement, psychological testing, and counseling interventions (Danish, Petitpas, & Hale, 1995).

The development of psychological skills to enhance performance has historically served as the foundation for sport psychology practice (Andersen et al., 2001), and, for the most part, it is based on the classic cognitive and behavioral therapy literature. The models sport psychologists use, however, are not based on cognitive-behavioral therapy but rather position the sport psychologist primarily as an educator who teaches psychological skills to athletes, teams, and coaches. The reason for this approach may relate to the settings in which sport psychology is often practiced, such as during training and at competitions (Andersen, 2000).

The term "sport psychology" can mean different things to different people. To a coach or athlete, it may refer to the actions of a practitioner who is brought in to help the team or individual prepare for an important game. To a sport scientist, it may describe the branch of the discipline that focuses on the brain and central nervous system and their influence on sporting performance. To a sport psychologist, the term may describe a discipline of psychology that applies psychological theories and methods to understanding physical exercise in general and competitive sport in particular. Each working definition is appropriate for its own target audience. Whereas some focus on practical application, others highlight professional concerns, and still others consider the discipline in its entirety. This diversity of interpretations, and its disparate sources of influence, continue to be reflected in both structure and practice in the discipline of sport psychology.

We must also ask, Whom is sport psychology for? Again, the answer depends entirely on whom you ask. According to some, its primary audience should be those who take part in sport. To others, sport psychology should feed the disciplines and professions associated with sport science or perhaps applied psychology. Others argue that it should not be *for* anyone in particular but should aim to advance scientific knowledge as an end in itself. Because there is no simple answer to the question, restricting ownership to any single constituency is not likely to help the discipline develop. Instead, it may be most useful to adopt a more flexible and pragmatic approach, arguing that the psychology of sport, whether applied or academic, can be tailored to meet the needs of a variety of potential users, both inside and outside the world of sport.

Main Theoretical Perspectives

The early years of sport psychology tended to be characterized by the adoption and subsequent application of theories that had originated elsewhere in psychology. The pioneers of sport psychology in the 1960s and 1970s normally came from an academic background in physical education and the sport sciences, and they drew heavily on existing psychological theories and models that appeared to them to be relevant to the topic in question. For example, Hull's drive theory of motivation and the Yerkes-Dodson law (the inverted-U hypothesis) became the mainstays for explaining competitive anxiety in sport, Atkinson's achievement motivation theory dominated discussion of participation motivation, and Zajonc's drive theory was used to interpret the effects of social influence on sport performance (Martens, 1975).

Very often, these adopted theories were developed to consider personal and social phenomena in specific contexts—including educational, occupational, and clinical settings—and the justification for generalizing to other contexts, including sport, was not always obvious. One prime example is Locke and Latham's work on goal setting, which was developed to consider motivation at work but then commonly applied to the world of sport despite the obvious dissimilarities between the two contexts.

During the late 1970s and 1980s, sport psychology tended to cherry-pick from the rich crop of available psychological theories. This selectivity may have led to a somewhat blinkered view of the discipline and its accumulated knowledge, as well as a tendency to develop sophisticated levels of expertise but only in narrowly defined domains. This tendency may have limited the potential for cross-fertilization of ideas from other psychological disciplines and slowed the response time to new developments outside of sport psychology.

Though traditional perspectives did serve as valuable catalysts for research activity, it was not long before sport-specific theories and models began to emerge, as the difficulties associated with the wholesale borrowing of theories became more apparent. As a consequence, beginning at the end of the 1970s, an increasing number of theories emerged that were dedicated to understanding sport behavior (Feltz, 1987). This trend has continued, with increasingly sophisticated models being developed to understand complex phenomena including, as outlined in the next section, anxiety, mental practice, and team dynamics.

Critical Findings

The relationship between anxiety and athletic performance has attracted a great deal of attention from researchers over the past century (Thomas, Mellalieu, & Hanton, 2008). Traditionally, in sport psychology, the relationship between anxiety and performance was regarded as being linear and indirect (i.e., the more anxious athletes are, the worse they perform). But since the advent of more sophisticated theoretical models in the 1980s, a different picture of the anxiety–performance relationship has emerged. This shift in understanding is evident in several ways. First, a crucial factor that mediates the relationship between anxiety and performance is the way in which athletes interpret the anxiety they experience. In general, if they perceive it as energizing performance, then it will probably help them do well; however, if they see it as a threat to performance, then they will probably do badly (Jones, Meijen, McCarthy, & Sheffield, 2009). Second, anxiety is now believed to be a multidimensional construct with cognitive, somatic, and behavioral components. Perhaps unsurprisingly, these aspects of anxiety may have different effects on skilled performance. For example, catastrophe theory suggests that a high degree of cognitive anxiety (or worry) is not always detrimental to performance. This view is shared by the processing efficiency model, which argues that worry can sometimes motivate anxious performers to invest more effort in the tasks they are performing. But this increased investment of effort may come at a price, namely a concomitant decline in processing efficiency. Third, in order to adequately explore the effects of anxiety on performance, researchers will have to use indexes of processing efficiency, as is evident, for example, from certain aspects of visual search behavior (A.M. Williams, Vickers, & Rodrigues, 2002), along with measures of overall task performance. Finally, most models of anxiety in sport agree that skilled performance tends to unravel when athletes think too much about themselves (self-consciousness) or about the mechanics of the tasks they are trying to perform ("paralysis by analysis"). According to Onions (1996), the word *anxiety* is derived from the Latin *angere*, which means "to choke," and of course the term "choking" is now widely used in the sporting community as a colloquial synonym for the sudden deterioration of athletic performance due to excessive anxiety (Hill, Hanton, Matthews, & Fleming, 2010).

Psychological interest in the area of mental practice (or imagery) is as old as psychology itself. For example, William James (1890) observed that, through imaginative anticipation, people could learn to skate in the summer and swim in the winter. During the 1890s, various expressions of the ideomotor principle were proposed. This principle suggested that people's thoughts have muscular concomitants. Thus in 1899 Beaunis (cited in Washburn, 1916) proposed that it was well known that "the idea of a movement suffices to produce the movement or make it tend to be produced" (p. 138). Similarly, Carpenter (1894) claimed that low-level neural impulses are produced during imagined movement and that these impulses are identical in nature (but lower in amplitude) to those emitted in actual movement. Clearly, these references show that mental practice was well established as a research topic in the early years of experimental psychology, and it is referred to at present as a systematic form of covert rehearsal, in which people imagine themselves performing an action without engaging in the physical movements (Moran, 2009).

Unfortunately, as a result of the behaviorist manifesto (Watson, 1913), which attacked "mentalistic" constructs such as imagery, interest in mental practice declined around the 1920s. This lull in imagery research continued until the advent of the cognitive revolution in psychology in the 1960s, when the first comprehensive reviews of mental practice began to emerge (Richardson, 1967a, 1967b). Since then, partly as a result of the development of objective measures of imagery processes—for example, the mental rotation task devised by Shepard and Metzler (1971)—visualization has attracted a resurgence of interest from theoretical and applied sport psychologists. In fact, research on mental practice is not confined to the world of sport; for example, the potential utility of mental rehearsal has been recognized in the domain of stroke rehabilitation (Page, 2001) and military training (Druckman & Swets, 1988).

In the social psychology of sport, group dynamics have been a focus for research for a considerable time, and studies of team cohesion (Carron, Hausenblas, & Eys, 2005) have been groundbreaking in psychology as a whole, offering genuine insight into the nature of group cohesion in general. The research reveals that cohesion itself is multifaceted and includes at least two primary dimensions—task and social cohesion—as well as secondary dimensions contingent on the type of group (e.g., Cota, Evans, Dion, Kilik, & Longman, 1995). Research also shows that a number of factors interact to determine levels of group cohesion and that cohesion is not a particularly reliable predictor of group performance or success (e.g., Carron, Bray, & Eys, 2002). Factors identified as influencing group or team cohesion include group size, physical proximity among members, the costs incurred in joining the group, leadership styles, competition, success, and similarity. This last factor—similarity, or homogeneity—has been the focus of considerable debate, and some authors have argued that it encourages cohesiveness (Eitzen, 1975), whereas others maintain that it may inhibit healthy group development (Janis, 1982).

The concept of team identity has not attracted as much attention in sport psychology, though fans' identification with teams is better researched. In social psychology itself, work on social identity in small groups has been prominent since the 1970s. According to the dominant perspective, social identity theory (Tajfel, 1982), the more closely an individual identifies with, and hence defines him- or herself in terms of, group membership, the more that person will be inclined to maximize differences between the ingroup and the outgroup. This dynamic is likely to be reflected in competitiveness and effort expended in striving for common goals. Thus the extent to which players identify with a club or a team is likely to exert considerable influence on performance, but as yet it has not been investigated widely in sport psychology.

Key Debates

Given its subject matter, sport psychology cannot avoid being defined as an applied, practical science, and consequently there has been an almost constant dialogue about how best to translate theory into practice and at what price. Rainer Martens (1979a) of the University of Illinois (and more recently of the publishing company Human Kinetics) published an article in the *Journal of Sport Psychology* titled "About Smocks and Jocks." His paper was a call for sport psychology to become more relevant to those engaged with sport, along with an acknowledgment that traditional approaches might not have helped to make the subdiscipline more accessible to sportspeople or to develop our common stock of knowledge. The earlier discussion of the schism between pure and applied sport psychology reveals how difficult the process of translating theory into practice can be, but there are encouraging signs that the gap may be narrowing with growing acceptance of the legitimacy of alternative roles for various types of sport psychologists, as well as appropriate structures for ensuring the regulation of core professional competencies.

Recognition of different roles for sport psychologists is not new. In 1984, Robert Singer, then president of the International Society of Sport Psychology, outlined three roles that could be played by sport psychologists: basic researchers, educational sport psychologists (who use their background in physical education to educate athletes and coaches), and clinical sport psychologists (who draw on their training to counsel or help sportspersons). To this list, we could easily add a fourth role—occupational psychology—since those who possess training in industrial and organizational psychology also have much to offer to the world of sport and especially to professional sport.

Each division of psychology brings certain skills and experience with certain types of intervention. Educational psychologists are adept at identifying behavioral and emotional problems among young people, in particular, and at developing programs to resolve these difficulties. In addition, all educational psychologists must have spent time teaching prior to their professional psychological training and thus can also bring those skills to their work in coach and athlete education programs. Clinical psychologists normally provide therapy in either individual or group settings, very often using cognitive-behavioral techniques to effect change. It has long been recognized that their counseling skills can easily be transferred into sport settings (Lavallee & Cockerill, 2002), where intervention programs can make the difference between average and above-average performance for athletes. The role of clinical psychology is acknowledged in the accreditation procedures that operate in North America and the United Kingdom. A unique category has been established for clinical sport psychologists, with qualification depending not only on the common criteria for all sport psychologists but also on appropriate qualification in clinical psychology. Increasingly, clinical psychologists have recognized the positive relationship between exercise and mental health, and a considerable number now operate as exercise psychologists, either advocating exercise as a form of therapy for clinical disorders or identifying the role of exercise in relation to other psychological and physical problems (e.g., body shape and weight control).

Across the globe, it is unlikely that the demand for sport psychology has ever been higher. As teams and individuals constantly strive to find the winning edge, it becomes increasingly likely that a sport psychologist will be involved to help find that edge. However, these powerful market forces can be dangerous, especially when demand has the potential to outstrip supply. In these circumstances, caution must be exercised in both promoting and developing the subject, with appropriate regulation of those who describe themselves as sport psychologists and due regard to the subject's limitations and weaknesses alongside its strengths.

While applied sport psychologists engage in the same range of activities and services as professionals in other areas of applied psychology, they also face numerous practical issues and interventions unique to their field (Sachs, 1993). But are the services of sport psychologists so distinctive that they require unique standards for ethical conduct? In 1987, Zeigler put forward the case that a code of ethics designed specifically for applied sport psychologists was a vital aspect of the overall professionalization of the field. Since then, others have suggested that the application of psychology ethical codes often leads to conflicts between practitioners involving boundaries of practice and title usage (e.g., Whelan, Meyers, & Elkin, 1996). It is fair to say that the creation of unique codes of ethics in the field, and no agreed-upon code of ethics for the field, has given sport psychologists some autonomy; however, sport psychology professionals still frequently (and unfortunately) find themselves in ethical dilemmas for which no clear rules exist to guide their behavior.

A further concern relates to the sport psychologist's competence, whether in terms of knowledge of other sport sciences, of psychology, or of the sport itself. In relation to psychological expertise, there is a serious danger that a sport psychologist may find her- or himself unwittingly crossing the boundaries of professional competence. An applied psychologist must always recognize where these boundaries lie. To overstep that mark may not only be harmful to the client but also make the practitioner vulnerable to a charge of professional negligence.

The question of who is qualified to practice sport psychology has been an issue of debate ever since the field began to provide professional services to athletes and coaches. Numerous position statements have been written on this topic, including the United States Olympic Committee guidelines (1983), which perhaps constituted the first systematic attempt to provide credentials for sport psychologists. The field has also started to address the issue of certification, which is the attempt to codify a common standard of preparation and practice. The primary objective of certification is to provide a standard by which the public can accept, on the basis of reliable evidence, that an individual has attained specified professional competencies and a means by which certified and noncertified individuals can be compared. Credentials, on the other hand, are related to a title or claim of competence and include statutory designations (e.g., those enacted by a legislative body) that are protected by law and nonstatutory designations (e.g., recognition by professional organizations) that are not protected by law. Certification is not based on laws per se but is generally established by academic or professional organizations (Zaichkowsky & Perna, 1996).

Probably more than any other scientific discipline, psychology as a whole is characterized by methodological pluralism—in this case, the use of a wide range of techniques for understanding, predicting, and interpreting human behavior and experience. Empirical methods (based on systematic observations) can include both the quantitative (How much or many?) and the qualitative (Why?); they can also involve numerous techniques, including the experimental (e.g., laboratory, field, or natural) and the nonexperimental (e.g., archival research, case studies, surveys, discourse analysis, content analysis, grounded analysis, interviews, focus groups). Some of these techniques are used in attempts to identify general laws as to how people behave (nomothetic approaches), others focus on determining individual responses and interpretations in particular contexts (idiographic approaches), and still others consider not behavior but the meanings associated with our actions (hermeneutic approaches). None of these methods or perspectives is intrinsically better than another; rather, good research is characterized by judicious use of a combination of appropriate methodologies. Indeed, psychology has become increasingly open minded about the utility of a range of alternative methods, thus reducing reliance on simple and sovereign techniques, most especially controlled laboratory experiments.

The approach to research methods currently being adopted by sport psychologists follows the pattern that has characterized psychology as a whole for the last 50 years: In the same way that the field adopted only selected psychological theories and models, it has also tended to rely on a restricted range of methods and to afford primacy to traditional, quantitative procedures. On a positive note, adherence to traditional methods, along with a preoccupation with measurement, has ensured a degree of rigor and the establishment of a set of high standards that maintain the quality of published work. On the downside, the field has historically exhibited intolerance for alternative approaches, which may have stifled innovation and creativity. The primary reliance on experimental procedures may also have encouraged reductionism, where a small number of variables are teased out for analysis but the bigger picture is lost from view.

Historically, the psychology of sport has been preoccupied with measurement, as evidenced by the hundreds of published studies attempting to quantify the personality of the athlete (Ruffer, 1976) and, more generally, by the number of sport-specific psychological measures available for use. The *Directory of Psychological Tests in the Sport and Exercise Sciences* (Ostrow, 1996) lists several hundred, dealing with topics including motivation, attitudes, confidence, anxiety, body image, and aggression.

The issues associated with psychological testing have led to a number of interrelated debates. First, the field has considered whether sound rationale exists for using a particular test with a particular population. Early research tended not to dwell on this question; instead, researchers tended to use one of a number of standard psychological tests (e.g., the Eysenck Personality Inventory). Hindsight has revealed these endeavors to be generally disappointing, and recent years have seen a steady decline in this particular type of work. There is also a strong consensus that, for whatever research purpose tests are used, it is not appropriate to rely on psychological tests to select participants, and this was one of a number of concerns associated with the development of the Athletic Motivation Inventory by Ogilvie and Tutko (1966). The scale was purported to measure traits associated with high athletic achievement (drive, aggression, determination, responsibility, leadership, self-confidence, emotional control, mental toughness, coachability, conscience development, and trust) and was made available to coaches who returned completed questionnaires to the authors for scoring and interpretation. How this information was then used was not controlled, and despite the poor reported association between scores and performance (e.g., H. Davis, 1991) concern arose that players' profiles could have been influential in subsequent selection decisions by coaches.

The general decline in the use of psychological tests could relate in part to an important question that should precede testing: What is the theoretical perspective that underpins the research? The majority of early research that used tests, though seemingly atheoretical, implicitly subscribed to a trait approach to personality, which posits that we are defined psychologically by our scores on a finite number of personality traits and that these traits and their significance remain relatively constant over time. This perception of the static nature of personality has been challenged in psychology and replaced by more dynamic, interactionist, and idiographic approaches, including, for example, personal construct theory. By 1980, a challenge was beginning to emerge in sport psychology itself. Morgan (1980) summarized this debate in an article titled "Sport Personology: The Credulous-Skeptical Argument in Perspective." Though debate continued for many years, the pendulum has swung gradually toward the skeptics, who duly acknowledge some individual psychological differences between athletes and nonathletes, between athletes in different sports and in different positions on teams, and between winners and losers, but who question the capacity of psychological tests to capture these differences or changes over time and context.

Another question that should be addressed prior to testing is that of what test to use. Initially, one must determine the psychometric robustness of the instrument, which is normally defined in terms of reliability (are test scores consistent over time and context?), validity (does the test measure what it purports to measure?), and standardization (can the test be administered uniformly, and are established norm tables of scores available for different populations?). Next, one must decide whether to use a general or sport-specific test. Increasingly, the trend has been away from general measures and toward tailored instruments designed to measure specific, sport-related characteristics. A considerable number of sport-specific scales are available (Ostrow, 1996), but issues associated with their reliability and validity have yet to be resolved. Certainly, the use of more focused measures of specific sport-related skills would appear to be a move in the right direction, but caution must be exercised.

The final issue concerns who to test and when. Traits are typically regarded as stable characteristics, yet increasing evidence suggests that involvement in sport and exercise may affect psychological functioning and health and thus that personality characteristics may change over time. One of the most common tests used by sport psychologists was originally designed to consider mood states, which fluctuate over time and place, but has often been employed to define the psychological profile of a successful athlete. The Profile of Mood States (POMS) (LeUnes & Burger, 1998) measures six mood states. A positive "iceberg profile" is associated with elevated scores on vigor and lower scores on tension, depression, anger, fatigue, and confusion. The accumulated evidence in recent years of research is, not surprisingly, mixed (Beedie, Terry, & Lane, 2000). For example, there is little to show that POMS can discriminate between successful and unsuccessful athletes, though athletes in general do appear to have a more positive profile than nonathletes and there is some support for the suggestion that an iceberg profile is associated with above-average performance for an individual athlete, especially in open-skill (i.e., open-to-the-environment) sports. However, the use of a measure of mood state to determine a personality profile has to remain questionable, and it exemplifies the difficulties associated with attempting to measure psychological determinants of physical performance.

Over the last few years, evidence has indicated that the exclusive reliance on quantitative methods may have lessened and that, at long last, appeals for a more eclectic approach to data gathering (e.g., Martens, 1979b) may be having an effect. The psychology of sport is still some way from embracing alternative methodologies, however, and qualitative techniques have yet to make significant inroads into the literature. Nevertheless, with ever-growing appreciation of these legitimate alternatives, the future looks promising.

Contemporary sport psychology is incredibly diverse, and this diversity is reflected in the continued growth in professional organizations and journals, each with its own orientation. In addition, the number of practicing sport psychologists worldwide has increased dramatically (Lidor, Morris, Bardaxoglou, & Becker, 2001), and more than 100 postgraduate degree programs in applied sport psychology have been established in no fewer than 44 countries in recent years (Sachs, Burke, & Schweighardt, 2011). Slowly at first, and then ever more rapidly, the field has gained a position of influence in the world of sport. The role of the sport psychologist is now widely valued and accepted by athletes, coaches, administrators, and others involved in sport and exercise (Morris & Thomas, 2003). Practicing sport psychologists are also beginning to recognize the needs of others outside of these areas, particularly groups that can benefit from various kinds of psychological support to help them to compete at the highest levels (e.g., business professionals, military personnel). Such advances have led the field to become more accessible in, and accountable to, mainstream psychology.

Summary

We live in exciting times for the psychology of sport. The field now enjoys a more confident sense of identity and purpose than at any time in its past, and a growing body of knowledge genuinely takes sport as its primary focus. This body of knowledge has brought fresh vitality to a field that previously could stand accused of remaining too exclusive for too long. With the influx of new ideas and new perspectives, the parent discipline of psychology is no longer far removed from the proceedings. At the same time, as sport psychology has matured, it has been less characterized by a desire to unceremoniously borrow packaged ideas from psychology in an effort to provide simple answers to complex phenomena. Now, the mood is shifting, and, like other psychological subdisciplines, sport psychology is becoming more critical and self-reflective in recognition of the complexity of the world with which it deals.

References

Andersen, M.B. (Ed.). (2000). *Doing sport psychology*. Champaign, IL: Human Kinetics.

Andersen, M.B., Van Raalte, J.L., & Brewer, B.W. (2001). Sport psychology service delivery: Staying ethical while keeping loose. *Professional Psychology: Research and Practice, 32*, 12–18.

Beedie, C.J., Terry, P.C., & Lane, A.M. (2000). The Profile of Mood States and athletic performance: Two meta-analyses. *Journal of Applied Sport Psychology, 12*, 49–68.

Benjamin, L.T., Jr., & Green, C.D. (2009). Introduction: The origins of sport psychology. In C.D. Green & L.T. Benjamin, Jr. (Eds.), *Psychology gets in the game: Sport, mind, and behavior, 1880–1960* (pp. 1–19). Lincoln : University of Nebraska Press.

Carpenter, W.B. (1894). *Principles of mental physiology*. New York: Appleton-Century-Crofts.

Carron, A.V., Bray, S.R., & Eys, M.A. (2002). Team cohesion and team success in sport. *Journal of Sports Sciences, 20*, 119–128.

Carron, A.V., Hausenblas, H.A., & Eys, M.A. (2005). *Group dynamics in sport* (3rd ed.). Morgantown, WV: Fitness Information Technology.

Cota, A.A., Evans, C.R., Dion, K.L., Kilik, L., & Longman, R.S. (1995). The structure of group cohesion. *Personality and Social Psychology Bulletin, 21*, 572–580.

Danish, S.J., Petitpas, A.J., & Hale, B.D. (1995). Psychological interventions: A life developmental model. In S. Murphy (Ed.), *Sport psychology interventions* (pp. 19–38). Champaign, IL: Human Kinetics.

Davis, H. (1991). Criterion validity of the Athletic Motivation Inventory: Issues in professional sport. *Journal of Applied Sport Psychology, 3*, 176–182.

Davis, S.F., Huss, M.T., & Becker, A.H. (2009). Norman Triplett: Recognizing the importance of competition. In C.D. Green & L.T. Benjamin, Jr. (Eds.), *Psychology gets in the game: Sport, mind, and behaviour, 1880–1960* (pp. 98–115). Lincoln : University of Nebraska Press.

Druckman, D., & Swets, J.A. (1988). *Enhancing human performance: Issues, theories, and techniques*. Washington, DC: National Academy Press.

Eitzen, D.S. (1975). Group structure and group performance. In D.M. Landers, D.V. Harris, & R.W. Christina (Eds.), *Psychology of sport and motor behavior* (pp. 262-270). University Park, PA: Pennsylvania State University Press.

Feltz, D.L. (1987). Advancing knowledge in sport psychology: Strategies for expanding our conceptual frameworks. *Quest, 39*, 243–254.

Gardiner, E.N. (1930). *Athletics of the ancient world*. Oxford, UK: Oxford University Press.

Garfield, C.A., & Bennett, H.Z. (1984). *Peak performance*. Los Angeles: Tarcher.

Gill, D.L. (1997). Sport and exercise psychology. In J. Massengale & R. Swanson (Eds.), *History of exercise and sport science* (pp. 293–320). Champaign, IL: Human Kinetics.

Green, C.D. (2009). Coleman Roberts Griffith: "Father" of sport psychology. In C.D. Green & L.T. Benjamin, Jr. (Eds.), *Psychology gets in the game: Sport, mind, and behaviour, 1880–1960* (pp. 202–229). Lincoln: University of Nebraska Press.

Griffith, C.R. (1926). *The psychology of coaching*. New York: Scribner's.

Griffith, C.R. (1928). *Psychology and athletics*. New York: Scribner's.

Hanin, Y., & Martens, R. (1978). Sport psychology in the USSR. *NASPSPA Newsletter, 3*, 1–3.

Hastorf, A.H., & Cantril, H. (1954). They saw a game: A case study. *Journal of Abnormal and Social Psychology, 49*, 129–143.

Hill, D.M., Hanton, S., Matthews, N., & Fleming, S. (2010). Choking in sport: A review. *International Review of Sport and Exercise Psychology, 3*, 24–39.

Howard, G.E. (1912). Social psychology of the spectator. *American Journal of Sociology, 8*, 33–50.

James, W. (1890). *Principles of psychology*. New York: Holt, Rinehart & Winston.

Janis, I. (1982). *Victims of groupthink*. Boston: Houghton Mifflin.

Jones, M.V., Meijen, C., McCarthy, P.J., & Sheffield, D. (2009). A theory of challenge and threat states in athletes. *International Review of Sport and Exercise Psychology, 2*, 161–180.

Kremer, J., & Moran, A. (2008). Swifter, higher, stronger: The history of sport and exercise psychology. *The Psychologist, 21*, 740–742.

Lavallee, D., & Cockerill, I.M. (Eds.). (2002). *Counselling in sport and exercise contexts*. Leicester: British Psychological Society.

LeUnes, A., & Burger, J. (1998). Bibliography of the Profile of Mood States in sport and exercise research, 1971–1998. *Journal of Sport Behavior, 21*, 53–70.

Lidor, R., Morris, T., Bardaxoglou, N., & Becker, B. (Eds.). (2001). *The world sport psychology sourcebook*. Morgantown, WV: Fitness Information Technology.

Martens, R. (1975). *Social psychology and physical activity*. New York: Harper & Row.

Martens, R. (1979a). About smocks and jocks. *Journal of Sport Psychology, 1*, 4–99.

Martens, R. (1979b). Science, knowledge, and sport psychology. *The Sport Psychologist, 1*, 29–55.

Moran, A. (2009). Cognitive psychology in sport: Progress and prospects. *Psychology of Sport and Exercise, 10*, 420–426.

Morgan, W.P. (1980). Sport personology: The credulous-skeptical argument in perspective. In W.E. Straub (Ed.), *Sport psychology: An analysis of athlete behavior* (2nd ed., pp. 330–339). Ithaca: Mouvement.

Morris, T., & Thomas, P. (2003). Approaches to applied sport psychology. In T. Morris & J. Summers (Eds.), *Sport psychology: Theory, applications, and issues* (2nd ed.). Brisbane: Jacaranda Wiley.

Murphy, S.M. (Ed.). (1995). *Sport psychology interventions*. Champaign, IL: Human Kinetics.

Ogilvie, B.C., & Tutko, T. (1966). *Problem athletes and how to handle them*. London: Pelham Books.

Onions, C.T. (Ed.). (1996). *The Oxford dictionary of English etymology*. Oxford, UK: Clarendon Press.

Ostrow, A.C. (Ed.). (1996). *Directory of psychological tests in the sport and exercise sciences* (2nd ed.). Morgantown, WV: Fitness Information Technology.

Page, S.J. (2001). Mental practice: A promising restorative technique in stroke rehabilitation. *Topics in Stroke Rehabilitation, 8,* 54–63.

Patrick, G.T.W. (1903). The psychology of football. *American Journal of Psychology, 14,* 104–17.

Richardson, A. (1967a). Mental practice: A review and discussion, part 1. *Research Quarterly, 38,* 95–107.

Richardson, A. (1967b). Mental practice: A review and discussion, part II. *Research Quarterly, 38,* 263–273.

Roberts, G.C., & Kiiecik, J.C. (1989). Sport psychology in the German Democratic Republic: An interview with Dr. Gerd Kanzag. *The Sport Psychologist, 3,* 72–77.

The role of psychology in sport and exercise psychology [Special issue]. (1996). *American Psychological Association Monitor, 27*(7).

Ruffer, W.A. (1976). Personality traits of athletes. *The Physical Educator, 33,* 211–214.

Sachs, M.L. (1993). Professional ethics in sport psychology. In R.N. Singer, M. Murphy, & L.K. Tennant (Eds.), *Handbook of research on sport psychology* (pp. 921–932). New York: Macmillan.

Sachs, M.L., Burke, K.L., & Schweighardt, S.L. (Eds.). (2011). *Directory of graduate programs in applied sport psychology* (10th ed.). Madison, WI: Association for Applied Sport Psychology.

Shepard, R.N., & Metzler, J. (1971). Mental rotation of three-dimensional objects. *Science, 171,* 701–703.

Singer, R.N. (1984). What sport psychology can do for the athlete and coach. *International Journal of Sport Psychology, 15,* 52–61.

Sport and exercise psychology [Special issue]. (1995). *Australian Psychologist, 30*(2).

Sport and exercise psychology [Special issue]. (2002). *The Psychologist, 15*(8).

Sweet, W.E. (1987). *Sport and recreation in ancient Greece: A sourcebook with translations.* Oxford, UK: Oxford University Press.

Tajfel, H. (Ed.). (1982). *Social identity and intergroup relations.* Cambridge, UK: Cambridge University Press.

Thomas, O., Mellalieu, S.D., & Hanton, S. (2008). Stress management in applied sport psychology. In S.D. Mellalieu & S. Hanton (Eds.), *Advances in applied sport psychology: A review* (pp. 124–161). Oxford, UK: Routledge.

Triplett, N. (1898). The dynamogenic factors in pacemaking and competition. *American Journal of Psychology, 9,* 505–523.

United States Olympic Committee. (1983). USOC establishes guidelines for sport psychology services. *Journal of Sport Psychology, 5,* 4–7.

Vanek, M., & Cratty, B.J. (1970). *Psychology and the superior athlete.* New York: Macmillan.

Van Raalte, J.L., & Brewer, B.W. (Eds.). (1996). *Exploring sport and exercise psychology.* Washington, DC: American Psychological Association.

Washburn, M.F. (1916). *Movement and mental imagery.* Boston: Houghton Mifflin.

Watson, J.B. (1913). Psychology as the behaviorist views it. *Psychological Review, 20,* 158–177.

Weinberg, R.S., & Gould, D. (2007). *Foundations of sport and exercise psychology* (4th ed.). Champaign, IL: Human Kinetics.

Whelan, J.P., Meyers, A.M., & Elkin, T.D. (1996). Ethics in sport and exercise psychology. In J.L. Van Raalte & B.W. Brewer (Eds.), *Exploring sport and exercise psychology* (pp. 431–447). Washington, DC: American Psychological Association.

Williams, A.M., Vickers, J., & Rodrigues, S. (2002). The effects of anxiety on visual search, movement kinematics, and performance in table tennis: A test of Eysenck and Calvo's processing efficiency theory. *Journal of Sport & Exercise Psychology, 24,* 438–455.

Williams, J.M. (Ed.). (1986). *Applied sport psychology.* Mountain View, CA: Mayfield.

Williams, J.M. (Ed.). (2010). *Applied sport psychology: Personal growth to peak performance* (6th ed.). Mountain View, CA: Mayfield.

Zaichkowsky, L., & Perna, F. (1996). Certification in sport and exercise psychology. In J.L. Van Raalte & B.W. Brewer (Eds.), *Exploring sport and exercise psychology* (pp. 395–411). Washington, DC: American Psychological Association.

Zeigler, E.F. (1987). Rationale and suggested dimensions for a code of ethics for sport psychologists. *The Sport Psychologist, 1,* 138–150.

II

Community: Place, Space, Image, and the Social

Part II focuses on questions of community—of how individuals make communities and communities make people. Hence, this section attends to the nature and extent to which local, national, and global communities fragment or share a sense of togetherness. It also considers whether emotional and communal identification extend across societies. These issues and concerns are both reflected in and reinforced by sport subcultures and sport worlds more generally. Because people and communities are contoured by places, spaces, images, and societies, we draw here on the social science knowledge provided by anthropology, sociology, geography, and media studies. Each of these disciplines provides compelling evidence regarding the role that sport plays in providing a sense of identification, belonging, and community. This section of the book also examines questions of power, culture, control, and the manifest and latent functions of sport.

In chapter 4, Alan Klein highlights how the use of an anthropological perspective illuminates the interconnections between places and communities. Klein astutely observes that there is no sport without culture and that there is no culture without sport or, at the very least, play. The usefulness of anthropology lies in studying not only non-Western body cultures but also Western sport forms. Highlighting play and games of the past and the present, Klein insightfully shows both how local places and spaces are marked by unique features and meanings and how these play and game forms involve links between societies and across time.

This latter theme is also picked up by Joseph Maguire in chapter 5, which highlights how sociologists critically examine the role, function, and meaning of sport in the lives of people and the communities they form. Sociologists share with anthropologists an interest in studying sport both within specific locations and across societies. Furthermore, sociologists share with historians (see chapter 1) a concern with describing and explaining the emergence and diffusion of sport over time. In doing so, sociologists identify the processes of socialization into, through, and out of sport and investigate the values and norms of dominant, emergent, and residual cultures and subcultures of and in sport. Crucial in this regard are questions regarding how power is exercised, and by whom, and how the structured nature of societies places limits, and creates possibilities, for people's involvement in sport in different places and spaces.

The work of geographer Christopher Gaffney in chapter 6 also highlights the importance of space and place in discussing how the study of sport needs a geographic perspective, even as geography can use the study of sport to explore wider geographic concerns. In particular, Gaffney insightfully notes the profound relationships between cultural landscapes, cultural identities, gender roles and relations, matters of political economy, architecture and design, and sport. That is, as he succinctly notes, sport is inherently geographic; games and sports are played in places bounded by space and time, each of which is a fundamental component of geographical investigation. For students of sport, taking a geographical perspective thus enhances our knowledge of sport places, spaces, interaction, meaning, and identities.

A knowledge of such places and spaces would not be complete without an understanding of the images that relate to the identities and communities forged in such locations. Here, as David Rowe rightfully observes in chapter 7, the study of the media and sport is vital. Rowe expertly presents media studies as an interdisciplinary field that draws from the social sciences and humanities more broadly. Rowe makes a compelling case that society itself has been mediated—in the arenas of politics, civic society, and everyday life. Using sport as an example par excellence, Rowe shows how over the past two centuries the sociocultural phenomenon of sport has been transformed by the media from local, small-scale events to worldwide spectacles. Sport is now located not in one place culturally or geographically but mediated into multiple spaces of daily existence. Furthermore, the economics of sport and its modes of presentation are permeated by a media-sport complex concerned with the production and consumption of sport both locally and globally. In seeking to understand the importance of the media in modern societies and the world of sport in such societies, it is crucial to understand the role, function, and actions of the media in terms of their ownership, production codes, content (audio, textual, and visual), and audience (size, profile, and knowledgeability).

Thus as each of these chapters probes questions of how individuals make the communities that form them, they capture the fact that place, space, and image are interconnected aspects of societal relations. The study of sport reveals how these dynamics play out amid the prevailing power relations of various social groups.

CHAPTER 4

Anthropology of Sport

Alan Klein, PhD

To the growing feast of sport scholarship, anthropology brings three dishes: cross-cultural analysis, a transnational orientation, and ethnographic methodology. Anthropology brings to the study of sport a way of understanding the subject through a sociocultural lens. There is no sport without culture, and one could argue that there is no culture without sport. Culture infuses all facets of this expansive institution—from the emotions associated with apparel worn by fans and the pre- and postgame behavior of sport crowds to the style of play on fields and pitches and the ways in which players (men and women) develop their desire, identity, and dedication to their sport.

This chapter examines how the field of social and cultural anthropology has fared over the past century—in particular, the ways in which sport anthropologists have had greater effect in neighboring disciplines than in their natal field. It also looks at the current contributions of sport anthropology and how it might serve to guide future research.

Foundations in Sociocultural Anthropology

Renowned anthropologist Eric Wolf once pointed out that "[a]nthropology, ambitiously entitled The Science of Man, did lay special claims to the study of non-Western and 'primitive' peoples" (Wolf, 1982, p. 16). In so claiming, Wolf reiterated a generally understood principle of the social sciences, in which "sociology studies the West, while anthropology studies the rest." As a generalization—and despite a growing interest in Western settings—this artificial division still holds, and it has prevented anthropologists from appreciating the role of contemporary sport.

Anthropology's orientation toward non-Western societies was spawned by 19th-century colonialism. Indeed, the professional development of anthropology was fueled by information produced regarding the "curious" customs and beliefs of people being brought under the dominion of one European nation after another (and, later, the United States). Anthropology reciprocated by providing colonial empires with a rationale for their handling of other cultures, as anthropologists of the day pursued questions that sorted cultures into categories of evolutionary complexity. Hence, customs and beliefs were contrasted in terms of how closely (thus supposedly more evolved) or distantly (less evolved) they compared to industrializing European nations (primarily Britain). In the United States, professional interests branched off into concern with how cultural attributes diffused from one society to another. Everywhere, however, early anthropology examined a global range of societies in search of principles that governed how societies operated and changed.

Anthropology's Relationship to Play and Sport

By the 20th century, British anthropology had come to focus on the study of structural social relations in Britain's colonial empire. Some of the finest examples of ethnography come from this time: Evans-Pritchard's study of the Nuer in Africa (1940), Malinowski's study of the Pacific Trobriand Islanders (1922), and Radcliffe-Brown's work on the Andaman Islanders off the coast of India (1922). These societies were struggling to retain internal cohesion in the face of change, and anthropologists looked at how their institutions worked to promote equilibrium. In the United States, anthropologists influenced by Franz Boas (the father of modern American anthropology) were frantically trying to gather information on Native American tribes because of the prevailing belief that they would soon vanish.

The anthropological preoccupation with the "other" (the non-West) was linked to two concerns—first, what anthropology could do to understand influences both within and between cultures; and second, the unique way in which anthropologists went about plying their trade: the creation of ethnography.

Being identified with the victims of progress rather than the perpetrators gave anthropologists a distinct view of the world as well as a wide swath of the globe for their domain, and for much of the 20th century they left the study of the West to their sociological cousins. No other discipline has at its core a preoccupation with understanding so full a range of societies and cultures in the way that anthropology does. Sociology and history may be amenable to cross-cultural study, but neither builds its identity on the global study of it. Moreover, no other discipline has fetishized the notion of culture as has anthropology; this is particularly the case for American anthropology. From the time of Boas to the present, anthropologists have focused their attention on the study of what they have termed culture patterns, cultural cores, and representations.

In addition, whatever their differences, all anthropologists embrace ethnography in conducting their affairs. Ethnography is both a product of doing anthropology and the way in which one goes about doing it. At the core of it lies the participant-observer method, in which the anthropologist immerses him- or herself into the culture—learning its language, behaviors, and practices—and engages in the culture in a blend of traditional and modern ways.

Since the 1960s, anthropology has increasingly taken a critical and self-reflexive direction, and the nature of whom and what we study and whom and what we bring to our studies has become central. As part of this "crisis of representation," as it can be termed, anthropologists seemingly left no interpretive stone unturned as they followed theorists such as Geertz (1973a, 1973b) and Marcus and Fischer (1999) in attempting to understand just what the relationship is between the anthropologist and the studied culture—and how each alters the other. Lost in the process has been the idea that the anthropologist is all-knowing and expert. Rather, the current view posits meaning and interpretation as evolving through layers of questioning, not only of one's subject of study but also of oneself in relation to that subject. Ethnography has increasingly shared the stage with the idea of glimpsing larger theory, and this awakening includes a directing of the anthropological gaze toward the West.

Historically, anthropologists saw the study of play as a distinct sidebar, even a frivolous endeavor, and this view was evinced, predictably, by the scarcity of work in the area. The reasons are easy to understand. Play, as an area of study, simply seemed too light to matter. In Johan Huizinga's classic *Homo Ludens: A Study of the Play Element in Culture,* he separates play from work as one might separate sacred from secular: "not being 'ordinary' life it (play) stands outside the immediate satisfaction of wants and appetites" (1955, p. 18). It seems that most anthropologists had long since decided that such statements really only meant that play, relative to the work-a-day experience, were insignificant.

Sport, as a later development, concerned anthropologists even less. Historian Allen Guttmann's (1979) thought-provoking book on the evolution of sport highlights important differences between play and sport practices. Most critically, he argues, along with other sport scholars (e.g., Elias & Dunning, 1986), that sport is a child of modernity and the West. As such, it has culturally distinct core features: it creates secularity, conditions of relative equality of competition, specialization of roles, standardized rules and organized bodies to oversee their enforcement, quantification of achievement, and the creation of the "record" as a standard of excellence. In most respects, Guttmann's criteria for sport reflect a general orientation toward work and the creation of professionalism that should lend sport an air of seriousness that play does not possess. However, the notions of play that anthropologists have occasionally studied reflect very different forms of competition, which helps us understand why anthropology has not embraced sport studies as much as other disciplines have.

Modern Anthropology of Sport

Kendall Blanchard and Alyce Cheska (1982) are credited with writing the first—and so far only—book-length overview of the anthropology of sport (a revised edition published in 1995 was authored by Blanchard). Their book was a valiant attempt to legitimize the study of sport in the field of anthropology; sadly, however, it served to underscore the weakness of such study. In an effort to strengthen his argument, Blanchard (1995) fuses studies of play with those of sport, which provides him the wherewithal to argue for a pedigree that validates sport as part of the historic development of the discipline. Hence, studies of competitive games among Native Americans, such as James Mooney's (1890) Cherokee study, count, in Blanchard's estimation, and thus help establish a presence in the field.

In documenting the earliest anthropological efforts to study games, Blanchard (1995) cites Sir Edward Tylor, one of the founders of anthropology, who wrote articles about games in both 1879 and 1896. Following the fashion of the times, these pieces showed connections in games played between societies and through time, indicating that people had been engaged in cultural exchange for some time. Indeed, cultural diffusion studies—showing how ideas, artifacts, and practices moved from one group to another—were all the rage around the turn of the 20th century, and some of these studies used games as one among many indices of diffusion. Beyond this, however, anthropologists felt there wasn't much to say about games.

For the first 70 or so years (until about 1950), the occasional piece on sport would find its way into anthropology journals without a great deal of fanfare. For example, Culin (1907), Weule (1925), Firth (1931), Lesser (1933), and Opler (1944) all wrote about sport in tribal societies. However, considering the overall amount of anthropological work produced during that period of time—including the creation of numerous journals, annual reviews, and books—this was not even a blip on the radar screen. Still, for Blanchard, it served as proof that interest had continued unabated. The watershed year, in Blanchard's mind, was 1959, when Roberts, Arth, and Bush published an article titled "Games in Culture." As a comparative study of 50 tribes, it sought to correlate games with other cultural attributes but continued the trend of studying small-scale societies and their supposedly curious interest in games (as opposed to serious sport). At a time when the world was beginning to experience transnational sport through soccer and cricket, Roberts and colleagues remained blind to the possibility of examining sport in industrialized settings. Blanchard, however, overlooked one anthropological study of note that ran counter to this trend: Frankenburg's *Village on the Border* (1957), a study of politics, religion, and sport in a North Welsh village that continued the British social anthropological interest in structural relations. Frankenberg chronicled the local soccer club's connections to local political divisions and even gender-based divisions. This was a breakthrough study in the anthropology of sport by virtue of its location (the West), its interest in sport as opposed to games, and its linking of sport to hotly contested political life.

Four years later and an ocean away, Robin Fox published a provocative article titled "Pueblo Baseball: A New Use for Old Magic" (1961), in which he explored the ability of a tribal people to integrate the modern sport of baseball into their traditions. Fox pointed to cultural linkages between industrial-era sport and anthropological conventions around tribal cultures. Among the Hopi, who eschewed competition, Fox showed how the competition inherent in baseball articulated with their interest in the use of magic, so that when the sporting event moved in a tense direction—as, for instance, one side pulled ahead of the other—the losing side argued that witchcraft was at work and went about attempting to prove its assertions. In so doing, the Hopi subordinated baseball to their cultural preoccupation with witchcraft and the social implications of witchcraft accusation.

The single most important examination in the fledgling anthropology of sport was Clifford Geertz's "Deep Play: Notes on a Balinese Cockfight" (1973a). In its ability to weave complex cultural themes into its deciphering of this tribal sport, Geertz's article is considered a minor classic in the field of anthropology. Geertz uses economist Jeremy Bentham's view of "deep play" (gaming stakes that are so steep as to seem irrational to engage in) as a vehicle for understanding cultural themes. His ability to uncover layer after layer of meaning is nothing short of masterful by any standard. Geertz's use of a gaming venue to demonstrate his profound new vision of the field (interpretive anthropology) should have ushered in a serious interest in sport, but, to most sport anthropologists' surprise, it did not.

There was further minor stirring in 1973 in the form of an interdisciplinary group of sport scholars (primarily kinesiologists but also historians and anthropologists) gathered in Canada to establish the Association for the Anthropological Study of Play (TAASP). As with several other cross-disciplinary attempts, such as the North American Society for the Sociology of Sport, TAASP was peopled primarily by physical educators who had either an interest or a bit of training in one or another social science. The organization lasted 20 years and managed to publish a journal before evaporating without fanfare. These are the developments that Blanchard cites as evidence of the golden future just out of reach—the athletic El Dorado. The period of benign neglect continued through the 1970s but started showing signs of decay in the succeeding decade.

Post-1970: The Athletic El Dorado and the Anthropologists Who Seek Him

The legendary man of gold stands for all of the futile—but irrepressible—searches of humankind, with specific reference to Spanish conquistadores. The history of neglect that has haunted sport anthropology has not extinguished it. Optimists continue to come forward, certain that the illusive validation is just around the bend. The preceding section can be roughly characterized as the early history of the anthropology of game and sport, when the field was in effect an occasional effort without serious undertakings in anything approaching the needed critical mass. This section looks at anthropologists who have changed the way in which sport anthropology is carried out, in part by daring to publicly declare their primary identity as sport specialists.

A strange thing happened in the 1990s: the occasional sport articles matured into the publication of a spate of sport ethnographies and anthologies written by anthropologists (e.g., Klein, 1991; Alter, 1992; Brownell, 1995). Interspersed among these book-length monographs, their authors and other anthropologists also published more than 30 articles and chapters (e.g., Bolin, 1992; Dyck, 1995; Appadurai, 1995). The anthropological import of these contributions is made manifest by the range of cultures represented from locations around the world, including China, the Dominican Republic, Mexico, Argentina, India, the United Kingdom, Canada, and the United States.

The anthropologists featured in the following discussion have two things in common. First, as sport anthropologists, they have abandoned what I call the "cockfighting in Bali" approach, in which anthropologists focused on indigenous games and sports, for one that examines modern, industrial sport. Second, a trend emerges, wherein anthropologists treat their sport subject matter in a transnational fashion, which is to say that sport is increasingly seen as an ongoing interaction between societies.

John MacAloon: The Pioneer

The origin of any serious effort to make the anthropology of sport resonate in the discipline lies in John MacAloon's (1981) pioneering book on Pierre de Coubertin, the founder of the modern Olympics. This monograph was equal parts anthropology, history, and social thought, making it an unlikely candidate for conventional anthropology—which is precisely the import of MacAloon's work. Staunchly interdisciplinary, he didn't shy away from the crisis of legitimacy that accompanies any such effort. *The Great Symbol: Pierre de Coubertin and the Origins of the Modern Olympic Movement* was a remarkable merger of disciplines that located this 19th-century French aristocrat in a changing Europe and drew together the threads of ritual, symbolic interpretation, and social history in examining what Ranger and Hobsbawm (1983) would have to consider a classic example of "invented tradition"—the modern Olympics. More specifically, for anthropology, MacAloon's book was an exposition of Victor Turner's notions of ritual in the spectacle of the modern Olympics, which was shown in its fullest sense as a center of transnational spectacle and ritual that resonated culturally.

If MacAloon was somewhat relegated to the periphery by mainstream anthropologists for his unconventional research, he was well regarded in sport studies, and his work served as a model for understanding the Olympics. His ability to court other audiences was a bit hindered by the general chippiness of his personal style. He was, for instance, asked to deliver a keynote address at the 1986 North American Society for the Sociology of Sport meeting, where he proceeded to raise a furor by critiquing the field of sport sociology: "Sport sociologists have yet to take sport as seriously as their society does all around them. We must stop perceiving ourselves as *Quixotic* if we are ever to cease acting and writing like *Sancho Panzas*" (1987). His attempt to soften the slap by referring to "we" and "ourselves" was not believed for a moment, since he wasn't even a member of the organization. Lost in his presentation of self was the power of his message—insistence on theorizing the subject in such a way that assumptions are questioned, for that was his approach to relevance and, ultimately, to respect.

MacAloon has continued his work on the Olympics, publishing steadily during the intervening period (e.g., 2006a, 2006b, 2008). His stature also grew sufficiently that he was brought into the International Olympic Committee (IOC) as a founding member of the IOC Research Council that is part of the IOC's Olympic Studies Centre. Some in anthropology now think that the import of his work on the Olympics is gradually dawning on the discipline.

Susan Brownell

A simple way to gauge the impact of one's work is to determine whether it can guide succeeding generations along the path it has created. Susan Brownell was indirectly but importantly influenced by MacAloon's abiding anthropological interest in the Olympics. Brownell's primary interests, however, were formed by her family's links to China and her personal involvement in sport. A former track-and-field athlete, she competed at the collegiate level both in the United States and in China, at Beijing University. Her first book (1995) was a breakthrough of sorts. Brownell was the first anthropologist to publish ethnography of Chinese sport (specifically, its track-and-field sporting institution). Her approach to the participant-observer method was carried out at a level rarely seen in the field. Brownell detailed the means by which athletes were culturally and socially molded to fit the state's notion of what a representative of China should be like. In *Training the Body for China* (1995), she chronicled the relationship between athletes and bodies using Foucauldian notions of "disciplining" (Foucault, 1977). Brownell fused all this with her abiding interest in gender (1996, 1999, 2000), thus opening a new and important portal in the anthropology of gender. With the awarding of the 2008 Olympic Games to China, Brownell launched a project (2008) that sought to understand the Games in the context of a rapidly changing China. In the same year, she replaced MacAloon at the IOC's Research Council.

Brownell has always been very much aware of the marginalization of sport anthropology: "treatments of sports [in anthropology] were typically peripheral to issues regarded as more central to the discipline. . . . [T]here is no professional journal on the anthropology of sport, nor is there an international organization of scholars; there is not even an association of that title under the American Anthropological Association" (2008, p. 105). For Brownell, however, the crux of the problem lies in what she sees as the undertheorizing of sport scholarship in the past.

Alan Klein

During graduate school in the mid-1970s, Klein came into contact with two faculty members at SUNY Buffalo, Allen Tindale and Phillips Stevens, who were also members of TAASP. They abided by the traditional anthropological view that "sport" meant "play." Though not wanting to study arcane sport in a tribal context, Klein hoped to tap into his own sporting past in high school and college baseball, but he paid no more attention to the subject until he encountered the documentary film *Pumping Iron* in 1977. That exposure launched a seven-year study, beginning in 1979, of the bodybuilding scene at Gold's Gym in Venice, California. Initially envisioned as an ethnographic exploration of narcissism, the study eventually grew to take a larger look at hegemonic masculinity. Klein's articles began appearing in the mid-1980s (1985, 1986, 1987, 1989), and the monograph came out in 1993. Along the way, Klein became firmly ensconced in his identity as a sport anthropologist. In his second ethnography, he used dependency models and cultural resistance to look at Dominican baseball. The result, *Sugarball: The American Game, the Dominican Dream* (1991), approached baseball as a venue for understanding social and political anthropology.

Discovering, as each novice sport anthropologist quickly does, that his anthropological audience was limited, Klein found support among sport sociologists, in particular the North American Society for the Sociology of Sport. Most of the 1990s found Klein engaged in the study of a unique sporting situation—a binational Mexican League baseball team on the Texas–Mexico border—and Klein used this next ethnography to examine nationalism in a nuanced way (1997). By the turn of the century, Klein was interested in globalization and preparing an ambitious project that took him through five continents and eight countries to chronicle how Major League Baseball goes about globalizing. *Growing the Game: Globalization and Major League Baseball* (2006) examines the idea that globalization is not ubiquitous and can be altered to fit local cultural requirements. From time to time, Klein allowed himself to imagine a significant presence for sport anthropology, but he has remained pessimistic about it ever occurring. For him, it is better to find interdisciplinary succor.

Eduardo Archetti

Archetti left his native Argentina to study anthropology in France, where he received his PhD in social anthropology. Opting to remain in Europe, he pursued a career in development studies at the University of Oslo. There, he became a fixture in anthropological circles. At mid-career, Archetti developed a research interest in the areas of masculinity and soccer (Archetti & Romero, 1994, Archetti, 1996), and he explored the complex interchange between nationalism and masculinity in his ethnography *Masculinities: Football, Polo, and Tango in Argentina* (1998). In this groundbreaking book, he advanced the discussion of masculinity through the revealing contexts of same-sex (soccer and polo) and cross-sex (tango) relations. From the mid-1990s into the early 2000s, Archetti used his anthropological sensibilities to delve into soccer violence and nationalism (e.g., 1997).

Gary Armstrong

Sport studies are more respected across the Atlantic than in the United States. Gary Armstrong is an anthropologist in the United Kingdom whose career has been entirely focused on the study of soccer. His ethnography of soccer hooliganism (1998) is widely acclaimed as an ethnographic tour de force, and it launched his career in England. Armstrong's case stands in stark contrast to that of sport anthropologists in the United States in that his study of hooliganism became part of a rich tradition of studies seeking to understand this phenomenon in a social control context; in other words, Armstrong moved into a field that already had legitimacy, which allowed the scholarly community to appreciate the extent of his contribution.

Joseph Alter

By contrast, American Joseph Alter failed while attempting to do something in the United States comparable to what Armstrong did in the United Kingdom. Alter's study of Indian wrestling is an excellent ethnography and is in many ways much more traditional and more nuanced than Armstrong's work, but Alter encountered American anthropology's anti-athleticism. His work (1997) looks deeply at the symbolic significance of Indian wrestling to views of the body. He also explores the relationship between sexuality, male celibacy, and nationalism in postcolonial India (2000). He found it very difficult to gain a toehold in the field in part because this kind of research had no currency in the discipline, and he shed his sport anthropology cloak and reinvented himself as a medical anthropologist. Properly chastened, perhaps, Alter found a position at the University of Pittsburgh.

George Gmelch

The lesson to be learned is that one enters sport anthropology at one's own peril. It is best undertaken when one has a measure of security (i.e., tenure). George Gmelch is such a case. He began his career (PhD, 1974) studying tinkers (or travelers) in the Irish countryside, then went on to study migration in Barbados. By the late 1980s, Gmelch was firmly entrenched in cultural anthropology and successfully mainstream, but something gnawed at him.

Unknown by most in the discipline was the fact that Gmelch was a former professional baseball player who had never left the sport far behind. The only hint of this past came in a remarkably well-known piece called "Baseball Magic," originally published in *Society* (1972), in which Gmelch illustrated how Malinowski's (1922) views of magic among the Trobriand Islanders also have currency among contemporary baseball players. Because it was one of the first sport pieces to merge modern Western notions with traditional anthropological theory, the article remains widely reprinted.

This spectacularly successful piece remained unconnected to Gmelch's "legitimate" interests until he finally returned to his roots 25 years later by publishing ethnographies about nonplayers who work in ballparks (Gmelch & Weiner, 1998) and about life in the minor leagues of U.S. baseball (Gmelch, 2001). The richness of Gmelch's ethnographies stem from his success in fusing anthropological practice with his previous incarnation as a ballplayer. He continues to work both his mainstream interests and, unabashedly, his bornagain baseball interests, most recently in the form of an anthology about international baseball (Gmelch, 2006).

Anne Bolin

Like Gmelch, Anne Bolin began her anthropology career in an established field—in this case gender studies—in which she garnered a baseline of acceptance. And like Gmelch, Bolin practiced sport (bodybuilding), which she kept off to the side. By the 1990s, she began publishing in the area of women's bodybuilding (1992, 1998a, 1998b). Together with Granskog, she edited *Athletic Intruders* (2003), which examined female athletes from a range of perspectives. Bolin's work has since gone on to look at sexuality, but she periodically returns to women's bodybuilding (e.g., 2011).

Noel Dyck

Canadian anthropologist Noel Dyck built his career on Native American studies, then in the late 1990s established sport as a second area of interest, and he has contributed significantly enough to be considered one of only a handful of anthropologists courageous enough to be identified as sport anthropologists (2000). As a proponent of sport anthropology, Dyck has striven to gain disciplinary respect for the study of sport and games. His own work has focused on children and sport (2006), but his manifesto for the rise of sport anthropology was laid out in the introduction to his edited collection, *Games, Sports, and Cultures*, in which he noted that "anthropological treatments of sport have become increasingly sophisticated and better known within the field of sport studies" (2000, p. 16).

William Kelly

William Kelly established his career in Japanese studies after earning his degree in anthropology in 1980. Beginning in the mid-1990s, however, he began to research Japanese baseball, particularly the history and present patterns of professional baseball in Osaka and Kobe. Kelly is now finishing a historical ethnography of one of the Kansai baseball clubs, the Hanshin Tigers, titled *The Hanshin Tigers and the Practices of Professional Baseball in Modern Japan*. Kelly's work (1998, 2000, 2004, 2007) has looked at various aspects of the sport in terms of culture change. For instance, he has examined cultural notions of samurai that were claimed for Japanese baseball and the notion that, as a rule-bound institution, sport is not capable of being changed as it moves between cultures. Japanese baseball practitioners, he pointed out, "indigenized" the game and made it their own. Kelly also introduces the useful notion of "uncanny mimicry" to understand the striking blend of cultural attributes and responses to baseball found in Japan.

Taken together, these anthropologists represent a range of approaches to sport anthropology, but, with the exception of the Europeans, we note the continued difficulty—both individually and collectively—of gaining a measure of respect in the discipline for their sport research. If legitimacy and acceptance are, as argued by both MacAloon and Brownell, a function of being theoretically sophisticated or ethnographically rich, then this body of work should have succeeded in establishing a firm toehold, yet it has not.

Looking Outward

I am led to the conclusion that too much energy has been expended internally in trying to meet a basically unachievable goal; in the process, we lose sight of even more important achievements and alliances. I refer to the rewarding relationships that most sport anthropologists have fashioned with colleagues in sociology and history. These cross-disciplinary connections were forged out of the subject studied. Sport is an excellent setting for looking at several key areas in the social sciences, most notably globalization (transnationalism), nationalism, and gender and body issues.

Globalization (Transnationalism)

Sport scholars with sociological ties have put together an impressive catalog of studies that have advanced our understanding of how globalization works. Beginning with the work of Joseph Maguire (1990), exploration of the relationship between sport, transnationalism, and global currents has proceeded apace, with related work taking place in other disciplines. Despite following the figurationalist school, sociologist Maguire's magnum opus on globalization looks at "global flows" in a way that is reminiscent of Appadurai (1991). Maguire's globalization schema weave in political structures, media, economics, and migration. Sport sociologist David Andrews' work (Andrews & Ritzer, 2007) continues this examination of local–global relationships in sport, albeit in a manner more focused on cultural areas. Indeed, local–global ties and global flows are central to anthropology's approach to globalization. In recent years, sport anthropology has begun to weigh in. For example, Klein's work on the globalization of Major League Baseball (MLB) chronicled the strategies employed by MLB in going global (2008, 2009, 2010). Using ethnographic methods, rare in such studies of sport, Klein conducted multi-sited research in eight nations (2006). He attempted to sharpen the focus on definitions of globalization by thinking of it as existing along a continuum, at one end of which globalization is merely a contemporary manifestation of neoliberal process (Klein refers to this as "testicular globalization"), while at the other end it is more decentralized and open to the sharing of power.

Nationalism

According to sport historian Allen Guttmann (1995, 2002), the partnership between sport and nationalism dates to the very beginnings of modern sport. With its base in international competition and a heavy reliance upon the symbols and ceremonies accompanying these international events, sport has been considered a classic venue for exploring how nationalism is built, the forms it takes, and the extent to which it produces political outcomes. Historians Ranger and Hobsbawm (1983) have provided a wonderful concept— "invented tradition"—in which practices of recent vintage take on the look of antiquity and serve to provide common identity among people in large national settings. In fact, international sporting events are especially laden with ritual and iconography that have the look of antiquity.

Anthropologists have kept pace with this thinking. MacAloon's studies of the Olympics intensively scrutinize the areas of culture, ritual, and nation (2013). Using Victor Turner's model for the study of ritual, MacAloon has explored the liminal and liminoid (reaffirming versus transformative) capacities of Olympic ceremonies. The implications for nationalism are powerfully apparent.

Susan Brownell's (2008) work on Chinese sport carries MacAloon's work into the 21st century. Brownell's access to China at the time it staged the 2008 Olympics enabled her to delve into China's sensitivity to outside views of itself—views that are ethnocentrically laden and politically tender. Again, anthropologists are often so well situated on the ground that their ethnographies provide badly needed accounts to the rest of the social sciences. The example of China's use of sport is woven, through and through, with various forms of nationalism. Aware of the worldwide appeal of the Olympics, Chinese authorities took every opportunity to promote China as a modern and desirable member of the world community. The Games also fueled China's national pride. Because rituals and ceremonies are designed to project ideal views of the host nation to the eyes of the world, Brownell examines all of this in the context of the social and political tensions that recurred in the weeks and months leading up to the Games.

The study of sport as a postcolonial phenomenon is illustrated in Appadurai's (1995) examination of Indian cricket, which shows how easily the meaning of sport can undergo metamorphosis to become a symbol of an emerging nationalism. This postcolonial orientation was used by historian Louis Pérez (1994) in his examination of Cuba's adoption of American baseball and its morphing of the meaning of the game from an element of American cultural identity to one of an emerging Cuban nationalism.

Argentinean Eduardo Archetti's comparative study of soccer and tango emphasizes soccer's democratic elements and interprets the game as an institution that offers Argentineans a respite from authoritarian politics (1999). Archetti's ethnographic work on soccer examined fans and their discourse to understand the unique role played by Argentinean soccer.

Joseph Alter studied kabaddi, Indian wrestling, as an indigenous form that literally and figuratively embodies the notion of India's nationalism (2000). But the nationalism Alter invokes is less concerned with postcolonial modernity; rather, he sees Indian wrestling as a tradition-bound form of nationalism that he reinterprets as "foreign" to Indians through its reliance on formal sport. As such, kabaddi exists in a dialectical relationship with modern sport forms.

Klein's (1997) study of a professional Mexican League baseball team straddling the border between Mexico and the United States explores multiple definitions of nationalism. This team—the Tecos—has home fields in both Nuevo Laredo, Mexico, and Laredo, Texas; it also engages with two national constituencies and features a Mexican owner and a Texan general manager, as well as players from both countries. Through his ethnography, Klein showed how the national antagonism—what Klein terms "autonationalism"—that exists at a range of levels is countered by national bonding (binationalism and transnationalism). This plays out in the ways in which the two sides come together whenever they are confronted by a presence from outside the Texas/Mexico border region. Ethnographically, Klein shows that the auto-nationalistic tensions are dealt with internally by the team and that micro-analysis (ethnography) is an excellent way of exploring macrolevel tensions.

Gender and the Body

The complex role of the body in politics and sport was presented to sport scholars over a quarter of a century ago by Hoberman (1984), and anthropologists have since added key facets of understanding in this rewarding area of study. We have noted Alter's study, which found that kabaddi Indian wrestlers' physiques were treated as the embodiment of Indian working-class nationalism, but Alter's work was also an ethnography of the body. His treatment of Gandhi's body as a vehicle through which to understand Indian nationalism (e.g., connecting fasting and Indian ideas of emptiness, or the relationship between Gandhi's celibacy and his notions of nonviolence) echoes that of Hoberman. Similarly, Brownell's treatment of nationalism and the training of Chinese athletes underscores the role of the state. Her work is also heavily concerned with the ways in which the body is disciplined and guided by the state.

In the nexus of sport, body, and gender, the ties between sociologists and anthropologists have been fruitful. Sport sociologists such as Cheryl Cole (Cole & Birrell, 1990) and Nancy Theberge (1991) played an early role in "reading" the body in terms of a range of issues pertaining to gender. In anthropology, Anne Bolin's (1992, 1998) work on female bodybuilders followed suit and added important dimensions of ethnographic insight, as did Brownell in China.

The free-flowing interchange between sociology and anthropology has also benefited the examination of masculinity, sport, and body. Messner's (1995) pioneering work in sociology was joined by Klein's (1992) ethnographic studies of bodybuilders and Mexican baseball players (1995), as well as Alter's work in India. Also relevant here is Eduardo Archetti's work on Argentinean soccer and masculinity; Argentinian fans fight each other through chants that seek to emasculate rivals. Collectively, those works point sport studies in a fruitful direction.

Summary

The comparative social and cultural dimensions associated with anthropology are particularly attractive in the 21st century, where national boundaries are rendered increasingly superfluous. Sport, it may be argued, is at the forefront of globalization, and understanding how it reflects local cultural matters or the more homogenous notions of powerful transnational currents in essential. Globalization, nationalism, and gender are promising directions that young scholars may build upon. It is also important that we make certain to keep abreast of developments in related fields. Knowing what sport historians, sport sociologists, and others are working on will not only prevent us from reinventing the wheel, but promote a synergy that will be theoretically invigorating.

I encourage sport anthropologists to be less concerned with gaining the respect of their natal field and to embrace the larger community of sport scholars. As a discipline, we can make a contribution that reaches throughout the social sciences. Through the careful application of ethnography, theorization of culture, and cross-cultural analysis, sport scholarship stands to advance throughout the 21st century.

References

Alter, J. (1992). *The wrestler's body: Identity and ideology in North India*. Berkeley: University of California Press.

Alter, J. (1997). Seminal truth: A modern science of male celibacy in Northern India. *Medical Anthropology Quarterly, 11*(3), 275–298.

Alter, J. (2000). *Gandhi's body: Sex, diet, and nationalism in India*. Philadelphia: University of Pennsylvania Press.

Andrews, D., & Ritzer, D. (2007). The grocal in the sporting glocal. In R. Giulianotti & R. Robertson (Eds.), *Globalization and sport* (pp. 67–93). New York: Wiley.

Appadurai, A. (1991). Decolonizing the production of culture: Cricket in contemporary India. In S. Kang, J. MacAloon, & R. DaMatta (Eds.), *The Olympics and cultural exchange* (pp. 163–190). Seoul: Hanyang University Press.

Appadurai, A. (1995). Playing with modernity: The decolonization of Indian cricket. In C. Breckenridge (Ed.), *Consuming modernity: Public culture in a South Asian world* (pp. 23–48). Minneapolis: University of Minnesota Press.

Archetti, E. (1996). Playing time and masculine virtues in Argentinean football. In M. Melhuss & K. Stolin (Eds.), *Machos, mistresses, and Madonnas: Contesting the power of Latin American gender* (pp. 36–56). London: Verso.

Archetti, E. (1997). The moralities of Argentinean football. In S. Howell (Ed.), *The ethnographies of morality* (pp. 99–127). London: Routledge.

Archetti, E. (1999). *Masculinities: Football, polo, and tango in Argentina*. Oxford, UK: Berg.

Archetti, E., & Romero, A. (1994). Death and violence in Argentinean football. In R. Giulianotti, N. Bonney, & M. Hepworth (Eds.), *Football, violence, and social identity* (pp. 37–67). London: Routledge.

Armstrong, G. (1998). *Football hooligans: Knowing the score*. Oxford, UK: Berg.

Blanchard, K. (1995). *The anthropology of sport* (rev. ed.). New York: Bergin & Garvey.

Blanchard, K., & Cheska, A. (1982). *The anthropology of sport*. New York: Bergin & Garvey.

Bolin, A. (1992). Flex appeal, food, and fat: Competitive bodybuilding, gender, and diet. *Play and Culture, 5*(4), 378–400.

Bolin, A. (1998a). Muscularity and femininity: Women bodybuilders and women's bodies in cultural historical context. In K. Volkwein (Ed.), *Fitness as cultural phenomenon* (pp.187–212). New York: Waxmann.

Bolin, A. (1998b). Vandalized vanity: Feminine physiques betrayed and portrayed. In F. Mascia-Lees & P. Sharpe (Eds.), *Tattoo, torture, adornment, and disfigurement: The denaturalization of the body in culture and text* (pp.79–99). Albany: State University of New York Press.Bolin, A., & Granskog, J. (Eds.). (2003). *Athletic intruders: Ethnographic research on women, culture, and exercise.* Albany: SUNY Press.

Bolin, A. (2011). *Buff bodies and the beast.* In: *Critical readings in bodybuilding.* A. Locks and N. Richardson. Routledge: 29-58.

Brownell, S. (1995). *Training the body for China: Sports in the moral order of the People's Republic.* Chicago: University of Chicago Press.

Brownell, S. (1996). Representing gender in the Chinese nation: Chinese sportswomen and Beijing's bid for the 2000 Olympics. *Identities, 2*(3), 223–247.

Brownell, S. (1999). Strong women and impotent men: Sports, gender, and nationalism in Chinese public culture. In M. Yang (Ed.), *Spaces of their own: Women's public sphere in transnational China* (pp. 70–92). Minneapolis: University of Minnesota Press.

Brownell, S. (2000). Why should an anthropologist study sports in China? In N. Dyck (Ed.), *Games, sports, and cultures* (pp. 43–64). Oxford, UK: Berg.

Brownell, S. (2008). *Beijing's Games: What the Olympics mean to China.* Lanham, MD: Rowman & Littlefield.

Cole, C., & Birrell, S. (1990). Double fault: Renee Richards and the construction and naturalization of difference. *Sociology of Sport Journal, 7,* 1–21.

Culin, S. (1907). *Games of the North American Indian* (Twenty-Fourth Annual Report of the Bureau of American Ethnology, 1902–1903). Washington, DC: Smithsonian Institution.

Dyck, N. (1992). Parents, consociates, and the social construction of children's athletics. *Anthropological Forum, 7*(2), 215–229.

Dyck, N. (Ed.). (2000). *Games, sports, and cultures.* Oxford, UK: Berg.

Dyck, N. (2006). Athletic scholarships and the politics of child rearing in Canada. *Anthropological Notebooks, 12,* 65–78.

Elias, N., & Dunning, E. (1986). *The quest for excitement: Sport and leisure in the civilizing process.* Oxford, UK: Blackwell.

Evans-Pritchard, E. (1940). *The Nuer.* Oxford, UK: Clarendon.

Firth, R. (1931). A dart match in Tikopia: A study in the sociology of a primitive sport. *Oceania, 1,* 33–59.

Foucault, M. (1977). *Discipline and punish.* New York: Random House.

Fox, R. (1961). Pueblo baseball: A new use for old magic. *Journal of American Folklore, 74*(1), 9–16.

Frankenberg, R. (1957). *Village on the border: A social study of religion, politics, and football in a North Wales community.* Long Grove, IL: Waveland.

Geertz, C. (1973a). Deep play: Notes on a Balinese cockfight. In C. Geertz (Ed.), *The interpretation of cultures* (pp. 412–453). New York: Basic Books.

Geertz, C. (1973b). *The interpretation of cultures*. New York: Basic Books.

Gmelch, G. (1972). Baseball magic. *Society, 8*(8), 39–45.

Gmelch, G. (2001). *Inside pitch: Life in professional baseball*. Lincoln, NE: Bison Books.

Gmelch, G. (Ed.). (2006). Baseball without borders: The international pastime. Lincoln, NE: Bison Books.

Gmelch, G., & Weiner, J. (Eds.). (1998). *The working lives of baseball people*. Washington, DC: Smithsonian Press. Guttmann, A. (1978). *From ritual to record*. New York: Columbia University Press.

Guttmann, A. (1979). *From ritual to record: The nature of modern sports*. New York: Columbia University Press.

Guttmann, A. (1995). *Games and empires*. New York: Columbia University Press.

Guttmann, A. (2002). *The Olympics: A modern history*. Champaign: University of Illinois Press.

Hoberman, J. (1984). *Sport and political ideology*. Austin: University of Texas Press.

Huizinga, J. (1955). *Homo ludens: A study of the play element in culture*. Boston: Beacon Press.

Kelly, W. (1998). Blood and guts in Japanese professional baseball. In S. Linhard & S. Fruhstuck (Eds.), *The culture of Japan as seen through its leisure* (pp. 95–111). Albany: State University of New York Press.

Kelly, W. (2000). Caught in the spin cycle: An anthropological observer at the sites of Japanese professional baseball. In S. Long (Ed.), *Moving targets: Ethnographies of self and community in Japan* (pp. 122–151). Ithaca, NY: Cornell University Press.

Kelly, W. (Ed.). (2004). *Fanning the flames: Fans and consumer culture in contemporary Japan*. Albany: State University of New York Press.

Kelly, W. (2007). Is baseball a global sport? America's "National Pastime" as a global sport. *Global Networks, 7*(2), 44–61.

Klein, A. (1985). Pumping iron. *Society, 22*(6), 68-75.

Klein, A. (1986). Pumping irony: Crisis and contradiction in bodybuilding. *Sport Sociology Journal, 3*(2), 112–133.

Klein, A. (1987). Fear and self-loathing in Venice: Narcissism, fascism, and bodybuilding. *Journal of Psychoanalytic Anthropology, 10*(2), 117–138.

Klein, A. (1989). Juggling deviance: Hustling and homophobia in bodybuilding. *Deviant Behavior, 10*(1), 11–27.

Klein, A. (1991). *Sugarball: The American game, the Dominican dream*. New Haven, CT: Yale University Press.

Klein, A. (1992). "Man makes himself": Self-objectification and alienation in bodybuilding subculture. *Play and Culture, 14*(4), 326–337.

Klein, A. (1993). *Little big men: Bodybuilding subculture and gender construction*. Albany: State University of New York Press.

Klein, A. (1995b). Tender machos: Masculine contrasts in the Mexican Baseball League. *Sociology of Sport Journal, 12*(4), 370–389.

Klein, A. (1997). *Baseball on the border: A tale of two Laredos*. Princeton, NJ: Princeton University Press.

Klein, A. (2006). *Growing the game: Globalization and Major League Baseball*. New Haven, CT: Yale University Press.

Klein, A. (2008). Globalizing sport: Assessing the World Baseball Classic. *Soccer & Society, 9*(2), 158–169.

Klein, A. (2009). The transnational view of sport and social development: The case of Dominican baseball. *Sport in Society, 12*(9), 1118–1132.

Klein, A. (2010). Sport labour migration as a global value chain: The Dominican case. In J. Maguire & M. Falcous (Eds.), *Sport and migration* (pp. 88–101). London: Routledge.

Lesser, A. (1933). *Pawnee ghost dance hand game: A study of cultural change* (Columbia University Contributions to Anthropology: 16). New York: Columbia University Press.

MacAloon, J. (1981). *The great symbol: Pierre de Coubertin and the origins of the modern Olympic movement*. Chicago: University of Chicago Press.

MacAloon, J. (1987). An observer's view of sport sociology. *Sport Sociology Journal, 4*(2), 105.

MacAloon, J. (2006a). Anthropology at the Olympic Games. In A. Klausen (Ed.), *Olympic Games as performance and public event* (pp. 9–25). Oxford, UK: Berghahn.

MacAloon, J. (2006b). Muscular Christianity after 150 years. *International Journal of the History of Sport, 23*(5), 687–700.

MacAloon, J. (2008). Legacy as managerial/magical discourse in contemporary Olympic affairs. *International Journal of the History of Sport, 25*(14), 2060–2071.

MacAloon, J. (Ed.). (2013). Bearing light: Flame relays and the struggle for the Olympic movement. London: Routledge.

MacClansy, J. (Ed.). (1996). *Sport, identity, and ethnicity*. Oxford, UK: Berg.

Maguire, J. (1990). More than a sporting touchdown: The making of American football in Britain, 1982–1989. *Sociology of Sport Journal, 7*(3), 213–237.

Maguire, J. (1999). *Global sport: Identities, societies, civilizations*. London: Polity.

Malinowski, B. (1922). *Argonauts of the Pacific*. New York: Dutton.

Marcus, G., & Fischer, M. (1999). *Anthropology as cultural critique*. Chicago: University of Chicago Press.

Messner, M. (1995). *Power at play: Sports and the problem of masculinity*. Boston: Beacon Press.

Mooney, J. (1890). The Cherokee ball game. *American Anthropologist, 3*(1), 105–132.

Opler, M. (1944). The Jicarilla Apache ceremonial relay race. *American Anthropologist, 46*(1), 75–97.

Pérez, L. (1994). Between baseball and bullfighting: The quest for Cuban nationalism. *Journal of American History, 81*(2), 493–517.

Radcliffe-Brown, A. (1922). *The Andaman Islanders*. Glencoe, IL: Free Press.

Ranger, T., & Hobsbawm, E. (Eds.). (1983). *The invention of tradition*. Cambridge, UK: Cambridge University Press.

Roberts, J., Arth, M., & Bush, R. (1959). Games in culture. *American Anthropologist, 61*(4), 595–609.

Theberge, N. (1991). Reflections on the body in the sociology of sport. *Quest, 61*(2), 110–131.

Tylor, E. (1879, May). A history of games. *The Fortnightly Review,* 739–749.

Tylor, E. (1896). On American-lot games, as evidence of Asiatic intercourse, before the time of Columbus. *International Archives of Ethnography, 9,* 55–67.

Weule, K. (1925). Ethnologie des Sports. In Geschichte des Sportes aller volken und zeiten, Leipzig, 92–130.

Wolf, E. (1982). *Europe and the people without history.* Berkeley: University of California Press.

CHAPTER 5

Sociology of Sport

Joseph Maguire, PhD

Sociologists of sport examine the role, function, and meaning of sport in the lives of people and the societies they form; they also describe and explain the emergence and diffusion of sport over time and across societies (Jarvie, 2012). In doing so, they seek neither to praise nor to blame sport per se—rather they seek to capture how things really are in sport, for better and worse. In this way, sociologists of sport identify the processes of socialization into, through, and out of modern sport and investigate the values and norms of dominant, emergent, and residual cultures and subcultures in sport. On this basis, they explore how the exercise of power and the stratified nature of societies both limit and create possibilities for people's involvement in and experience of sport as performers, officials, spectators, workers, or consumers. Taken as a whole, sport worlds form an interlocking set of structured processes, or figurations, that enable and constrain—but not in equal measure—the lives of people and the communities and nations they form.

Though grounded in sociology, the sociology of sport encompasses research in a range of disciplines in the humanities and social sciences that also find expression in this collection: history, political science, social geography, anthropology, social psychology, and economics. It also draws on research from cultural studies, postmodernism, media studies, and gender studies. The sociology of sport is both theoretically driven and empirically grounded (Smith, 2010). It overlaps with, and is informed by, work on the body, culture, and society more broadly, which some advocates view as physical cultural studies. It also contributes to the formation of policy aimed at making global sport processes less wasteful and more beneficial to individuals and communities. Increasingly, there is an explicit emphasis on the need for social justice in and through sport. Aligned to this is the aim in some research to show how the ownership and control of sport need to be more democratically based and accountable and that the decisions of the power elite should be more transparent (Jarvie, 2012; Maguire, 2013).

Sociologists of sport generate knowledge that, rather than focusing solely on the performance efficiency of elite athletes, also enables critical examination of the costs, benefits, limits, and possibilities of modern sport for all involved. Furthermore, in studying sport in the same way in which they examine religion, law, or medicine, they seek to highlight aspects of the general human and societal condition (Malcolm, 2012). Sport, then, is used as a setting in which to explore, refine, and enhance our knowledge and understanding of broader questions concerning human and societal relationships. Yet, sociological research also seeks to debunk popular myths about sport, critically appraise the actions of the more powerful groups involved in sport, and inform social policy regarding sport. Advice is offered to but not always accepted by government agencies, those conducting public inquiries, and those issuing commission reports on topics such as drugs, violence, and health education. In part, this stems from the critical debunking role that underpins the sociological perspective. Such advice also raises questions about which side sport sociologists are on, because sociologists also act as advocates for athletes' rights and responsibilities and have provided knowledge for groups who challenge inequalities of gender, class, ethnicity, age, and disability, particularly with respect to access, resources, and status. In addition, sociologists of sport have argued for the better use of human and environmental resources to ensure that there is a sporting future for generations to come (Coakley & Pike, 2009). The success that sociologists have achieved varies across the globe, but, given over 50 years of systematic research, a substantial empirical and theoretical database exists about the workings of sport.

Given that sport brings people together yet also divides them along existing societal and cultural lines, sociologists probe the coexistence of cooperation with confrontation, power, and control. The struggles that shape sport provide rich case studies highlighting broader social questions. For example, consider the question "What is sport?" For sociologists, answering such a question requires one to understand the set of social practices adhered to in a set of conventions. That is to say, an understanding of what sport *is* requires an analysis of the society that produces it. Sport, then, is a form of collective action involving a host of people connected in particular figurations and creating particular forms of sport products and performances (Maguire, 2013). The field has attended to the conventional understandings that mark sport subcultures, govern sport practices, and give sport a relative autonomy while also critically examining the extent to which sport worlds are free from the political and economic contexts in which they are situated. The intimate and extensive relations between sport and other social worlds must be traced. For example, sport worlds are interconnected with issues of domestic and foreign policy, big business, environmental degradation, the medicalization of social life, and the socialization of citizens (Coakley, 2004).

Sport is, then, a distinctive world, a suspension of everyday life, yet it is also highly symbolic of the society in which it exists, and it is embedded in wider political-economic and sociocultural currents. Here, people experience a form of exciting significance that is rarely encountered in their daily lives. In sport, individuals and communities conduct a symbolic dialogue that reveals things about themselves and other nations (Maguire, 2013). From this vantage point, sport is a modern morality play that reveals fundamental truths about us as individuals, about our societies, and about our relations with others. Thus sport moves us emotionally and matters to us socially. It involves mimetic activity that provides a distinct setting that allows emotions to flow more easily. Excitement is elicited by the creation of tensions that can involve imaginary or controlled but real danger, as well as mimetic fear, pleasure, sadness, or joy. This controlled decontrolling of excitement allows for moods to be evoked in distinct settings, and such moods are the siblings of those aroused in real-life situations (Elias & Dunning, 1986; Maguire, 2013).

Such events as tiebreaks in tennis, penalty shootouts in soccer, and sudden death playoffs in golf evoke a range of emotions, so much so that by the end of the contest we are emotionally drained. And, unlike with a well-performed play or well-acted film, people know that what they are witnessing in sport is real and that the outcome was not determined beforehand—although with the increase in betting scandals in sports such as cricket and soccer, the evidence suggests that this is not always the case. When sport is associated with matters of deep cultural and personal significance, it becomes important to fans. Major sporting events are thus mythic spectacles where fans are provided with the opportunity for collective participation and identification that serves as a means of celebrating and reinforcing shared cultural meanings. It is precisely because sport is a distinct world that seemingly suspends the everyday world that it can be used to celebrate shared cultural meanings expressed through and embodied by sport participants. The fact that teams and individual sport participants represent a nation is highlighted by the anthems, emblems, and flags often associated with sporting contests. For sociologists using a symbolic interactionist perspective, social life can be conceived of as a game through which identities are established, tested, and developed, and thus sport can be viewed as an idealized form of social life. Its rules and codes of play (e.g., golf etiquette) allow for a fair contest and a true test of ability. The best expression of this dynamic is the "true" champion playing an authentic match with integrity. In such a context, it is possible to establish an identity with greater consensual and authentic certainty than in everyday social life itself. People insist on the authenticity and integrity of the contest—on the strict formal rules and their fair enforcement—because they want any differences of worth between them to be based on merit. In real life, however, class, race, gender, and religion interfere and rig the game of social life and its outcomes. Thus victors and losers are profane, deceptive illusions. But on the field of play, it is claimed, sport outcomes are sacred; they are real and authentic. This is also why champions seek to defeat fellow champions: That is the true test, because honor and respect cannot be achieved by knowing in advance that you will defeat an inferior opponent (Hughson, 2009).

Sport is thus viewed by some sociologists as a symbolic dialogue. It symbolizes the strict requirements of the way in which a dialogue should be conducted (Ashworth, 1971). It involves a dramatic representation of who people are and who they would like to be. The stadium is a theater in which individuals and social groups experience a range of emotional pleasure and exciting significance—the excitement of the well-played game, uncertain in its outcome but significant in what people have invested in it emotionally, morally, and socially. Sport participants act as people's heroes, expressing both the myths and the revered social values of societies and the sport ethic that underpins involvement in sport. They have to take risks in order to exhibit the hallmarks of bravery and courage and show integrity. Yet as the sociological account of sport reveals, there are other sides of the sport experience as well. This chapter, therefore, provides a brief overview of the development of the sociology of sport. It also reviews some key concepts and theoretical perspectives, examines critical findings and key debates, and considers future directions (Jarvie, 2006). By necessity, this overview is a selection and thus is limited to literature primarily published in English (and therefore does not do justice to significant research conducted in, for example, French, German, Spanish, Japanese, or Korean). For the past 50 years researchers in these, and other, countries have accumulated a substantial database regarding the role, function, and meaning of sport (Jarvie, 2012).

Historical Development and Core Concepts

Although the first texts on the sociology of sport appeared in the 1920s, the subdiscipline did not develop until the 1960s in Europe and North America (Caillois, 1961; Loy & Kenyon, 1981; Loy, McPherson, & Kenyon, 1981; Stone, 1971; Yiannakis & Melnick, 2001). In 1965, a small number of scholars from both physical education and sociology formed the International Committee for the Sociology of Sport (ICSS). Around the same time, theoretical and empirical work began to be presented at annual symposiums, conferences, and congresses. Researchers from various sociological backgrounds began to develop sociological definitions of sport, conduct pioneering work in diverse aspects of sport, and develop courses and programs at the undergraduate, master's, and doctoral levels. In the years since, the field has also developed theoretical and empirically based case studies regarding sports in various societies.

Research areas now include, among others, sport and socialization; sport and social stratification; sport subcultures; the political economy of sport; sport and deviance; sport and the media; sport, the body, and the emotions;

sport violence; sport politics and national identity; and sport and global-ization (Young, 2012; Maguire, 2013). The subdiscipline has developed a sophisticated understanding of how people become involved in sport; what barriers they face; and how gender, class, ethnicity, and sexual relations play out in sport (Hall et al., 1991). Scholars have also developed considerable knowledge about how sport is mediated, contoured by a complex political economy, and bound up in global identity politics.

The sociology of sport is internationally represented today by the International Sociology of Sport Association (ISSA, formerly ICSS), which publishes the *International Review for the Sociology of Sport*. This body is a research committee of the International Sociological Association (ISA) and an official committee of the International Council of Sport Science and Physical Education (ICSSPE). ISSA currently includes 250 members from around the globe. It presents annual conferences, including congresses held in conjunction with the World Congress of Sociology and its own world congresses, which have been staged around the globe. As an international umbrella organization, ISSA consults with national and regional groups. Some national groups are federated with the national sociological association of that country or with a sport science or physical education organization. Such groups have a direct link to ISSA either through ISA or ICSSPE. There are also regional groups in areas such as Asia and North America, the best known of which is the North American Society for the Sociology of Sport (NASSS), which publishes the *Sociology of Sport Journal*. European researchers are linked to the European College of Sport Science and the European Asso-ciation for Sociology of Sport, which publishes the *European Journal for Sport and Society*.

The subdiscipline has also produced various edited works, handbooks, and textbooks in North America and Europe. The sociology of sport is also established in Asia, particularly in Japan and Korea, and, more recently, scholars from South America have formed their own association (Asociación Latinoamericana de Estudios Socioculturales del Deporte). In addition, col-leagues in Africa and Australia are using a sociological perspective to help make sense of the social problems that beset sport and to understand how sport illuminates wider sociological issues (Burnett, 2012; Cornelissen, 2011; Keim, 2003; Lawrence & Rowe, 1986).

Main Theoretical Perspectives

To study sport without theoretically informed inquiry is simply to describe and reproduce the status quo. Theory can be understood, variously, as a guide and compass, a craft, and a lifelong apprenticeship. Theory can also be understood as a structure by which sociologists build explanations about the sport worlds people inhabit. It can help sociologists understand the limits and possibilities in individual lives by placing biography in the context of larger historical processes and social structures. Doing so enables us to understand that sport is not natural but socially constructed. Theory can also serve as a guide in the necessary dialogue between past and present sport cultures, thus allowing us to imagine what a different sporting future might look like. Rather than being read in isolation, theory needs to be read with a view to capturing the continuities and differences between theorists and within theories (Maguire & Young, 2002; Molnar & Kelly, 2012).

Thinking in terms of and engaging with a structured account of theory allow students to see how the sociological enterprise has developed and enables them to examine the craft of various sociological practices (Jarvie & Maguire, 1994). Considered in this way, theories need to be read in clusters with the underlying aim of seeing both linkages and differences. Though theory cannot provide "the answers" in the study of sport, it can equip students to know which questions have to be asked, which questions are worth asking, and in what order or sequence. That sport is sociologically worthy of study seems beyond dispute. Sport worlds hold major cultural, economic, social, and political significance. Many people across the globe enjoy sport, revel in its positive dimensions, or are exploited by the power elite and the social practices that underpin and characterize it. In seeking to comprehend this significance, theorizing—for *thinking* with sociological theory—is imperative. What follows here provides a brief survey of some (by no means all) of the main theories that have considered sport as a social institution since the 1960s.

Functionalist Approach

When the sociology of sport developed as an academic subdiscipline in the 1960s, the theories used to explain sport were, unsurprisingly, the dominant ones of the time. In North America, particularly the United States, functionalist accounts held sway (Eitzen & Sage, 1989; Lever, 1984; Sage, 1970; Malcolm, 2012). Thus North American accounts of sport in the 1960s and 1970s tended to emphasize that sport reflected society and that society itself was based on a social order in which consensus and shared values were evident. Functionalist accounts approached society as made up of a system of interrelated parts that contribute to the satisfaction of system needs and thus to social order. In mainstream functionalist accounts, the social function of religion, education, and law, for example, were assessed in terms of their contribution toward meeting the functional prerequisites of society. Sport was viewed in a similar vein. In this approach, its social function was, and is, seen in terms of how, as both a social institution and a source of personal expression, it contributes to social stability and socialization. Parallels were also drawn between the roles of sport and religion. Considered in this way, sport functions as a surrogate religion in acting as a form of social glue that brings and binds people together (Coles, 1975; Stevenson & Nixon, 1972).

Though this approach fell increasingly out of favor in Europe and North America in the 1980s, its influence lingered into the 1990s in Korean and Japanese accounts of sport. More recently, it is arguable that some of the underlying assumptions of this approach have found expression in the use of the concept of social capital to assess the potential of sport to solve wider societal and even global problems (Putnam, 2000).

Marxist Accounts

In contrast to the functionalist accounts provided in North America in the 1960s, European sociology increasingly turned to Marxist accounts to explain the conflicts and inequalities evident within and between societies (Bairner, 2007). Drawing on the work of Karl Marx and others, writers such as Jean-Marie Brohm (1978) and Paul Hoch (1972) focused on the role of economic interests and the exploitative relations built into the capitalist system. Marxist accounts attended to how economic resources were unequally distributed, to the role that social class plays in societies, and to how power was based on the ownership and control of the economic means of production. In this light, participation in and consumption of sport were seen to reflect and reinforce class relations: The power elite in the wider society have their equivalents in sport, the system of sport is used to maintain the interests of the powerful, and its consumption is viewed as distracting those in the working class from taking a more critical stance against the inequalities of the capitalist system. Indeed, sport itself was viewed as distorted by the role of capital and broader political and economic interests. The play element of sport was undermined, and sport had become, much like religion more broadly, the opiate of the masses (Rigauer, 1981; Carrington & McDonald, 2008).

Though they reached quite different conclusions about the function and meaning of sport, functionalist and Marxist accounts both tended to downplay the role of the individual in shaping his or her life and sporting involvement; by and large, they concluded, sport reflected society and reinforced the existing status quo. Critique and countercritique between these paradigms are still features of the sociology of sport today (Morgan, 1994). In Marxist circles, however, academics began to question whether the account offered was too economistic and deterministic. Instead, in the research of Richard Gruneau (1983) and in the later work of John Hargreaves (1986) for example, attention was increasingly given to the role of culture throughout the late 1980s and 1990s. Therefore, neo-Marxist and cultural studies accounts of sport superseded classical or orthodox Marxist accounts, and researchers increasingly attended to the role of sport in wider cultural relations. Power was now viewed as contested, exploitation was resisted, and alternative subcultural responses were provided. Sport was viewed as a site where culture was indeed produced and reproduced but also transformed. Sporting subcultures were investigated to assess the extent to which people were repressed or empowered, and particular attention was given to the resistance offered by people at the margins of societies. Arguably, the sentiments of neo-Marxists and cultural studies scholars found expression in the more postmodern studies of sport that came to the fore in the 1990s and 2000s (Andrews, 1993, 2000; Markula & Pringle, 2006; Rail, 1998). Indeed, postmodern studies that examine sport in terms of identity politics, consumption, the body, and globalization have become very popular, especially in North America, and in some ways have supplanted classical Marxist accounts of how best to understand the role and meaning of sport in and across societies (Hughson, 2012). Given the central role of capital in North American sport, this is rather surprising: In some respects what is currently missing is an account of North American sport anchored in a classical Marxist framework (Sage, 2011).

Feminist Perspectives

Postmodern accounts of sport have also been influenced by feminist perspectives (Flintoff & Scraton, 2002), which developed later than the functionalist and Marxist accounts and which, since the 1970s, have changed considerably in terms of their view of the societal basis of patriarchy, the role that sport plays in this regard, and what solutions are offered to overcome gender exploitation (Hall, 1996). As with other perspectives, feminism is not one thing, but all of the approaches in this perspective agree on the centrality of gender to understanding society. The overall approach has grown in prominence in Western societies and in the academy since the 1980s. Initially, liberal feminists were concerned with ensuring that women had equal access to and equal treatment in sport. Throughout the 1990s, as the feminist approach grew in popularity, some scholars, such as Jennifer Hargreaves (1994), combined Marxist and feminist approaches and used a class and gender analysis to raise questions about the role that sport played not just in reflecting the inequality of society but, in some instances, exacerbating inequality. In particular, such studies focused on the role that hegemonic masculinity plays in the biased nature of sporting ideology and content.

The solution to this problem was framed not simply in terms of access, status, or resources but rather in reconceptualizing the meaning and function of sport (Hall, 1996). Arguing that sport was inherently unequal and unhealthy, radical feminists argued for separate development and alternative body cultures (Hall, 1996). More recently, this latter emphasis has gelled with postmodern concerns regarding the body, identity, sexuality, and consumption (Markula, 2005). By and large, however, these approaches have tended to be a much more prominent interest of Western scholars and, as yet, have not taken significant hold elsewhere.

Symbolic Interactionist Approach

The approaches just discussed have tended to emphasize, to a greater or lesser degree, how sport reflects and reinforces society, but there is also a long-standing approach, again dating from the 1960s, that examines sport in terms of how society is created through the exchange of meaning, identity, and culture in interaction with others. Drawing on the work of George Herbert Mead (1934), Erving Goffman (1959), and others, this symbolic interactionist approach, though less prominent in the sociology of sport, has provided a counterpoint to more macro and deterministic explanations of the meaning and function of sport. Focusing on small-scale social settings, this approach examines the meanings, identities, and (sub)cultures created in and through interaction (Donnelly & Young, 1988). Attention is given to how social worlds, including sport, are socially constructed by the expression, interpretation, and exchange of meaning (Klein, 1993). This approach has proved particularly valuable in probing socialization into, through, and out of sport (Curry, 1991; Fine, 1987). Researchers working in this tradition have also fruitfully explored the symbolic side of sport—how it represents identities at the local, national, and global levels. Perhaps its biggest weakness is its inability to explain how these microsettings—in which the agency of the individual is emphasized and meanings are constructed and exchanged—relate to wider social structures and issues of power and inequality. Despite this, there is much merit in this approach when probing the meaning and identity politics associated with specific sport subcultures.

Agency and Structure:
The Work of Elias and Bourdieu

Two other perspectives that directly address this issue of the relationship between individual agency and social structure have also been extensively used in sociology of sport. These approaches derive from the work of the European social theorists Norbert Elias and Pierre Bourdieu. Eliasian (that is, figurational or process) sociologists highlight the chains of interdependence that people form and in which they live out their lives. While people are active in the ongoing development of interdependence, such chains act back on people in both enabling and constraining ways. In examining social change, figurationalists probe the power balances in figurations that influence relationships between individuals, social groups, and societies—and between those who are established and outsiders. Developed by Elias and Eric Dunning (1986) and others, this approach has examined the emergence and global diffusion of modern sport, the expression of violence by sport participants and spectators (Atkinson & Young, 2008), the role that sport plays as a male preserve in affirming masculinity and male power, the connections between sport and the medicalization of the body (Waddington, 2000), the significance of global sport to local and national identities, and the meaning and importance of sport in terms of individual and group quests for exciting significance (Maguire, 2013).

With an intent somewhat similar to that of Elias, Bourdieu sought in his general theory to resolve the tension between the individual and society. For him and for researchers inspired by his framework, the building blocks for understanding society lie in probing the connections between the accumulation and investment of capital, the formation of a person's habitus, and the gaining and maintaining of distinction. Unlike more Marxist accounts, Bourdieu was keen to highlight that the accumulation and investment of capital involved cultural and social elements as well as economic ones (Bourdieu, 1984). That is, though an understanding of the distribution of wealth and income was a necessary part of any analysis, one also needed to consider the gaining of cultural capital (formal qualifications and informal high-status knowledge) and the presentation of an individual's social capital as expressed in and through his or her body (e.g., in terms of accent, demeanor, and body language). Together, these forms of social capital construct social fields in which individuals share with others common life chances, experiences, and tastes. The embodied set of social memories, or habitus, of an individual reflects and reinforces the ongoing struggle for distinction, power, and status in societies. Sport plays a significant role in both the form of a person's habitus and the accumulation of distinction (Bourdieu, 1984; Wacquant, 1992). For Bourdieu and his followers, the social function of sport is to reflect the use and investment of social capital and the differential rewards that flow from such investment. Sport itself is also marked by the struggle to gain and maintain status—different sports and sport settings require and confer differential distinction on their participants and consumers (Kay & Laberge, 2002).

Research drawing on Elias and Bourdieu shares a commitment to using theory and evidence in an integrated manner; to probing the interconnections between the body, emotions, and society; and to addressing questions of power, culture, and control in everyday life. Though usually used as distinct perspectives, there is also merit in drawing together these approaches when focusing on questions of habitus, field or figurations, and distinction or zones of prestige, emulation, and resistance (Maguire, 2005).

Areas of Study

The foregoing discussion gives an incomplete account of the range of social theories used in the sociological study of sport, and other approaches have also been used to explain the relationship between sport, culture, and society (Jarvie & Maguire, 1994; Maguire & Young, 2002; Malcolm, 2012; Molnar & Kelly, 2012). Nevertheless, this review does highlight how the sociology of sport both uses and contributes to wider sociological theory. Informed by these approaches, sociologists have focused on the following areas:

- Culture and socialization into, through, and out of sport
- The relationship between sport and stratification—particularly with reference to social class, gender, and race or ethnicity, but also in terms of disability
- The body and the emotions—focusing on the able and the disabled body, the technologized body, the medicalized body, the consuming body, and bodies and identity politics
- The role that sport plays in the generation and expression of deviance: violence by participants and spectators, drugs, pain, and injury
- The connections between sport and local, national, and global spaces and places, with particular reference to issues of political economy, migration, national identity, and the media (Whannel, 2008)

A Sociological Account of Sport: Critical Findings

Any study of sport that is not a study of the society in which that sport is located is a study performed out of context. In order to make sense of society—and how sport both reflects and reinforces societal structures and subcultures—one must bring to bear theoretical insight and empirical inquiry of the kind described in this chapter. The facts about sport and society do not speak for themselves, and sociological theories help us both make sense of our observations and develop analysis and explanations for the patterns we observe. The interplay between theory and evidence lies at the heart of the sociological imagination, which seeks to make sense of history, biography, and social structures (Sugden & Tomlinson, 2002). Hence, the study of sport sheds light both on the subcultures of particular sports and on the society in which they are located. Through the seemingly mundane and unserious aspects of sport, the sociologist can see serious aspects of society and the human condition.

This power can be illustrated with reference to the role and significance of champions in sport. What is it to be a sporting champion, and why do champions mean so much to people in various cultures and civilizations, both Western and non-Western? A champion usually refers to someone who is the first among all contestants or competitors, and in this regard the term refers to the ability of an individual or team to win a contest. Yet the origin of the word, in English, indicates a different usage and offers a clue to why champions are so much more important to us than their sheer ability to win and why people attach such meaning to them. The word's first usage emerged in the context of the medieval tournament—where the warrior would act as a champion of others and would defend, or *champion*, a cause (Hughson, 2009). Athletes, then, are not simply champions of their sport but also of their local community, nation, and, sometimes, humanity as a whole. One example is the American boxer Muhammad Ali. A champion is said to possess special gifts and exude a certain charisma: He or she performs a kind of miracle by achieving the seemingly impossible. Athletes become modern heroes—symbolic representations of contemporary cultural values and who some people would wish to be. Champions are talented individuals, but as heroes they are people whose lives tell stories to fellow citizens and to people from other nations (Huizinga, 1955).

People from diverse cultures appreciate excellence and desire to achieve it or at least share in it. Champions, by representing communities or nations, make people vicariously fulfilled human beings. They are framed as modern heroes because sport has become a forum in which communal self-revelation occurs. That is, modern sport is viewed by some sociologists as a form of surrogate religion and popular theater in which occurs the communal discovery of who people think they are. Sport stadiums are contemporary venues in which champions are observed by spectators or watched by viewers: People thus experience sacred moments of exciting significance while seemingly leaving behind the profaneness of ordinary life. In this sense, society needs its champions as heroes. They perform the manifest function of achieving sporting success for themselves and their local community and nation. But they also perform a more latent role: They are meant to embody the elements that a society values most. As idealized creations, they provide inspiration, motivation, direction, and meaning for people's lives. Champions as heroes act to unify a society, bringing people together with a common sense of purpose and values. That is how *modern* sport developed. Pioneers in the 19th century linked sport to Western muscular Christianity in terms of unselfishness, self-restraint, fairness, gentlemanliness, and moral excellence. This in itself supplemented traditional notions of chivalry such as honor, decency, courage, and loyalty. These qualities are some of the very attributes associated with what people describe as "true" champions. Yet, reality also intrudes into this setting.

That is, threats exist to the manifest and latent functions of champions as heroes. These threats stem from issues associated with authenticity and integrity. The status of the champion relies upon the authenticity of the contest; if the contest is tarnished by corruption, cheating, drug taking, or betting scandals, then the hero is diminished in our eyes. The contest is no longer either a mutual quest for excellence or society's forum in which communal self-revelation occurs. Authenticity is also lost when a sport becomes too make-believe, is rigged, or becomes too predictable. Professional wrestling may produce so-called champions, but they are not taken seriously, and they are not heroes. In addition, if the champion represents a state system that the people do not support, then their respect is withheld; alternatively, athletes can become signs of resistance and offer glimpses of a different social system or different social values (Dyck, 2000).

A champion can, as hero, embody the elements that a society holds most dear, but his or her integrity can be undermined in several ways. Champions may be flawed geniuses—either because they suffer from hubris and feel they need not dedicate themselves to the required level and intensity of preparation and performance or because their private lives intrude on their status as heroes. Whatever the cause, society's idealized image of them as athletes can be shattered; the cyclist Lance Armstrong is a case in point. In addition, our champion may be less a hero and more a celebrity—famous but not heroic. David Beckham's media representation may be seen in this light, though even here his status appears to oscillate between celebrity and hero. In such a case, fame is short lived, and the athlete fails one of the tests of a true champion as hero—the test of time. Indeed, a celebrity sport star can be famous yet be neither a champion nor a hero, and thus be easily forgotten. In order to understand why champions mean so much and what effect they have, the role that sport plays in society has to be considered (Horne, Tomlinson, Whannel, & Woodward, 2012). This is where sociological theory helps and why insights from this subdiscipline are crucial to developing a rich understanding of sport and society (Coakley, 2004; Tomlinson, 2005, 2007).

Future Directions and Key Debates

This review makes clear that sport is sociologically worthy of study. This is neither to praise, nor to blame, the present state of sport. As a phenomenon, for better and for worse, sport cannot be avoided. Sporting practices permeate nursery and kindergarten provision and are part of the formal curricula in schools. Sport clubs structure local community lifestyles and relationships, and elite sport matters economically and politically—both domestically and in terms of foreign relations and nation-building. Sport worlds both reflect and reinforce existing social relations but can, on occasion, also be used to challenge and oppose the existing social order within sport and the wider society. In seeking to grasp the complexity of these sets of interrelations, the case has been made for theorizing—for *thinking* with sociological theory about sport.

Indeed, people across diverse cultures and societies have contributed to the making of contemporary sport cultures. There is, then, both a temporal and a spatial dimension to sport (Guttmann, 2004). Just as the shape of the sporting present was made in the past, so a sporting future can be shaped in the present. Sport structures, cultures, and experiences in the future can be similar to those of today, or they can be made anew. Similarly, they can be made such as to enhance the positive aspects of contemporary sport, or they can reinforce, or make worse, what we already experience as negative features. Power resources are unevenly distributed within and between societies. Class, gender, race, ethnicity, and "disability" are but some of the fault lines along which sport is splintered (Collins & Kay, 2003). Nevertheless, specific actions—for example, consumer boycotts, targeted media campaigns, and political movements—can and do make a difference. Thus it is important to hold out hope that things can change and that the sociological study of sport can make this goal less difficult to achieve. Why is this the case? The struggle to change what counts as possible and pleasurable in sport begins with consciousness raising and the gaining of new knowledge—just what the sociological study of sport seeks to do. By so doing, those studying for physical education and sport, exercise, and health science degrees can be motivated to demand that the sport elite be held accountable, that their decisions be made transparent, and that their positions be more democratically based (Kidd, 2008).

Educating in this way fosters a recognition that people have a responsibility to themselves and to others, to share good practice, to use the sporting arena on land and water in an environmentally sensitive way, and to cherish body traditions from across the globe in a culturally sensitive manner (Coakley & Pike, 2009). This stance points up the need to develop green notions of sport that can sustain both people, in their experience of sport as embodied individuals with a healthy habitus, and the planet and its varied habitats. Sport cultures and structures need to balance local needs with global interdependence. This is the challenge that faces us, and it is one that sociological accounts of sport need to more fully address (Tomlinson, 2007).

Summary

This chapter has highlighted the social significance of sport—to individuals, communities, and nations—and has shown how a sociological perspective helps make sense of this significance. By probing the connections between biography, history, and social structures, the sporting lives of people and the status of sport within their communities can be more effectively examined and explained. Sport worlds are seen not only to reflect and reinforce, but also, on occasion, to help overcome the barriers and opportunities people face in society. In order to more adequately explain how and in what ways sports are embedded in these wider societal processes, the case for thinking with theory was made. As the chapter made clear, there are competing theories that highlight and emphasize different aspects of the dynamics involved.

Taken together, such theories help explain the role, function, and meaning of sport within societies and cross-culturally. In examining and applying social theories, students will find that such knowledge can also empower citizens to make more informed choices about their sport practices and how sport more broadly can be made more accountable to the needs and interests of people across the globe.

References

Andrews, D. (1993). Desperately seeking Michel. *Sociology of Sport Journal, 10*(2), 148–167.

Andrews, D. (2000). Posting up: French post-structuralism and the critical analysis of contemporary sporting culture. In J. Coakley & E. Dunning (Eds.), *Handbook of sports studies* (pp. 106–138). London: Sage.

Ashworth, C. (1971). Sport as symbolic dialogue. In E. Dunning (Ed.), *Sociology of sport* (pp. 40–46). London: Cass.

Atkinson, M., & Young, K. (2008). *Deviance and social control in sport.* Champaign, IL: Human Kinetics.

Bairner, A. (2007). Back to basics: Class, social theory and sport. *Sociology of Sport Journal, 24,* 20–36.

Brohm, J.-M. (1978). Sport: A prison of measured time. London: Pluto Press.

Bourdieu, P. (1984). *Distinction: A social critique of the judgement of taste.* Harvard: Harvard University Press.

Burnett, C. (2012). *Stories from the field: GIZ/YDF footprint in Africa.* Pretoria, South Africa: Van Schaik.

Caillois, R. (1961). *Man, play, and games.* Glencoe, IL: Free Press.

Carrington, B., & McDonald, I. (Eds.). (2008). *Marxism, cultural studies, and sport.* London: Routledge.

Coakley, J. (2004). *Sports in society: Issues and controversies* (8th ed.). Boston: McGraw-Hill.

Coakley, J., & Pike, E. (2009). *Sports in society: Issues and controversies* (1st UK ed.). Boston: McGraw-Hill.

Coles, R. (1975). Sport as a surrogate religion. In M. Hill (Ed.), *A sociological yearbook of religion in Britain* (Vol. 8, pp. 20–39). London: SCM Press.

Collins, M., & Kay, T. (2003). *Sport and social exclusion.* London: Routledge.

Cornelissen, S. (2011). More than a sporting chance? Appraising the sport for development legacy of the 2010 FIFA World Cup. *Third World Quarterly, 32*(3), 503–529.

Curry, T. (1991). Fraternal bonding in the locker room: A profeminist analysis of talk about competition and women. *Sociology of Sport Journal, 8,* 119–35.

Donnelly, P., & Young, K. (1988). The construction of and confirmation of identity in sport subcultures. *Sociology of Sport Journal, 5,* 223–240.

Dyck, N. (2000). *Games, sports, and cultures.* Oxford, UK: Berg.

Eitzen, S. & *Sage,* G. (1989). *Sociology of North American sport.* Dubuque, IA: Wm. C. Brown,

Elias, N., & Dunning, E. (1986). Quest for excitement: Sport and leisure in the civilizing process. Oxford, UK: Blackwell.

Fine, G.A. (1987). *With the boys: Little League Baseball and preadolescent culture.* Chicago: University of Chicago Press.

Flintoff, A., & Scraton, S. (2002). *Gender and sport: A reader.* London: Routledge.

Goffman, E. (1959). The presentation of self in everyday life. Garden City: Anchor Books.

Gruneau, R. (1983). *Class, sports, and social development.* Amherst: University of Massachusetts Press.

Guttmann, A. (2004). *From ritual to record: The nature of modern sports.* New York: Columbia University Press. Hall, M.A. (1996). Feminism and sporting bodies: Essays in theory and practice. Champaign IL: Human Kinetics.

Hargreaves, J. (1986). *Sport, culture, and ideology.* Cambridge, UK: Polity.

Hargreaves, J. (1994). *Sporting females: Critical issues in the history and sociology of women's sports.* London: Routledge.

Hoch, P. (1972). Rip off the big game. New York: Anchor Books.

Horne, J., Tomlinson, A., Whannel, G., & Woodward, K. (2012). *Understanding sport* (2nd ed.). London: Routledge.

Hughson, J. (2009). On sporting heroes. *Sport in Society, 12*(1), 85–101.

Hughson, J. (2012). Sport, leisure, and culture in the postmodern city. *Cultural Trends, 21*(2), 183–185.

Huizinga, J. (1955). *Homo ludens: A study of the play element in culture.* Boston: Beacon Press.

Jarvie, G. (2006). *Sport, culture, and society: An introduction.* London: Routledge.

Jarvie, G. (2012). *Sport, culture, and society* (2nd ed.). London: Routledge.

Jarvie, G., & Maguire, J. (1994). *Sport and leisure in social thought.* London: Routledge.

Kay, J., & Laberge, S. (2002). The "new" corporate habitus in adventure racing. *International Review for the Sociology of Sport, 37*, 17–36.

Keim, M. (2003). *Nation building at play: Sport as a tool for social integration in post-apartheid South Africa.* In Sport, Culture and Society, Vol. 4, Meyer & Meyer, Aachen (Germany),

Kidd, B. (2008). A new social movement: Sport for development and peace. *Sport in Society, 11*(4), 370–380.

Klein, A. (1993). *Little big men: Bodybuilding subculture and gender construction.* Albany: State University of New York Press.

Lawrence, G., & Rowe, D. (Eds.). (1986). Power play: The commercialisation of Australian sport. Sydney: Hale & Iremonger.

Lever, J. (1984). *Soccer madness.* Chicago: University Chicago Press. Loy, J., & Kenyon, G. (Eds.). (1981). *Sport, culture, and society: A reader on the sociology of sport* (2nd ed.). Philadelphia: Lea & Febiger.

Loy, J., McPherson, B., & Kenyon, G. (1981). *Sport and social systems.* New York: Addison-Wesley. Maguire, J. (2005). *Power and global sport: Zones of prestige, emulation and resistance.* London: Routledge.

Maguire, J. (2013). *Reflections on process sociology and sport.* London: Routledge.

Maguire, J., & Young, K. (Eds.). (2002). *Theory, sport, & society*. Boston: JAI.

Malcolm, D. (2012). *Sport and sociology*. London: Routledge.

Mead, G.H. (1934). *Mind, self, and society*. Chicago: University of Chicago Press.

Markula, P. (2005). *Feminist sport studies: Sharing experiences of joy and pain*. New York: State University of New York Press.

Markula, P., & Pringle, R. (2006). *Foucault, sport, and exercise*. London: Routledge. Molnar, G., & Kelly, J. (2012). *Sport, exercise, and social theory: An introduction*. London: Routledge.

Morgan, W.J. (1994). *Leftist theories of sport*. Champaign: University of Illinois Press.

Putnam, R. (2000). *Bowling alone: The collapse and revival of American community*. New York: Simon & Schuster.

Rail, G. (1998). *Sport and postmodern times*. Albany: State University of New York Press.

Rigauer, B. (1981). *Sport and work*. New York: Columbia University Press.

Sage, G. (Ed.). (1970). Sport and American society: Selected readings. Reading, MA: Addison-Wesley.

Sage, G. (2011). Globalizing sport: How organizations, corporations, media, and politics are changing sport. Boulder, Co: Paradigm.

Smith, E. (Ed.). (2010). *Sociology of sport and social theory*. Champaign, IL: Human Kinetics.

Stevenson, C., & Nixon, J. (1972). A conceptual scheme of the social functions of sport. *Sportwissenschaft, 2*, 119–32.

Stone, G. (1971). Wrestling: The great American passion play. In E. Dunning (Ed.), *The sociology of sport* (pp. 301–335). London: Cass.

Sugden, J., & Tomlinson, A. (2002). *Power games: A Critical sociology of sport*. London: Routledge.

Tomlinson, A. (2005). *Sport and leisure cultures*. Minneapolis: University of Minnesota Press.

Tomlinson, A. (2007). *The sport studies reader*. London: Routledge.

Wacquant, L. (1992). The social logic of boxing in black Chicago: Towards a sociology of pugilism. *Sociology of Sport Journal, 9*, 221–254.

Waddington, I. (2000). *Sport, health, and drugs: A critical sociological perspective*. London: Spon.

Whannel, G. (2008). *Culture, politics, and sport: Blowing the whistle, revisited*. New York: Routledge.

Yiannakis, A., & Melnick, M. (2001). *Contemporary issues in sociology of sport*. Champaign, IL: Human Kinetics.

Young, K. (2012). *Sport, violence, and society*. London: Routledge.

CHAPTER 6

Geography of Sport

Christopher Gaffney, PhD

Sport is inherently geographic. Games and competitions occur in places and are bounded by space and time, both of which are components of geographic investigation. The Romans, Byzantines, Greeks, Maya, and Toltec all left their stadiums behind for us to marvel at—ancient geographers writing their landscapes for us to read. More recently, the global diffusion of modern sport landscapes that followed in the wake of expanding global economies and their associated empires in the 19th and 20th centuries was so profound as to render unremarkable the presence of baseball stadiums in Nicaragua, rugby pitches in Fiji, and soccer fields in the Himalayas.

Despite the ubiquitous nature of sport, the traditional disdain of academic geographers for "popular" investigations made sporting landscapes and cultures invisible within the discipline for many years. Indeed, despite the obviously profound relationships between cultural landscapes, cultural identities, gender roles and relations, political economy, architecture, and sport, an identifiable "geography of sport" did not emerge until the last decade of the 20th century. As an example of the dearth of geographic studies of sport, the fourth edition of *The Dictionary of Human Geography* (Johnston, Gregory, Pratt, & Watts, 2000) treated the topic in only two paragraph with only two references.

However, even though the generalized absence of academic geography in the world of sport has limited the geography of sport as a subdiscipline, an identifiable tradition of sport geography has contributed to the development of increasingly robust and complex investigations. This trajectory is explored in the first part of this chapter, which then turns to core concepts, theoretical perspectives, key findings, and future directions.

Historical Trajectory of the Geography of Sport

The first identifiable geographic work to focus on sport in the United States was Albert Carlson's treatment of skiing in New England (Carlson, 1942).

This study was fairly typical of early geographic approaches to sport in that it examined the interaction of sporting practice with the landscape, identified spatial boundaries, and imagined the production of a unitary geography of skiing. That is, the geography was considered as a fixed object to be observed and analyzed, not as an ever-shifting series of relationships; this approach reflected the overall thinking regarding sport within the discipline at the time. Published as it was in the midst of World War II, this article makes one wonder what impact it made. It and other early forays into sport should be considered as bland geographic treatments of sport rather than as studies specifically organized to examine sporting practice.

For many decades, geographers limited their explorations of sporting worlds to side notes or curiosities. Meanwhile, the mania for quantitative analysis that defined cultural geography in the 1960s limited the analytic tools that geographers were able to employ in their work. During this era, John Rooney's article "Up From the Mines and Out From the Prairies: Some Geographical Implications of Football in the United States" used quantitative data to arrive at generalized conclusions regarding the impact of American football (Rooney, 1969). Rooney is credited with giving birth to the geography of sport, though his opus is better characterized as cartographic than as analytic or critical.

Rooney followed his initial explorations with the 1974 book *A Geography of American Sport: From Cabin Creek to Anaheim*. This text, which examined regional variations of sport practices and player origins in the United States, did much to open sport to geographic investigation, yet, as one reviewer observed, "the strengths and weaknesses of this book reflect the present underdeveloped state of the geography of sport" (Mitchell, 1989). The tradition that Rooney started has endured, and purely cartographic examinations of the spatial patterns of sport dominated sport geography as a field of study into the 1980s. Most of the works conducted in this tradition have not built upon Rooney's self-critical reflection that "the challenge of explaining the patterns is much greater than that of identifying them" (Rooney, 1969, p. 492); nonetheless, they have offered visually compelling narratives of sport, region, and place.

Richard Pillsbury, who would later collaborate with Rooney on the *Atlas of American Sport* (1992), published a similar study on the regional variation of stock-car racers and racetracks in the United States. Pillsbury's analysis is somewhat more sophisticated, problematizing changes in regional variation, but it falls short of a more profound geographic analysis that would explain changes in the cultural complex as something more than information to be gleaned from cartography (Pillsbury, 1974).

Because of the absence of a sustained geographic tradition in sport studies, we need to look to other disciplines to understand some of the developments that would later take root in geography. In 1977, the anthropologist

Clifford Geertz published his classic *The Interpretation of Cultures*, in which he examined Balinese cockfighting as part of a larger social complex. His trenchant analysis continues to be a touchstone for social scientists seeking to use sporting practices as a window onto the patterns and processes of the cultures that produce and sustain them. Cultural geographers were not very attuned to the interventions of anthropology in the realm of sport, and it would be some time before geographers joined their colleagues in history and anthropology in taking sport as a serious object of study.

In a 1978 book chapter titled "Association Football and the Urban Ethos," Lincoln Allison referred to sport studies as an academic blind spot, indicating that it was not only geographers who were remiss in their analysis of sporting phenomena. Allison's historical analysis explored changing conditions of urban life in Manchester and São Paulo as a result of rapid industrialization and linked the morphology of these exploding urban centers to the development and institutionalization of sporting cultures. Allison recognized both that "the change in social relations which [urbanization] involves includes spatial, social, and economic dimensions" and that "organized, professional sports with a mass following are particularly appropriate recreation patterns for modern, urban societies" (Allison, 1978, p. 220). Though based in urban history, this contextualization of sporting cultures and spaces led the way for a more complex, nuanced, and integrated geography of sport. While Allison does well to identify association football as existing in a kind of symbiotic relationship with the modern city and to frame its practice as inherently spatial, social, and economic (not to mention political), it is curious that he later drops the ball by suggesting that "football can only be understood in terms of what it *means* to players and spectators and that meaning can only be understood in terms of emotions whose anthropology predates modern societies" (p. 223, original emphasis). The key linkages and lacunae for further research that are identifiable here are discussed later in the chapter. For now, it is enough to note that the disconnections between observation, analysis, and interpretation are emblematic of the relatively strict divisions between academic disciplines that characterized the era, as well as the nearly complete absence of geographic studies to draw from when considering the production of urban space and sporting culture.

The British geographer John Bale can be considered the vanguard of modern (and postmodern) sport geography, though his earlier works owe much to the cartographic traditions of early sport geography. Bale's first major book, *Sport and Place* (1982), engaged in the same kind of regional cartographic analysis as had Rooney and Pillsbury, and his regional differentiation of sport in Great Britain committed the same kinds of error as its predecessors had—namely, a valuing of description over analysis and a lack of critical insight into the processes of diffusion and adaptation that the work describes. Regional differentiation and locational models were not without their uses, however, as several studies employed geographic modeling and economic models to predict ideal locations for sport teams and facilities; see Bale (1988) for a more detailed account of this history and the variety of geographic treatments of sport in the 1980s. Bale's call for a "recognition of the significance of sport in modern society" and "an integration of notions of popular culture, localism, and cultural geography" (1988, p. 519) would be taken up, albeit slowly, by cultural geographers over the next two decades.

As the role and texture of place became more predominant in geographic thinking, researchers, particularly historians and sociologists, began producing an increasing number of studies identifying sport as a mechanism for geographic, class, and ethnic identification. Indeed, interdisciplinary attention was called for by the creation of a global cultural complex of sport due to the expansion of national and international sport cultures through faster telecommunications and economies of scale, as well as the extended reach of the International Federation of Association Football (FIFA) and the International Olympic Committee (IOC). In this climate, the interests of historians, particularly urban social historians, began to cross-pollinate with those of cultural geographers. An example of the kind of work produced by this hybridization is Steven Riess' *City Games: The Evolution of American Urban Society and the Rise of Sports* (1989). Riess, a historian, drew from sociology, anthropology, geography, and urban studies to examine the origins of modern sport practice. With a clear focus on the intersections of the spatial, the social, the political, and the urban-managerial, he weaves together a complex urban, spatial, and social history of sport.

In the United Kingdom, the rise of hooliganism in the 1980s brought the management and architecture of stadiums and urban spaces into sharper focus. The 1989 Taylor Report, delivered to the Thatcher government following a series of stadium disasters (exacerbated by Thatcherite economic and social policies), declared that the solution to hooliganism was the restructuring of stadium architecture. The remodeling of much-loved, though aging and uncomfortable, stadiums stimulated a series of geographic studies examining the role of the stadium in the urban landscape. These studies tended to be of two kinds. The identifiably geographic studies (published in geography journals) dealt with the "externalities" of stadiums: their urban, social, and economic impacts beyond the gates (Mason & Robbins, 1991; Chase & Healey, 1995). The other type explored the textures of "stadiums as place" and the importance of fan cultures and identities. This latter group did not necessarily focus on geographic aspects of sport and society, but the implicit relationships between place and identity in sport connected the contributions from journalists (Hornby, 1992; Buford, 1992; Kuper, 1994), anthropologists (McClancy, 1996; Gellner, 1989), sociologists (Giulianotti & Williams, 1994; Mangan, 1996), historians (Prebish, 1993), and globalization theorists (Williams, 1995).

John Bale (1993) was the first to categorically assess the changes in stadium architecture that would soon sweep the globe. That Bale published his 1992 article "Cartographic Fetishism to Geographical Humanism: Some Central Features of a Geography of Sport" in *Innovation: The European Journal of Social Science Research* is indicative of the disciplinary center of sport geography (Bale, 1992). Sport was also being addressed by geographers concerned with the subfield of the structuration of sport along spatiotemporal axes; the most relevant work in this regard is Weiss and Schulz's *Sport in Place and Time* (1995).

During the 1990s, the explosion of telecommunication technology, cable television, and emerging markets in Eastern Europe and Asia made sport an ever more complicated social, economic, cultural, political, and globalized phenomenon. Though geographers were slow to react, evidence appeared that a more generalized interdisciplinary approach was beginning to emerge. One of the first texts to combine sociological, historical, geographical, and anthropological perspectives was Bale and Maguire's 1994 book *The Global Sports Arena: Athletic Talent Migration in an Interdependent World*. This work is an important text for sociologists, anthropologists, and geographers of sport not only because of its groundbreaking approaches to the themes of migration and globalization but also because of its global perspective—top scholars contributed works from Latin America, Europe, Africa, and North America. The book is particularly notable for Bale and Maguire's comprehensive analysis of the contemporary geographical theories applied to sport studies. Among the concepts and theories employed in this comparative volume—with which students of sport geography should be conversant—are global systems (p. 11), dependency theory (pp. 13–14), world systems theory (p. 15), and notions of hegemony and empire (pp. 15–16). Missing from this list are concepts such as the "production of space" (Lefebvre, 1973; Harvey, 1989), "spaces of flows," and theories of diaspora, representation, and transnational identity. Some of these approaches have been incorporated into later works in sport geography (Shobe, 2008a; Gaffney, 2008), but the generalized absence of deeper theoretical modeling continues to limit the field's ability to produce a more complete geography of sport.

Following his work with the sport geographer Bale, Maguire published a seminal article titled "Common Ground? Links Between Sports History, Sports Geography, and the Sociology of Sport" (1995). In reflecting on his experience in collaborating with scholars from other disciplines, Maguire suggests that the linking of the social, the spatial, and the temporal allows scholars to "see small-scale interaction not in isolation, but in the larger context of a network of interdependencies that stretch across time and space" (p. 17). Indeed, this is one of the fundamental projects of cultural geography. When sporting complexes are considered within these theoretical models, scholars have been able to demonstrate that sport is not peripheral or incidental, not merely a curiosity or a footnote in the academic literature, but rather a fundamental and constitutive element of human endeavor—and thus that sport studies can be theoretically robust and sophisticated.

Landscape studies have long been a central theme within the tradition of human geography in the United Kingdom and North America, and this tradition has been adapted by geographers who have looked increasingly at urban dynamics in an age of accelerated globalization. Within sport geography, one of the first texts to make use of this fortuitous analytic turn was Bale and Moen's *The Stadium and the City* (1995). This compendium treats stadiums as complex, contradictory, symbolic, and integrated elements of the urban, political, economic, and social fabrics. Geography has always been a synthetic discipline, and *The Stadium and the City* helped open sport geography to multiple fields of inquiry. It is no accident that this text emerged out of a wave of postmodernist studies and the "cultural turn" in geography. Beginning in the early 1990s, Bale had begun to look more closely at stadiums, and the closer he looked the more he discovered (Bale, 1993, 1994), and *The Stadium and the City* opened the possibility for a wide range of scholars to investigate a singular geographic object in its physical context.

The contributors to that seminal volume examine the stadium in the following ways: as a fundamental component of modernity (Nielsen), as integral to metropolitan life (Maguire), within the trajectory of urban political economy (Toft), as reflective of demographic and residential trends (Horak), as a symbol of state power (Brownell), as a tool for urban development (Schimmel), as a sacred place (Jorgensen), as a site for spectacularized entertainment (Kidd), as reflective of changing social values (Moen), within the context of changing governmental regulations (Williams), as a microeconomic space (Aldskogius), as a component of urban economic systems (Baade, Anderson), as a spatial metaphor for contemporary society (Bale), and as a spatial mechanism that produces and reinforces social hierarchies (Bale). Far from the dry accounting of the early sport geographers, the developing understanding of the stadium as one of the most complex spaces in urban society began to foreground sport spaces as an object of study. This shift in focus was to have important implications for sport geography at large.

The Stadium and the City marked the development of sport geography into a more complete and competent field of endeavor. These scholars recognized that urban and cultural geographers possessed academic tools that could be used to interpret and relate the complex intersections of sport stadiums with urban political economy, socioeconomic class and grassroots movements, environmental impacts, media, and political power. The cultural turn in applied human geography also opened the possibility for sport geography to take the lead in developing critical studies of race, gender, class, and the spatial dynamics of sport.

Anthropologists, cultural theorists, and sociologists were ahead of sport geographers in understanding the role of sport in producing and maintaining unequal power relations. Again, it is impossible to separate these studies from an accounting of the geography of sport, since they were (and are) based upon many of the same theorists that define the discipline today. For instance, Burstyn's *The Rites of Men: Manhood, Politics, and the Culture of Sport* (1999) reflected a growing trend among postmodernist and poststructuralist theorists to employ French social theorists such as Michel Foucault, Pierre Bourdieu, and Guy Debord to explain sporting relations and structures. These theorists engaged in many of the same kinds of analysis as cultural geographers but took sport as a frame of reference.

The global sport boom of the 1990s and 2000s was echoed by a commensurate rise in publications by journalists (deMause & Cagan, 2008), sociologists (Delaney & Eckstein, 2003), economists (Noll & Zimbalist, 1997), communication and media theorists (Trumpbour, 2007), urban planners (Essex & Chalkley, 2004), and others addressing the role of stadiums in urban cultures in the United States. These texts are implicitly geographic in that they deal with the intersection of urban political economy, media, urban boosterism, localized identities, and the use of sport as a mechanism for urban (re)development.

The tremendous boom in stadium construction in Europe, Asia, and North America—in addition to the increasing scope and scale of mega-sporting events—placed the development of sporting facilities at the center of an increasingly heated debate regarding the use of public funds for stadium construction. As explored later in the chapter, the study of public financing for sport infrastructure generated rich economic data and methodologies that are being employed to investigate the complex and costly impacts of mega-sporting events such as the World Cup and the Olympics (Horne & Manzenreiter, 2002, 2006).

As feminist critiques and perspectives became a more central component of geographic inquiry, the connections between sport and gender were increasingly apparent within the discipline. Vertinsky (1994) built upon the pioneering work of geographer Doreen Massey to interrogate the ways in which sport and gender are mutually constitutive. Her later contributions with John Bale (e.g., Bale & Vertinsky, 2004) began to explore the microgeographies of sporting places as sites of conflict, control, and power—issues that should be central components of the geography of sport. Gaffney (2008) developed a complex model to analyze relationships between the development of a predominantly masculine public space, public culture, and the emergence and evolution of soccer stadiums in Argentina. The role of gender in the production of sporting practice and sport places deserves much more attention, especially in terms of exclusion, inclusion, and the socialization of sexuality in sporting contexts.

Core Concepts

The major difficulties in defining the core concepts of a geography of sport are strongly correlated with the difficulties in identifying geography as a discipline at large. The word *geography* literally means "earth writing," and nearly anything can and does come under its aegis. The lack of a precise definition is both a strength and a weakness of the discipline, and one of the fundamental challenges for geographers is that of establishing methodological parameters. The most generalized distinctions within the discipline lie within three major headings: the physical, the cultural or human, and techniques (e.g., geographic information systems [GIS], geographic information science [GISc], remote sensing). Sport geography typically lies within the cultural and human dimension, though some research has been undertaken regarding the effect of atmospheric conditions on the flight of baseballs (Chambers, Page, & Zaidins, 2003) and the impacts of environmental conditions on athletic performance.

Within the cultural dimension, several core concepts define the parameters of research, discourse, and dialogue. The sections that follow look at these broad dimensions by asking a series of questions about each one that are suggestive of its component parts. The questions guide you through a particular vision of the geography of sport, and many other points of departure and connections could be chosen for each of the themes. None of these themes is independent of the others, and the relative weight given to each one depends on the context of a given topic and the predilection of the geographer. As identified by the Association of American Geographers and the UK Council for Graduate Education, the five core themes of geography are as follows: location, human–environment interaction, place, movement, and region.

Location

Where is, for example, a stadium? What continent, country, region, state, province, department, county, city, latitude, longitude? What and where are the boundaries? Are they permeable? Why is it where it is? What is around it? Who decided to build the stadium and why? What series of decisions, geographic realities, economic possibilities, and social conditions combined to make the stadium a reality? What and where are the other spaces associated with the stadium? Who labors there and how? What other urban and social infrastructures support the stadium? How does the location of a stadium affect real estate values, residents' quality of life, traffic, and environmental quality? How much is the stadium worth? How much money, how much information, how many people, and how many goods flow through this place? Who wins? Who loses? Have you been there? What was the score?

Human–Environment Interaction

How has sport transformed and affected the landscape? What are the environmental externalities of sporting landscapes? What does "sustainable" design in sporting infrastructure mean? What are the relationships between conservation movements, outdoor recreation, economic expansion, and tourism? What are the effects of large-scale events on social and physical infrastructures? How are geographic way-finding mechanisms incorporated into tourist landscapes? What are the signs and symbols (semiotics) of a city that guide our interpretation of the environment? What effect does training at high altitudes have on the body and mind? What does a level playing field imply?

Place

How does sport define a city, town, or region? What are the place-based signs associated with sport? Could Old Trafford be in London or Wembley in Manchester? Where is Safeco Field? American Airlines Arena? How do stadiums and their surroundings create feelings of topophilia (love of place) or topophobia (fear of place)? How do personal relationships with sporting places change over time? What is the social memory of a stadium? How do stadiums embody, create, and respond to cultural change? What is the role of national parks in shaping a cultural landscape? How does the law influence the form and function of sport in a given locale? How are place-based cultural identities formed and transmitted through sport? What are the distinctions between sport space and sport place? How are these distinctions formed and transformed in the conceptual and physical realms of sport?

Movement

What are patterns of athletic talent migration? How do international and national laws influence the movements of professional athletes? Why and how are the game movements of rugby different from those of football? What percentage of a team's budget is allocated to travel? Are the movements of referees similar to those of players? How do fans, members of the media, police, and vendors mobilize for a sporting event? What infrastructures, technologies, and tactics facilitate, direct, or limit movement in a given scenario? Who moves within what spaces and how? How are ideals of social mobility through sport communicated and performed in a highly controlled environment? How do we train, educate, and discipline bodies to move through sport spaces?

Region

Why is baseball prevalent in East Asia, the Caribbean, and Latin America, but not in Africa, Europe, South Asia, or the Middle East? How are regional variations in language, culture, and landscape reflected through sport? What are the diffusion patterns of sport culture within a region, and what factors influence its spread? What role do transportation networks play in defining sport regions? What geographic and political logics lie behind FIFA's division of the world into five qualifying regions? Why does FIFA place Australia and Palestine in Asia but Israel and Turkey in Europe? Do identifiable regional sporting identities exist, and if so what are their measurable qualities? What factors cause regional differentiation in sporting practices? How do regional religious cultures influence expressions of sexuality and gender in sport worlds?

The five central themes of human and cultural geography are intended to serve as a structuring mechanism for geographic investigation and teaching, but they are not sufficient for conducting geographic investigations of sport. The lines of inquiry suggested by the preceding questions are based on the author's experiences and interests, but the broad nature of each theme allows for innumerable points of departure. The conclusions one reaches have much to do with the theoretical perspectives that direct a given study; some of these perspectives are explored in the following section.

Main Theoretical Perspectives

Geography is too complex a discipline to allow a definitive overview here of the range of approaches that characterize it, but we can identify some critical frameworks employed as tools in analyzing sporting phenomena. Each item addressed here forms part of a critical geography of sport within the broader academic context of human and cultural geography. Critical geographies are distinguished from other types of geographic investigation by the fact that they seek to define and transform relations of power as they are articulated in space. For complementary explorations and definitions of these themes, *The Dictionary of Human Geography* (Gregory, Johnston, Pratt, Watts, & Whatmore, 2009) is a definitive and inexhaustible resource.

Space, place, and time are interrelated and inseparable components of geographic investigation. Theorizing the interaction of the three brings together multiple disciplines within the social sciences and gives researchers a series of problems to consider before tackling specific cultural phenomena. Sport spaces and sport places change over time and are laden with cultural signifiers, memories, and meaning. Geographers have long addressed the distinctions between space and place and the role that each plays in the formation of human culture, and the major contributions in this field have come from derivative investigations in phenomenology. Studies of the relationships between sport, time, and space have also revealed important clues about the ways in which athletes use these core geographic components in their performances. In fact, these basic geographic concepts figure so heavily in the ordinary discourses of sport that they are often neglected. Yet the language we use to describe sport and sporting movements is based in a geographic understanding of the world. The greatest athletes in the world have a heightened awareness within the context of the bounded spaces, places, and times of their sport.

Extensibility

The concept of extensibility refers to the ways in which humans can extend their geographic presence through communication. The more an individual is able to use media of communication, the more extensible he or she becomes. The act of talking or sign making, for example, extends one's self beyond the body into the world at large. An individual's extensibility can be measured by the scope of communication technologies one is able to use. When we consider the different extensibility levels of those with access to electronic media versus those without, we begin to see patterns of economic and political power manifest themselves within the realm of the individual.

Within sport, the concept of extensibility can be variously applied. If we think, for example, of the wearing of a replica jersey, an individual is communicating messages of identity, belonging, and space and place to a wider audience. If that jersey bears a player's name, the extensibility of the player reaches an audience that is impossible to define in its entirety. When we think of the television, radio, and Internet audiences for an event such as the World Cup, we are presented with an impossibly complex matrix of relationships that extend forward and backward in time and space.

The concept of extensibility can also be attributed to architecture, as buildings communicate messages and meanings to the larger world. In this context, the importance of sport becomes evident. The hypermediation of sporting phenomena ensures that sport places are among the most extensible ones that humans have created. Though the concept of extensibility has been applied only recently in the world of sport, it opens possibilities for new understandings of the multifaceted ways in which sporting landscapes and cultures interact with and help create the world around us.

Production of Space

Production of space is one of the most complicated concepts in geography, and I give a very abridged version here. Building on Lefebvre's (1973) categorical definition, three intersecting kinds of space must be considered when looking at how any given space is produced.

The first kind of space is productive and spatial practice—the physical moving of things and rearranging of objects in order to create a desired space. The elements of productive space are related to capital investment, architecture, urban planning, engineering, materials, and labor.

The second type is representative space—the ideologies, ideas, and messages that a space communicates. Representative spaces communicate ideas about the ordering of the world, the role of public space in urban societies, the role of the state, and larger ideological and discursive frames (e.g., modernism, postmodernism). These larger frameworks shape not only the interpretation but also the use and function of space.

The third category is space of interpretation and resistance. This final element of the triad involves the practical (and impractical) use of space by the full range of social actors that influence the form and function of space. It includes the ways in which space is actualized or used on a daily basis, allowing for individuals and groups to restructure the intended uses of a particular space, thus transforming and appropriating it.

We can use Lefebvre's spatial trialectic to examine the evolution of sporting spaces. In the context of the Industrial Revolution, for example, the production of sporting spaces resulted from rapid urbanization, a desire for institutional discipline in private schools, new ideas of leisure associated with capitalist time consciousness, and an expanding global economy. In a simpler example, a golf course is produced by physical labor, communicates messages of leisure and capital, and is variously interpreted and employed by multiple social actors. In another example, in the latter half of the 20th century, ideas of modernity and progressive technology influenced the shape, form, and function of many cities. The construction of car-dependent landscapes was understood as a sign of industrial, economic, and social progress—not as a threat to the environment, to personal safety, or to culture. In the case of the United States, the production of these landscapes resulted in the proliferation of suburban stadiums paired with huge parking lots and completely disconnected from urban environments.

The production and reproduction of a given sporting landscape somewhere on the globe should be understood as particular response to the specific forces of production that have given birth to it. The varied interpretations and uses of sport—and the various economic and cultural contexts in which they occur—require that researchers situate geographic spaces within the complex and contradictory productive elements.

Urban Political Economy

Urban political economy encompasses the ways in which political and economic forces shape the urban landscape. The principal axes along which this shaping occurs are the FIRE sector (finances, insurance, real estate), municipal government (zoning, code, enforcement, budgeting), urban infrastructure, and the BMS triangle (business, media, sport). Each of these subfields contains levels of nuance that merit deeper attention.

To use the example of the BMS triangle in the context of the United States, we observe that urban growth regimes (coalitions of economic and political capital) have a disproportionate influence on political and economic policy in their cities. In order to attract more businesses to the area (to maximize economic and demographic growth), the business community pushes the city government to, say, subsidize the building of a new stadium for professional sport, and the facility is widely perceived as holding symbolic and cultural capital that will be attractive to business executives who make location decisions. Because of their influence as advertisers in a city's electronic and print media, the stadium supporters' agenda is not examined critically, since it also benefits the media to have a professional sport franchise to cover cheaply and thus attract a larger audience. The government calls for a referendum on public financing to build the stadium in order to attract the sport team, which is itself a franchise of a monopolistic holding company (e.g., Major League Baseball, Major League Soccer, the National Football League, the National Basketball Association, or the National Hockey League). Meanwhile, business leaders bankroll the public relations drive for the referendum, and members of the media deliver the emotive discourse of sport to the population. Opposition groups such as social movements or NIMBY coalitions are stigmatized as anti-sport, and the publicly funded stadium project, even if defeated at the polls, eventually comes to fruition. The sport franchise moves into the stadium at exorbitantly low rent, accumulating most of the revenue from the stadium, and taxpayers are left to pay construction and maintenance costs while teams and leagues collect record profits. This basic scenario played out repeatedly in an extended period of stadium construction across North America that began with Baltimore's Oriole Park at Camden Yards, completed in 1992, and culminated in the completion of the US$1.3 billion Cowboys Stadium in Arlington, Texas, in 2009.

When this process is combined with the redevelopment of degraded areas through rezoning, special economic development designations (or business investment districts), or new infrastructure projects, the real estate sector swings into action, causing speculation, gentrification, and dislocation. In some instances, stadiums are undertaken as part of a more generalized urban reform project, and, rarely, have been used to anchor successful urban redevelopment projects. The debt servicing on public stadiums is generally passed on through regressive sales taxes or tourist taxes, thus affecting those who are poor more than those who are wealthy and diminishing the overall amount of money in circulation in the economy. There is no evidence to support the claim that stadiums or other sport installations have a significant positive effect on a city's economy; to the contrary, in the case of hosting mega-events such as the Olympics or the World Cup, the costs can be crippling.

While not true in all cases, the vast majority of stadiums in the United States are single-use buildings with little or no integration into the urban fabric. Furthermore, the development of transportation infrastructure that leads from tourist areas or parking lots to the stadium generally serves to exacerbate rather than ameliorate chronic traffic problems. Nonetheless, the public subsidies given to private sporting enterprises form an integral part of the urban political economy of cities in the United States, and the gross proliferation of sports stadiums that resulted from the machinations of urban political economy can be generally said to have exacerbated already grave socioeconomic divides in North America.

Global Political Economy

Global political economy is one of the major drivers of the global expansion of sport. The processes and operations of a global political economy are similar to those just outlined for urban political economy, but they take place on a larger scale and intersect with urban or metropolitan-scale processes at intervals that promise the largest return on capital investment. In the world of sport, we can read the processes of global political economy in a multitude of sectors, including equipment production, athletic talent migration, and global mega-event production.

Equipment Production

It is no secret that large companies such as Nike, Adidas, Reebok, and others locate their factories in South and East Asia in order to take advantage of cheap labor and lax environmental regulations. These conditions allow companies to maximize profit margins while providing relatively cheap goods for wealthier consumers. The presence of shoe, clothing, and soccer ball manufacturing in Indonesia, Vietnam, Pakistan, Bangladesh, and China is not accidental; rather, it results from straightforward economic and political logics that tend to reflect the balance of economic and political power on regional and global scales.

Athletic Talent Migration

Generalized balances of power within a global political economy are also reflected in patterns of athletic talent migration. In the examples of Brazil and Argentina, athletic talent originates in South America and flows to wealthier countries (typically for North American basketball or European, Asian, or Middle Eastern soccer). Since athletic careers are relatively short, athletes almost always choose to maximize their salary whenever possible. The economic conditions for top-level athletes in Brazil and Argentina are relatively unfavorable, whereas foreign markets (with wealthy consumers and advertisers) are marked by high demand for athletic talent. This contrast discourages top-level European talent from seeking employment in South America (though there is some interregional migration that reflects the regional political economy); it also re-creates conditions not dissimilar to those affecting the export of natural resources that gain value as they are successively refined, accruing more value as they move away from their place of origin. The nexus of economic and political power within world sport not only reflects but also *is* an element of the unbalanced structure of a global political economy.

For instance, medal-winning Olympic athletes generally come from a minority of wealthy nations (roughly identified as the G-20 nations) that compete in sports requiring specialized training facilities, scientific diets, and training, while the vast majority of the world's athletes lack the necessary infrastructures to compete on a global level. The development of youth soccer talent is somewhat immune to the vagaries of infrastructure, though at higher competitive levels the necessity for highly professional facilities and management becomes paramount. The more sport infrastructure a country has, the more it can engage in international competitions.

Global Mega-Events

A third example of the global political economy of sport can be observed in the selection of host countries and the logics of production for global mega-events such as the FIFA World Cup and the Olympic Games. If we consider the geographic trajectory of mega-events in the quarter century that includes the recent wave of accelerated globalization, a pattern becomes clear reflecting the logics of a global political economy. The assumption here is that the various drivers of a global political economy of sport (international sport federations, multinational corporations, national governments, and national and international media) are motivated principally by the accelerated accumulation of wealth and power. Here, I discuss selected Summer Olympic Games, though many other mega-events could be inserted in the trajectory I describe.

Barcelona hosted the 1992 Summer Olympics, and the urban and social transformations that accompanied those Games continue to serve as a model for refashioning metropolitan regions. The purported success of the Olympic development model in Barcelona is qualified, since the major changes in the city were not welcomed by all parties. However, the Olympics concerted with the long-term planning that Barcelona's city government undertook in the mid-1980s. Barcelona's strategic plan came together with new techniques in urban entrepreneurialism—a model of urban political economy in which a city is run as a for-profit company, slashing unprofitable services. The government and business leaders of Barcelona incorporated Olympic planning into long-term goals for the city and used the Olympics to overcome social, economic, and political obstacles to massive urban reform projects. Post-1992 Barcelona has become a global icon of sophisticated cosmopolitanism and one of the most popular tourist destinations in the world.

Since 1992, cities have tried to copy the Barcelona model by using the Olympics and other mega-events as top-down drivers of social and economic change. They make the mistake, however, of crediting the refashioning of the urban landscape and the commercial success of Barcelona as the prime mechanism for developmental change. While it is true that Olympic infrastructures are frequently the most visible, this fact could result from their hyperexposure in the media during the Games. The Spanish tourist market is also the second largest in the world (after France), receiving more than 50 million tourist visits a year, and Barcelona occupies a strategic and protected anchorage in the Mediterranean Sea, thus attracting cargo and cruise ships. These factors must be considered when characterizing or qualifying the success of the Barcelona Olympics development model.

In an age of accelerated capitalism, mega-events have opened new markets and new opportunities to exploit national and regional economies or offer the IOC and FIFA the chance to leave the greatest "games legacy." The Olympics are increasingly used as a tool for development that inevitably benefits already privileged social groups and produces or exacerbates social, economic, and political inequalities. The World Cup has been less effective as a developmental model and has begun to have negative impacts when similarly employed.

The 1996 Atlanta Olympics were mounted with a vision similar to that of Barcelona's but lacked the long-term strategic planning and dense urban model of the Catalan capital. Widely considered a failure in terms of urban planning, the Atlanta Games exerted an effect that was both minimal and prejudicial. Multiple low-income neighborhoods near Olympic sites were eliminated, and residents were given little or no voice in the planning or relocation process. The Centennial Olympic Stadium was leased at favorable rates to Ted Turner (then owner of CNN and the Atlanta Braves) in perpetuity, and many of the promised improvements in transportation infrastructure never arrived. The Olympics did nothing to encourage smart growth or to incorporate Olympic projects into a larger urban planning regime. Rather, the Atlanta suburbs have continued to explode in scale and scope, giving metropolitan Atlanta the worst traffic conditions in the United States. The crass commercialism of the Atlanta Olympics generated record profits for the IOC and the local organizing committee and ushered in (much as had the 1984 Los Angeles Games and USA World Cup of 1994) an era of rapacious accumulation during mega-events that has yet to abate.

The 2004 Athens Olympics resulted in a radical transformation of the Greek capital marked by massive public spending on transportation, tourism, and sport infrastructure. Part of the logic for bringing the Olympics (back) to Greece was sentimental, but supporters also promised large financial rewards through real estate speculation and infrastructure development. The Greek economy was retooled for tourism, and the specter of terrorism loomed over the event, increasing irrecoverable security costs to more than US$1 billion. While the IOC considered the Games to be successful, the majority of the Olympic installations went over budget and were not built with post-Games use in mind. Many thousands of people were forcibly dislocated to make way for Olympic installations, and transportation infrastructure was oriented to bring people to and from venues rather than attending to the needs of the population. The heavy debt undertaken by the Greek government in order to prepare for the Olympics nearly disqualified the nation from acceptance into the European market as its borrowing during the run-up to the Games exceeded the eurozone limit of 3 percent. The debt-financing of the Olympic Games also almost certainly contributed to a wider crisis of European governance and to the reduction of public services as part of austerity measures imposed upon the Greeks.

Following the 2004 Olympics, and in part stimulated by then-record spending, Greece has entered into default on its debt, and its financial troubles have been exacerbated by the collapse of the tourist economy in the wake of the global economic crisis that began in 2008. During the years preceding the Olympics, the discourse of promise was prominent in touting economic and social development and infrastructure modernization through hosting a mega-event. What resulted, however, are little-used sport infrastructures and an exacerbation of latent socioeconomic divides through the imposition of austerity measures in an attempt to control government spending.

Beijing 2008 was the most extravagant and costly Olympic Games ever mounted. The capturing of the Olympics was considered a major international triumph for the Chinese government and a reflection of Chinese political and economic ascendancy during the previous 30 years. The Chinese government promised a lavish Olympics, and it delivered by spending more than US$40 billion, a small drop in the increasingly large bucket of China's economy. However, the 2008 Beijing Games should not be considered simply in monetary terms, which were significant, but also in terms of the social costs of hosting a mega-event. By some estimates, more than 1.5 million people were forcibly relocated from their homes as historic neighborhoods were demolished to make way for new beltways, metro lines, and Olympic public spaces. The spectacular architecture of the Beijing National Stadium (also called the Bird's Nest) and the National Aquatics Center (the Water Cube) quickly became international symbols of the new China, yet less than a year after the Olympics the stadium was sold to private developers to be turned into a shopping mall. The spectacularization of Beijing has been studied by geographers and urban planners as part of a wider literature that addresses the role of sport in processes of globalization and city marketing (Broudehoux, 2004).

The Chinese government used the opportunity of the Olympics to promote China on a global stage, setting off global protests regarding human rights abuses, the occupation of Tibet, and other issues. The restructuring of old Beijing was facilitated by the arrival of the Games, and the city's chronic pollution problems were swept under the carpet for three weeks but were not addressed with long-term solutions in mind.

In the wake of the global economic crisis that began just after the Beijing Olympics, the organizers of the 2012 London Games began a damage mitigation campaign in the midst of their revitalization and development plans. While spending lavishly to host the 2012 Olympics, the national government started to impose austerity measures to ward off a debt crisis. The London Games had as their primary goal the accelerated "redevelopment" and "recuperation" of areas in East London, with an eye toward maximizing rent and stimulating consumer-oriented commerce. Unfortunately, as Raco and Tunney (2010) have demonstrated, the programs of forced and indirect displacement have been prejudicial against low-income merchants and residents. Production of Olympic space in London has been privileged over stewardship of the lived space of residents, thus accelerating processes of dispossession and accumulation in the interest of global spectacle.

The cycles and processes of mega-event production are beginning to precede the events themselves by more and more years. In Rio de Janeiro, the process of reshaping the city to host the 2016 Olympics began in the late 1990s. Since the announcement in 2009 of what will be the first South American Summer Olympics, Rio de Janeiro has undergone massive restructuring in preparation for the event: Rezoning, forced relocations, military occupation of strategic parts of the city, hosting of international conferences, monumental architectural plans, and dozens of other techniques and tactics have been employed by the local organizing committee in conjunction with three levels of government to "prepare" urban space for the production of an Olympic City. The outlook for the city is not positive, because the Olympics will enforce and create radically uneven geographies of access to labor markets, environmental amenities, and public space (Gaffney, 2010).

Scholars from multiple disciplines are converging around these new expressions of global political economy to understand and influence the ways in which global sport is radically affecting local places. The intersection of actors at multiple scales in search of economic, cultural, and political capital through sport exerts increasingly pejorative effects on ordinary lives. In the 21st century, in every place where the global economy of sport intersects with the local, the interests of capital take spatial form, frequently with devastating results.

Architecture and Landscape

The concept of architecture need not be limited to buildings but can be extended to the environment itself. All architecture, as an intentional expression of human culture, expresses meaning. The relationship between form and function in architecture means that function cannot generally be separated from appearance, though the use of facades can disguise usage norms. Sporting architecture often accounts for some of the most expensive, identifiable, and recognizable features of the urban landscape, and sport geographers must have a working vocabulary of architectural periods, styles, and technologies.

The concept of landscape is fundamental to humanistic geographic research. The term has been widely employed by geographers to describe a bounded set of territories and social relations; it has also been successfully criticized as sexist and masculine, thus serving to reproduce a "gaze" that re-creates unequal power relationships, reinforces distanced relationships between humans and nature, and aids in the collection of geographic information that serves the interests of nation building, colonialism, and empire.

Landscape studies have focused on regional variations in cultural patterns, urban spaces, and agricultural lands. Landscape approaches to geographic phenomena are necessarily interdisciplinary in that they treat the ways in which geographic space has changed over time; the various social, economic, cultural, and political factors that combine to produce it; and the meanings embedded within it.

Gender, Sexuality, and the Body

The study of gender, sexuality, and the body should be an integral component of critical geographic analyses of sport. This area should be one in which we strengthen the interdisciplinary linkages between geography, sociology, and anthropology, since the spatiality of gender relations and the movement and control of bodies in space, especially in a disciplinary context, are fundamental to an understanding of the social and cultural messages of sport. The performative sexuality of athletes and the communication of gender norms in sport spaces are inexorably connected to the formation and performance of gender and sexual identities in the nonsporting world. The persistence of heterosexism and homophobia in the media and the well-documented difficulties faced by LGBTQ athletes who want to be as openly sexual as their heterosexual teammates exert profound spatial as well as cultural and personal effects.

Memory and Identity

Memory and identity are fundamental to the study of geographic places. Because of the emotive nature of sport and the transformative potential of mass participation in a singular event, sport space is imbued with *feeling*— a difficult concept for social scientists to analyze. The rituals and cycles of sport create something much more than the sum of their objective parts.

The strength of team identities and allegiances within individuals and collectives can be surprisingly powerful, moving beyond the ordinary bounds of human rationality. The collective nature of sport space allows communities and individuals to create memories there and to return to those spaces to re-create, reimagine, reproduce, and transform culture. Yet the social memory of sport is nearly always one of conflict (involving winners and losers) and is transmitted in ways that are complex and even contradictory. The development of museum sites within stadiums around the globe is a response to a more generalized need to preserve social memory and construct places in which we can self-consciously anchor collective identities. However, museumization is only one method of preserving social memory. The memories and identities associated with sport are constantly shifting, and the spatial character of the memories and emotions of sport is a theme that geographers have yet to consider.

Key Debates and Critical Findings

The geography of sport was relatively slow to develop into a theoretically robust academic category. In recent years, however, a number of important studies have analyzed the inherently spatial character of sport and the larger impact of sport on cities, landscapes, identities, politics, economy, and culture (Shobe, 2008a; Gaffney, 2010). Most of the pioneering work being done by geographers is happening outside of the United Kingdom and United States, and South African and Brazilian geographers are taking the lead.

We know that mapping projects are an important element of sport geography, and, though several national atlases of sport have been produced, a global atlas of sport is badly needed, as are updated and integrated regional and local maps. Yet geographers must take care not to allow their investigations to remain at the level of cartographic fetishism. Maps are necessary—but not sufficient—elements of a critical analysis of sporting phenomena.

The key debates in sport geography are focusing on the political economy of sport and the role of sport mega-events in urban planning agendas. Attention has been focused on the role of sport as a development strategy due to the increasing scope and scale of the World Cup and the Olympics; their relatively opaque planning processes; and their realization in countries with a historical lack of democratic institutions, high economic growth, and massive income disparities—for example, South Africa's 2010 World Cup, Delhi's 2010 Commonwealth Games, Sochi's 2014 Olympics, Brazil's 2014 World Cup, Rio's 2016 Olympics, and Russia's 2018 World Cup (Black, 2010). The role of the public sphere in directing public investment is of critical concern to the debate surrounding the use of sport as a development tool.

The development strategy of mega-events is deeply tied to the workings of the global economy and the constant search by diverse agents for symbolic, cultural, and political capital. The itinerant nature of mega-events and the dependent position of so-called emerging economies have created a global competition between cities to attract these events as a way of gaining international media attention and unleashing projects for infrastructure and real estate that would otherwise encounter insuperable political barriers. The hidden agendas of powerful coalitions also affect "First World" cities, such as London and Vancouver, and tend to weaken democratic institutions and limit public participation to volunteerism or paid spectatorship, thus increasing profits for the corporations involved while generating affective relationships with the event.

These urban-scale impacts are related to the global production of sporting equipment, whether it be the manufacture of Adidas footballs in Pakistan or Nike shoes in Vietnam. The production of sporting equipment has profound effects on local labor dynamics, though with uneven repercussions that have disproportionately negative effects on women and girls. The constant search for the lowest point of production by multinational clothing and sports equipment manufacturers should be a growing focus of sport geographers in conjunction with labor and human rights activists.

One of the ironies of producing world-class sporting facilities in the developing world is that the opportunity cost for sport development is usually borne by members of the local population, who lose out on opportunities for more a democratic spatial distribution of, and access to, sporting facilities. The funneling of public funds to elite sport activity exacerbates the already differential access to sport and leisure generated by wide income gaps. Access to sport and leisure is a principal determinant of individual health, and it is notable that regions of cities that offer fewer recreational facilities also tend to have fewer public services in general. Thus, mega-events, with their multibillion-dollar expenditures on elite sport, represent an enormous opportunity cost for lower-income residents and for society as a whole.

The observation of sport has evolved considerably in 40 years, reflecting the increasing complexity of sporting worlds. The best texts we have regarding sport in the ancient world come from historians who could use a helping hand from geographers to spatialize temporal investigations. Two of the most pertinent texts in this regard are Cameron's *Circus Factions* (1976) and Mumford's *The City in History* (1961). In looking back at these texts, as well as works about the history of Mayan ball courts, one is struck by the many similarities between ancient and modern sporting practices. In the 21st century, it is possible to read the premature deaths of American football players and the bodily sacrifices of mixed martial arts fighters as forms of human sacrifice not too distant from those undertaken in supposedly less civilized eras.

Geographers need to undertake and become involved in more comparative studies, both across cultures and across time. Several strong interdisciplinary examples exist, but they almost always exclude geographers and geographic perspectives (Miller & Crolley, 2007). For example, a major interdisciplinary work on sport by Tiesler and Coelho (2008) did not include a single schematic or spatial representation (map) or a single contribution from a geographer. This is an astounding lacuna given that the book featured traditional geographic fields of study such as transnational identity and migrant populations, colonialism, labor migration patterns, and cultural transformation and new economies of scale. Why aren't geographers asked to contribute to such texts?

Future Directions

A new, critical geography of sport should explore possibilities in multiple directions. The first obstacle is to recognize that intradisciplinary inertia need not prevent geographers from seeking out colleagues in other disciplines. The increasingly profound effect of sport on cultural and urban landscapes requires that geography and geographers remain open to inputs from multiple perspectives in order to help resolve the conflicts and contradictions of modern sport. Several excellent examples of collaborative interdisciplinary work have emerged, the most important of which is the 2009 compendium *Development and Dreams: The Urban Legacy of the 2010 World Cup* (Pillay, Tomlinson, & Bass). This analysis of the South African experience of hosting the World Cup treats themes and concepts that should serve as a model for future investigations of mega-events as they unfold. Such events begin long before the world turns its attention to the contests, and geographers should be deeply involved in conducting and participating in the relevant academic and public debates.

In the realm of teaching, geographers should be connecting with film studies and communication theory. Excellent points of departure can be found, for example, in an increasing number of documentary films (e.g., *Fahrenheit 2010, Pelada, The Other Final, Pelé Eterno*) and reality-based fictions (e.g., *Fever Pitch, Looking for Eric, Offside*) that facilitate discussions of issues such as urban history, socioeconomic conditions of a given time and place, cultural memory, gender politics, and the significance of sport in daily life. As academic consciousness becomes increasingly aware of sport, more opportunities will arise for increasingly complex studies and projects. One such project involves engaging in multiple forms of urban and social research to explore the intersection of the local and the global that is opened up by sport mega-events. Researchers will find a continually evolving field that allows for comparative studies, across cities and countries, of topics as diverse as labor relations, democratic participation, countercartographies, tourism and leisure studies, transportation management, architecture, sport management, marketing, housing, finance, and urban governance. Geographers' ability to speak to and across many fields of study will push sport geography to the front of debates surrounding the future of global cities (Darnell, 2012).

The next generation of sport-related projects undertaken by geographers will indicate the strength and future directions for the discipline. There is not much cohesion to the current approaches that we can categorize as belonging to a unitary geography of sport. Some geographers do study sport, but that does not necessarily make them sport geographers—a term with circumscribed expectations and effects within the academy. This is not to say, however, that geographers do not possess identifying characteristics; for instance, space and place matter profoundly to them. Every geographic study includes spatial aspects, and the fact that every sport occurs in a designated space and place at a particular time means that almost no element of sport can escape the geographic eye.

Summary

This chapter defines the historical trajectory, core concepts, key terms, current realities, and future directions of sport geography. Because geography is a plastic, synthetic discipline, geographers are able to bring together multiple perspectives and approaches. Similarly, the range of sport subjects and study areas is unlimited, and it is waiting for the next geographer to enter the field.

- As a synthetic discipline, geography draws from many fields of study in order to analyze phenomena using a perspective based in complex theories of space.
- The geography of sport is a relatively underdeveloped subfield within geography that offers tremendous possibilities for expansion and connection with other disciplines.
- Sport affects urban and social landscapes in ways that are complex and contradictory, and there is always a need for geographic analysis of sporting phenomena.
- As the social, political, and urban repercussions of major sporting events and facilities continue to grow, geographers will be well positioned to undertake critical analyses in the realms of public policy, urban planning, labor studies, sport management, transportation modeling, logistics, and impact studies.

References

Bale, J.R. (1982a). Sport and place: A geography of sport in England, Scotland, and Wales. Lincoln: University of Nebraska Press.

Bale, J.R. (1982b). Sports history as innovation diffusion. *Canadian Journal of the History of Sport, 15,* 38–63.

Bale, J. R. (1993). Sport, space and the city. New York: Routledge.

Bale, J.R. (1993). Cartographic fetishism to geographical humanism: Some central features of a geography of sport. *Innovation in Social Sciences Research, 5*(4), 71–88.

Bale, J.R. (1996). Space, place, and body culture: Yi-Fu Tuan and a geography of sport.

Bale, J.R. (1998). The place of "place" in cultural studies in sports. *Progress in Human Geography, 12*(4), 507–524.

Bale, J., & Maguire, J.A. (1994). *The global sports arena: Athletic talent migration in an interdependent world.* London: Cass.

Bale, J., & Moen, O. (1995). *The stadium and the city.* Keele, Staffordshire, UK: Keele University Press.

Bale, J., & Vertinsky, P. (Eds.). (2004). *Sites of sport: Space, place, experience.* London: Routledge.

Black, D. (2010). The ambiguities of development: Implications for "development through sport." *Sport in Society, 13*(1), 121–129.

Broudehoux, A.-M. (2004). *The making and selling of post-Mao Beijing.* London: Routledge.

Buford, B. (1992). Among the Thugs. New York: W.W. Norton.

Burstyn, V. (1999). *The rites of men: Manhood, politics, and the culture of sport.* Toronto: University of Toronto Press.

Cameron, A. (1976). *Circus factions: Blues and Greens at Rome and Byzantium.* Oxford, UK: Oxford University Press.

Carlson, A.S. (1942). Ski geography of New England. *Economic Geographer, 18,* 307–320.

Castells, M, & Susser, I. (Eds.). (2002). The Castells reader on cities and social theory. London: Blackwell.

Chambers, F., Page, B., & Zaidins, C. (2003). Atmosphere, weather, and baseball: How much farther do baseballs really fly at Denver's Coors Field? *The Professional Geographer, 55*(4), 491–504.

Chase, J., & Healey, M. (1995). The spatial externality effects of football matches and rock concerts: The case of Portman Road Stadium, Ipswich, Suffolk. *Applied Geography, 15*(1), 18–34.

Darnell, S. (2012). *Sport for development and peace.* London: Bloomsbury.

DeChano, L.M., & Shelley, F.M. (2004). Using sports to teach geography: Examples from

Delaney, K., & Eckstein, R. (2003). *Public dollars, private stadiums: The battle over building sports stadiums.* New Brunswick, NJ: Rutgers University Press.

deMause, N., & Cagan, J. (2008). *Field of schemes: How the great stadium swindle turns public money into private profit* (rev. ed.). Lincoln: University of Nebraska Press.

Essex, S., & Chalkley, B. (2004). Mega sporting events in urban and regional policy: A history of the Winter Olympics. *Planning Perspectives, 19*(2), 201–232.

Gaffney, C. (2008). *Temples of the earthbound Gods: Stadiums in the cultural landscapes of Rio de Janeiro and Buenos Aires.* Austin: University of Texas Press.

Gaffney, C. (2010). Mega-events and socio-spatial dynamics in Rio de Janeiro: 1919–2016. *Journal of Latin American Geography, 9*(1), 7–29.

Gellner, E. (1989). Plough, sword and book: The structure of human history. University of Chicago Press,

Geertz, Clifford. (1977). *The interpretation of cultures*. New York: Basic Books.

Giulianotti, R. (1999). Football: A sociology of the global game. London: Polity.

Giulianotti, R. & Williams, J. (1994). Games without frontiers: Football, identity and modernity. Aldershot. Arena,

Gregory, D., Johnston, R., Pratt, G., Watts, M., & Whatmore, S. (Eds.). (2009). *The dictionary of human geography* (5th ed.). London: Wiley-Blackwell.

Harvey, D. (1989). The urban experience. Johns Hopkins University Press.

Hornby, N. (1992). Fever Fitch. Riverhead Books. New York.

Horne, J., & Manzenreiter, W. (Eds.). (2002). *Japan, Korea, and the 2002 World Cup*. London: Routledge.

Horne, J., & Manzenreiter, W. (Eds.). (2006). *Sports mega-events: Social scientific analysis of a global phenomenon*. London: Blackwell.

Kuper, S. (1994). Football against the enemy. Orion. London.

Lefebvre, H. (1991). The production of space. Wiley-Blackwell. Oxford, Cambridge.

Maguire, J. (1995). Common ground? Links between sports history, sports geography, and the sociology of sport. *Sporting Traditions, 12*(1), 3–25.

Mangan, J,A.(1996). Tribal identities: Nationalism, Europe and sport. Frank Cass. London.

Mason, C. & Robins, R. (1991). The spatial externality fields of football stadiums: the effect of football and non football use at Kenilworth Road, Luton. Applied Geography, 11.

McClancy, J, (Ed.). (1996). Sport, identity and ethnicity. Berg. Oxford.

Miller, R., & Crolley, L. (Eds.). (2007). *Football in the Americas: Fútbol, futebol, soccer*. London: Institute for the Study of the Americas.

Mitchell, L.S., & Smith, R.V. (1989). The geography of recreation, tourism, and sport. In G.L.

Mumford, L. (1961). *The city in history*. New York: Marnier Books.

Noll, R. & Zimbalist, A. (1997). Sports, jobs and taxes: The economic impact of sports teams and stadiums. Brookings Institution Press. Washington, D.C.

Pillay, U., Tomlinson, R., & Bass, O. (Eds.). (2009). *Development and dreams: The urban legacy of the 2010 World Cup*. Cape Town: HSRC Press.

Pillsbury, R. (1974). Carolina thunder: A geography of Southern stock car racing. *Journal of Geography, 73*(1), 39–47.

Prebish, C. (1993). Religion and sport: The meaning of sacred and profane. Greenwood Press. Connecticut,

Riess, S. (1989). *City games: The evolution of American urban society and the rise of sports*. Champaign: University of Illinois Press.

Rooney, J.F., Jr. (1969). Up from the mines and out from the prairies: Some geographical implications of football in the United States. *Geographical Review, 59*(3), 471–492.

Rooney, J.F., Jr. (1974). *A geography of American sport: From Cabin Creek to Anaheim.* Reading, MA: Addison-Wesley.

Rooney, J.F., Jr., & Pillsbury, R. (1992). *Atlas of American Sport.* New York: Macmillan.

Shobe, H. (2008a). Football and the politics of place: Football Club Barcelona and Catalonia, 1975–2005. *Journal of Cultural Geography, 25*(1), 87–105.

Shobe, H. (2008b). Place, identity, and football: Catalonia, *Catalanisme,* and Football Club

The Hillsborough Stadium Disaster. (1989). The Inquiry by the Rt. Honorable Lord Justice Taylor: Interim Report. Her Majestry's Stationary Office. London.

Tiesler, N., & Coelho, J. (Eds.). (2008). *Globalised football: Nations and migration, the city and the dream.* London: Routledge.

Trumpbour, R. (2007). *The new cathedrals: Politics and media in the history of stadium construction.* Syracuse, NY: Syracuse University Press.

Vertinsky, P. (1994). The Social Construction of the gendered body: Exercise and the exercise of power. *International Journal of the History of Sport, 11*(2), 147–171.

CHAPTER 7

Media Studies and Sport

David Rowe, PhD

Media studies is a classic example of an interdisciplinary field shaped by a common set of concerns rather than by prescribed theories, concepts, and methods. By way of illustration, a recent 10th anniversary issue of the journal *Television & New Media* (Miller, 2009) invited 52 scholars from around the world to succinctly state their vision under the title "My Media Studies." The outcome was a diverse set of prescriptions offered by media studies scholars from many disciplines, as many based in the humanities as in the social sciences. What they held broadly in common was the orientation that first animated the field of media studies. Essentially, the contributions revealed that media studies is a specific, targeted response to a development under modernity that has exerted thoroughgoing global consequences—the extraordinary growth of the institution of the media and the pronounced insinuation of media symbols, texts, rituals, and practices into the lives of populations throughout the world. Indeed, the neologism "mediatization" has been proposed to capture this development (Lundby, 2009; Schulz, 2004), thus emphasizing that no adequate analytical understanding of the contemporary world can downplay the media's role in shaping both ways of seeing and the phenomena being seen—and thereby being changed through exposure and representation—in intricate, reflexive spirals of signification.

Clearly, then, media studies is concerned with much more than the development of technologies of communication. The proliferation of ways of representing the world beyond immediate physical, sensory experience in print and electronic form is not regarded as a neutral process of evolutionary communicative efficiency; rather, it raises profound questions of media representation and power (as famously argued by McLuhan, 1964). As Roger Silverstone (1999, p. 2) argues in his manifesto for the study of the media:

> *[I]t is because the media are central to our everyday lives that we must study them. Study them as social and cultural as well as political and economic dimensions of the modern world. Study them in their ubiquity and complexity. Study them as contributors to our variable capacity to make sense of the world, to make and share its meanings.*

In terms of the key questions and disciplines addressed in this section of the book, Silverstone sees the media as related to the following: the construction of identities of self and other, a focus that he associates with anthropology; the formation and mutation of communities, which have long been analyzed by sociologists and geographers the growth and distribution of capital, which is of deep interest in political economic approaches in several disciplines, especially economics; and matters of governance and politics addressed by political science, among other academic disciplines that return always to orders of power:

> *It is all about power, of course. In the end. The power the media have to set an agenda. The power they have to destroy one. The power they have to influence and change the political process. The power to enable, to inform. The power to deceive. The power to shift the balance of power: between state and citizen; between country and country; between producer and consumer. And the power that they are denied: by the state, by the market, by the resistant or resisting audience, citizen, consumer. (Silverstone, 1999, p. 143)*

Silverstone's eloquent advocacy of media studies is devoted to general questions, but if society itself is becoming mediatized, then the process is found in all spheres, from formal politics such as elections to the politics of everyday life inherent in the experience of work and play. To take an example (which could be randomly selected, but hasn't been here), we might ask, Which sociocultural phenomenon has been transformed by the media from a fragmented collection of relatively small, local events to the world's largest spectacles; has been insinuated into multiple spaces of daily existence; has seen the media dominate its economics and modes of presentation; has become highly dependent itself on the institution that represent it—indeed, has become so integrated into the media as to be virtually inseparable from them? That phenomenon, of course, is sport.

Over the last two centuries, the media (especially broadcast television) have become central to sport and consequently have demanded the engagement of media studies (Wenner, 1998). Sport has raised—urgently—all the key questions that animate media studies, and it is important to understand the intertwined histories of this interdisciplinary field and its object of analysis. First, though, we should trace something of the history of media studies' concerns and perspectives.

Historical Connections and Questions in Media Studies

Media studies emerged during the 20th century as a specific inter-disciplinary response to the increased importance and influence of the media. Traditional social science disciplines such as sociology, psychology, and economics had been concerned with the media as, principally and respectively, social institutions, individual influences, and industrial organizations, but media studies foregrounded the media in an unprecedented manner. In so doing, however, media studies did not become a rival discipline; indeed, it is increasingly difficult to seal off any discipline in the manner typical of the early 20th century's taxonomies of knowledge systems. Media studies drew eclectically on a variety of disciplines and subdisciplines, ranging from psychoanalysis to management, and combined approaches and methods (including textual analysis and ethnography) in seeking to understand the significance of the media in contemporary societies. The impetus behind this intellectual inquiry was more a matter of anxiety than of optimism. It was feared, especially after the use of sophisticated media propaganda by the Nazis prior to and during World War II, that the mass media and the mass communication that flowed from them created a mass culture (the term "mass" carried negative connotations of a formless crowd) with the potential for manipulating the citizenry to think and act in ways prescribed by the controllers of media organizations and messages (Swingewood, 1977). Control of the commanding heights of the media—whether by states, governments, elite groups, or private corporations—could, it was feared, deliver effective control of whole societies without necessarily resorting to instruments of military repression (Curran & Seaton, 2009).

This anxiety was exacerbated by successive technological developments, as newspapers were joined in the media marketplace by the more immediate forms of radio and television. The last, because of its ability to simulate experiences of seeing and hearing and its immediate appeal to large sections of the population, stimulated deep concern about "brainwashing" (another wartime concept) of the populace. While some welcomed the new communicative possibilities of the media as enhancing democracy, education, and pleasure, others (on both the right and the left politically) worried that the media, captured by powerful forces, would in turn imprison the minds, prescribe the values, and determine the behavior of human subjects (O'Shaughnessy & Stadler, 2008). Marxian thinkers (especially those of the Frankfurt School, notably Theodor Adorno) were concerned that the capitalist class could subdue the proletariat by installing false consciousness in them—for example, distracting them from class struggle through the manipulated, uncritical consumption of entertainment. Those of a more conservative disposition also saw this process as the degradation of profound cultural values and the triumph of superficial pleasures that eroded a strong moral sense of social order (Rowe, 1995; Swingewood, 1977).

A populace stripped of its capacity to think and to challenge (though of course there was disagreement about what should be thought about and challenged) was seen as vulnerable to, alternately, mob behavior and mindless passivity. The centrality of the media to anxieties among intellectuals—and evident anxieties in the workings and statements of governments, police forces, and the judiciary—is well illustrated by the rapid and extensive uptake of the concept of "moral panic" proposed by Stanley Cohen in the early 1970s. Cohen (2002) presented a persuasive case for the integral role of the news media in establishing which issues among the many competing options come to dominate the news agenda and which social groupings acquire the status of "folk devil" among "moral entrepreneurs":

> Societies appear to be subject, every now and then, to periods of moral panic. A condition, episode, person or group of persons emerges to become defined as a threat to societal values and interests; its nature is presented in a stylized and stereotypical fashion by the mass media; the moral barricades are manned by editors, bishops, politicians and other right-thinking people; socially accredited experts pronounce their diagnoses and solutions; ways of coping are evolved or (more often) resorted to; the condition then disappears, submerges or deteriorates and becomes more visible. Sometimes the object of the panic is quite novel and at other times it is something which has been in existence long enough, but suddenly appears in the limelight. Sometimes the panic passes over and is forgotten, except in folk-lore and collective memory; at other times it has more serious and long-lasting repercussions and might produce such changes as those in legal and social policy or even in the way the society conceives itself. (Cohen, 2002, p. 9)

This famous passage is careful to avoid what could be called media-centrism—the misleading idea that the media operate outside of societal structures and practices (Critcher, 2003; Rowe, 2009). Instead, it demonstrates the ways in which the mass media operate to select and project particular images of the world that interact dynamically with other social, cultural, and political institutions among the relations of power that, as Silverstone posits, are always at the heart of any analytical project. In the British context, in particular, Cohen's work (among that of others in the so-called labeling tradition of sociological theory) on the media's propensity for "amplification" of social questions and disputes connects in various ways with the more explicit neo-Marxist and critical institutional approaches of those (e.g., the Glasgow University Media Group, 1976, and the University of Birmingham's Centre for Contemporary Cultural Studies [Hall, Critcher, Jefferson, Clarke,

& Roberts, 1978]) who addressed the "agenda setting" role of the media. The interest here focuses on the media's capacity not so much to tell the population what to think but to channel what it *might* think—and not think—about. According to Stuart Hall and his associates, this task relies on a process of communication by which information is encoded in particular ways—for example, representations of socially produced inequality as inevitable and natural—so that it will be decoded as such by many of the citizens who are themselves oppressed.

This approach within media studies (and within the broader field of communication studies) has tended to be associated with European perspectives that combine political-economic and ideological critique and are frequently contrasted with those from North America. The latter have a more consistent connection with technically oriented functionalist perspectives concerned with the media's socially integrative orientation, as well as the ways in which the positive and negative effects of media messages can be empirically measured (Fiske, 1990). Of course, this is a very rough distinction—the United States has produced such critical media studies work as Noam Chomsky and Edward Herman's (2002) condemnation of media propaganda by means of "manufacturing consent" and Robert McChesney's (2008) political-economic critique of the media. But the distinction indicates the ways in which media studies has tended to cluster around traditions that, to a significant degree, mirror the deep division within sociology between conflict-oriented and functionalist approaches (Bottomore, 1987). The equivalent of an interactionist approach (elements of which appear in Cohen, 2002) can be found where the primary interest focuses on how mediation can be accomplished in particular settings without any rigorous emphasis on wider structural causation.

The three most important applied issues in media studies have revolved around the effect of the media on political attitudes and behavior; their potential for encouraging, even to the point of mimicry, violent and antisocial behavior; and, especially since the arrival in the mid-20th century of highly industrialized music, film, and television industries, the notion that they can "tranquilize" the citizenry in a manner resembling the dystopian projections of the future by authors such as George Orwell and Aldous Huxley. Mediated sport, as a popular cultural form that arose in tandem with industrialized entertainment, has been consistently regarded as implicated in all of these issues. For example, under the guise of harmless fun transported by media technologies into the family home, sport can be critiqued as the bearer of covert ideologies that include national chauvinism, racism, sexism, and homophobia (Birrell & McDonald, 2000). The media's dramatization of sport and the celebration of many contact sports—for example, through highly excitable broadcast commentary on male codes of soccer—can be seen as endorsing and encouraging violence (Bryant, 1989; Bryant, Zillmann, & Raney, 1998). Furthermore, the very popularity of sport within media space has been criticized as a "bread and circuses" diversion of the populace that might lead it away from the deeper engagement with political questions that is the marker of an evolving, sophisticated society (Eco, 1986).

The following sections flesh out these debates in engaging with interdisciplinary media studies as it has developed and been practiced, relating them where possible to the specific subject of this book: sport. Though media studies was slow to appreciate the importance of analyzing sport—initially concentrating instead on the news media, politics, and the implications of changes in technology and genre—it has in the last two decades produced a large international literature about sport in the social sciences and humanities (Billings, 2011) that has begun to match its overall importance to the media as a social institution. In seeking to grasp the dual development of media studies and sport, the next section briefly outlines the concepts proposed as key tools for analyzing the media as an institution, a set of practices and routines, and an "engine" of meanings and values in relation to which virtually no contemporary human subject can claim to be entirely indifferent or dissociated.

Understanding Media: Core Concepts

As noted earlier, one central factor in the emergence of media studies was the appreciation that the establishment of capitalism, industrialism, and formal state institutions under modernity brought an enormous capacity and drive to overcome the limitations of face-to-face communication by sending messages, simultaneously if possible, to a vast cohort of dispersed recipients who would probably never meet or resemble each other. These units of communication are conceived as *texts* but are seen as being far more diverse than the traditional idea of a written work to be read in linear fashion (that is, line by line, left to right, and front page to last, as prescribed in Western, though not in all, protocols of literary training). A text here might be anything—a passage of song, for example, or a moving visual image—that needs to be "read" (i.e., interpreted) in order to ascertain its meaning or meanings (Gillespie & Toynbee, 2006). Recognizing the plurality of meanings is central to media studies because it indicates that the world is not just "out there" waiting to be discovered but is actively constructed within human societies; thus the media and the texts they produce are inherently social (Holmes, 2005). In the case of watching, say, a soccer match on television, viewers experience an audiovisual text with various components to which they relate differently depending on which team they support. What might be regarded as a routine sports report in a newspaper can be analyzed for more than its literal meaning; one might consider, for example, how the reader is positioned by the journalist in terms of gender (e.g., the conventional implication that the reader is male) or the ways in which sport is related to wider issues of politics and society (e.g., the oft-seen curious mixture of demanding that politics and sport should be kept apart while actually linking them through assumptions about sport's positive functional role in promoting social solidarity) (Boyle & Haynes, 2009). Thus, mediated sport texts are seen as consisting of mini "sign systems" that need to be decoded in order to understand their meanings and significance.

Because mediated sport texts are produced in such profusion, it is also necessary not to treat them as unique, never-to-be-repeated communicative objects but to search for patterns that show them as being organized into highly predictable types known as *genres*. For example, a radio or television broadcast of a live sport event usually involves a build-up in which commentators and analysts anticipate what will occur, followed by description and discussion of the event while it occurs, and then a postmortem exploring what happened and why, what was good and bad, and what the result's implications are. Both broadcasters and audiences are familiar with these routines, which could be described as a pact between the media producer and the audience based on mutual expectations of what will be produced and consumed (Brookes, 2002; Rowe, 2004b). Indeed, sport program genres are usually so formulaic as to take on a quality of being eternal and natural. But what if the rules are broken and elements of surreal comedy are introduced or the usual forms of sporting language and tone are circumvented? One key function of media studies, then, is not only to identify the conventional ways in which the media render the world to audiences but also to denaturalize the conventional texts and genres that almost become part of the cultural "furniture."

Questioning the innocence of everyday popular media culture in sport (e.g., match reports, live commentary, still photographs, action sequences, and player profiles) demands an interrogation of, to invoke the influential concept brought to the field by Barthes in 1957, its mythologies. In media studies, as in other areas of critical academic inquiry, myths (the building blocks of full-blown mythologies) can mean common (though not universally held) untruths and misapprehensions (Watson, 1998)—for example, that watching a particular television program involving violence will cause all children instantly to imitate what they have seen, or that only women watch and enjoy daytime soap operas. But media myths are more than just the products of prejudice and ignorance—they are integral to turning confusing and contradictory aspects of the world into a largely unquestioned common sense (Hall, 1997). Thus, a night's viewing of prime-time television might represent white people as the authoritative commentators in news and current affairs and as the heroes and heroines of drama programs, whereas nonwhite people might be presented as the problems being commented on and the villains that the white protagonists have to kill or capture. On the basis of such media representations (H. Gray, 2004), more extensive readings of the world—mythologies—might be favored, such as that the world relies on inherently law-abiding white people to control nonwhite people who have an inherent potential to be criminally destructive, apart from those who are willing to act in a support role for their white superiors in dealing with their nonwhite peers.

In the light of such highly charged accounts of the world that posit some people and types as ranking above or below others, mythologies communicated through the media (though not entirely created by them) are manifested as ideologies—that is, they have tangible political and social consequences that encourage (without entirely determining) acceptance of values, attitudes, and actions that tend to support (consciously or unconsciously) the interests of those who are already in power and who already have the media at their disposal. In an example from the world's biggest sport media moment, the entrance of the athletes into the arena at the opening ceremony of the Summer Olympic Games is communicated to the world by the principal Olympic broadcaster (which, for several decades, has been the U.S. media corporation NBC). This "feed" (a revealing term in itself) structures the television experience for the rest of the world, while enabling television commentary on the event to be customized by countries that can insert their own commentary or, if they lack the requisite resources, carry commentary provided by another country (Moragas Spà, Rivenburgh, & Larson, 1995). The media representation of the event, therefore, tends to reflect the structure of power in the world at large *through* the world of sport (Tomlinson & Young, 2006)—for example, national teams that are smaller and less internationally prominent are likely to receive little attention. For obvious reasons, countries and their broadcasters privilege their own national interests, and dominant nations are prone to represent others, especially "minor" world and sport powers, as incidental, less important, and exotic—or barely to mention them at all. Such familiar media routines, drawing on a seemingly ordinary world order, carry over into the world of politics through mythologies and ideologies that are at their most effective when they are accepted unconsciously and in areas of culture that claim to be nonpolitical. Thus, media studies is above all concerned with the politics of representation in any context, from nightly news programs to situation comedies, from televised soccer matches to children's cartoons. There exists a range of explicit or implied sociocultural theories (i.e., systematic, generalizable propositions about the world, and in particular the relationship between cause and effect) that requires closer attention.

Media Powers and Routines: Main Theoretical Perspectives

The approaches used in media studies are characterized by their varying orientations and media specializations, as well as the main relationships they address between media, culture, and society. In macrotheoretical terms, the contrasting positions adopted within media studies are rather like those that have historically marked out the territory of sociology and the subdiscipline of sport sociology (Coakley, Hallinan, Jackson, & Mewett, 2009). Thus, as noted earlier and applied here to sport, there is both a functionalist approach, which is connected to the more technocratic strands of the larger field of communication studies and is principally concerned with the contribution of the mediation of sport to social integration and order, and a conflict perspective, whose point of departure is media sport's contribution to the reproduction and maintenance of social inequalities and asymmetries of power (Rowe, 2004b). Media studies has been most attracted to a critique of media power using a range of theoretical positions, such as Marxism-inspired hegemony theory, Foucauldian analyses of media discourse, feminist critiques of the gender order that the media are argued both to represent and promote, and critical race theory concerning the complicity of the media with racist stratification and ideology (O'Shaughnessy & Stadler, 2008).

Much of the theoretical disputation revolves around objections to radical critiques of the media from those who, while in some ways sympathetic, see them as rather one-dimensional, totalizing, or overly negative accounts of how the media work to produce texts and as being too dismissive of the capacity of ordinary citizens to reflect critically on the media that they encounter and use on a daily basis. For example, the well-known pioneering work of John Fiske and John Hartley (together and separately) has resisted propositions that audiences are "victimized" by powerful media forces, preferring instead to see them as active, creative, possessed of the resources to resist the imposition of meaning and pleasure, and able to create their own (Fiske, 1989; Fiske & Hartley, 2003; Hartley, 1996, 2008). Thus, the theoretical positions and research findings evident in media studies often consist of divergent readings of media power, process, and experience.

In terms of application to sport, the range of approaches used in media studies may in part reflect how sport itself is viewed prior to its processing through the media. It has often been pointed out that sport tends to be treated in an elitist way within intellectual culture because of its emphasis on the body, whereas many academics who specialize in sport have a romantic attitude toward it, especially among men for whom it is a formative aspect of conventional masculinity (Miller, 1998). Such tensions can cause the same sport media texts to be read in very different ways. For example, the 2008 Beijing Olympics might be seen as providing important communicative opportunities for the world to develop a better understanding of China that enhances peace and prosperity; at the same time, an almost diametrically opposed position could claim that the Games exacerbated the political repression of China's Tibetan citizens and obscured the continuing obstruction of the right to political expression among China's citizenry under the guise of the Olympic slogan "One World, One Dream" (Qing & Richeri, 2010). Given that most people in the world are highly dependent on media coverage for much of their knowledge of China—media, after all, construct images of place for those who are distant and also influence perceptions of place even for those who are physically present in a geographical location and have already received a range of interpretive clues (Dayan & Katz, 1992)—the coverage of the event becomes something of a battleground for alternative perspectives.

There is a generally uneven fit between these contending positions, and thus the matters raised are never entirely settled but instead constantly provoke debates and demands for further inquiry, though some positions may take on the character of orthodoxy; for example, few media studies scholars can legitimately argue that the media coverage of female athletes is adequate in either quantitative or qualitative terms (Creedon, 1994). Media studies researchers and scholars, therefore, are highly attuned to questions of who is producing media texts and for what purposes, the range of texts available, and their associated perspectives and ideologies. It is most useful here to reflect on the ways in which these debates are played out across various sport media phenomena in the analytical context of media studies.

Critical Findings and Key Debates in Sport and Media

In broad social science terms, the main areas of concentration in media studies are media sport production and institutions, media sport texts and forms, and media sport audiences and their relationships. This is not to argue that it is impossible to discuss production, text, and audience at the same time but that, for reasons of both researcher interest and expertise and the manageability of research activities, media studies work tends to coalesce around a limited range of phenomena within its purview. For some, the most important question is Who makes and profits from media sport? Without such an apparatus, there is no object or practice to be analyzed. Two types of institution, public and private, have been crucial to the production of media sport, and the balance of influence has varied across space and time. Thus, for example, in Europe and Asia, national governments have tended to pioneer the development of sport television and radio (Whannel, 1992), whereas private companies were primarily responsible for the sport press. In the United States, on the other hand, public involvement in media sport has been weak except with regard to regulating the commercial market in the name of competition—a function that, ironically, involves exempting sport in some instances from antitrust legislation in order to preserve the competitive balance of sport leagues such as the National Football League and the National Basketball Association (Chandler, 1988).

Considerable capital is needed in order to show sport events live or to employ sport journalists. In some cases, the state has underwritten the cost of the former because sport is one of the most powerful and relatively peaceful vehicles for representing the nation and for at least temporarily uniting disparate groups within a country. One instance of this nation-building role of sport can be seen in association football in Europe, especially given that most nations, despite myths that they can be traced back to antiquity, are in fact modern entities formed in the 19th century and often later remodeled substantially while remaining conflict prone in various respects. Indeed, the media have often been foregrounded as crucial not merely to reflecting the preexisting nation but to actively constituting it, a process in which mediated sport plays a crucial role (Bairner, 2001).

Sport, Media, and Nation Building

To take a fairly recent example, the Euro 2008 soccer tournament surprised some observers when Catalans, many of whom would prefer to be independent of the current Spanish nation-state (as has been indicated by large pro-independence majorities in several unofficial referendums in Catalonia), uncharacteristically supported the national team. Spain's victories were vibrantly celebrated in public spaces like La Rambla, "Barcelona's famous boulevard and a site as significant to Catalan identity as any" (Keeley & Burke, 2008). There were also signs of support for a unified national team in other culturally distinctive regions with independent aspirations like Galicia, and even in the Basque Country, where a long campaign (currently discontinued) of political violence has been waged by the separatist Euskadi Ta Askatasuna (ETA) organization and popular support for independence remains strong. Similarly, after Spain won the 2010 FIFA World Cup, "many fans celebrated even in Bilbao and Barcelona. These people were not binning their regional identities. Rather, they felt both Basque and Spanish, or Catalan and Spanish" (Kuper, 2012). The sport-media nexus can, then, in some circumstances prompt an unlikely (though perhaps temporary) reconciliation with the nation among those who seek departure from it.

As this example indicates, the form of cultural power that mediated sport contests can command attracts national governments because the abstraction that is the sovereign nation-state becomes paradoxically concrete in the symbolic space of mediated sport. This is why virtually all nations subsidize in some way their participation in international sport competitions such as the Olympic Games and the World Cup, which are now guaranteed to be carried to all continents and to penetrate even those nations where private ownership of television sets is still limited. Nations such as South Africa, host of the 2010 World Cup, are anxious to involve even their most marginalized and impoverished citizens in the spectacle through public viewing sites. The sport's supranational body, the Fédération Internationale de Football Association (FIFA), with 208 member nations—like the International Olympic Committee (IOC), with its 205 national Olympic committees—emphasizes and enforces the principle of maximizing free-to-air television coverage for the world citizenry.

Ownership and Control of Media Sport

Of course, a larger global television audience means, in principle, that sport organizations can charge greater sums to media companies for broadcast rights. This revenue—with its associated sponsorships made possible by media exposure of brands, goods, and services—has become the greatest economic force in sport. An alternative business model involves a reduction in aggregate audience in favor of a smaller one that pays directly for the sport broadcast service. For this reason, even in countries where the government has been historically committed to free access to major sport events for citizens through (public or commercial free-to-air) television, substantial pressure has arisen to allow subscription services to take over sports broadcasting as a highly lucrative venture in commercial terms (Scherer & Whitson, 2009; Scherer & Rowe, 2014).

This movement, where such a structure did not already exist from the start (whether due to strong state control of electronic media or to a more commodified arrangement where sport broadcasting is funded not by taxation revenue but by advertising or direct subscription payments from consumers), has created significant debates within media studies (Rowe, 2004a). A compulsory licensing system for television set owners, such as that operating in the United Kingdom to support the publicly owned British Broadcasting Corporation (BBC), is an uncommon arrangement that is frequently criticized by orthodox market economists (who regard such forms of "hypothecation" as distortions of the free market and instances of unwarranted state interference in the media industry) and by commercial media proprietors and executives. The latter frequently argue that they are disadvantaged by state subsidies for media programs and services that compete directly with them and thus should be limited only to media content—in this case, sports of little ongoing appeal to a large audience—that could never be expected to break even financially but may have some social utility (News Corporation, 2008). Such disagreements over public and private involvement, and over missions and roles in the media, are of deep relevance to media studies (Price & Raboy, 2003).

It can be claimed that the retreat of the state and increasing deregulation are inevitable and desirable enhancements of the efficiency of service delivery and the extension of consumer choice that have occurred in a range of social institutions, including health, education, telecommunication, and other utilities—and that they are responsive to such processes as globalization that militate against the state control and regulation that prevailed in earlier stages of development of the polity and economy (as summarized in Miller, Lawrence, McKay, & Rowe, 2001). Such trends also invite critique as the unfettered operation of the logic of capital accumulation that, especially within a critical analytical framework based on social class, erodes social and cultural citizenship rights of the (by definition) non-elite majority of the populace (Scherer & Rowe, 2012). From this perspective, the so-called siphoning of free sport television content by pay platforms is viewed as the capture of sport and of organic sport fandom by transnational capital, especially the most conspicuous and commercially aggressive of media corporations, the Rupert Murdoch–controlled News Corporation (Andrews, 2006). The power and influence exercised over sport by media conglomerates such as News Corporation are very considerable and tend toward monopoly. For example, in 2011, the company was poised to acquire full ownership (from a previous holding of 39 percent) of the highly profitable subscription broadcaster BSkyB, which had generated much of its surplus through acquiring the exclusive or predominant rights to major sport properties, notably the English Premier League. News Corporation, however, withdrew from the BSkyB takeover after it was revealed that one of its UK newspapers, the now-defunct *News of the World*, had illegally hacked into the phones of many people. Among the established or alleged victims of this practice were several people involved in sport, including Gordon Taylor, then chief executive of the Professional Footballers' Association, and footballers (i.e., soccer players) Sol Campbell, Peter Crouch, Paul Gascoigne, Jermaine Jenas, and Wayne Rooney (see Leveson Inquiry, 2012). The abandonment (or, perhaps, postponement) of the BSkyB takeover obstructed News Corporation's ambition of consolidating and extending its market position in European subscription television, in which sport is a pivotal generator of profit.

The ownership and control of media sport, from such political-economic perspectives, take in all the possibilities of extracting, in Marxist terms, surplus value from a range of exchanges, including cross-promotion of media content and services between print, electronic, online, and communication platforms, as well as both vertical and horizontal integration of the production and consumption chain. This vertical integration means, for example, owning a club and a sport league, as well as acquiring the media rights to them, whereas the horizontal integration might involve owning a range of broadcast and new media rights to key sports that create dominance across the media sport market. Here, as noted earlier, the state, in the form of national competition authorities or supranational regulators (e.g., the European Union), may intervene, although such moves run substantially against the drift of the neoclassical economic model that has gathered strength in many societies in various world regions since the late 1970s. Therefore, media studies, both in general and where applied directly to sport, is profoundly implicated in debates about the relative powers of the state and the market in the cultural sphere (Boyle & Haynes, 2004).

Organizing and Operating the Sport Media

But ownership and control mean more than just holding the reins in producing media sport texts; they also involve specific institutional and organizational practices that shape texts prior to their reception by audiences. These issues may be addressed at scales ranging from the historical and geographical conventions of sport media representation, to upper-organizational decision making, to the routines of editors and journalists in the electronic and print media. In the case of the conventions of representation, the look, sound, and register of sport presented through the media vary substantially according to where it has been produced and what contextual expectations are operative. For example, the brasher popular culture and dominance of commercial sport media in the United States produced televisual representations of sport in that country in the early and mid-20th century that were detectably different from those typical of the United Kingdom (Goldlust, 1987), where a commitment to a more restrained approach to broadcasting mirrored its development by the state and was carried over for a considerable time even when commercial television began to occupy a prominent position in televised sport (Chandler, 1988; Whannel, 1992).

Media imperialism, international influence, and globalization mean that virtually no national sports television system can be sealed off from others. Within this reality, change occurs both exogenously and endogenously, and differences occur within countries and between media (Bairner, 2001; Maguire, 1999). For example, the British tabloid newspaper coverage of sport has for some time been notable for a rambunctiousness that is considerably at odds with the BBC's sober approach across its television, radio, and online platforms. During the 2010 World Cup in South Africa, for instance, when the goalkeeper for England made an embarrassing mistake in the opening match against the United States, a typical BBC headline was "World Cup 2010: Robert Green Vows to Bounce Back" ("World Cup," 2010). By contrast, the British popular tabloid press vied for the most denunciatory headlines and stories, and even some "quality" newspapers took part. As one international press agency noted in a story titled "From Tainted Glove to Hand of Clod: Brits Lash Robert Green's Howler,"

> *Britain's Sunday newspapers blasted Robert Green for the goalkeeping blunder that cost England a victory in the opening World Cup game against the US.*

The weekly press printed frame-by-frame images of Green's error, with the front pages of the News of the World *and the* Sunday Mirror *both reading "Hand of Clod," accompanied by a giant picture of Green.*

"Tainted Glove," said the Sunday Mirror. *"Worst Howler Ever," said another headline. "Calamity keeper Robert Green gifted one of the all-time blunder goals as the jinx of the England goalies struck again," it said.*

The Sunday Times *referenced the Gulf of Mexico tragedy, saying the error was "one disastrous spill the Yanks won't complain about." It was a "howler that will haunt him for the rest of his career." ("From Tainted Glove," 2010)*

Such stories also highlight another area of analytical interest in media studies—intertextuality—whereby one text takes on meaning by referencing another. In this case, apart from the reference to the oil spill, "'Hand of Clod' [is] a play on the 'Hand of God' goal scored by Diego Maradona that knocked England out of the 1986 World Cup" ("Tabloids," 2010), and "Tainted Glove" is a pun on the pop song "Tainted Love." Similarly, the *News of the World's* description of the game as "Shock 'N' Draw" was a reference to the "shock and awe" tactic adopted by the U.S. military during its 2003 invasion of Iraq. In media studies, communicated meanings are analyzed not as self-evident but as constructed out of a complex interaction of signs, codes, associations, myths, and ideologies that are perpetually in the process of being made and remade; as such, they are always to some degree open to reinvention, reinterpretation, and miscomprehension (Bignell, 2002).

The notoriety of the British tabloids, with their often cruel and ribald puns and intertextual jokes, stems in part from their origins in the sensationalist news sheets of the 18th century (Curran & Seaton, 2009) but also from the fierce national commercial competition between them, which has far exceeded that in the television world (and, indeed, is more intense than that of the United States' more regional- and city-oriented press). This sensitivity to historical, social, cultural, and economic context is needed within media studies in order to avoid legitimate social science accusations of mediacentricity—that is, the implausible notion that the media can be separated from the world and even that the world revolves around the media. Instead, there is a reflexive relationship between the media as a social institution and other institutions with which media organizations are in constant contact (Maguire, 2005). In the case of media sport, then, there will inevitably be resistance to change, as well as hangovers of earlier eras when the representation of sport events and athletes was sporadic and limited in scope. But it cannot avoid being caught up in such wide-ranging transformations and trends as urbanization, industrialization, technologization, privatization, and globalization (Horne, 2006; Miller et al., 2001; Whannel, 2008).

Change and Continuity in Media Sport Texts and Cultural Politics

How precisely, though, will these changes in media sport production affect media sport texts? We cannot assume that alterations to production arrangements will automatically result in measurable changes in the qualities displayed by sport-related television, photography, and print reportage, but neither is it feasible that they will remain immune to such influences and subject only to immutable craft-based rules of media work. Both continuities and changes in media sport texts are, therefore, of key concern, as is their effect on what can broadly be called the politics of media sport representation. It is possible to focus on sport news stories and live commentaries without giving much attention to how they came to be produced, but such textualist approaches leave themselves open to critique on the grounds of idealism and partiality. For this reason, media studies also attempts to understand the cultural politics of media sport in light of its conditions of production and by means of close interrogation of the ideological ramifications of what they reveal about sporting and social relations. This connection between text and context is crucial, since it resists the tendency—evident in some other disciplines, including the more traditional approaches within the study of literature, painting, and even film—to detach the cultural object from the web of historical and social relations that make it meaningful in the first place. For this reason, attention has been given to the organizational sites and labor practices involved in the manufacture of media sport texts (Billings, 2008; Lowes, 1999; Silk, Slack, & Amis, 2000).

This does not mean, however, that media texts are exempted from close interrogation. In media studies—with its seminal interest in the power of messages disseminated to large, diverse, and heterogeneous audiences—sport is typically viewed as a popular vehicle for carrying social meanings, myths, and ideologies. For example, content analyses consistently reveal that men's sport overwhelmingly dominates women's in the media (Schultz-Jorgensen, 2005; Horky & Nieland, 2011). With some exceptions, such as the Olympics (an unusual multisport event featuring men's, women's, and mixed events), and major tennis tournaments, sport on television is massively male centered. This is not just a matter of quantity. It is also important to capture, understand, and analyze how masculinity and femininity tend to be represented in the sport media; for example, are men seen as pivotal and heroic whereas women are cast as marginal and playing supportive roles? Is undue concentration placed on the sexual appearance of women, thus reproducing an oppressive beauty myth that is patriarchal in nature? Alternatively, are there spaces within media sport where different images of what it means to be male or female challenge prevailing stereotypes? By asking such questions, the field of media studies explores and critiques, as in other areas of representation (though not, of course, forgetting that media organizations also tend to be male dominated and thus likely to produce media texts that, consciously and unconsciously, reflect that position), the gender order of the sport media (Bernstein, 2002; Bruce, Hovden, & Markula, 2010); Davis, 1997).

Just as gender is a key dimension of social power and inequality within both sport and its media representation, many other social variables are also of keen interest to media studies scholars. Social class, for instance, is a key constituent of the social order that stratifies sport in terms of who can participate and in which kinds of sport—a set of structural relations that are made manifest in mediated sport. One could propose, for example, that the representation of affluent, individual, noncontact sports such as tennis and golf contrasts with that of sports that are more accessible, team based, and contact based, such as American football and rugby, and with that of individual contact sports such as boxing that involve the real possibility of injury and even death. From a Marxian perspective, such differences can be read as reflecting the division between the bourgeoisie and proletariat in terms of their material comfort, their contrasting emphases on mental ability or brute strength, and the cultural capital that accumulates around certain sports of "distinction" that are presented as elegant and graceful. In other words, the representation of sport in the media may inscribe "subterranean" class relations that are unconsciously communicated in ways not necessarily obvious to those who are exposed to them (Crawford, 2004).

Mediated Sport Gossip and Scandals

Of course, one might object that since the late 20th century in games associated with working-class culture, some elite athletes (the tiny minority of professionals who have prospered during the generally short period of active sport life available to them) have become extraordinarily well rewarded and acquired celebrity status. Again, though, intense media coverage of their conspicuous consumption and style choices, and those of their wives and girlfriends (so-called WAGs), often bears the stamp of the traditional class analysis that ridicules the tastes of the nouveau riche (Whannel, 2001). Similarly, the analytics of media representation in sport are applied to constructions of race and ethnicity that naturalize hierarchies, including those involving the Western media's treatment of race and postcolonialism (Andrews & Jackson, 2001; Baker & Boyd, 1997) and heterosexist treatments of sexuality. The latter invite disparaging attitudes toward athletes who do not fit comfortably into the binary world constructed by sport—a world marked by substantial sexual segregation predicated on heterosexuality, yet uneasy with the resulting same-sex intimacy of locker rooms, and thus generally representing homosexual athletes as predatory and voyeuristic (Miller, 2001).

While the sport media have generally been found to be conservative and even reactionary with regard to many social questions of equality and identity, this is not to argue that the media sports cultural complex (Rowe, 2004b) is predictable and uniform. Investigative journalism—though much of it emanates from outside the "sports desk"—can expose corruption and exploitation, while the close scrutiny of sport organizations and athletes as part of the blanket coverage they receive creates the conditions for conspicuous sport scandals that erupt into debates about issues of considerable importance (Boyle, 2006). For example, when in November 2009 the golfer Tiger Woods was revealed as serially unfaithful to his wife, the prurient press coverage of his many sexual encounters nonetheless invited critical analyses of issues such as the image creation of sport celebrities, the expectations of alignment between image and personal conduct, and the politics of sport celebrity sponsorship and product endorsement. Similarly, outbreaks of racism, both proven and suspected, and both and on and off the field of play—most famously in recent times involving the sending off of French captain Zinedine Zidane during the 2006 World Cup Final after he headbutted opponent Marco Materazzi for alleged (though disputed) racist (and certainly sexist) comments—have placed the often hidden issue of racism squarely at the center of global media debates about the ethics of sport (Rowe, 2010).

There are many other examples of matters where close attention to, and deconstruction of, diverse media sport texts have been interpreted as necessary because they are crucially implicated in pressing social questions of the day. However, such textual research and scholarship can be criticized as informing more about the mind-set of the analyst than about the issues being analyzed. That is, media studies practitioners may tend to be selective in their interpretations of the meanings and implications of texts and to read them in ways that are partial, biased, or overly complicated. It is certainly reasonable to be duly skeptical about the causal relationships between media structures, practices, texts, and audience interpretations. For this reason, audience reception is addressed by some media studies researchers, either in combination with those that analyze media production and texts, or as a specific subfield that takes less interest in media production and concentrates instead on what audiences take from the media and the ways in which they interpret and use media content.

Audiences and Audience Relations

This approach is especially important because, except where it isolates people as fans of media genres with little in the way of lives outside of their fandom, it insists on probing how people read and respond to media sport texts in different ways in relation to their social origins and identities. To return to issues of gender, for example, this approach asks such questions as why men tend to watch more sports than women on television and why gender-based preferences show up in the sports that people watch; it also seeks to explain what may seem to be "perverse" or supposedly non-gender-appropriate tastes in media sport. Indeed, one can ask whether some sport-related broadcasts and publications are actually *seen* as sexist, racist, or otherwise biased, and, if so, how, for example, female sport fans might negotiate their marginalization and subordination in many such media sport texts. Similar questions are asked about how sports forcibly introduced by imperial and colonial powers (as in the case of cricket on the Indian sub-continent and in the Caribbean) and then broadcast by the media controlled by their successors may be responded to positively and embraced by peoples who might otherwise be expected to despise and reject them. Alternatively, media studies research might also ask whether sports broadcasts designed to elicit nationalistic or xenophobic audience responses are efficacious or perhaps produce readings opposite of those intended. With regard to media sport, such audience and reception research (Nightingale, 2010) has tended to focus on sport fandom, especially the ways in which contemporary sport fans are "interpellated" (that is, identified and addressed) by the media, and also on how they mobilize the media themselves, through such endeavors as webzines and fan sites, to communicate with each other (J. Gray, Sandvoss, & Harrington, 2007; Hermes, 2005).

In taking account of audience engagements with sport media, researchers can use a range of approaches, including those that focus on uses and gratifications and cultivation analysis (Ruddock, 2001), to help overcome the gap between analyst interpretation and audience experience. This does not mean, however, that the complex questions surrounding sport and media can be neatly resolved, given that many variables interact both consistently and intermittently, both predictably and by chance. These variables include differences in the type of sport media text; fans' histories and positions in relation to them; variations in response across time and space; social variables, such as gender and age, that overdetermine readings of texts; the larger and immediate environment in which media encounters occur; and the psychological and personality variations that lead apparently similar human actors to respond differently to the same text. Seemingly unequivocal empirical findings—for example, that exposure to aggressive sport encounters on television provokes aggressive behavior among some viewers—often lead to disputes about causality (over, say, predisposing factors such as an aggressive orientation), cultural variability (the need for comparative case studies), and duration (immediate stimulation versus lasting impact); for more, see various contributions to section three in Raney & Bryant (2006).

The dynamic nature of media studies lies in the extraordinarily diffi-cult task of matching media production, textuality, and reception in their myriad forms to human attitudes and behavior in their variously linear and nonlinear causal manifestations. This task is made even more difficult by the constantly changing nature of the media terrain. Media studies, as noted, was given initial impetus by anxiety that whole human populations could be manipulated and dominated by small interest groups (notably, ruling classes, totalitarian governments, and commercial entertainment corporations) through being exposed to the same messages with the same collective effect by means of sophisticated media technologies and propaganda techniques. This so-called hypodermic syringe model of media effects was quickly revealed to be inadequate (if it were so, variations in human behavior and thought would have disappeared long ago), and it was superseded by more cautious, qualified analyses of issues such as the conditions under which media messages might be most effective, the different kinds of impact that the media might have (by, for example, limiting the range of possible options and responses to political issues), and the differential influences evident among demographic groupings. But even as debates over media influence continued, the media themselves mutated constantly and created new modes of production and consumption. In the electronic media, for example, extensions to bandwidth and digitization, alongside the maturation of media markets and outlets for public debate, have meant not only that many citizens across the globe can access literally thousands of radio stations and television channels but also that they can use freely available media technologies to become broadcasters and media communicators themselves thanks to the most important emergent media technology of the 21st century—the Internet. It is not surprising, given its sociocultural standing, popular appeal, and related economic power, that sport is in the vanguard of these profound changes in the media that became familiar in the last century and have become increasingly unpredictable and multifaceted in the current one (Leonard, 2009).

Conclusion: Sport and Media Studies in Transition

Media studies has not created a single body of knowledge with regard to sport (or other media-dependent cultural forms) that constitutes a clearly delineated set of parameters and a consensual, evolutionary process of discipline development. Instead, it consists of a set of primary concerns about the relationships between sport, media, and society. There is a broad consensus that sport and media have been mutually transformative but some dispute whether their relationship constitutes a more or less equal codependency or, as is more common, the colonization and domination of sport by media. This media-sport nexus, it is generally agreed, is becoming ever more intimate but is also subject to periods of crisis that are analogous to—and often directly stem from—pressing problems in the wider spheres of society, culture, economy, and polity. The main points of contestation concern the implication of media sport in a range of sociocultural relations and the extent to which, in its various guises, the media sports cultural complex constitutes a progressive or reactionary force in human affairs. However, as noted earlier, it is difficult to make easily generalizable propositions, given that the term *media*, in part, is one of convenience that is used in an effort to capture very diverse phenomena, including, for example, books, feature films, satellite television, and websites. These phenomena are also subject to the influences of profoundly different cultural contexts and to constant changes wrought by new technologies and audience relations. Thus, if knowledge gaps exist in media studies, they can be almost welcomed as signs of its continuing vibrancy and relevance.

The most powerful current sport medium, television, can be regarded as a classic instance of a mass medium—a small number of people controlling the messages sent to the multitudes. Yet, apart from the aforementioned disputes about how these media messages are received and used, the messages themselves and the contexts of their delivery are in flux. Two of the principal causes of this dynamic media sport environment are the globalization and transnationalism that have begun to challenge Western domination of the sport media across the world. While major Western media companies such as News Corporation, NBCUniversal, and ESPN have large, growing global interests that especially target the growing Asia-Pacific region (Rowe, 2011), there is a corresponding development in the activities of Asian sport media enterprises such as Al Jazeera Sports, Zee Entertainment Enterprises, and China Central Television both within and beyond Asia.

Multichanneling (mostly by subscription) has created considerably greater choice in terms of which sports can be watched and when, including by means of 24-hour sport channels (Nicholson, 2007). Domestic recording devices, from video recorders to inbuilt television hard drives, have enabled time-shift viewing that allows viewers to watch programs when it is convenient for them. Digitization has enabled viewers to choose camera angles and simultaneous multi-event watching, as well as three-dimensional perspectives, and the Internet and mobile telephony have made it possible to catch live sports and highlights on computer screens. Even more significant, the idea of who gets to make media sport is changing. The Internet has enabled fans to become citizen sport journalists, tweeters, and bloggers and to create their own websites with substantial texts and video material; meanwhile, sport organizations and clubs have been able to turn themselves into developing media companies with their own television channels and much-viewed websites. At the same time, athletes can, sometimes to the consternation of sport organizations anxious to protect contracts with sponsors and media companies, bypass the mainstream media and communicate directly with fans through microblogging and other social media practices.

The emergence of social media in sport is important, then, because it has weakened—though not dissolved—the dependence of sport fans on major media organizations. Broadcast television remains powerful, but reliance on a single screen to view sport action, and on professional commentators to interpret it, is in retreat. Instead, sport fans can communicate with each other via Twitter, Facebook, YouTube, and other social media under a new digital regime of networked media sport (Hutchins & Rowe, 2012). These practices do not necessarily erode television audiences for major sport events—indeed, social media can help create the "buzz" that draws more people to the Super Bowl or the Football Association (FA) Cup Final. But their attention is likely to be divided between large television screens, computers, tablets, smartphones, and even game consoles. Efforts to track and capitalize on these sport audience trends are now major concerns for media sport companies that may not themselves be primarily concerned with broadcast television.

Telecommunication companies have entered the field of media sport by using the possibilities of technological convergence to reconfigure the communication industry sector. In addition, gaming has introduced strong collective fantasy aspects to media sport that have even led to actual soccer clubs being acquired and "played with" in ways that complicate simulation and "the real" (Hutchins & Rowe, 2009, 2010; Leonard, 2009). Thus, we need to understand changes in the sport media environment that are closer to networking than to traditional notions of a one-way flow between media and audience. We also need a much greater appreciation of the changed conditions that are creating new arrangements for media sport production, reception, and use—without, as is common, exaggerating the speed, durability, and consistency of change (for example, television audiences for major sport events have never been larger). There is a danger that technophilia encouraged by exciting new gadgets will stimulate complacent assumptions that regard enduring questions of power, access, and representation as outmoded (Hutchins & Rowe, 2012). Media studies, properly understood, can provide social science sport study with four valuable lessons: that the media-sport nexus is now indissoluble; that the media are constantly in a state of transformation; that media production, interpretation, and use are always, everywhere deeply social; and that, whatever the utopian possibilities of new media technologies and applications, it is, as noted earlier in Silverstone's words, "all about power, of course. In the end."

References

Andrews, D.L. (2006). *Sport, commerce, culture: Essays on sport in late-capitalist America.* New York: Lang.

Andrews, D.L., & Jackson, S.J. (Eds.). (2001). *Sport stars: The cultural politics of sporting celebrity*. London: Routledge.

Bairner, A. (2001). *Sport, nationalism, and globalization: European and North American perspectives*. Albany: State University of New York Press.

Baker, A., & Boyd, T. (Eds.). (1997). *Out of bounds: Sports, media, and the politics of identity*. Bloomington: Indiana University Press.

Barthes, R. (1973). *Mythologies* (A. Lavers, Trans.). London: Paladin. (Original work published 1957)

Bernstein, A. (2002). Is it time for a victory lap? Changes in the media coverage of women in sport. *International Review for the Sociology of Sport, 37*, 415–428.

Bignell, J. (2002). *Media semiotics: An introduction* (2nd ed.). Manchester: Manchester University Press.

Billings, A.C. (2008). *Olympic media: Inside the biggest show on television*. London: Routledge.

Billings, A.C. (Ed.). (2011). *Sports media: Transformation, integration, consumption*. New York: Routledge.

Birrell, S., & McDonald, M.G. (Eds.). (2000). *Reading sport: Critical essays on power and representation*. Boston: Northeastern University Press.

Bottomore, T. (1987). *Sociology: A guide to problems and literature* (3rd ed.). London: Allen and Unwin.

Boyle, R. (2006). *Sports journalism: Context and issues*. London: Sage.

Boyle, R., & Haynes, R. (2004). *Football in the new media age*. London: Routledge.

Boyle, R., & Haynes, R. (2009). *Power play: Sport, the media, and popular culture* (2nd ed.). Edinburgh: Edinburgh University Press.

Brookes, R. (2002). *Representing sport*. London: Arnold.

Bruce, T., Hovden, J., & Markula, P. (Eds.). (2010). *Sportswomen at the Olympics: A global content analysis of newspaper coverage*. Rotterdam: Sense.

Bryant, J. (1989). Viewers' enjoyment of televised sports violence. In L.A. Wenner (Ed.), *Media, sports, & society* (pp. 270–289). London: Sage.

Bryant, J., Zillmann, D., & Raney, A.A. (1998). Violence and the enjoyment of media sports. In L.A. Wenner (Ed.), *MediaSport* (pp. 252–265). London: Routledge.

Chandler, J.M. (1988). *Television and national sport: The United States and Britain*. Champaign: University of Illinois Press.

Chomsky, N., & Herman, E.S. (2002). *Manufacturing consent: The political economy of the mass media*. New York: Pantheon.

Coakley, J., Hallinan, C., Jackson, S., & Mewett, P. (2009). *Sports in society: Issues and controversies in Australia and New Zealand*. Sydney: McGraw-Hill.

Cohen, S. (2002). *Folk devils and moral panics: The creation of the mods and rockers* (3rd ed.). London: Routledge.

Crawford, G. (2004). *Consuming sport: Fans, sport, and culture*. London: Routledge.

Creedon, P.J. (Ed.). (1994). *Women, media, and sport: Challenging gender values*. Thousand Oaks, CA: Sage.

Critcher, C. (2003). *Moral panics and the media*. Buckingham, UK: Open University Press.

Curran, J., & Seaton, J. (2009). *Power without responsibility: Press, broadcasting, and the Internet in Britain* (7th ed.). London: Routledge.

Davis, L.A. (1997). *The swimsuit issue and sport: Hegemonic masculinity in Sports Illustrated*. Albany: State University of New York Press.

Dayan, D., & Katz, E. (1992). *Media events: The live broadcasting of history*. Cambridge, MA: Harvard University Press.

Eco, U. (1986). *Travels in hyperreality*. New York: Harcourt Brace Jovanovich.

Fiske, J. (1989). *Understanding popular culture*. Boston: Unwin Hyman.

Fiske, J. (1990). *Introduction to communication studies* (2nd ed.). London: Routledge.

Fiske, J., & Hartley, J. (2003). *Reading television: 25th anniversary edition*. London: Routledge.

From tainted glove to hand of clod: Brits lash Robert Green's howler. (2010, June 14). *The Australian*. www.theaustralian.com.au/sport/world-cup-2010/from-tainted-glove-to-hand-of-clod-brits-lash-robert-greens-howler/story-fn4l4sfy-1225879204739.

Gillespie, M., & Toynbee, J. (2006). *Analysing media texts*. Maidenhead, UK: Open University Press.

Glasgow University Media Group. (1976). *Bad news*. London: Routledge.

Goldlust, J. (1987). *Playing for keeps: Sport, the media, and society*. Melbourne: Longman Cheshire.

Gray, H. (2004). *Watching race: Television and the struggle for blackness*. Minneapolis: University of Minnesota Press.

Gray, J., Sandvoss, C. , & Harrington, C.L. (Eds.). (2007). *Fandom: Identities and communities in a mediated world*. New York: New York University Press.

Hall, S. (Ed.). (1997). *Representation: Cultural representations and signifying practices*. London: Sage.

Hall, S., Critcher, S., Jefferson, T., Clarke, J., & Roberts, B. (1978). *Policing the crisis: Mugging, the state, and law and order*. London: Macmillan.

Hartley, J. (1996). *Popular reality: Journalism, modernity, popular culture*. London: Arnold.

Hartley, J. (2008). *Television truths: Forms of knowledge in popular culture*. Oxford, UK: Blackwell.

Hermes, J. (2005). *Re-reading popular culture*. Oxford, UK: Wiley-Blackwell.

Holmes, D. (2005). *Communication theory: Media, technology, and society*. London: Sage.

Horky, T., & Nieland, J.-W. (2011). First results of the International Sports Press Survey 2011. Play the Game initiative of the Danish Institute for Sport Studies. http://www.playthegame.org/fileadmin/image/PTG2011/Presentation/PTG_Nieland-Horky_ISPS_2011_3.10.2011_final.pdf.

Horne, J. (2006). *Sport in consumer culture*. Basingstoke, UK: Palgrave Macmillan.

Hutchins, B., & Rowe, D. (2009). From broadcast rationing to digital plenitude: The changing dynamics of the media sport content economy. *Television & New Media, 10*, 354–370.

Hutchins, B., & Rowe, D. (2010). Reconfiguring media sport for the online world: An inquiry into "Sports News and Digital Media." *International Journal of Communication, 4*, 696–718. http://ijoc.org/ojs/index.php/ijoc/article/view/758/443.

Hutchins, B., & Rowe, D. (2012). *Sport beyond television: The Internet, digital media, and the rise of networked media sport.* New York: Routledge.

Keeley, G., & Burke, J. (2008, June 28). Spain revels in new spirit of unity as football team heals divisions. *The Observer.* www.guardian.co.uk/world/2008/jun/29/spain.spain.

Kuper, S. (2012, June 17). Spain's football unity shows regions the way. *Financial Times.* www.ft.com/cms/s/0/b1a368a6-b89b-11e1-a2d6-00144feabdc0.html#axzz2RQIiaDMO.

Leonard, D.J. (Ed.). (2009). New media and global sporting cultures [Special issue]. *Sociology of Sport Journal, 26*(1).

Leveson Inquiry: Culture, Practice, and Ethics of the Press. (2012). www.levesoninquiry.org.uk/.

Lowes, M.D. (1999). *Inside the sports pages: Work routines, professional ideologies, and the manufacture of sports news.* Toronto: University of Toronto Press.

Lundby, K. (Ed.). (2009). *Mediatization: Concept, changes, consequences.* New York: Lang.

Maguire, J. (1999). *Global sport: Identities, societies, civilizations.* Cambridge, UK: Polity.

Maguire, J. (2005). *Power and global sport: Zones of prestige, emulation, and resistance.* London: Routledge.

McChesney, R.W. (2008). *The political economy of media: Enduring issues, emerging dilemmas.* New York: Monthly Review Press.

McLuhan, M. (1964). *Understanding media: The extensions of man.* New York: McGraw-Hill.

Miller, T. (1998). *Technologies of truth: Cultural citizenship and the popular media.* Minneapolis: University of Minnesota Press.

Miller, T. (2001). *Sportsex.* Philadelphia: Temple University Press.

Miller, T. (Ed.). (2009). My media studies [Special issue]. *Television & New Media, 10*(1).

Miller, T., Lawrence, G., McKay, J., & Rowe, D. (2001). *Globalization and sport: Playing the world.* London: Sage.

Moragas Spà, M. de, Rivenburgh, N.K., & Larson, J.F. (1995). *Television in the Olympics.* London: Libbey.

News Corporation. (2008). *NewsCorp Annual Report 2008.* www.newscorp.com/AR2008Flash/NC08.html.

Nicholson, M. (2007). *Sport and the media: Managing the nexus.* Oxford, UK: Elsevier.

Nightingale, V. (Ed.). (2010). *Handbook of media audiences.* Oxford, UK: Blackwell.

O'Shaughnessy, M., & Stadler, J. (2008). *Media and society: An introduction* (4th ed.). Melbourne: Oxford, UK University Press.

Price, M.E., & Raboy, M. (2003). *Public service broadcasting in transition: A documentary reader.* The Hague: Kluwer Law International.

Qing, L., & Richeri, G. (Eds.). (2010). *Encoding the Olympics: Comparative analysis on international reporting of Beijing 2008; A communication perspective.* London: Routledge.

Raney, A.A., & Bryant, J. (Eds.). (2006). *Handbook of sport and media.* New York: Routledge.

Rowe, D. (1995). *Popular cultures: Rock music, sport, and the politics of pleasure.* London: Sage.

Rowe, D. (2004a). Fulfilling the cultural mission: Popular genre and public remit. *European Journal of Cultural Studies, 7,* 381–399.

Rowe, D. (2004b). *Sport, culture, and the media: The unruly trinity* (2nd ed.). Maidenhead, UK: Open University Press.

Rowe, D. (2009). The concept of the moral panic: An historico-sociological positioning. In D. Lemmings & C. Walker (Eds.), *Moral panics, the press, and the law in early modern England* (pp. 22–40). New York: Palgrave Macmillan.

Rowe, D. (2010). Stages of the global: Media, sport, racialization, and the last temptation of Zinedine Zidane. *International Review for the Sociology of Sport, 45,* 355–371.

Rowe, D. (2011). *Global media sport: Flows, forms, and futures.* London: Bloomsbury Academic.

Ruddock, A. (2001). *Understanding audiences.* London: Sage.

Scherer, J., & Rowe, D. (Eds.). (2014). *Sport, public broadcasting, and cultural citizenship: Signal lost?* New York: Routledge.

Scherer, J., & Whitson, D. (2009). Public broadcasting, sport, and cultural citizenship: The future of sport on the Canadian Broadcasting Corporation? *International Review for the Sociology of Sport, 44,* 213–229.

Schultz-Jorgensen, S. (2005). The world's best advertising agency: The sports press. [Summary of The International Sports Press Survey 2005]. House of Monday Morning and the Play the Game initiative of the Danish Institute for Sport Studies. www.playthegame.org/upload/sport_press_survey_english.pdf.

Schulz, W. (2004). Reconstructing mediatization as an analytical concept. *European Journal of Communication, 19,* 87–101.Silk, M., Slack, T., & Amis, L. (2000). Bread, butter, and gravy: An institutional approach to televised sport production. *Culture, Sport, Society, 3,* 1–21.

Silverstone, R. (1999). *Why study the media?* London: Sage.

Swingewood, A. (1977). *The myth of mass culture.* London: Macmillan.

Tabloids target Green 'keeper: Hand of clod. (2010, June 13). *USA Today.* http://usatoday30.usatoday.com/sports/soccer/2010-06-13-2542168294_x.htm.

Tomlinson, A., & Young, C. (Eds.). (2006). *National identity and global sports events: Culture, politics, and spectacle in the Olympics and the football World Cup.* New York: State University of New York Press.

Watson, J. (1998). *Media communication: An introduction to theory and process.* Basingstoke, UK: Macmillan.

Wenner, L.A. (Ed.). (1998). *MediaSport.* London: Routledge.

Whannel, G. (1992). *Fields in vision: Television sport and cultural transformation*. London: Routledge.

Whannel, G. (2001). *Media sport stars: Masculinities and moralities*. London: Routledge.

Whannel, G. (2008). *Culture, politics, and sport: Blowing the whistle revisited*. London: Routledge.

World Cup 2010: Robert Green vows to bounce back. (2010, June 13). BBC Sport. http://news.bbc.co.uk/go/pr/fr/-/sport2/hi/football/world_cup_2010/8737289.stm.

PART

III

Capital: Wealth, Power, and Resources

The questions of community and identity explored in part II are bound up in issues relating to capital, status, wealth, power, and resources. Thus the issues raised by anthropologists, geographers, sociologists, and media theorists also relate to the concerns examined by the disciplines surveyed in part III. Here, economists, political scientists, and international relations experts probe the ways in which wealth, power, and resources are generated, distributed, and used in sport contexts.

In chapter 8, Stefan Szymanski makes an important distinction with regard to the study of economics and that of sport. Much of what is studied in sport economics can be viewed as the use of sporting examples to highlight a general proposition or theory from the discipline. For Szymanski, however, sport is also characterized by what he terms a "peculiar economics," in which competitors need to cooperate with their rivals in order to produce the sporting contest, which then has economic worth. In other economic spheres, such acts would be seen as a form of collusion, which would raise profitability but harm the interests of consumers. In sport, however, rivals must work together to produce a saleable product. How this form of cooperation is enacted varies cross-culturally, and differing economic models are on display. Thus economists examine models relating to professional sport, performance measurement in sport, impact studies of and on sport, the economics of health and physical activity, and the use of sport to illustrate broader economic theories.

Jonathan Grix's penetrating contribution in chapter 9 touches on some of the concerns raised in part II but also addresses issues raised in the field of economics. Exploring issues of power, the use (and misuse) of resources, and the distribution of wealth, Grix surveys the areas of sport and political science, sport policy, and politics and sport. Highlighting the complex and contradictory nature of political science, he probes the commonsense (and ideological) assumption that sport and politics should or do not mix. Drawing on examples and case studies, Grix provides a telling argument that sport and politics interweave and that in order to make sense of this reality students need a political science perspective.

The interconnectedness of sport and politics is also demonstrated by Roger Levermore and Aaron Beacom in their discussion of international relations (IR) in chapter 10. Levermore and Beacom highlight the utility of an IR perspective as a means both for understanding the character of contemporary international sport and for enhancing an appreciation of the nature of international relations. In doing so, they examine issues of governance and the rise of nongovernmental actors in international politics, community development, and the dynamics of international assistance. Such concerns link with questions of community highlighted in part II. This chapter also has direct relevance to the politics and economics of development and sport debates.

CHAPTER 8

Economics and Sport

Stefan Szymanski, PhD

Economics, classically defined, is the study of the allocation of scarce resources among competing ends (Robbins, 1932). Given that resources are everywhere scarce, and that the ends of humans are almost unlimited, the study of economics can be taken to cover "all purposive human behavior" and has therefore been dubbed (by some economists) the "imperial science" (e.g., Stigler, 1984). From the perspective of an economist, then, what is distinctive about the study of sport (a special case) rather than it being just another part of this imperial project (a case study)?

The toolkit of the economist typically consists of a model of rational agents seeking to maximize some objective function subject to constraints, which results in a set of demands and supplies for goods and services, which in turn combine in some way to produce an equilibrium. This, at least, is the agenda of mainstream, neoclassical economics; various dissenting streams also exist, but, for good or ill, they receive little attention from the majority of academic economists. The nature of this equilibrium is that no one should believe that he or she could have done better by making an alternative feasible choice, given the choices of others (a Nash equilibrium). This equilibrium (if it exists) is assumed to be the natural focal point toward which behavior in the real world is likely to converge (a testable hypothesis), and the equilibrium can then be compared with the allocation of resources that would arise if a benevolent and omniscient social planner allocated resources optimally (the basis for policy analysis).

Much of what is studied in sport economics can be thought of as standard analysis, where sporting examples illustrate a general proposition from economics—for example, testing whether athletes respond to increased financial incentives or whether the odds offered in bookmaking are efficient (in a financial markets sense). However, sport is also characterized by a "peculiar economics," in which competitors (in a sporting sense) need to collaborate with their sporting rivals in order to produce the sporting contest. This dynamic is most pertinent in the case of professional team sports, where individual teams are often organized as commercial enterprises. In all other commercial enterprise, collaboration between rival businesses is seen as a collusive device that will raise profitability and harm the interests of consumers, but in the case of sport the product (a contest) cannot be produced without some form of collaboration (e.g., agreeing on the rules of the game). Indeed, no other form of commerce requires rivals to work together in order to produce a saleable product. Integrating this peculiar economics into a mainstream framework represents a significant challenge both at the level of theory and at the level of policy.

For the purposes of this survey, the subject has been divided into five main areas. The chapter begins by presenting models of professional sport leagues, which is where economic analysis was first explicitly applied to sport. Then follows a discussion of performance measurement in sport. For many economists, this has been a bit of a hobby, but as the economic value of sport activities has grown, so has interest in applying statistical and economic methods to team performance. Next, we consider the economic impact of sport facilities and events, which has been a major focus of policy making and sport. The fourth segment is a discussion of the economics of health, sport, and physical activity, an area that is becoming an important focus of research. Finally, examples are gathered under the general heading "illustrating economic theory," and they include some significant contributions to the fields of labor economics, game theory, and finance theory.

Sport economics as a field of research has grown dramatically over the last 20 years. In 1990, there were probably no more than a few dozen studies of any significance, whereas today there are hundreds and thus this review is inevitably selective. To give some idea of the present scope of study, Andreff and Szymanski (2006) edited a large collection of reviews contributed by many of the leading authors in the field. Zimbalist (2001) also put together a collection of significant early papers in the field, and more recent papers can be found in a collection by Andreff (2011). In addition, *The Oxford Handbook of Sports Economics* (Shmanske & Kahane, 2012) provides an up-to-date overview of many issues.

Professional League Model: Theory and Policy

Most economists agree that sport economics originates with Simon Rottenberg's article about the baseball players' labor market (1956). This article dealt with a central issue in professional sport—the competitive balance defense. Back in 1876, William Hulbert had founded the National League of Professional Baseball Clubs as a closed commercial enterprise on the basis that an elite group of clubs agreed to play a fixed schedule of games to produce a league champion. In 1879, Hulbert introduced the reserve clause, which, on the grounds that the free movement of players within the league undermined the profitability of teams, effectively prevented a player from joining another club without the permission of his current employer. In 1890, the U.S. Congress passed the Sherman Antitrust Act, which, among other things, prohibited restrictive agreements (i.e., the formation of cartels) between competing organizations. Around this time, the National League began to proclaim a new motive for the reserve clause—the need to limit competition in the interest of the weaker teams. Without rough parity (competitive balance) among the teams, the argument goes, the outcome of sporting competition would become predictable and fans would lose interest; see Sullivan (1995) for the original statements by Hulbert and Albert Spalding. Hence restrictive arrangements, which would otherwise fall afoul of the competition law because they exploit consumers, are in this case claimed to benefit consumers; this is the competitive balance defense, the claim that restrictive agreements between members of a league are required as a means of achieving sufficient parity so that fans do not lose interest.

Players bitterly resented the reserve clause, which they rightly believed held down their wages, and periodic disputes erupted between owners and players. In 1951, Congress investigated baseball, and the resulting Celler Hearings (*Hearings*, 1952) aired the views of owners, players, and other interested parties. Team owners argued specifically that if players were free to sell their services in an open market, the best players would inevitably migrate to the teams in the largest cities, which had the largest fan bases and therefore the greatest capacity to pay, thus rendering small-market teams uncompetitive. Not only would the small teams lose support, they said, but total attendance at baseball games would fall due to the lack of competitive balance. Rottenberg, an economist at the University of Chicago, rejected this argument. He imagined a world in which wins increased revenues (because fans want to see their team win) and playing talent produced wins (the more talented the team, the more it wins). Each player, he argued, would migrate to the team that valued his services the most, regardless of whether that team owned the right to decide the player's destination (thanks to the reserve clause) or the player was free to sell his services to the highest bidder. He reasoned that in the first situation, a player whose ability could generate, say, $10,000 of revenue for one club (because of his ability to raise the performance and thus attract more fans) but only $5,000 for his present club (because of its smaller fan base) would be sold (for a fee between $5,000 and $10,000). In the second situation, the large-market club would offer to pay the player a high wage to get him to change clubs. Thus the recipient of the payment might differ, but the outcome would be the same.

Sport economists have since pointed out that this represents a special case of the more general Coase theorem, which states that in the absence of transaction costs the ownership of resources will have no effect on the economic activities to which they are ultimately allocated (Coase, 1960). Rottenberg's proposition has become known in the sport economics literature as the invariance principle, meaning that the competitive balance of a league will be invariant in the midst of the contractual relationships governing not only player services but also the stream of income derived from league competition. El-Hodiri and Quirk (1971) claimed to extend the invariance principle, using a formal economic model, to the sharing of gate revenues (see also Quirk & El-Hodiri, 1974). The argument in this case is that while the sharing of revenues reduces the return on winning (assuming that gate revenues increase with wins), it does so for each team in an equal and opposite way, and so the distribution of wins is unchanged.

This view became something of an orthodoxy until the late 1990s (e.g., Vrooman, 1995; Fort & Quirk, 1995), but it has been challenged on two fronts. First, Késenne (1996), building on the earlier work of Sloane (1969, 1971), argued that in a European context it made more sense to think of teams as win maximizers rather than using the standard American assumption of profit maximization. Under this assumption, the invariance principle no longer holds, since clubs will spend all income they receive on talent, and any revenue sharing between high- and low-income teams will tend to equalize team quality and outcomes. Perhaps more surprising, Szymanski and Késenne (2004; see also Szymanski, 2003, 2004) showed that when the underlying game theoretic framework is formally set out, gate sharing under the assumptions previously adopted leads to a more unequal distribution of talent. The reason for this is that teams impose a pecuniary externality on each other (the more my team invests in talent, the more your team loses, and therefore the less income your team generates), and the size of the externality is greater for a small-market team than for a large-market one (when a small team takes a larger share of wins, the revenue loss to large-market teams is greater than the revenue loss to the small-market team when the large-market team takes a larger share of wins).

This result has generated a good deal of controversy, and claims have been made to the effect that it is merely an artifact of the way that European leagues, where talent moves from one league to another, differ from American major leagues, where all the best talent in a given sport plays in one league only (Eckard, 2006; Vrooman, 2007; Fort & Winfree, 2009). However, the result is an example of a better-known result in the literature on contests that is known as the paradox of power (Hirshleifer, 1991). Another way to pose the question about competitive balance is to ask whether the choices of individual members of a league will lead to too much, too little, or just the right amount of competitive balance, where the optimal competitive balance is defined as that which maximizes total attendance at league matches. The paradox of power suggests that there will be too much competitive balance because weak teams overinvest as compared with strong teams (Szymanski, 2006).

More recently, P. Madden (2011) has suggested that more attention should be paid to the process of wage negotiation. The standard model assumes that players are paid the market-clearing wage (where supply equals demand), but P. Madden shows that when wage negotiation is introduced explicitly, a wider range of outcomes is possible.

One important innovation in recent years among sport economists is that of referring more carefully to the substantial literature on economic contests (Szymanski, 2003). An economic contest is a situation where two or more contestants compete for a prize. This literature goes back to Tullock (1980) and provides the theoretical framework for thinking about sporting competition; it is also closely connected to the auction literature (e.g., Konrad, 2007).

From a policy perspective, the theoretical disputes have tended to mask a broader consensus. Almost all of the economists cited so far have taken a skeptical view of the restraints entered into by professional sport leagues in the name of competitive balance. In North America, these restraints have been wide ranging, including roster limits, draft rules, salary caps, revenue sharing in relation to gates, merchandising, and broadcast income. Economists have noted that these measures are likely to have a positive influence on the level of profitability of a league (whether or not they affect competitive balance), often at the expense of a player's bargaining power and earning capacity.

Empirical research in economics on the demand for professional sport has examined a number of contributory factors, including price, income, quality of services offered, availability of substitutes, and degree of competitive balance; for a review, see Borland and MacDonald (2003). Most studies find that demand is price-inelastic (meaning that an increase [or decrease] in price will cause a proportionately smaller decrease [or increase] in demand), which itself poses something of a puzzle. Given that the marginal cost of a seat for a game in a stadium is approximately zero (no costs are saved if the seat is not filled), economic theory suggests that the ticket price should be set where the price elasticity of demand equals minus one, which is also the price that maximizes total revenue. In other words, it appears that stadium owners could profitably raise prices. Several explanations have been advanced to explain this apparent paradox, the most plausible being that owners generate profits from other goods and services sold to ticket holders (e.g., car parking, food and beverages, merchandise) and thus that effectively discounting the ticket price may be a sensible way to maximize the total profit extracted from fans (e.g., Fort, 2004).

A number of studies have examined the impact of new stadiums on fan demand, and most have identified a significant honeymoon effect in which attendance is boosted for a number of seasons following the new facility's opening (e.g., Clapp & Hakes, 2005). One difficulty lies in separating the effect of the new stadium itself from the effect of team quality, since frequently owners invest in a better team when they have a new stadium. Better players also tend to attract larger gates, both because the performance of the team improves (and fans tend to follow more successful teams) and because fans like to see stars, which means that attendance also tends to be affected by the quality of the visiting team.

However, perhaps the most important research question has been whether the competitive balance of matches affects attendance. This question can be studied at the level of the individual game or at the level of the league as a whole. Given the reliance placed by leagues and policy makers on the concept of competitive balance, it is perhaps surprising to discover that the empirical support for this reliance is not very strong. Studies at the level of the game have tended to rely on either prematch betting odds or the previous records of the teams in question, and most of these results tend to show that attendance increases as the home team's probability of winning increases and that demand tends to reach a peak around the 70 percent level, which represents a very unbalanced contest (Forrest & Simmons, 2002; Rascher & Solmes, 2007). In other words, as expected, home team fans like to see the home team win. If all teams possessed an equal share of talent in the league, home advantage would mean that home teams won more than 50 percent of the time but probably not 70 percent of the time. Moreover, since large-market teams tend to increase their attendance by more when they win than do small-market teams, some asymmetry in playing strengths is likely to be ideal. A small number of studies have looked at competitive balance in a league as a whole over the long term, and they have failed to show convincingly that more competitive balance raises demand (e.g., Schmidt & Berri, 2001). Contrary to popular opinion, then, an equally balanced league is unlikely to be more attractive to fans than an unbalanced one. The question of how much imbalance is optimal remains open.

Most of the literature discussed here has been developed in the context of North American professional sport, and until the 1990s there were relatively few contributions from Europeans (the main exceptions being the work of Sloane and Késenne mentioned earlier). This dearth can be explained by the fact that until the 1990s, European professional sport, which is dominated by soccer, generated very little income and could barely be considered a commercial activity. What transformed European professional sport, especially soccer, was the deregulation of broadcast markets in the 1980s due to the development of satellite technology. Prior to this change, most countries in Europe, unlike the United States, had either a state monopoly of broadcasting or only limited competition. Since analog technology limited the number of channels that could be shown, monopoly broadcasters faced a shortage of capacity rather than a shortage of content, and hence were willing to pay relatively little for broadcast rights. At the same time, professional leagues were fearful that broadcasting might reduce attendance, so their incentive to sell games was limited. Satellite (and later, cable) transformed the market structure by dramatically enhancing capacity (thanks to digital technology) and increasing competition between broadcasters. Soccer was seen as one of the principal drivers for getting viewers to pay for content (which, if available, used to be free), and the income generated from broadcasting expanded significantly. The marketing effect of increased broadcast coverage also tended to increase demand for attendance, which tended to increase despite rising ticket prices. At the same time, leagues based in the larger broadcast markets (Germany, Italy, England, Spain) saw their spending power increase significantly relative to that of the smaller markets (e.g., the Netherlands, Portugal, Scotland, Sweden). For more on this transition, see Szymanski and Kuypers (1999) and Andreff and Staudohar (2000).

This change provoked a reassessment by the courts and by the European Commission of a number of commercial practices that were previously unchallenged. In 1995, the European Court of Justice ruled that the existing rules in soccer relating to player transfers and restrictions on the number of foreign players per team violated European Union laws relating to the free movement of labor. Likewise, a number of competition authorities across Europe investigated the practice of collective selling of broadcast rights. While these issues had been addressed in U.S. litigation in previous decades, European legal analysis needed to take account of specific attributes of European sport—namely, the integration of professional sport within national governing bodies responsible for all levels of sport and its long-term development; the existence of promotion and relegation mechanisms that link different levels of competition to each other (notably absent in North America); the significant role played by international representative competition in the organization of sport; and the more limited role of commercial objectives in the management of clubs (many of which are owned by fans). A number of published papers have considered the structure of labor market contracts in Europe in light of the Bosman ruling (e.g., Jeanrenaud & Késenne, 1999) and analyzed the effect of collective selling of broadcast rights (e.g., Forrest, Simmons, & Szymanski, 2004). More generally, a number of articles have been published about the European model of sport (e.g., Hoehn & Szymanski, 1999; Andreff & Staudohar, 2000). In recent times, a great deal of discussion in Europe has focused on the financial problems experienced by soccer clubs and the demand for increased financial regulation (e.g., Lago, Simmons, & Szymanski, 2006).

Outside of Europe and North America, the major contributions in the field have come from Australia, which is home to professional leagues in a wide range of sports (cricket, rugby league, rugby union, soccer, and basketball) and a very strong sporting culture. While the sporting institutions developed initially along British (European) lines, they have more recently tended to adopt American approaches. Surprisingly little has been written on the economic organization of Australian sport.

Productivity Studies

The productivity of professional athletes and their teams has been a key interest of sport economists. The first study in this field is generally acknowledged to be G. Scully's 1974 paper on pay and performance in Major League Baseball. His methodology involved estimating the relationship between team success (win percentage) and various performance statistics (e.g., team slugging average, team strikeout-to-walk ratio) using linear regression methods. Each player's personal contribution to winning could then be estimated using his own performance statistics and the coefficients derived from the regression. G. Scully then estimated the relationship between winning and revenues, so that a monetary value could be placed on each player's contribution to winning. G. Scully's motivation was to analyze the extent to which players' salaries reflected the economic value of their services (marginal revenue product) given that player salaries were at that time still restrained by the reserve clause, and indeed he found that marginal revenue products were nearly 10 times larger than salaries paid. A subsequent study by Zimbalist (1992) found that salaries had risen much closer to estimated marginal revenue product, as might have been expected following the introduction of veteran free agency in the late 1970s.

Generally speaking, it is hard to obtain financial data on the value of a win, but the first stage of G. Scully's approach—regressing success on some collection of variables of interest—has been widely replicated for a number of purposes. One popular research stream concerns the impact of managerial performance on outcomes. For more detail, see G. Scully (1994), Fizel and D'Itri (1997), and Kahn (1993) for baseball; Dawson, Dobson, & Gerrard (2000a) for soccer; and Berri et al. (2009) for basketball. Another line of research involves measuring team efficiency with respect to variables of interest in order to rank teams independently of their performance in sporting competition itself. Thus, for example, while it is known in European soccer that some teams have far greater resources than their competitors, it is possible to rank clubs by the efficiency with which they use the resources they have. This literature has two main strands. The first, known as stochastic frontier analysis, uses a regression approach and identifies organizations that outperform the average by the largest amount, controlling for other contributions (see Cornwell & Schmidt, 2008, for a review). The disadvantage of this approach is that it requires the researcher to define exactly how output (in this case, sporting performance) is produced. This problem is avoided by the second commonly used approach, known as data envelopment analysis (DEA), in which linear programming is used to calculate the inputs required to produce a given output for each production unit so that the relative efficiency of production units can be compared. Examples of using stochastic frontier approaches include Dawson, Dobson, and Gerrard (2000b); Kahane (2005); and Barros and Leach (2006b). Examples using DEA analysis include Haas (2003a, 2003b); Haas, Kocher, and Sutter (2004); Espitia-Escuer and García-Cebrián (2004); Barros and Leach (2006a); and García-Sánchez (2007). One problem with this literature is that of determining a use to which the results can be put. It is one thing to say that a poor team is relatively more efficient than a wealthy team, but this fact may make little difference if the wealthy team always wins the match.

The use of statistical analysis to measure performance holds more than merely academic interest. As Guttmann (1978) observed, quantification and obsession with records are characteristics of modern sport. Many fans are interested in measurement not merely for the sake of making comparisons but also for the possibility that statistics can be used to predict performance. Perhaps the most famous popularizer of statistics in sport is Bill James, who in 1977 started publishing the *Bill James Baseball Abstract*, which looks at performance in baseball (e.g., James, 1982). The Society for American Baseball Research, founded in 1971, also contributed to the development of statistical analysis in sport; indeed, its acronym (SABR) gave rise to the term "sabermetrics" to describe statistical analysis in baseball. The approach reached an even wider audience with the publication in 2003 of Michael Lewis' book *Moneyball*, which described the use of statistics by Billy Beane, the general manager of the Oakland A's, to identify characteristics of players that were undervalued in the player market. The book claimed that this approach enabled Oakland to field a more competitive team with a relatively low budget, and subsequent research by Hakes and Sauer (2006) showed not only that the alleged anomaly on which Beane had based his strategy actually existed in the data but also that after the publication of *Moneyball* the anomaly became widely known and then disappeared (as would be predicted if the market responded efficiently to the new information).

Statistical analysis of other sports in order to identify performance is becoming popular, especially as more sophisticated and detailed measures of performance become available. Examples include Berri, Schmidt, and Brook (2006) and Berri and Schmidt (2010) for basketball and Carmichael, Thomas, and Ward (2000) for soccer.

Economic Impact: Measurement, Theory, and Policy

Modern spectator sport plays a large role in many people's emotional lives, even to the point where sport may seem to dominate day-to-day life. It is therefore natural to suppose that sport holds great economic significance in terms of its contribution to GDP. Certainly, there is evidence that sport activities in general (including participation in sport) play a significant role in the economy; for example, the Sport Industry Research Centre (2010) estimates that 2.2 percent of gross value added in the United Kingdom's economy is attributable to sport. However, spectator sport contributes only a fraction of the total.

The main issue in sport economics has not focused on the overall contribution of sport to the economy but on the impact of specific new sport facilities and the hosting of major sport events (the two are often tied together). In North America, it has long been claimed that a new sport stadium will bring economic benefits to the local economy thanks to employment in the construction industry when the facility is being built, visitors to the facility once it is completed, and a more general "halo" effect due to the presence of a major facility. These claims are used as leverage to extract economic support from local taxpayers for the initial investment.

Economists have long been skeptical about such arguments on theoretical grounds. The essential economic notion here is one of opportunity cost—the value of resources in their next-best alternative use. It is not denied that economic facilities and events can generate much revenue, but it is suggested that the opportunity cost of the resources is often at least as great as, if not greater than, the economic benefits produced. Stadium facilities are typically very expensive to build and are often used for a relatively small period during the year; thus they may not be very productive as compared with alternative infrastructure investments. The value of revenue generated by paying spectators and sport-related activities can be large, but frequently these benefits are spread over a large area, since many of the suppliers are not local. Some have argued that sport facilities produce multiplier effects—a Keynesian notion positing that expenditures create incomes for suppliers, incomes that are then used partly to fund more expenditure, thus creating income for another round of suppliers, and so on. However, the benefit of multiplier effects may turn out to be rather muted by the impact of taxes and spending on imports. These theoretical arguments have been explored by several economists—for example, Crompton (1995), Noll and Zimbalist (1997), Porter (1999), Siegfried and Zimbalist (2000), and Hudson (2001).

Nonetheless, those in favor of building facilities and hosting events usually come armed with consultants' reports suggesting that facilities will have large multiplier effects and significant, long-term, beneficial impact. These are ex ante forecasts, and there now exists a substantial array of ex post studies searching for significant economic impacts. Most of the best studies of this issue originate from the United States, where new stadiums have frequently been constructed to house major sport league franchises in large cities, and the economic development of these cities can be compared with that of similar cities that were not home to similar investments. To cite several examples, Baade and Dye (1988) examined the effect of professional sport facilities on manufacturing employment, real value added in manufacturing, and new capital expenditure in metropolitan areas in the United States; Baade and Dye (1990) looked at the impact on personal incomes in metropolitan areas; Baade (1996) considered the effect on employment and income in metropolitan areas; Coates and Humphreys (1999) examined the impact on level and growth rate of per capita income in metropolitan areas with major league franchises; Coates and Humphreys (2001, 2002) looked at the impact of strikes and playoff appearances on real per capita incomes; and Coates and Humphreys (2003) probed the sectoral breakdown within the local economy. In all of these studies, the aggregate effect of a sport facility or franchise on the local economy was negligible, and the last of these papers provides a plausible explanation—the benefits that the "amusement and recreation" sector generates for the local economy in terms of employment and output is generally offset by negative effects on other parts of the local economy. Individuals allocate a budget for entertainment, and when a given form of entertainment is present, individuals may substitute it for alternatives that are less easily available or less attractive. The net effect is approximately zero.

The apparent lack of significant *economic* benefits arising from sport facilities does not mean that such facilities are not worth having. Whether or not a cultural artifact enhances incomes, it may still be socially valuable if it enhances human well-being. One way of approaching this issue is to ask how much individuals are willing to pay in order to host a franchise or event or to build a stadium. Examples of research along this line include Johnson and Whitehead (2000,and Johnson, Groothuis, and Whitehead (2002) who used survey evidence to estimate how much people in Lexington, Kentucky, would be willing to pay to have either a new basketball arena or a minor league baseball stadium. Atkinson, Mourata, Szymanski, and Ozdemiroglu (2008) used a similar method to identify how much people in London, Manchester, and Glasgow would be willing to pay to host the 2012 Olympics in London. These studies identified a substantial willingness to pay, though not enough in either case to cover the cost of facilities. These results might suggest that political support for such expenditures from taxes is misplaced. Critics might argue that there is a big difference between what people say they are willing to pay and what they actually would pay if faced with the choice (one might suspect that stated preferences would tend to overstate the willingness to pay).

Hedonic regression methods, which attempt to estimate the value of an amenity by looking at the prices of related goods, have also been applied in this area. Carlino and Coulson (2004) found that the costs of rental property close to sport stadiums were significantly higher than in cities without stadiums, implying a substantial willingness to pay for these amenities, although Coates, Humphreys, and Zimbalist (2006) have challenged the validity of these findings. Finally, economists have started to look at well-being in relation to sport events and facilities by using the large international survey data that exist on subjective well-being. Porsche and Maennig (2008) document a significant "feel-good factor" in Germany associated with hosting the World Cup in 2006, and Kavetsos and Szymanski (2010) found that individuals' self-reported well-being appeared significantly higher in the immediate aftermath of hosting a major international soccer championship.

Finally, there has been an increasing number of studies on the impact of mega-events, notably the Olympic Games and the World Cup; see, for example, Hotchkiss et al. (2003), Baade and Matheson (2002, 2004), Preuss (2004), J.R. Madden (2006), and Allmers and Maennig (2009). Generally, these studies discover negligible economic benefits associated with mega-events.

Sport, Physical Activity, and Well-Being

Professional sport represents a tiny fraction of all sporting activity; in other words, a large portion of the population in most countries participates in sport, whether as children in school or after-school clubs or as adults. This participation generates significant economic activity, and in recent years academics from a variety of disciplines related to health (medicine, psychology, sociology, and economics) have focused on the effect of sporting activities.

Sport is, of course, only one kind of physical activity; others include work, housework, and walking or cycling to work or for recreation. The medical benefits of physical activity in general have long been recognized (e.g. Oja, Vuori, & Paronen, 1998; Cervero & Duncan, 2003; Pucher & Dijkstra, 2003; Biddle, Goreley, & Stensel, 2004; Bassett, Pucher, Buehler, Thompson, & Crouter, 2008) and supported by government policy (e.g., Pate et al., 1995; Smith & Bird, 2004; Wendel-Vos et al., 2004). Of particular interest have been the rising levels of obesity, especially in wealthier nations, in the face of increasingly sedentary lifestyles and cheap food.

Economists tend to see sporting activities in the context of a wider set of social objectives that the individual may embrace. Grossman (1972, 1999) suggested a model in which individuals have a demand for health based on the other activities that it supports (employment, leisure activities), and sport participation can be seen as a contributory factor aimed at achieving a target level of health. However, individuals may also participate in sport because it generates satisfaction in its own right, independent of health benefits. Recent research in economics has focused on individual happiness, which is typically measured through surveys of individual self-reported life satisfaction. These surveys have been carried out across many countries for several decades and have generated many new insights into human behavior (e.g., Frey & Stutzer, 2002).

In this context, sport as physical activity may be important because it can help control obesity and thus improve both health and happiness (Oswald & Powdthavee, 2007) or because there is a direct link between sport participation and increasing happiness (e.g., Gerdtham & Johannesson, 2001; D. Scully, Kremer, Meade, Graham, & Dudgeon, 1999). Rasciute and Downward (2010) suggest that some physical activities may improve health but do little to improve happiness (e.g., cycling to work), whereas sport may jointly increase happiness and health. This distinction has important policy implications, since it seems likely that people are more likely to engage in activities that make them happy.

Perhaps the most important challenge in this area of research is to establish the direction of causality. Fairly consistent evidence suggests that sport participation, health, and happiness are closely correlated (e.g., Humphreys & Ruseski, 2007), but it is unclear whether we should think that causation runs from sport participation to happiness or vice versa (and much the same can be said for the link between health and happiness and between sport participation and health). These questions have important implications for government policy and other issues, such as the supply of sport facilities (e.g., Forrest & McHale, 2009). Establishing causality within the framework of happiness surveys involves significant statistical problems (e.g., Huang & Humphreys, 2010; Kavetsos, 2011), and this will continue to be a research focus for some years to come.

Illustrations of Economic Issues

For the most part, the studies discussed so far have taken sport as their primary focus of research. However, this is not always the case; for example, research on managerial performance in sport teams is often aimed at drawing more general conclusions about managerial incentives. In fact, a number of fields in economics have used sport markets as a kind of laboratory in which to test economic theories, and this approach has been most evident in the field of labor economics. Sport is ideal for this purpose due to the quantity and quality of data available on the performance and remuneration of athletes, coaches, and managers (e.g., Kahn, 2000; Rosen & Sanderson, 2001).

Discrimination

One of the earliest applications of sport data was made in the study of discrimination in labor markets (e.g., Pascal & Rapping, 1972). This literature focused not just on the estimation of pay differences between black and white players in sports such as baseball, basketball, and American football but also on the way in which discrimination interacted with market forces (for an early survey, see Kahn, 1991). Thus while evidence showed that black players were underpaid relative to equivalently talented white players, especially in basketball, economists focused on the issue raised by Becker (1971) that discriminators would face a penalty in the marketplace by having to pay more to hire talent than nondiscriminators would pay (e.g., Hanssen, 1998). For example, it has been argued that the breaking of the color barrier in baseball was motivated in part by the desire to hire cheaper players (e.g., Gwartney & Haworth, 1974).

Generally, evidence on discrimination has focused on salaries (e.g., Hamilton, 1997; Kahn & Sherer, 1988; Gius & Johnson, 1998), but others have addressed issues including promotion (Bellemore, 2001), retention (Kahn, 2006), coaches (J.F. Madden, 2004; Kahn, 2006), career length (Groothuis & Hill, 2004), and referees (Price & Wolfers, 2007). Another important issue in discrimination studies (e.g., Bodvarsson & Partridge, 2001) has been the identity of the discriminator: Is it the team owner, players, coaching staff, or fans themselves? Researchers who have studied fan discrimination include Burdekin, Hossfeld, and Smith (2005), Foley and Smith (2007), Hanssen and Andersen (1999), Brown and Jewell (1994), Burdekin and Idson (1991), and Coleman, DuMond, and Lynch (2008).

All of these studies deal with racial discrimination in North American sport, and relatively few such studies have been conducted of soccer markets in Europe or elsewhere. Exceptions include Szymanski (2000), who found evidence of salary discrimination in the 1970s and early 1980s, as well as Wilson and Ying (2003) and Goddard and Wilson (2009). Some studies have identified a wage premium for players of particular nationalities—especially South Americans—whose style of play is often considered more attractive to fans even if it is not more likely to produce success in competition (e.g., Frick, 2007; Pedace, 2008).

Gambling

There is a close analogy, if not identity in many cases, between financial markets and betting markets. In each case, an investment is made in expectation of a risky return, and perhaps the only real difference is that gamblers are usually presumed to derive direct pleasure (utility) from risk taking, whereas investors in financial markets are assumed to be purely motivated by the financial returns (e.g., Friedman & Savage, 1948; Conlisk, 1993). For an early review of gambling markets, see Sauer (1998).

One of the key issues in the finance literature is the efficiency with which publicly available information is incorporated into the price of financial assets. If the efficiency is low, then in principle it is possible to devise an investment strategy based on public information that generates a guaranteed return. Gambling markets have been extensively studied to see whether such guaranteed returns can be found there (e.g., Ali, 1977, 1979; Asch, Malkiel, & Quandt, 1982; Gabriel & Marsden, 1990; Dolbear, 1993; Busche, 1994; Dixon & Pope, 2004; Forrest, Goddard, & Simmons, 2005).

By and large, the evidence has shown that betting markets are close to being efficient in the sense of incorporating all available information, but there is some evidence of anomalies (e.g., Thaler & Ziemba, 1988). Of particular interest has been the favorite–long shot bias—the observation that the publicly available odds tend to understate the probability that the favorite will win (e.g., Hurley & McDonough, 1995; Williams & Paton, 1997). Some interesting research has sought to rationalize this observation (e.g., Shin, 1992; Ottaviani & Sørensen, 2003), which implies that systematically betting on favorites will generate guaranteed profits.

Game Theory

A particularly interesting application of sport data has been made to the testing of propositions from game theory, which deals with situations where the payoff (e.g., profit, happiness) of each player in the game depends on the actions of the other players (as well as their own actions). In such cases, the formulation of a strategy involves considering the best response to the actions of the other players. In many situations, this best response is what is called a pure strategy, which means taking a single action calculated to maximize the player's payoff, but it is possible to show in theory that in many situations the player's best response is a mixed strategy, which involves selecting an action with some probability. This is as if people decided what to do by flipping a coin even though the player is not indifferent to the final outcome (also known as randomization).

Theorists have found it hard to persuade a skeptical world that real players will adopt such strategies. In laboratory conditions where volunteers play simple games for small sums of money, there is some evidence of randomization, but the evidence has tended to show that players do not choose the optimal strategies identified in theory. Sport provides a number of situations where mixed strategies make sense and where the actions of players can be tested to see whether they are optimal. One example involves soccer penalty kicks, where a strategy of always kicking to the same side of the goal is clearly inferior to sometimes shooting to the left and sometimes to the right; however, the pattern followed by penalty takers must also be random, since simply alternating between left and right would be a predictable strategy and thus would increase the chance that the goalkeeper would save the ball. Independent research by Chiappori, Levitt, and Groseclose (2002) and Palacios-Huerta (2003) showed that penalty takers do indeed seem to follow mixed strategies that are indistinguishable from optimal mixed strategies.

Similarly, Walker and Wooders (2001) found that tennis players also demonstrate an optimal mixed strategy in their choices about whether to return the ball to the left or right side of the court.

Conclusions

It is suggested at the start of this chapter that economics can be considered an *imperial* social science, always seeking out new fields of inquiry into which to expand its hegemony. The chapter documents the recent expansion of economic analysis into every manner of sport-related activity, including, for example, professional league sports, public infrastructure projects, and health and public welfare. Whatever the validity of economic approaches as compared with the alternatives, economists tend to wield significant influence on businesses and governments, who often seek the protection of economic analysis to justify their actions. Increasingly, people who never thought about economic models—from disgruntled fans of bankrupt soccer clubs to boosters seeking to attract the next major sporting event to their city—have found themselves needing to understand the economic approach to analyzing sport. At the same time, economists have found themselves increasingly working with researchers from other social and natural sciences—for example, with sociologists on issues such as crowd violence and hooliganism and with physiologists on the benefits of physical activity.

There is no doubt that this expansion will continue, and it seems that a clear pattern has emerged. The principal route to career advancement in academic economics is through publication of articles in peer-reviewed journals. A small community of researchers, mainly in North America and Europe, have established journals and associations to pursue the specific issues that arise in sport. Mainstream economics journals publish this material relatively rarely, given that it tends to reflect a narrower interest in sport; however, these journals do increasingly publish innovative papers, often written by researchers who do not have a specific interest in sport but are using data generated from sport activities. This "sport laboratory" effect seems to be making the academic study of sport economics more and more respectable.

There remain many unanswered questions and avenues for research, and speculation about future directions must inevitably reflect the preferences of the writer. My own opinion is that in the past too much research in sport economics has focused on data collection, without enough consideration of theoretical underpinnings. In many cases, this has resulted from the fact that the data are too poor to permit structural analysis or to address the ever-present problems of identification and inferring causality. I think that the richer data sets beginning to emerge offer the prospect that more careful testing of theory will become feasible.

The most important area for future research, in my opinion, is the relationship between sport and physical activity. Although this has not been the traditional focus of the field, it is surely one of the most important policy issues facing governments today. Is the promotion of sport an effective way to promote healthy lifestyles among the populace? If so, how? Convincing answers to these questions promise very high returns.

References

Ali, M. (1977). Probability and utility estimates for racetrack bettors. *Journal of Political Economy, 85*(4), 803–815.

Ali, M. (1979). Some evidence of the efficiency of a speculative market. *Econometrica, 47*(2), 387–392.

Allmers, S., & Maennig, W. (2009). Economic impacts of the FIFA soccer World Cups in France 1998, Germany 2006, and outlook for South Africa 2010. *Eastern Economic Journal, 35*(4), 500–519.

Andreff, W. (Ed.). (2011). *Recent developments in the economics of sport*. Cheltenham, UK: Elgar.

Andreff, W., & Staudohar, P. (2000). The evolving European model of professional sports finance. *Journal of Sports Economics, 1*(3), 257–276.

Andreff, W., & Szymanski, S. (Eds.). (2006). *Handbook on the economics of sport*. Cheltenham, UK: Elgar.

Asch, P., Malkiel, B., & Quandt, R. (1982). Racetrack betting and informed behavior. *Journal of Financial Economics, 10*, 187–194.

Atkinson, G., Mourata, S., Szymanski, S., & Ozdemiroglu, E. (2008). Are we willing to pay enough to "back the bid"?: Valuing the intangible impacts of London's bid to host the 2012 Summer Olympic Games. *Urban Studies, 45*(2), 419–444.

Baade, R. (1996). Professional sports as catalysts for metropolitan economic development. *Journal of Urban Affairs, 18*(1), 1–17.

Baade, R., & Matheson, V. (2002). Bidding for the Olympics: Fool's gold? In C.P. Barros, M. Ibrahimo, & S. Szymanski (Eds.), *Transatlantic sport: The comparative economics of North American and European sports* (pp. 127–151). London: Elgar.

Baade, R., & Matheson, V. (2004). The quest for the Cup: Assessing the economic impact of the World Cup. *Regional Studies, 38*(4), 341–352.

Baade, R.A., & Dye, R.E. (1988). An analysis of the economic rationale for public subsidization of sports stadiums. *Annals of Regional Science, 22*(2), 37–47.

Baade, R.A., & Dye, R.E. (1990). The impact of stadiums and professional sports on metropolitan area development. *Growth and Change, 21*(2), 1–14.

Barros, C.P., & Leach, S. (2006a). Performance evaluation of the English Premier Football League with Data Envelopment Analysis. *Applied Economics, 38*, 1449–1458.

Barros, C.P., & Leach, S. (2006b). Analysing the performance of the English F.A. Premier League with an econometric frontier model. *Journal of Sports Economics, 7*, 391–407.

Bassett, D.R., Jr., Pucher, J., Buehler, R., Thompson, D.L., & Crouter, S.E. (2008). Walking, cycling, and obesity rates in Europe, North America, and Australia. *Journal of Physical Activity and Health, 5*, 795–814.

Becker, G. (1971). *The economics of discrimination* (2nd ed.). Chicago: University of Chicago Press.

Bellemore, F.A. (2001). Racial and ethnic employment discrimination: Promotion in Major League Baseball. *Journal of Sports Economics, 2*, 356–368.

Berri, D., Michael, A., Leeds, A. Marikova, E., Mondello, M. (2009.) The Role of Managers in Team Performance. *International Journal of Sport Finance, Fitness Information Technology, 4*(2), 75-93, May.

Berri, D., & Schmidt, M. (2010). *Stumbling on wins.* Upper Saddle River, NJ: FT Press.

Berri, D., Schmidt, M., & Brook, S. (2006). *The wages of wins: Taking measure of the many myths in modern sports.* Palo Alto: Stanford University Press.

Biddle, A.J.H, Goreley, T., & Stensel, D.J. (2004). Health-enhancing physical activity and sedentary behaviour in children and adolescents. *Journal of Sports Sciences, 22*, 679–701.

Bodvarsson, Ö., & Partridge, M.D. (2001). A supply and demand model of co-worker, employer, and customer discrimination. *Labour Economics, 8*(2), 389–416.

Borland, J., & Macdonald, R. (2003). Demand for sport. *Oxford Review of Economic Policy, 19*, 478–498.

Brown, R. W., & Jewell, K. T. (1994). Is there customer discrimination in college basketball? The premium fans pay for White American players. *Social Science Quarterly, 75*(2), 401-413.

Burdekin, R., and Idson, T.L., (1991). Customer Preferences, Attendance and the Racial Structure of Professional Basketball Teams. *Applied Economics,* 23:1, Part B, 179-186.

Burdekin, R.C., Hossfeld, R.T., & Smith, J.K. (2005). Are NBA fans becoming indifferent to race? Evidence from the 1990s. *Journal of Sports Economics, 6,*144–159.

Busche, K. (1994). Efficient market results in an Asian setting. In D. Hausch, V. Lo, & W.T. Ziemba (Eds.), *Efficiency of racetrack betting markets* (pp. 615–616). New York: Academic Press.

Carlino G., & Coulson, E. (2004). Compensating differentials and the social benefits of the NFL. *Journal of Urban Economics, 56*(1), 25–50.

Carmichael, F., Thomas, D., & Ward, R. (2000). Team performance: The case of English Premiership Football. *Managerial and Decision Economics, 21*(1), 31–45.

Cervero, R., & Duncan, M. (2003). Walking, bicycling, and urban landscapes: Evidence from the San Francisco Bay Area. *American Journal of Public Health, 93*(9), 1478–1483.

Chiappori, P.A., Levitt, S.D., & Groseclose, T. (2002). Testing mixed strategy equilibrium when players are heterogeneous: The case of penalty kicks. *American Economic Review, 92,* 1138–1151.

Clapp, C.M., & Hakes, J.K. (2005). How long a honeymoon? The effect of new stadiums on attendance in Major League Baseball. *Journal of Sports Economics, 6,* 237–263.

Coase, R. (1960). The problem of social cost. *Journal of Law and Economics, 3,* 1–44.

Coates, D., & Humphreys, B.R. (1999). The growth effects of sports franchises, stadia, and arenas. *Journal of Policy Analysis and Management, 18*(4), 601–624.

Coates, D., & Humphreys, B.R. (2001). The economic consequences of professional sports strikes and lockouts. *Southern Economic Journal, 67*(3), 737–747.

Coates, D., & Humphreys, B.R. (2002). The economic impact of postseason play in professional sports. *Journal of Sports Economics, 3*(3), 291–299.

Coates, D., & Humphreys, B.R. (2003). The effect of professional sports on earnings and employment in the services and retail sectors in U.S. cities. *Regional Science and Urban Economics, 33,*175–198.

Coates, D., Humphreys, B., & Zimbalist, A. (2006). Compensating differentials and the social benefits of the NFL: A comment. *Journal of Urban Economics, 60*(1), 124–131.

Coleman, B. J., DuMond, J.M., & Lynch, A.K. (2008). An examination of NBA MVP voting behavior: Does race matter? *Journal of Sports Economics, 9*(6), 606–627.

Conlisk, J. (1993). The utility of gambling. *Journal of Risk and Uncertainty, 6*(3), 255–275.

Cornwell, C., & Schmidt, P. (2008). Stochastic frontier analysis and efficiency estimation. *The Econometrics of Panel Data: Advanced Studies in Theoretical and Applied Econometrics, 46*(3), 697–726.

Crompton, J.L. (1995). Economic impact analysis of sports facilities and events: Eleven sources of misapplication. *Journal of Sport Management, 9*(1), 14–35.

Dawson, P., Dobson S., & Gerrard, B. (2000a). Stochastic frontiers and the temporal structure of managerial efficiency in English soccer. *Journal of Sports Economics, 1*(4), 341–362.

Dawson, P., Dobson S., & Gerrard, B. (2000b). Estimating coaching efficiency in professional team sports: Evidence from English Association football. *Scottish Journal of Political Economy, 47*(4), 399–421.

Dixon, M.J., & Pope, P.F. (2004). The value of statistical forecasts in the UK association football betting market. *International Journal of Forecasting, 20,* 697–711.

Dolbear, T., Jr. (1993). Is racetrack betting on exactas efficient? *Economica, 60*(237), 105–111.

Eckard, E.W. (2006). Comment: Professional team sports are only a game: The Walrasian fixed-supply conjecture model, contest-Nash equilibrium, and the invariance principle. *Journal of Sports Economics, 7,* 234–239.

El-Hodiri, M., & Quirk, J. (1971). An economic model of a professional sports league. *Journal of Political Economy, 79,* 1302–1319.

Espitia-Escuer, M., & García-Cebrián, L.I. (2004). Measuring the efficiency of Spanish First-Division soccer teams. *Journal of Sports Economics, 5,* 329–346.

Fizel, J., & D'Itri, M. (1997). Managerial efficiency, managerial succession, and organizational performance. *Managerial and Decision Economics, 18*(4), 295–308.

Foley, M., & Smith, F.H. (2007). Consumer discrimination in professional sports: new evidence from major league baseball. *Applied Economics Letters, 14*(13), 951-955.

Forrest, D., Goddard, J., & Simmons, R. (2005). Odds-setters as forecasters: The case of English football. *International Journal of Forecasting, 21,* 551–564.

Forrest, D., & McHale, I. (2009). *Public policy, sport, and happiness: An empirical study.* Working paper, Salford University.

Forrest, D., & Simmons, R. (2002). Outcome uncertainty and attendance demand in sport: The case of English soccer. *The Statistician, 51,* 229–241.

Forrest, D., Simmons, R., & Szymanski, S. (2004). Broadcasting, attendance, and the inefficiency of cartels. *Review of Industrial Organization, 24,* 243–265.

Fort, R. (2004). Inelastic sports pricing. *Managerial and Decision Economics, 25,* 87–94.

Fort, R., & Quirk, J. (1995). Cross subsidization, incentives, and outcomes in professional team sports leagues. *Journal of Economic Literature, 33*(3), 1265–1299.

Fort, R., & Winfree, J. (2009). Sports really are different: The contest success function and the supply of talent. *Review of Industrial Organization, 34,*69–80.

Frey, B.S., & Stutzer, A. (2002). Happiness and economics: How the economy and institutions affect well-being. Princeton, NJ: Princeton University Press.

Frick, B. (2007). The football players' labor market: Empirical evidence from the major European leagues. *Scottish Journal of Political Economy, 54,* 422–446.

Friedman, M., & Savage, L.J. (1948). The utility analysis of choices involving risk. *Journal of Political Economy, 56*(4), 279–304.

Gabriel, P., & Marsden, J. (1990). An examination of market efficiency in British racetrack betting. *Journal of Political Economy, 98*(4), 874–885.

García-Sánchez, I.M. (2007). Efficiency and effectiveness of Spanish football teams: A three stage-DEA approach. *Central European Journal of Operations Research, 15,* 21–45.

Gerdtham, U-G., & Johannesson, M. (2001). The relationship between happiness, health, and socioeconomic factors: Results based on Swedish microdata. *Journal of Socio-Economics, 30,* 553–557.

Gius, M., & Johnson, D. (1998). An empirical investigation of wage discrimination in professional basketball. *Applied Economics Letters, 5*(11), 703–705.

Goddard, J., & Wilson, J.O.S. (2009). Racial discrimination in English professional football: Evidence from an empirical analysis of players' career progression. *Cambridge Journal of Economics, 33,* 295–316.

Groothuis, P.A., & Hill, J.R. (2004). Exit discrimination in the NBA: A duration analysis of career length. *Economic Inquiry, 42*(2), 341–349.

Grossman, M. (1972). On the concept of health capital and the demand for health. *Journal of Political Economy, 80,* 223–255.

Grossman, M. (1999). *The human capital model of the demand for health.* Working paper 7078, National Bureau of Economic Research.

Guttmann, A. (1978). From ritual to record: The nature of modern sports. New York: Columbia University Press.

Gwartney, J., & Haworth, C. (1974). Employer costs and discrimination: The case of baseball. *Journal of Political Economy, 82*(4), 873–881.

Haas, D.J. (2003a). Technical efficiency in Major League Soccer. *Journal of Sports Economics, 4,* 203–215.

Haas, D.J. (2003b). Productive efficiency of English football teams: A data envelopment approach. *Managerial and Decision Economics, 24,* 403–410.

Haas, D.J., Kocher, M.G., & Sutter, M. (2004). Measuring efficiency of German football teams by Data Envelopment Analysis. *Central European Journal of Operations Research, 12,* 251–268.

Hakes, J., & Sauer, R. (2006). An economic evaluation of the Moneyball hypothesis. *Journal of Economic Perspectives, 20*(3), 173–185.

Hamilton, B.H. (1997). Racial discrimination and professional basketball salaries in the 1990s. *Applied Economics, 29*(3), 287–296.

Hanssen, A. (1998). The cost of discrimination: A study of Major League Baseball. *Southern Economic Journal, 64*(3), 603–627.

Hanssen, A.F., & Andersen, T. (1999). Has discrimination lessened over time? A test using baseball's all-star vote. *Economic Inquiry, 37,* 326–352.

Hearings before the Subcommittee on Study of Monopoly Power of the Committee on the Judiciary of the House of Representatives (82nd Cong., 1st sess.), Serial no. 1, Part 6: Organized baseball. (1952). Washington, DC: U.S. Government Printing Office.

Hirshleifer, J. (1991). The paradox of power. *Economics and Politics, 3,* 177–200.

Hoehn T., & Szymanski, S. (1999). The Americanization of European Football. *Economic Policy,* No. 28, 205-233.

Hotchkiss, J., Moore, R.E., & Zobay S.M. (2003). Impact of the 1996 Summer Olympic Games on employment and wages in Georgia. *Southern Economic Journal, 69,* 691-704.

Huang, H., & Humphreys, B. (2010). Sports participation and happiness: Evidence from U.S. Micro Data. Working paper 2010-09, University of Alberta.

Hudson, I. (2001). The use and misuse of economic impact analysis: The case of professional sports. *Journal of Sport and Social Issues, 25*(1), 20–39.

Humphreys, B.R., & Ruseski, J.E. (2007). Participation in physical activity and government spending on parks and recreation. *Contemporary Economic Policy, 25*(4), 538–552.

Hurley, W., & McDonough, L. (1995). A note on the Hayek Hypothesis and the favorite-longshot bias in parimutuel betting. *American Economic Review, 85*(4), 949–955.

James, B. (1982). *The Bill James baseball abstract, 1982.* New York: Ballantine Books

Jeanrenaud, C., & Késenne, S. (Eds.). (1999). *Player market regulation in professional team sports.* Antwerp: Standaard Uitgeverij.

Johnson, B.K., Groothuis, P.A., & Whitehead, J.C. (2002). The value of public goods generated by a major league sports team: The CVM approach. *Journal of Sports Economics, 2*(1), 6–21.

Johnson, B.K., & Whitehead, J.C. (2000). The value of public goods from sports stadiums: The CVM approach. *Contemporary Economic Policy, 18*(1), 48–58.Kahane, L.H. (2005). Production efficiency and discriminatory hiring practices in the National Hockey League: A stochastic frontier approach. *Review of Industrial Organization, 27,* 47–71.

Kahn, L. (1993). Managerial quality, team success, and individual player performance in Major League Baseball. *.Industrial and Labor Relations Review, 46*(3), 531–547.

Kahn, L.M. (1991). Discrimination in professional sports: A survey of the literature. *Industrial and Labor Relations Review, 44*, 395–418.

Kahn, L.M. (2000). The sports business as a labor market laboratory. *Journal of Economic Perspectives, 14*(3), 75–94.

Kahn, L.M. (2006). Race, performance, pay, and retention among National Basketball Association head coaches. *Journal of Sports Economics, 7*, 119–149.

Kahn, L.M., & Sherer, P.D. (1988). Racial differences in professional basketball players' compensation. *Journal of Labor Economics, 6*, 40–61.

Kavetsos, G. (2011). Physical activity and subjective well-being: An empirical analysis. In P. Rodriguez, S. Késenne, & B. Humphreys (Eds.), *The economics of sport, health, and happiness: The promotion of well-being through sporting activities.* Cheltenham, UK: Elgar.

Kavetsos, G., & Szymanski, S. (2010). National well-being and international sports events. *Journal of Economic Psychology, 31*(2),158–171.

Késenne, S. (1996). League management in professional team sports with win maximizing clubs. *European Journal for Sport Management, 2*(2), 14–22.

Konrad, K. (2007). Strategy in contests: An introduction. WZB-Markets and Politics Working Paper No. SP II 2007-01.

Lago, U., Simmons, R., & Szymanski, S. (Eds.). (2006). The financial crisis in European football [Special issue]. *Journal of Sports Economics, 7*(3).

Lewis, M. (2003). Moneyball: The art of winning an unfair game. New York: Norton.

Madden, J.F. (2004). Differences in the success of NFL coaches by race, 1990–2002: Evidence of last hire, first fire. *Journal of Sports Economics, 5*, 6–19.

Madden, J.R. (2006). Economic and fiscal impacts of mega sporting events: A general equilibrium assessment. *Public Finance and Management, 6*(3), 346–394.

Madden, P. (2011). Game theoretic analysis of basic team sports leagues. *Journal of Sports Economics, 12*(4), 407–431.

Noll, R.G., & Zimbalist, A. (1997). *Sports, jobs, and taxes: The economic impact of sports teams and stadiums.* Washington, DC: Brookings Institution Press.

Oja, P., Vuori, I., & Paronen, O. (1998). Daily walking and cycling to work: Their utility as health enhancing physical activity. *Patient Education and Counselling, 33*, S87–S94.

Oswald, A., & Powdthavee, N. (2007). Obesity, unhappiness, and the challenge of affluence. *Economic Journal, 117*, F441–F459.

Ottaviani, M.., & Sørensen, P.N. (2003). Late informed betting and the favourite-longshot bias. Centre for Economic Policy Research Discussion Paper 4092.

Palacios-Huerta, I. (2003). Professionals play minimax. *Review of Economic Studies, 70*(2), 395–415.

Pascal, A.H., & Rapping, L.A. (1972). The economics of racial discrimination in organized baseball. In A.H. Pascal (Ed.), *Racial discrimination in economic life* (pp. 119–156). Lexington, MA.: Heath.

Pate, R.R., Pratt, M., Blair, S.N., Haskell, W.L., Macera, C.A., & Bouchard, C. (1995). Physical activity and public health: A recommendation from the Centers for

Disease Control and Prevention and the American College of Sports Medicine. *Journal of the American Medical Association, 275*(5), 402–407.

Pedace, R. (2008). Earnings, performance, and nationality discrimination in a highly competitive labor market as an analysis of the English professional soccer league. *Journal of Sports Economics, 9,* 115–140.

Porsche, M., & Maennig, W. (2008). The feel-good factor at mega sport events. Recommendations for public and private administration informed by the experience of the FIFA World Cup 2006. Hamburg Contemporary Economic Discussion Paper No.18, University of Hamburg.

Porter, P.K. (1999). Mega-sports events as municipal investments: A critique of impact analysis. In J. Fizel, E. Gustafson, & L. Hadley (Eds.), *Sports Economics: Current Research* (pp. 61–74). Westport, CT: Prager.

Preuss, H. (2004). *Economics of the Olympic Games.* London: Elgar.

Price, J., & Wolfers, J. (2007). Racial discrimination among NBA referees. National Bureau of Economic Research Working Paper 13206. Cambridge, MA: National Bureau of Economic Research.

Pucher, J., & Dijkstra, L. (2003). Promoting safe walking and cycling to improve public health: Lessons from The Netherlands and Germany. *American Journal of Public Health, 93*(9), 1509–1516.

Quirk, J., & El-Hodiri, M. (1974). The economic theory of a professional sports league. In R.G. Noll (Ed.), *Government and the sports business* (pp. 33–80). Washington, DC: Brookings Institution.

Rascher, D.A., & Solmes, J.P.G. (2007). Do fans want close contests? A test of the uncertainty of outcome hypothesis in the National Basketball Association. *International Journal of Sport Finance, 2,* 130–141.

Rasciute, S., & Downward, P. (2010). Health or happiness? What is the impact of physical activity on the individual? *Kyklos, 63*(2), 256–270.

Robbins, L. (1932). *An essay on the nature and significance of economic science.* London: Macmillan.

Rosen, S., & Sanderson, A. (2001). Labour markets in professional sports. *Economic Journal, 111,* F47–F68.

Rottenberg, S. (1956). The baseball players' labor market. *Journal of Political Economy, 44*(3), 242–258.

Sauer, R. (1998). The economics of wagering markets. *Journal of Economic Literature, 36*(4), 2021–2064.

Schmidt, M., & Berri, D. (2001). Competitive balance and attendance: The case of Major League Baseball. *Journal of Sports Economics, 2*(2), 145–167.

Scully, D., Kremer, J., Meade, M., Graham, R., & Dudgeon, K. (1999). Physical exercise and psychological well-being: A critical review. *British Journal of Sports Medicine, 32,* 11–20.

Scully, G. (1974). Pay and performance in Major League Baseball. *American Economic Review, 64,* 915–930.

Scully, G. (1994). Managerial efficiency and survivability in professional team sports. *Managerial and Decision Economics, 15*(5), 403–411.

Shin, H.S. (1992). Prices of state contingent claims with insider traders, and the favourite-longshot bias. *Economic Journal, 102,* 426–435.

Shmanske, S., & Kahane, L. (2012). *The Oxford handbook of sports economics* (Vols. 1–2). New York: Oxford University Press.

Siegfried, J., & Zimbalist, A. (2000). The economics of sports facilities and their communities. *Journal of Economic Perspectives, 14*(3), 95–114.

Sloane, P.J. (1969). The labour market in professional football. *British Journal of Industrial Relations, 7*(2), 181–199.

Sloane, P.J. (1971). The economics of professional football: The football club as a utility maximizer. *Scottish Journal of Political Economy, 17*(2), 121–146.

Smith, A., & Bird, S. (2004). From evidence to policy: Reflections on emerging themes in health related physical activity. *Journal of Sports Sciences, 22,* 791–799.

Sport Industry Research Centre (Sheffield Hallam University). (2010). 2004 sport satellite account for the UK. Working paper. London: Department for Culture, Media, and Sport.

Stigler, G.J. (1984). Economics—The imperial science? *Scandinavian Journal of Economics, 86*(3), 301.

Sullivan, D.A. (Ed.). (1995). *Early innings: A documentary history of baseball, 1825–1908.* Lincoln, NE.: University of Nebraska Press

Szymanski, S. (2000). A market test for discrimination in the English professional soccer leagues. *Journal of Political Economy, 108,* 590–603.

Szymanski, S. (2003). The economic design of sporting contests. *Journal of Economic Literature, 51,* 1137–1187.

Szymanski, S. (2004). Professional team sports are only a game: The Walrasian fixed-supply conjecture model, Contest-Nash equilibrium, and the invariance principle. *Journal of Sports Economics, 5*(2), 111–126.

Szymanski, S. (2006). Competitive balance in sports leagues and the paradox of power. International Association of Sport Economists Working Paper 0618.

Szymanski, S., & Késenne, S. (2004). Competitive balance and gate revenue sharing in team sports. *Journal of Industrial Economics, 52*(1), 165–177.

Szymanski, S., & Kuypers, T. (1999). *Winners and losers: The business strategy of football.* London: Penguin.

Thaler, R., & Ziemba, W. (1988). Anomalies—Parimutuel betting markets: Racetracks and lotteries. *Journal of Economic Perspectives, 2*(2), 161–174.

Tullock, G. (1980). Efficient rent seeking. In J. Buchanan, R Tollison, & G. Tullock (Eds.), *Toward a theory of rent seeking society* (pp. 97–112). College Station: Texas A&M University Press.

Vrooman J. (1995). A general theory of professional sports leagues. *Southern Economic Journal, 61*(4), 971–990.

Vrooman, J. (2007). Theory of the beautiful game: The unification of European football. *Scottish Journal of Political Economy, 54*(3), 314–354.

Walker, M., & Wooders, J. (2001). Minimax play at Wimbledon. *American Economic Review, 91,* 1521–1538.

Wendel-Vos, G.C.W, Schuit, A.J., Feskens, E.J.M., Boshuizen, H.C., Verschuren, W.M.M., Saris, W.H.M., et al. (2004). Physical activity and stroke. A meta-analysis of observational data. *International Journal of Epidemiology, 33*, 787–798.

Williams, L.V., & Paton, D. (1997). Why is there a favorite-longshot bias in British racetrack betting markets? *Economic Journal, 107*(440), 150–158.

Wilson, D.P., & Ying, Y.H. (2003). Nationality preferences for labour in the international football industry. *Applied Economics, 35*, 1551–1560.

Zimbalist A. (1992). *Baseball and Billions*. New York: Basic Books.

Zimbalist, A. (Ed.). (2001). *The economics of sport*. Cheltenham, UK: Elgar.

CHAPTER 9

Political Science and Sport

Jonathan Grix, PhD

It is fair to say that mainstream political science has been relatively slow to engage with the academic study of sport. This is surprising given the political nature of most sport disciplines, sporting events, their resourcing, and the instrumental use of sport by states both nowadays and throughout history. Active government intervention in sport—especially in terms of its development and funding—has increased greatly in the past 30 years, but political scientists have lagged in analyzing these developments. The majority of work carried out hitherto falls under the rubrics of public administration and policy studies, both of which are subcategories of political science. Policy is, of course, the end result of much political contestation, and many scholars have drawn upon the tools of policy studies to shed light on developments in this area. This chapter introduces the sparse work on sport from political science, the greater body of work on sport policy, and the area of study that one could term "politics and/of sport" or, simply, sport politics. This latter is an umbrella heading for a number of studies from outside the mainstream of political science with a central focus on the political aspects of sport.

The United Kingdom offers a good example of increasing government intervention in sport. Many of the developments discussed, however, are relevant and similar to those in a number of advanced capitalist states. The political salience of sport has increased since the 1960s—rapidly in the last two decades—and grassroots sport, including school and community sport and elite performance sport, have risen sharply up the political agenda. Moreover, after the Labour party came to power in 1997, the word "sport" featured, for the first time in British politics, in the title of a government department—the Department for Culture, Media, and Sport. In addition, the decision in 2005 to award London the 2012 Olympics added impetus to a process already under way, and sport has become a cross-departmental policy area that appears to offer the government an "extremely malleable resource to achieve . . . a wide variety of domestic and international goals" (Houlihan & Green, 2008, p. 3). Benefits claimed for sport include fighting obesity—hence reducing the burden on the National Health Service—as well as enhancing social inclusion, generating social capital, contributing to citizens' general well-being, and contributing to world peace. Given such "claim inflation," one would expect a wealth of data evidencing sport's potential. Sadly, this is not the case, and, apart from a section of literature in health studies, the evidence base for sport's ability to effect change is very limited indeed (see Coalter, 2007).

Elite sport funding has been greatly increased in a majority of advanced capitalist states as they attempt to use sporting success to bolster their image and international prestige (more on this later in the chapter). In the United Kingdom, elite sport has received unprecedented sums of funding (more than £300 million [roughly US$450 million] toward Olympic sports from 2008 to 2012) for the purpose of producing world-class athletes and Olympic medals (Department for Culture, Media, and Sport, 2008). The government's rationale and justification for such support of elite sport hinge on the idea that, among other things, the success of athletes produces among watching citizens a "feel-good factor" and thus the likelihood that they will be inspired to participate in sport; this, then, produces a pool of healthy people, from which the elite stars of the future will come. This supposed pattern I term a "virtuous cycle" of sport and discuss in more detail later in relation to the growing tendency of states to invest in elite sport (and the staging of mega-sporting events) as a resource for international prestige.

Before turning to the study of political aspects of sport by political scientists and other scholars, I introduce the discipline of political science, briefly outlining its focus of study. The interpretation of just what is political not only differs between academics but also greatly affects what is subsequently studied. I go on to suggest a way of dividing up political science according to key research paradigms and theoretical perspectives—and explain what these and other terms mean—before discussing some central concepts in political science and how they are, or could be, applied to the study of sport.

Core Concepts in Political Science

The term "political science" is as contested as the subject matter that falls under the scrutiny of those who practice it. Debates rage both over what is political and whether the discipline is truly scientific. For the purposes of this introductory section, I touch only briefly on these disputes. The first thing to note, however, is that no discipline is neatly confined to certain areas of study or to the use of specific research methods, theories, and methodologies. Much of the debate in political science, for example, is about just this: What counts as political? What is the "legitimate terrain of political enquiry?" (Hay, 2002, p. 59). If there is little agreement on this fundamental question, matters become more confusing when scholars discuss the way in which political science ought to go about finding out what it is they think worthy of study—be it an institution, an individual's behavior, or a policy decision.

These fundamental realities of the discipline are the same for all other academic branches of knowledge, and they touch on the foundations of research. Political scientists—and many sociologists—are very keen to discuss the ontological and epistemological underpinnings of research (Grix, 2002). These difficult-sounding concepts, once unpacked, relate simply to what I have already discussed. Ontology and epistemology can be considered as the foundations upon which research is built. Ontology is the starting point of all research, after which one's epistemological and methodological positions logically follow. A dictionary definition of the term usually describes it as something like "the image of social reality upon which a theory is based," which is not a great deal of help to those of us seeking clarity. Blaikie (2000, p. 8) offers a fuller definition, suggesting that ontological claims are "claims and assumptions that are made about the nature of social reality, claims about what exists, what it looks like, what units make it up and how these units interact with each other. In short, ontological assumptions are concerned with what we believe constitutes social reality." With this in mind, it is not difficult to understand how different scholarly traditions embedded in fundamentally different cultural contexts can have diverging views. If ontology relates to what Hay terms the "political question"—that is, what is political—then epistemology captures the claims made about knowledge. Blaikie (2000) once again provides a way through the impenetrable prose employed in discussing these metatheoretical issues when he states that epistemology refers "to the claims or assumptions made about the ways in which it is possible to gain knowledge of reality," or how these assumptions are perceived to exist according to our ontological positions (see Grix, 2010a, for more on these concepts).

Another area of contestation in political science is whether the study of politics ought to restrict itself to the study of the formal operation of politics, its institutions, and the sphere of government or be driven by a definition of politics that "sees it (the 'political') as a social process that can be observed in a variety of settings" (Stoker & Marsh, 2002, p. 9; see also Leftwich, 2004; Hay, 2002). This latter understanding of politics highlights the power relations between parties—be they state and subject, husband and wife, or employer and employee. Wherever power lies, politics is said to be present. Further debate revolves around the word *science* in the term "political science," and numerous books and articles have discussed whether and to what extent the discipline can claim to be scientific (see R.E. Goodwin & Klingemann, 2000, pp. 9–10). In general, scholars working from within a positivist epistemological tradition (for an overview of the assumptions upon which it is based, see a later part of this chapter) subscribe to the view that the study of politics can be scientific (see Burnham, Gilland Lutz, Grant, & Layton-Henry, 2008). This group also tends to favor the narrow definition of politics, whereas the broader understanding of politics is generally advocated by scholars working with perspectives in any of the anti-positivist research paradigms (Marxism, feminism, interpretivism).

Whichever definition of politics is used, both camps in the discipline are bound by their "concern with the analysis of the origins, forms, distribution and control of power" (Leftwich, 2004, p. 2). From this concern are derived other central concepts such as authority, legitimacy, government, and governance (see Houlihan, 2008). Given that sport has been used by governments to maintain authority and gain political legitimacy domestically and internationally, it is astonishing that the topic has received so little attention from the discipline of political science.

Study of Sport and Politics

Before we look at the political use of sport made by states, it is worth reflecting on the dearth of academic research conducted by the very people one would assume might analyze the politics of sport: political scientists and international relations scholars. There are, of course, a number of exceptions (notably, Allison, 1986; Levermore, 2004; Houlihan, 1991; for more, see Grix, 2010b, and Grix, 2013a); however, there is no political science or international relations "literature" as such within which one could place one's own work. Much of the (good) work that does exist has been penned by sociologists, sport studies scholars, and especially historians, although, as Hill (2003) points out, not much historical work has been undertaken on the formal aspects of politics. Allen Guttmann surveys the work that historians have done concerning politics and sport and picks out a number of major themes from the vast, and diverse, extant literature. Of his themes, the most relevant for the current discussion involve scholars who have studied sport under fascism or communism and those who have focused their attention on the politics of the Olympics (Guttmann, 2003). These themes clearly overlap, and the Olympics has become a political site used by a variety of political regimes to promote their particular brand of ideology—and an event that drives, steers, and dominates sport policy making and policy cycles. These facts make the lack of analysis of sport by political scientists and international relations scholars even more surprising; indeed, sport as a political resource has been used and manipulated for thousands of years—since the Ancient Greeks and Romans—either externally in interstate relations or internally as, among other things, part of an attempt to create a sense of nationhood among citizens. As Roger Levermore (2004) rightly points out (see also chapter 10 in this volume), elite sport usually represents a nation in international competition, and a national team is often equated with its nation; given, then, that much of the understanding of international relations is focused on the unit of analysis of the state, it is easy to see the potential value in analyzing and understanding elite sport.

Avery Brundage (president of the International Olympic Committee from 1952 to 1972) was adamant that sport and politics do not mix when he stated that "sport . . . like music and the other fine arts, transcends politics. . . . We are concerned with sports, not politics and business" (IOC 1968, 10). Unfortunately, this view does not hold up in the light of a history of boycotts (e.g., the Moscow and Los Angeles Olympics), murder (the Munich Olympics), and sport events mirroring political struggles (e.g., Hungary vs. the USSR in water polo in 1956; see Strenk, 1979, for an excellent overview of political events in sport). Despite these and myriad other examples of the political instrumentalization of sport and sporting events, the studies of politics, international relations, and sport still suffer from a "case of mutual neglect" (Taylor, 1986). Nonetheless, Olympic medal counts—and, to a lesser extent, those of the Commonwealth Games—are still used actively by states as a barometer of their standing in the (sporting) world (Hilvoorde, Elling, & Stokvis, 2010).

In the 21st century, holding a mega-event such as the Olympics is very much a political decision, and sport-related aspects come in a distant second. Calculations by the host city or nation are based on the perceived international prestige and credibility that can be gained, as with the "consumer-communist" Games in Beijing in 2008, or on the urban regeneration and legacy that can be leveraged, as with the 2012 London Games. (I say more about mega-events later in this chapter; for more on the problems of defining legacy, see Grix, 2013a.) Yet, despite the increasing instrumentalization of sport for political means in the last 20 years—and the key questions that arise about policy making, delivery, governance, power, and resource allocation (that is, very much the core focus of much of political science)—only a handful of political scientists have turned their attention to this area of study. One of the reasons appears to be that the academic study of sport suffers from many of the same legitimacy problems as those disciplines with names that include the word *studies*. Academics who work within area studies, gender studies, German studies, and so on can find themselves defending the methodological rigor of their research against attacks from scholars who work in traditional disciplines. The same applies for the student of sport, which, often seen as simply a hobby, is not recognized, by some, as a serious area of study. This appears to be particularly the case in the United Kingdom and the United States, where the analysis and dissemination of research on politics and sport are generally not carried out in mainstream political science journals but in those specializing in sport (for exceptions, see Allison, 1998; Houlihan & Green, 2009; M. Goodwin & Grix, 2011; Grix & Phillpots, 2011). An early U.S. example is an article penned by Andrew Strenk in 1979 that manages to tersely outline the political nature of sport, which arguably has since greatly increased. More than 30 years ago, then, Strenk argued that

> *the tremendous investments being made by some countries in sports centers, facilities, training and talent development programs, medical and drug research and competitions have generated extreme pressure for success. Enormous human and natural resources are being directed towards producing and supporting star athletes and teams. . . . The idea of unpolitical sports is, and always has been, a myth. Modern sports are, indeed, a "war without weapons." (p. 140)*

In the United Kingdom, Lincoln Allison is one of the few political scientists to have turned his attention to sport. His two edited volumes (1986, 1993) dealing with a wide variety of topics touching on sport and politics are indicative of the rapid politicization of sport. The initial book was titled *The Politics of Sport*, and the follow-up, which came just seven years later, was titled *The Changing Politics of Sport* (see also Polley, 1998). The wide range of topics analyzed by Allison and his colleagues—the majority of whom are *not* political scientists—reveals the extent to which politics permeates sport, from obvious angles such as state and sport, the "politics of the Olympics," and "national identity and sport" through to more specific aspects such as "sport and ideology," "sport and law," and "elite sport policy." Despite Allison's efforts and subsequent work, the study of sport by political scientists in the United Kingdom has been conspicuous by its absence.

In the United States, with its thousands of political scientists and one of the most successful elite sport systems in the world, the story is the same: Leading academics who have written on sport and politics come from disciplines other than political science—for example, sociology (Markovits & Rensmann, 2010; Coakley, 2004) and marketing (Chalip, 2006).

The gap left by political scientists has been filled, to some extent, by a wide range of diverse authors concentrating on a variety of topics, many involving analysis of the very essence of politics as captured by Lasswell's immortal phrase: "who gets what, when and how" (Lasswell, 1936). This project has been carried out in panoramic fashion by historians (Guttmann, 2003; Polley, 1998; Hill, 2002), sociologists (Dunning, 1999; Elias, 2000; Jarvie, 1991; Bloyce & Smith, 2010), economists (Gratton & Taylor, 2001), and sport policy specialists (Houlihan, 1991, 1997, 2002; Houlihan & Green, 2005; Coalter, 2007). Gilchrist and Holden (2011) are correct when they suggest that "sport politics," or the study of the politics of sport, is emerging as a recognizable focus of scholars from a wide variety of disciplines—mostly *not* political science and international relations. This nascent yet growing literature has vastly expanded the notions of the "political" discussed earlier in this chapter, moving into areas unthinkable to traditional advocates of academic disciplines (see Gilchrist & Holden, 2011, for examples). However, given the fact that sport is a cultural institution with such a wide reach, affecting many people's lives in a variety of ways (e.g., from player to spectator, gambler to match maker, politician to policy), it could be argued that an interdisciplinary approach is needed in order to fully understand sport's role in society.

It is neither my intention nor my task in what follows to present a review of the vast literature dealing with politics and sport across the academic disciplines (see Houlihan, 2002, for a good overview). Rather, I seek to introduce the study of sport using a specific concept from political science—that of governance—and to give an example of a political analysis of elite sport investment by states (in this case, the United Kingdom). Both small case studies illuminate a political science approach to the study of sport. First, however, I introduce the core research paradigms and research perspectives that make up the discipline of political science.

Research Paradigms and Theoretical Perspectives in Political Science

My task here is unusual in that I indicate the potential of a selection of political science perspectives for the study of sport, even if there is little actual literature applied to sport politics to point to by way of demonstration. A number of caveats ought to be discussed about the following depiction. First, as Hay (2002) rightly points out, the practice of rehearsing dominant paradigmatic perspectives may serve to reinforce the artificial divisions that already exist within the discipline and to divert attention away from other, innovative perspectives. However, the student should never feel bound by established approaches to research and should seek to question and even modify existing and established approaches. Second, carving up an academic discipline for the purpose of explanation always brings with it the certainty that scholars themselves will disagree with the categories, terminology, and emphasis. Despite these warnings, a discussion of the heart of a discipline without reference to dominant, previously dominant, and different bodies of literature would suffer from being unable to see the forest for the trees (see Grix, 2010a, for more on research paradigms and perspectives in social science).

I introduce three broad research paradigms (see also Marsh & Furlong, 2002; Guba & Lincoln, 1998; Robson, 2002) and not two as is often done (see Denscombe, 2002, for a division into two neat, opposing paradigms). These three are the research paradigms you are likely to encounter in the political sciences, and this overview can help you place the main academic perspectives according to the research paradigms within which they operate. This exercise necessarily involves oversimplification but offers a route through the bewildering array of isms and ologies frequently used in discussions of metatheoretical and methodological issues.

Any form of categorization is likely to be imprecise and to leave out more than it contains. Yet research paradigms—that is, our ways of understanding *what* one can know about something and *how* one can gather knowledge about it (i.e., ontology and epistemology)—are inherent in every approach to the study of society. Generally, in the philosophy of the social and human sciences, there are three broad paradigms: the positivist, postpositivist, and interpretivist positions (an interpretivist position is *also* postpositivist; however, as I seek to make clear, these three particular paradigms act as umbrella terms for specific approaches to social inquiry). These positions are often labeled differently, which makes the discourse on this topic confusing.

Why is it important to understand the core paradigms in research? According to Clough and Nutbrown, who advise us *not* to elaborate on the assumptions underpinning our research, such research paradigms, or metatheories, are "*post hoc* frameworks for characterising the means and concerns of a given study. . . . Hence the idea of choice *between* broad approaches characterised in this way is ultimately spurious" (2002, p. 15). This is seemingly difficult to square with the view, which I share, that "[m]etatheory should . . . be a central feature in all planning of social science study, and should not be introduced *ad hoc*, since there is otherwise a great risk of the work being conducted in an unsystematic and inconsequent manner. In other words there should always be a clear connection between the ontological and epistemological starting points and the practical research work" (Danermark, Ekström, Jakobsen, & Karlsson, 2002, p. 4). Again, our starting point in research affects the rest of the research process. For this reason, the following discussion outlines the central tenets of the core research paradigms and highlights other names and varieties by which they may be known.

The Core of Positivism

Positivism—and those research perspectives I have associated with it—have formed the most dominant research paradigm of the past century. This, and the fact that more recent paradigms use it as a marker against which they seek to differentiate themselves, has led to a wealth of literature on the subject. For this reason, it receives a little more space here than the other two paradigms. Positivism—which, technically speaking, is an epistemological approach—is a very broad term under which many different approaches to social inquiry are known. Its historical legacy is said to stretch back to Aristotle and has been developed, in a variety of ways, by such figures as Francis Bacon, René Descartes, Auguste Comte, Thomas Hobbes, David Hume, John Stuart Mill, and Emile Durkheim (Hughes & Sharrock, 1997). Many of these key figures looked upon natural science as a model for the human sciences, seeking in the process to unearth a unitary methodology of the social and natural sciences. Other terms related to this broad rubric include empiricism, objectivism, the scientific method—by which positivism is clearly influenced—naturalism, and a naturalist approach (Marsh & Furlong, 2002). Although significant qualitative differences exist between all of these approaches, they tend to subscribe to the broad principles described here.

Most positivists assume that there is no dichotomy between what we see (appearance) and how things really are (reality) and that the world is real and neither mediated by our senses nor socially constructed (in contrast to realism and interpretivism; see Marsh & Furlong, 2002). Furthermore, the belief in causal statements is shared by realism but contrasts with the approach taken by interpretivism. Positivism places an emphasis on empirical theory in the production of knowledge; it rejects normative questions (e.g., questions of values or trust) and believes that social science can be value free (i.e., it believes in the value neutrality of researchers when investigating the social world). There is understandable attractiveness in an approach seeking the precision, exactitude, and power of prediction promised by the natural sciences. The human sciences can be messy, people can be unpredictable, and factors leading to events can be hard to unravel. Positivism attempts to overcome this messiness by seeking rules and laws with which to render the social world understandable.

Two core political science perspectives fall under this broad umbrella: rational choice theory (RCT) and behavioralism. RCT shares many of the same core assumptions that underlie neoclassical economics, realism (i.e., the international relations variety), functionalism (sociology), and empiricism (history). RCT tends to focus on the individual as the key unit of analysis and shares the notions of rationality and objectivity that are often associated with the neoclassical perspective in economics. Within RCT are a wide variety of approaches, ranging from hard to soft, where the former attempts to emulate the mathematical calculus of neoclassical economists' analyses and the latter incorporates elements of other perspectives, for example, institutionalism. The belief in the logic and power of the market held by neoclassical economists is mirrored in RCT by a belief in the utility-maximizing potential of the individual, as he or she is guided in life by specific preferences, irrespective of the context in which choices are made. Finally, RCT can be seen as an attempt to "import the rigour and predictive power of neo-classical economics into political science," while also trying to "model (mathematically) the implications of human rationality for political conduct" (Hay, 2002, p. 8).

Behavioralism was a dominant and unchallenged paradigm in political science (particularly the United States) in the 1950s and 1960s, and it is closely linked with specific research strategies—for example, probability-sampling techniques intended to find out what shaped electoral choice (Burnham et al., 2008). Behavioralists saw themselves as using a scientific approach that focused heavily on the observable, the idea that theories ought to be testable, and the notion that scholars should seek the regularities that make up politics. The demise of this approach in late 1960s was brought on in part by a challenge from scholars rediscovering the study of institutions (on the varieties of institutionalism, see Hay, 2002; Burnham et al., 2008; and Marsh & Stoker, 2002). Of interest to our current discussion is the rebirth of aspects of behavioralism through the publication of the book *Nudge* by Thaler and Sunstein (2008). This text has greatly influenced the U.S. and UK governments and public policy delivery in health and sport. The nudge agenda is underpinned by the assumption that government can change people's behavior, without resorting to legislation, by simply changing the environment in which people act, work, and live in order to encourage them to do what the government would like. For example, the Cabinet Office in the United Kingdom now has a Behavioural Insights Team that looks into ways to make the populace more physically active, thereby hoping to save more than £900 million [roughly US$1.4 billion] a year (Cabinet Office, 2010). With 6 of 10 UK adults overweight—at an estimated cost of £4 billion (roughly US$6 billion) per annum to the National Health Service—it is easy to understand why the government would want to promote sport and physical activity.

However, the criticisms of the original behavioral perspective remain: These "insights" and their remedies (in this case, sport) cannot be taken in isolation. While the government is "nudging" people to be more physically active, it is cutting funding for interventions that have been shown to do just that (e.g., the free swimming and gym membership system for all council taxpayers). Coalter (2007) has written extensively on the lack of *real* evidence for the alleged ability of sport to solve a number of society's ills and the difficulty of isolating sport's effect from other variables that influence a person's well-being. Finally, approaches stemming from a positivist paradigm are much more likely to be favored by governments, who want short-term, observable results associated with quantifiable data. The latter is often thought of as objective and scientific and therefore nearer to the truth. As we shall see, however, scholars working in different paradigms would struggle with and refute this latter aspiration.

In general, there is very little positivist work on sport and politics. We have discussed the lack of political scientists studying sport, but even among the vast literature that looks at the political in sport from the perspective of other disciplines, few are avowedly positivist, and there is no body of literature to speak of. Wakefield and Sloan's research (1995) into team loyalty and spectator attendance is one of the few subscribing to the objectivity that this approach promises (cited in Gratton & Jones, 2004).

The Core of Interpretivism

Interpretivism, on the other hand, is a wide umbrella term under which a great deal of work on sport could be categorized, albeit mostly from scholars in neighboring disciplines; indeed, this term covers just as many variations of approach to social inquiry as does positivism. Under this heading, we can gather, to name but a few, relativism, phenomenology, hermeneutics, idealism (the philosophical doctrine), symbolic interactionism, constructionism, and *Verstehen* (understanding), which is usually associated with the work of Max Weber (see Outhwaite, 1986) and which is the opposite of "explanation," though Weber's explanatory understanding makes it difficult to classify his body of work as interpretivism (see also Neuman, 2000; Blaikie, 2000). The key influences cited in relation to the interpretivist paradigm include the influential German thinkers Immanuel Kant, G.W.F. Hegel, Weber, Wilhelm Dilthey, and Hans-Georg Gadamer and the American sociologists George Herbert Mead, Ervin Goffman, and, more recently, Barney Glaser and Anselm Strauss. Again, qualitative differences exist between all of these approaches, but they have several things in common, the first of which is an anti-positivist position; that is, they oppose or refute the assumptions upon which a positivist understanding of the world is based.

Many studies in the sociology of sport (see chapter 5) would fall under this broad heading (see Donnelly, 2002, for a terse summary of the development of interpretive sociological approaches to sport). My own work has built on what could be termed the "interpretive turn" in political science—a very recent development drawing explicitly on the assumptions that underpin this paradigm and developing an approach to understanding the British state that is very different from the dominant positivist approaches. The pioneers of a decentralized approach to the study of government and governance built on interpretive assumptions were Mark Bevir and Rod Rhodes (2003, 2006, 2008). It is difficult to get across to those outside of political science—and especially those with knowledge of interpretivism—how much of a paradigm shift Bevir and Rhodes instigated. To the onlooker versed in interpretivist thought, such is the lack of work from this orientation in the discipline that the debate in political science can come across as if Bevir and Rhodes had developed the epistemology themselves. I explain their intervention in more detail later in the example of using governance to understand sport; for now, suffice it to say that my own work has attempted to carve out a political-interpretive approach—one that is very close to, but not the same as, critical realism (discussed in the next section). I put forward the notion of work on the border between the epistemological position of interpretivism and that of critical realism (Grix, 2010c). My intention is to show that research entering this border area consists of an *incremental* move, or a *gradation,* toward an epistemological approach, depending on one's direction of travel. And herein lies the rub. The distinctions between epistemological positions are often too stark (either positivist or interpretivist). In real-world research, gradations exist between positions. The real implication in terms of how scholars undertake research is that an interpretivist position *nearer* the border with post-positivism would indicate an acceptance of, or an appeal to, a greater role of structures and institutions in an explanation of, for example, the governance and function of County Sports Partnerships (local government-funded agency networks geared toward increasing participation in sport and physical activity) in the United Kingdom than would a "regular" interpretivist approach (see Grix & Phillpots, 2011, for the actual research).

The practical benefit of conceptualizing the border area between epistemologies as gradational is that it allows for a more precise positioning of scholars' research and a clearer understanding of the philosophical underpinnings of the subsequent (empirical) inquiry.

The Core of Postpositivism: Critical Realism

Postpositivism can be understood as a research paradigm placed between positivism and interpretivism. Many textbooks choose the term "realism" to describe the paradigm between positivism and interpretivism. While the division of paradigms is necessary and admirable, the term "realism" is somewhat confusing, since it represents an *ontological* position shared in part by positivism and a number of perspectives under the label of postpositivism. More specifically, positivism and parts of postpositivism share a realist, foundationalist ontology, but positivism tends toward empirical realism— that is, it treats the world as consisting of observable objects, as a world with no unobservable qualities (Sayer, 2000)—whereas the postpositivist account we are interested in here tends toward a *critical* realism. One way of conceiving of critical realism as I use the term here, attributed to the thinking of the philosopher Roy Bhaskar, is to think of it as a broad research paradigm related to a variety of approaches under the heading "critical social science." There are a great number of realisms (e.g., scientific realism, transcendental realism; see Robson, 2002), all drawing from the basic tenets of realism, but I shall opt for the term "critical realism" in the following passages, since it appears to be the most influential strand of realism in the human sciences. Most commentators trace the historical antecedents of this approach back to the work of Karl Marx, Sigmund Freud, Theodor Adorno, and Herbert Marcuse. This paradigm has also been influenced by the Frankfurt School in Germany (see Neuman, 2000).

If I were to employ the term "critical social science," I would be able to capture a great deal of the extant literature on the politics of sport, albeit not from political scientists. Herein lies a problem of categorization, as many scholars would see themselves as "critical interpretivists," which would appear to straddle two of the epistemological positions outlined here. Since the 1970s, a powerful alternative to both positivism, with its search for regular laws, and interpretivism, with its emphasis on "the interpretation of meaning" (Sayer, 2000, pp. 2–3), has grown in importance. Put simply, critical-realist scholars have attempted to combine the "how" (understanding, which is linked to interpretivism) and the "why" (explanation, which is linked to positivism) approaches by bridging the gap between the two extremes (see May, 2001). They do this by adopting what is termed a "depth ontology"—that is, generative mechanisms or structures that are not always directly observable. An example of such a structure is patriarchy, which in itself is difficult to see, but the influence of patriarchy is something that can be studied. Critical realists do this "by not restricting its focus to directly observable causal links, the 'depth ontology' which realism offers is able to produce a much richer layer of explanatory variables and generative mechanisms than rival positivist explanations" (Kerr, 2003, pp. 122–123). Furthermore, critical realists seek to incorporate a notion of reflexive agency in their explanation, in which the agent interprets his or her own structural context.

In the work conducted on government politics and sport policy from a critical realist paradigm, Green and Houlihan stand out (2005, 2009). Their work on elite sport development broadly, and on the modernization of sport specifically, draws on the critical realist paradigm to sharpen their focus on both structure and agency, which are seen as mutually constitutive (Hay, 2002, p. 127; Grix, 2010b). The resulting research is clear and theoretically informed but not overburdened.

Emancipatory Perspectives

There is insufficient space here to outline research perspectives that do not fit into this neat three-way division: namely, feminist research and postmodernism. Suffice it to say that these two emancipatory approaches have both questioned the very assumptions upon which most mainstream research is based. They are not just different applications of theory to research practice; they also call many accepted norms and fundamentals of research into question. This, in turn, has led to a great deal of methodological reflection, justification, and clarification, which, if not taken too far, can be good for research as a whole. For example, much work on sport is carried out by critical feminists (see Talbot, 1995; Hargreaves, 1994, 2000), who would fit into the category of critical social science.

Applying Political Science and Sport: The Governance of Sport and the Politics of Mega-Events

The first example given here applies a key concept in political science (governance) to the study of sport with an added twist of attempting to shed light not just on the governance of sport but also on how such research can, in turn, shed light on political science concepts and the debates that surround them (e.g., regarding governance). The second example is a discussion about the political nature of elite sport funding, including that of sport mega-events. The point is to indicate the intricate political nature of sport and how it is bound up by the very core of what ought to be considered the terrain of political scientists: government, resource distribution, power, international prestige, and national identity.

There is usually a one-way relationship between mainstream social science disciplines and the study of sport, wherein concepts and theories of the former are brought to bear down on the latter (figure 9.1). Some of the best work to date on sport and politics has been carried out by Barrie Houlihan. Through his work on politics and policy, Houlihan has introduced the tools, theories, and methods of political science and policy studies, which, themselves, of course, are taken from a wide cross-section of social science disciplines, to the study of sport. In particular, Houlihan has, along with the late Mick Green, focused on the sport policy community, adopting and adapting tools from public policy and public administration research to the study of sport. This pioneering work has introduced sport scholars to the tools and concepts of political and policy studies, including advocacy coalition frameworks, policy networks, multiple streams analysis, comparative policy analysis, the government's modernization process, governance, social capital, and more (e.g., Houlihan, 1997; Green & Houlihan, 2005; Houlihan & Green, 2008; Houlihan & Green, 2009). Green went on to borrow the tools of policy transfer (2006), appropriate the notion of policy discourse (2004), and employ the concept of social investment state (2007a) in a series of illuminat-

▶ **Figure 9.1** Traditional studies of sport and politics.

ing articles interrogating sport politics. This use of the political science toolkit is in itself a very important task that has helped the study of sport and sport policy become more systematic and rigorous. Such borrowing from cognate disciplines takes place all the time. For example, social capital is a concept appropriated by political scientists from the neighboring discipline of sociology but made popular by the political scientist Robert Putnam, 1994, 2000. We need in-depth analyses of specific areas of sport—for example, doping in sport, the governance of sport, the role of sport in international affairs and identity building, and comparative sport systems.

Such studies are what one could call traditional in the sense that they draw insights, tools, and theories from a discipline and apply them to a subfield, in this case sport politics and policy; this is similar, for example, to the sub-discipline of the sociology of sport. The first example involves application of a borrowed political science concept (governance) to the study of sport. As I have discussed elsewhere, political scientists ought to see in sport a topic that can offer reflections back on the tools and debates in political studies (Grix, 2010b; see also Hill, 2003, for a similar idea in relation to political sport history). For example, if we turn things around and take a topic from sport—and there is a long list that would interest those working in political studies—as the independent variable through which to contribute to an understanding or explanation of some phenomenon in political studies, then, irrespective of whether you like sport or not, this ought to have a wider purchase and aid our understanding (figure 9.2).

▶ **Figure 9.2**　The subject of sport as an independent variable in understanding issues in British politics.

Example 1: Governance and Sport

In a number of recent articles, scholars have drawn on key debates in political science to discuss and explain developments in sport. Although I use the United Kingdom as an example, governance theory applies to all advanced democratic states. This example involves the Labour government's modernization process—part of a worldwide trend of reforming government's public policy and administration—and the effect on the governance of sport. This process, begun under conservatives, was continued by Labour from 1997 on and saw increasing influence of central government and its agencies in public policy, including sport development and policy (Houlihan, 2005, p. 177). The government white paper *Modernising Government* (1999), clearly set out the

> *vision of "modern" government [in which] policy making is more forward-looking, joined-up and strategic; public services are more responsive to the needs of users and are more efficient, effective and delivered to higher quality standards. (Sanderson, 2002, p. 62)*

As part of this modernizing process, national governing bodies of sport (NGBs) were required to professionalize their management and introduce "techniques, values and practices taken from the private sector" (Deem, 2001, p. 10). For Green and Houlihan (2006), "'modernization' programmes as a political rationality of government have emerged as one of the ways in which governments have sought to shape and sculpt the management and administration of NSOs [national sports organizations]—especially those identified as 'failing organisations'" (p. 50). Their more recent study concludes that New Labour's modernization project has led to a narrowing of UK Sport and Sport England's objectives and to their adoption of a number of businesslike principles (also see Grix, 2009 for a similar conclusion). Crucially, the authors pick up on the discourse that accompanied the rolling out of the modernization process. They refer to the simultaneous "rhetoric of empowerment and autonomy" and the "strengthening of the government's capacity to set the strategic direction for policy and also micro-manage the activities of units of the state" (Houlihan & Green, 2009, p. 681). This echoes the paradox found in sport policy governance, in that the outward appearance seemed to confirm a democratic "flowering" (Skelcher, 2000) of new parastatal bodies, and with it talk of (sport) actors enjoying "significant autonomy from the state" (Rhodes, 1997, p. 15), when in fact this is not the case, because asymmetrical power relations clearly still exist.

In work on the governance of sport, I have attempted to contribute to, build on, and develop Bevir and Rhodes' critique of the so-called governance narrative (2003, 2006, 2008; see also M. Goodwin & Grix, 2011; Grix, 2010c). The governance narrative refers to literature setting out to explain change in the British state. While the first wave of positivist governance narrative work pointed to major changes in the way the state was governed, Bevir and Rhodes offered an interpretivist response to the inadequacies of the conceptualization of British government in the form of the Westminster model (Bevir & Rhodes, 2003, 2006). The latter hierarchic model is, according to Rhodes, "no longer acceptable. We have to tell a different story of the shift from government with its narrative of the strong executive to governance through networks" (2007, p. 1247). I attempted to take the decentered approach advocated by Bevir and Rhodes—and latterly Richards (see Bevir

& Richards, 2009a, 2009b)—and contribute to it on three levels: conceptually, empirically, and methodologically.

First, I offered a way of conceptualizing and understanding policy sectors that do not conform to the governance narrative (e.g., sport and education, as well as social housing and health). The notion of asymmetrical network governance sought to capture the paradox in certain policy sectors, wherein outward signs of governance are empirically discernible, yet asymmetrical power relations remain the dominant mode of governing. Such outward signs of a shift from big government to governance by and through networks can be seen in the trend toward "agencification," including arm's-length agencies and the rapid growth of partnerships, networks, charities, advisory bodies, boards, commissions, councils, and other parastatal bodies involved in policy deliberation and delivery. Such a configuration can be understood in some policy sectors, perhaps paradoxically, as a state strategy to *enhance* control over policy. In such sectors, new governance has not resulted in a "hollowing out" of the state but rather an increased capacity for central steering (Grix & Phillpots, 2011).

Second, I offered empirical examples of asymmetrical policy communities from the sectors of education (together with M. Goodwin) and sport policy. These cases add to the stock of examples available to those seeking to develop the decentered approach, providing accounts of the governance of two national-level policy communities that as yet have not been thoroughly examined through the lens of the decentered approach to governance.

Finally, I assessed the analysis of both the sport and education cases via the decentered approach and suggested that a decentered approach that allows room for a causal role of structures and institutions in its explanation of changes in British politics could account for the seemingly deviant education and sport policy communities. Broadly, this contribution accepts decentered theorists' critique of the existing governance literature but advocates allowing for the role that institutions and structures play in changes in British politics alongside the ideas, culture, and beliefs of individual actors (see also the work of Marsh, Richards, & Smith, 2003; Marsh, 2008a, 2008b).

The sport policy community in this example provided a study of a weaker policy area—one not normally analyzed by governance theorists—in which policy taking is more common than policy making; hence the use of the concept of asymmetry to understand the manner in which it is governed. It also—along with the education policy community case study—highlighted the need to account for the role of structures in an explanation of how policy is made and delivered. The point here is that a case study of sport is used to feed back into the building of theory and the stock of conceptual tools used in political science—it is not just a simple case of peeking into the political science toolkit, selecting the tools we think are appropriate, and then applying them to a topic outside the discipline.

Example 2: Distributing Resources: Elite Sport and Mega-Events

The case of elite sport investment is slightly different. Here, I consider the political rationale for investing in elite sport and mega-events, bearing in mind that state investment is a finite resource. Sums invested in elite sport are *not* invested elsewhere, so the reasoning behind decisions about how to distribute resources is highly political (see Houlihan & Green, 2008).

Sport offers both an individual and a collective experience—something recognized by modern states that invest heavily in elite sport in order to engender a so-called feel-good factor among citizens that is said to exist in the collective experience of sporting events (Department for Culture, Media, and Sport/Strategy Unit, 2002). Riordan (1999) rightly points to the nation-building potential of sport when he suggests that sport

> *extends and unites wider sections of the population than probably any other social activity. It is easily understood and enjoyed, cutting across social, economic, educational, ethnic, religious and language barriers. It permits some emotional release (reasonably) safely, it can be relatively cheap and it is easily adapted to support educational, health and social-welfare objectives. (pp. 49–50)*

In addition to this inward-looking benefit from elite sport success, the outward-looking concept of international prestige is often invoked as part of the justificatory discourse for spending. Many states seek to use sport externally to promote the country's image, gain prestige, and even exert influence over other states (so-called soft power; see Nye, 1990; Grix & Houlihan, 2013; Grix, 2013a). Prestige has long been recognized by scholars as an "indispensable source of power" in international relations (Reinhold Niebuhr, cited in Kim, 2004, p. 40), one that works alongside traditional material forces of power such as guns and bombs. Sport is clearly part of a nation's package of measures available to improve and project its image abroad; success at (elite) sport is easily recognizable to other states, and it appears that in order to be considered a leading nation a state needs to produce internationally competitive athletes and teams (see Strenk, 1979). Internally, states seek to bind individuals around these collective, national experiences of sport success and engender both the feel-good factor and a cohesive identity akin to that of Benedict Anderson's "imagined communities" (Anderson, 1983; Nye, 1990).

The literature on elite sport development (ESD) is relatively new, and studies inquiring into *why* countries continue to invest heavily in supporting elite sport and hosting mega-events are few and far between in political science (early literature includes Green & Oakley, 2001; Green & Houlihan, 2005; Green, 2007b; Houlihan & Green, 2008; Grix & Carmichael, 2012). This is baffling, for if politics is in part about the struggle for resources and an analysis of who gets what, when, and how, then posing the unanswered question of why governments invest so much public money into elite sport ought to be second nature to students of the discipline. We ought to question both the uncritical acceptance of millions of dollars being pumped into elite sport and the concurrent discourse surrounding such investment that takes it as a given.

This is particularly the case in light of the fact that the rationales for state investment in elite sport (international prestige, identity formation) are not confined to advanced capitalist states. So-called emerging states are increasingly interested in using sport to accelerate their entry into the developed world. Take, for example, India's—and Delhi's—recent staging of the problematic Commonwealth Games in 2010. This could certainly be read as an attempt by a developing country to announce to the world that it has finally arrived. It appears that for developing countries the ability to stage a mega-sporting event is a rite of passage into the developed world. Unfortunately, a series of setbacks, collapsing infrastructure, environmental factors (including snakes and monkeys), and corruption appear to have scuppered India's ambition of holding an Olympics in the near future ("IOC Chief," 2010). Indeed, students of politics can find a veritable Aladdin's cave in such an event as the Delhi Games, the political context within which it took place, the political ambitions of the host nation, and the struggle for interests, resources, and influence that surrounded its staging. Allegations of bribery, backhanders (i.e., under-the-table payments), and crooked politicians were commonplace, and the question remains unanswered of how India could invest billions of dollars in a sporting event when a large part of its population—who did not get to see, use, or benefit from the event—has no access to clean running water (Burke, 2010).

Cross-country and cross-regime comparisons can help us understand similarities and differences between states and their instrumental uses of sport. We can also compare across time; for example, an analysis of both capitalist states and the authoritarian socialist East Germany and (consumer-) communist China reveals parallels in the key characteristics of elite sport systems and the rationales behind them (Dennis & Grix, 2012). Not only are the key characteristics of the sport models similar (i.e., sport science, talent identification, professional coaching, funding for full-time athletes), but also all regime types appear to strive for international prestige on the back of elite sport success. Most, albeit to differing degrees, attempt to use sport to generate pride in their nation (the elusive feel-good factor). Such comparisons of the rationale behind elite sport investment reveal that, despite local variations and differences, national models of sport could be said to be (generally) moving toward convergence (Houlihan & Green, 2008; Dennis & Grix, 2012).

The UK Example

The UK government in its sport policy documents has inextricably linked two aims: investment in elite sport is to promote the United Kingdom's image abroad and gain international prestige through elite sport success, and this success is thought to have a positive effect on UK citizens by way of making them feel good and inspiring them to participate in sport. Take, for example, the "official" UK government justification for investing some £600 million (roughly US$900 million) into elite sport over a 6-year period (2006–2012), about half of which went for the London Olympic funding cycle (2008–2012) following Britain's fourth-place ranking in Beijing in 2008 (Department for Culture, Media, and Sport, 2008). The justification is spelled out clearly in the Labour government's sport treatise, *Game Plan*:

> *Why should government invest in high performance sport? . . . as a driver of the "feel good factor" and the image of the UK abroad; as a driver for grassroots participation, whereby sporting heroes inspire participation.* (Department for Culture, Media, and Sport/Strategy Unit, 2002, p. 117)

The three key reasons given here for such investment—the production of a feel-good factor, the promotion of the country's image abroad (also termed "international prestige"), and the promotion of sport and physical activity participation among citizens—all have one thing in common: There is little evidence to support these claims about the efficacy of elite sport and sporting events. Despite this lack of evidence, it would appear that the majority of (Western) advanced ESD systems (including that of the United Kingdom) are based on the premise of what I term a "virtuous cycle of sport" (Grix & Carmichael, 2012). This cycle, as an elite policy discourse, has a convincing logic of circularity that appears commonsensical to the extent that the value of competing in the global "sporting arms race" (Collins & Green, 2007, p. 9) appears to be an unquestionable given. The virtuous cycle of sport touches and builds upon similar phenomena such as the double pyramid theory described by van Bottenburg (2002) and by authors in the so-called grey literature (conference papers, in-house papers, and so on). The double pyramid theory simply states that "thousands of people practising sport at the base lead to a few Olympic champions, and at the same time the existence of champion role models encourages thousands of people to take up some form of sport" (van Bottenburg, 2002, p. 2; see also Hanstad & Skille, 2010). The notion of a virtuous cycle of sport takes this analysis further, first by presenting the relationship between elite and mass sport as self-reinforcing and circular. I also embellish the model with reasons and motives behind government investment in elite sport (e.g., in order to gain international prestige). Moreover, I put forward the philosophy underpinning this cycle as the chief justificatory discourse behind investment in elite sport by states.

Thus, the virtuous cycle of sport holds that elite success on the international stage leads to prestige and that elite sport contributes to a collective sense of identity; this, then, boosts a greater mass sport participation, leading to a healthier populace, which, in turn, provides a bigger pool of talent from which to choose the elite stars of the future, thus ensuring elite success. The process then starts over again (see figure 9.3 for a pictorial overview).

So, what can abstraction and a few arrows and boxes tell us about sport? If we understand elite policy discourse as a virtuous cycle of sport, it helps explain governments' overemphasis on the ability of elite sport success to effect so much change (domestically and internationally). It also allows us to make generalizations about the majority of (usually advanced capitalist) states and their relationship with elite sport. Effectively, the virtuous cycle of sport spells out the elite sport discourse or narrative that appears dominant among policy makers, and it affords students of sport a pictorial overview of the causal claims made on behalf of sport.

Discussion of governments' use of sport mega-events is by no means restricted to the United Kingdom or to advanced capitalist states. In fact, there is a discernible trend toward sport "megas"—including so-called second-order events (Black, 2008), such as the Commonwealth Games— being awarded to "emerging" states. These states (e.g., China, Russia, Qatar, Brazil, India) have not promised that hosting such an event will lead to,

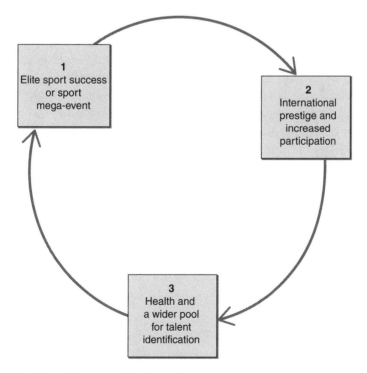

▶ **Figure 9.3** The virtuous cycle of sport.

for example, greater numbers of physically active citizens. It is fairly clear that their primary reason for bidding and hosting is international prestige. States clearly calculate that the return on what is usually a very expensive investment is value for money.

Deciding the Host

One final point of obvious political interest surrounding mega-events involves the decisions behind who gets to host them. This process has always been politically charged, but recent events have highlighted the inherently political nature of these decisions that go far beyond what happens on the playing field. Take, for example, the recent judgment of which countries would host the 2018 and 2022 World Cups. To the outsider, the script reads like a novel: In the driver's seat is a (male-dominated) organization that exhibits the key characteristics of secrecy, untransparency, wheeling-dealing, backhanders or under-the-table payments, and an aversion to paying tax. At the head is a septuagenarian who rules with an iron fist. This is not a description of the Mafia or of East Germany's politburo but of the organization in charge of the world's most popular sport and the world's biggest sporting event: FIFA (the International Federation of Association Football). Commentators picking over England's bid in the aftermath of its rejection in favor of "new lands" (Blatter, 2011) in the form of Russia (2018) and Qatar (2022), the latter being the smallest country ever to put on the event, pointed the finger of blame directly at the English media. Even the English soccer player Rio Ferdinand cited the timing of an exposé by the BBC program *Panorama* of corruption among FIFA officials as central to the bid's failure. The English media had flagged up and sought proof for what most people already know: FIFA, a charity, is, and has been for a very long time, surrounded by accusations of backstabbing, improper dealing, palm greasing, and profit seeking. Despite the tendency of the UK media to be insensitive, intrusive, and, at times, sensationalist, the manner in which FIFA functions as a world governing body should be the focus of far more academic attention—and a major inquiry.

Arranging the announcement of two future World Cup hosts at the same meeting allowed for even more back-room dealing, vote swapping, and alliances than usual. What this and the subsequent result have shown is that reform is needed in order to readdress the balance of politics and sport: FIFA appears to be too much about the former and too little about the latter. The power of such supranational organizations in sport and their ability to affect *national* sport offer an excellent case for students of politics.

Summary

This chapter attempts to do a number of things. First, it introduces the academic discipline of political science by discussing the area of the study of politics. Two broad views are discussed: One view is that political science is the study of the sphere of government, including its institutions; another, much broader conception understands politics as a process that can be observed in a wide variety of settings. These views are linked by the notion of power, and the study of sport and politics, or sport politics, transcends both: Governments use and invest in sport, and sport as a cultural institution in society is much broader than the narrow confines of government.

The chapter also provides an introduction to the core of political science—arranged by epistemological positions—by discussing how differing research perspectives are aligned according to their philosophical roots. Two short examples are offered to show the usefulness of a political analysis of sport: first, by drawing on and adapting one of the key debates in political science and public administration—that of governance—and applying it to a study of sport; and second, by illustrating how politics is central to questions about sport mega-events and the distribution of resources attached to them.

Sport politics, as a body of literature, is slowly emerging and developing, yet it is doing so without many political scientists contributing to it (see Grix, 2013a). There is clearly potential for students of politics to engage with the study of sport, which is mostly undertheorized, apart from the area covered by the sociology of sport. On the one hand, it is astonishing that political scientists—in particular, those interested in resource distribution, justice, national interest and identity, corruption, and democracy, to name but a few topics—have not turned their attention to the intrinsically political nature of sport, be it at the elite, grassroots, or community level. It is true that the multifaceted nature of sport requires more tools and understanding than a single academic discipline can offer. A full appreciation of, say, the staging of an Olympic Games and its legacy requires an understanding of the political, economic, and social contexts in which it takes place and of the psychological mechanisms at play in both the external image of the host nation and the internal effect of the events on the attitudes of the host citizens. Nonetheless, political science, and the tools it offers, can play a major part in developing such an understanding of the increasingly important part that sport plays in society, as states of all political hues become more and more involved with it.

References

Allison, L. (Ed.). (1986). *The politics of sport.* Manchester, UK: Manchester University Press.

Allison, L. (Ed.). (1993). *The changing politics of sport.* Manchester, UK: Manchester University Press.

Allison, L. (1998). Sport and civil society. *Political Studies, 46,* 709–726.

Anderson, B. (1983). *Imagined communities: Reflections on the origin and spread of nationalism.* London: Verso.

Bevir, M., & Rhodes, R.A.W. (2003). *Interpreting British governance*. London: Routledge.

Bevir, M., & Rhodes, R.A.W. (2006). *Governance stories*. London: Routledge.

Bevir, M., & Rhodes, R.A.W. (2008). The differentiated polity as narrative. *British Journal of Politics and International Relations, 10*(4), 729–734.

Bevir, M., & Richards, D. (2009a). Decentring policy networks: A theoretical agenda. *Public Administration, 87*(1), 3–14.

Bevir, M., & Richards, D. (2009b). Decentring policy networks: Lessons and prospects. *Public Administration, 87*(1), 132–141.

Black, D. (2008). Dreaming big: The pursuit of "second order" games as a strategic response to globalisation. *Sport in Society, 11*(4), 467–480.

Blatter, S. (2011) Russia, Qatar Take World Cup to New Lands. Available from: http://in.reuters.com/article/2010/12/02/idININdia-53307220101202. Accessed 20 July 2012.

Blaikie, N. (2000). *Designing social research*. Cambridge: Polity Press.

Bloyce, D., & Smith, A. (2010). *Sport policy and development*. London Routledge.

Burke, J. (2010, August 3). Delhi battling human and financial cost of hosting Commonwealth Games. *The Guardian*. www.guardian.co.uk/sport/2010/aug/04/commonwealth-games-delhi-preparations.

Burnham, P., Gilland Lutz, K., Grant, W., & Layton-Henry, Z. (2008). *Research methods in politics*. Basingstoke, UK: Palgrave.

Cabinet Office (United Kingdom). (2010). Applying behavioural insight to health. www.cabinetoffice.gov.uk/resource-library/applying-behavioural-insight-health.

Chalip, L. (2006). Toward a distinctive sport management discipline. *Journal of Sport Management, 20*, 1–21.

Clough, P., & Nutbrown, C. (2002). *A student's guide to methodology*. Thousand Oaks, CA: Sage.

Coakley, J. (2004). *Sports in society*. Boston: McGraw-Hill.

Coalter, F. (2007). *A wider social role for sport: Who's keeping the score?* London: Routledge.

Collins, S., & Green, M. (2007). The Australian Institute of Sport. *Journal of the Academy of Social Sciences in Australia, 26*(2), 4–14.

Danermark, B., Ekström, M., Jakobsen, L., & Karlsson, J. (2002). *Explaining society. Critical realism in the social sciences*. New York: Routledge.

Deem, R. (2001). Globalisation, new managerialism, academic capitalism and entrepreneurialism in universities: Is the local dimension still important? *Comparative Education, 37*(1), 7–20.

Dennis, M., & Grix, J. (2012). *Sport under communism: Behind the East German "miracle."* Basingstoke, UK: Palgrave.

Denscombe, M. (2002). *Ground rules for good research: A ten-point guide for social researchers*. Buckingham, UK: Open University Press.

Department for Culture, Media, and Sport. (2008). Playing to win: A new era for sport. London: Author.

Department for Culture, Media, and Sport/Strategy Unit. (2002). *Game plan: A strategy for delivering government's sport and physical activity objectives.* London: Cabinet Office.

Donnelly, P. (2002). Interpretive approaches to the sociology of sport. In J. Coakley & E. Dunning (Eds.), *Handbook of sports studies* (pp. 77-91). London: Sage.

Dunning, E. (1999). *Sport matters: Sociological studies of sport, violence, and civilization.* London: Routledge.

Elias, N. (2000). *The civilizing process.* Oxford: Blackwell.

Gilchrist, P., & Holden, R. (Eds.). (2011). The politics of sport—Community, mobility, identity [Special issue]. *Sport in Society, 14*(2), 151–159.

Goodwin, M., & Grix, J. (2011). Bringing structures back in: The "governance narrative," the "decentred approach" and "asymmetrical network governance" in the education and sport policy communities, *Public Administration, 89*(2), 537–556.

Goodwin, R.E., & Klingemann, H.-D. (2000). *A new handbook of political science.* Oxford: Oxford University Press.

Gratton, C., & Jones, I. (2004). *Research methods for sport studies.* London: Routledge.

Gratton, C., & Taylor, P. (2001). *The economics of sport and recreation.* London: Routledge.

Green, M. (2004). Changing policy priorities for sport in England: The emergence of elite sport development as a key policy concern. *Leisure Studies, 23*(4), 365–385.

Green, M. (2006). From "sport for all" to not about "sport" at all?: Interrogating sport policy interventions in the United Kingdom. *European Sport Management Quarterly, 6,* 217–238.

Green, M. (2007a). Governing under advanced liberalism: Sport policy and the social investment state. *Policy Sciences, 40*(1), 55–71.

Green, M. (2007b). Olympic glory or grassroots development? Sports policy priorities in Australia, Canada, and the United Kingdom 1960–2006. *International Journal of the History of Sport, 24*(7), 921–953.

Green, M., & Houlihan, B. (2005). *Elite sport development. Policy learning and political priorities.* London and New York: Routledge.

Green, M., & Houlihan, B. (2006). Governmentality, modernization, and the "disciplining" of national sporting organizations: An analysis of athletics in Australia and the United Kingdom, *Sociology of Sport Journal, 23,* 47–71.

Green, M., & Oakley, B. (2001). Elite sport development systems and playing to win: Uniformity and diversity in international approaches. *Leisure Studies, 20*(4), 247–267.

Grix, J. (2002). Introducing students to the generic terminology of social research. *Politics, 22*(3), 175–185.

Grix, J. (2009). The impact of UK sport policy on the governance of athletics. *International Journal of Sport Policy, 1*(1), 31–49.

Grix, J. (2010a). *The foundations of research.* Basingstoke, UK: Palgrave.

Grix, J. (2010b). From hobbyhorse to mainstream: Using sport to understand British politics. *British Politics, 5*(1), 114–129.

Grix, J. (2010c). The governance debate and the study of sport policy. *International Journal of Sport Policy, 2*(2), 159–171.

Grix, J. (2013a). Sports politics and the Olympics. *Political Studies Review, 11*(1), 15–25.

Grix, J. (2013b). "Image" leveraging and sports mega-events: Germany and the 2006 FIFA World Cup. *Journal of Sport and Tourism, 17*(4), 289–312.

Grix, J., & Carmichael, F. (2012). Why do governments invest in elite sport? A polemic. *International Journal of Sport Policy and Politics, 4*(1), 73–90.

Grix, J., & Houlihan, B. (2013). Sports Mega-Events as Part of a Nation's Soft Power Strategy: The Cases of Germany (2006) and the UK (2012). *British Journal of Politics and International Relations.*

Grix, J., & Phillpots, L. (2011). Revisiting the "governance narrative": "Asymmetrical network governance" and the deviant case of the sport policy sector. *Public Policy and Administration, 26*(1), 3–19.Guba, E.G., & Lincoln, Y.S. (1998). Competing paradigms in qualitative research. In N.K. Denzin & Y.S. Lincoln (Eds.), *The landscape of qualitative research: Theories and issues* (pp. 3-19). Thousand Oaks, CA: Sage.

Guttmann, A. (2003). Sport, politics, and the engaged historian. *Journal of Contemporary History, 38*(3), 363–375.

Hanstad, D.V., & Skille, E.A. (2010). Does elite sport develop mass sport? A Norwegian case study. *Scandinavian Sport Studies Forum, 1,* 51–68.

Hargreaves, J. (1994). *Sporting females: Critical issues in the history and sociology of women's sports.* London: Routledge.

Hargreaves, J. (2000) *Heroines of Sport. The Politics of Difference and Identity,* London: Routledge.

Hay, C. (2002). *Political analysis.* Basingstoke, UK: Palgrave.

Hill, J. (2002). *Sport, leisure, and culture in twentieth-century Britain.* Basingstoke, UK: Macmillan.

Hill, J. (2003). Introduction: Sport and politics. *Journal of Contemporary History, 38*(3), 355–361.

Hilvoorde, I.V., Elling, A., & Stokvis, R. (2010). How to influence national pride? The Olympic medal index as a unifying narrative. *International Review for the Sociology of Sport, 45*(1), 87–102.

Houlihan, B. (1991). *The government and politics of sport.* London: Routledge.

Houlihan, B. (1997). *Sport policy and politics: A comparative analysis.* London: Routledge.

Houlihan, B. (2002). Politics and sport. In J. Coakley & E. Dunning (Eds.), *Handbook of sports studies* (pp. 213-=27). London: Sage.

Houlihan, B. (2005). Public sector sport policy: Developing a framework for analysis. *International Review for the Sociology of Sport, 40*(2), 163–185.

Houlihan, B. (2008) (Ed.). *Sport and society: A student introduction,* London: Sage.

Houlihan, B., & Green, M. (2008). *Comparative elite sport development: Systems, structures, and public policy.* Amsterdam: Butterworth-Heinemann.

Houlihan, B., & Green, M. (2009). Modernization and sport: The Reform of Sport England and UK Sport. *Public Administration, 87*(3), 678–698.

Hughes, J., & Sharrock, W. (1997). *The philosophy of social research* (3rd ed.). London: Longman.

IOC chief optimistic about CWG, says give India a chance. (2010, September 24). *Hindustan Times.* www.hindustantimes.com/StoryPage/Print/604196.aspx.

International Olympic Committee. (Ed.). (1968). *The speeches of President Avery Brundage,* Lausanne: IOC, p. 10.

Jarvie, G. (1991). *Sport, racism, and ethnicity.* Sussex: Falmer Press.

Kerr, P. (2003). Keeping it real! Evolution in political science: A reply to Kay and Curry. *British Journal of Politics and International Relations, 5*(1), 118–128.

Kim, Y. (2004). Does prestige matter in international politics? *Journal of International and Area Studies, 11*(1), 39–55.

Lasswell, H.D. (1936). *Politics: Who gets what, when, how.* New York: McGraw-Hill.

Leftwich, A. (Ed.). (2004). *What is politics?* Cambridge: Policy Press.

Levermore, R. (2004). Sport's role in constructing the "inter-state" worldview. In R. Levermore & A. Budd (Eds.), *Sport and International Relations* (pp. 1-30). London: Routledge.

Markovits, A.S., & Rensmann, L. (2010). *Gaming the world.* Princeton, NJ: Princeton University Press.

Marsh, D. (2008a). What is at stake? A response to Bevir and Rhodes. *The British Journal of Politics and International Relations, 10*(4), 735–739.

Marsh, D. (2008b). Understanding British government: Analysing competing models. *The British Journal of Politics and International Relations, 10*(2), 251–268.

Marsh, D., & Furlong, P. (2002). A skin not a sweater: Ontology and epistemology in political science. In D. Marsh & G. Stoker (Eds.), *Theory and methods in political science* (2nd ed.) (pp. 17-41). Basingstoke, UK: Palgrave Macmillan.

Marsh, D., Richards, D., & Smith, M. (2003). Unequal plurality: Towards an asymmetric power model of British politics. *Government and Opposition, 38*(3), 306–332.

Marsh, D., & Stoker, G. (Eds.). (2002). *Theory and methods in political science* (2nd ed.). Basingstoke, UK: Palgrave Macmillan.

May, T. (2001). *Social research: Issues, methods, and process.* Buckingham, UK: Open University Press.

Neuman, W.L. (2000). *Social research methods: Qualitative and quantitative approaches.* Needham Heights, MA: Allyn & Bacon,

Nye, J.S. (1990). Soft power. *Foreign Policy, 80,* 153–171.

Outhwaite, W. (1986). *Understanding social life: The method called Verstehen.* London: Allen and Unwin.

Polley, M. (1998). *Moving the goalposts—A history of sport and society since 1945.* London: Routledge.

Putnam, R. (1994). *Making democracy work: Civic traditions in modern Italy.* Princeton, NJ: Princeton University Press.

Putnam, R. (2000). *Bowling alone: The collapse and revival of American community.* New York: Simon & Schuster.

Rhodes, R.A.W. (1997). Understanding Governance. Milton Keynes, UK: Open University Press.

Rhodes, R.A.W. (2007). Understanding governance: Ten years on. *Organization Studies, 28*(8), 1243–1264.

Riordan, J. (1999). The impact of communism on sport. In J. Riordan & A. Krüger (Eds.), *The international politics of sport in the 20th century.* London: Spon Press.

Robson, C. (2002). *Real world research: A resource for social scientists and practitioner researchers* (2nd ed.). Cambridge, MA: Blackwell.

Sanderson, I. (2002). Making sense of what works: Evidence-based policy making as instrumental rationality? *Public Policy and Administration, 17*(3), 61–75.

Sayer, A. (2000). *Realism and social science.* London: Sage.

Skelcher, C. (2000). Changing images of the state: Overloaded, hollowed-out, congested. *Public Policy and Administration, 15*(3), 3–19.

Stoker, G., & Marsh, D. (2002). Introduction. In D. Marsh & G. Stoker (Eds.), *Theory and methods in political science* (2nd ed.) (pp. 1-16). Basingstoke, UK: Palgrave Macmillan.

Strenk, A. (1979). What price victory? The world of international sports and politics. *The ANNALS of the American Academy of Political and Social Sciences, 445*(1), 128–140.

Talbot, M. (1995). The politics of sport and physical education. In S. Fleming, M. Talbot, & A. Tomlinson (Eds.), *Policy and politics in sport, physical education, and leisure* (pp. 3-26). Brighton: Leisure Studies Association.

Taylor, T. (1986). Sport and international relations: A case of mutual neglect. In L. Allison (Ed.), *The politics of sport.* Manchester, UK: Manchester University Press.

Thaler, R.H., & Sunstein, C.R. (2008). *Nudge: Improving decisions about health, wealth, and happiness.* New Haven, CT: Yale University Press.

van Bottenburg, M. (2002, October). Sport for all and elite sport: Do they benefit one another? W.J.H. Mulier Institute—Centre for Research on Sports in Society. www.vanbottenburg.nl/downloads/147.%20Van%20Bottenburg%20-%20 Sport%20for%20all%20and%20elite%20sport.%20Do%20they%20benefit%20 one%20another.pdf.

CHAPTER 10

International Relations and Sport

**Roger Levermore, PhD,
and Aaron Beacom, PhD**

The status of international relations (IR) as a field of study has been a matter of intense debate for a number of years (Schmidt, 2002). Issues include dissension about whether IR constitutes a distinct academic discipline with clearly delineated, interlocking intellectual traditions or "a poorly marked out arena in which a multiplicity of research programs and strategies compete, co-exist or retain splendid isolation" (Plating, 1969, cited in Schmidt, 2002, p. 3). Nevertheless, IR has been in existence in some form for nearly 100 years, during which a range of theoretical models have emerged that facilitate the investigation of international issues. In this sense, the authors contend, IR does have a role to play in understanding the characteristics of international sport and in debates concerning relations between sport and so-called global society.

It is commonplace for the academic community to distinguish between international relations (generally abbreviated to IR) that refers to the academic discipline of that name and international relations as events in world politics (S. Smith, 2003). For the benefit of readers, this protocol is followed throughout the chapter. Only very recently have IR scholars begun to examine the relationship between sport and international society, preferring previously to focus largely on the "high politics" of government, global governance, and diplomacy. As if to emphasize this point, Calvocoressi (2010, p. 129) remarked that the use of table tennis in the 1970s as a tool for diplomacy between the United States and China represented one of the first times that sport and high politics had converged; it was his only reference to sport in the book. More recently, Nye (2011), in developing his thesis regarding the role of "soft power" in international politics, addressed the potential of the 2008 Olympic Games in Beijing to increase Chinese engagement in international diplomacy. Nevertheless, sport remains on the periphery of IR analyses, and academics from non-IR disciplines dominate what has been published to date. This chapter notes these limitations but also aims to stimulate debate concerning the opportunities for engaging with IR as a means both of understanding the characteristics of contemporary international sport and of enhancing our appreciation of the characteristics of international relations. Issues addressed in this book—governance and the rise of nongovernmental actors in international politics, community development and the dynamics of international assistance, identity in the globalization–localization debate, and trends in the international economy (especially the effect on distribution of capital)—have attracted widespread attention from IR scholars. We are concerned here with understanding the nature of international sport from the perspective of such debates.

The chapter begins by assessing significant developments in the discipline of IR, then considers the changing contours of the study of sport and the challenges faced in approaching such study from the perspective of a discipline that has not fully engaged with the role of sport in international society. Next, the chapter explores four key debates relating to sport and the themes of governance, community, identity, and capital.

Core Concepts and Main Theoretical Perspectives

IR as an academic discipline arose in UK and U.S. academic institutions in response to the chaos of the international system in 1919. That the First World War took place at all was seen to be a failure of the "balance of power" system, wherein great powers combined against each other in contending alliances and thus supposedly acted as deterrents to prevent the outbreak of total war. Early IR scholars were occupied with addressing this perceived failure of the balance of power system by considering alternative approaches. Of the four great debates that have arguably shaped the discipline, the first (1920s to 1940s) took place between idealists, who favored creating international institutions to supervise international relations as advocated by statesmen such as Woodrow Wilson (the League of Nations), and realists, who emphasized that states should remain the preeminent institutions dominating international relations (a debate chronicled by C. Levermore, 1924).

The two debates that followed dominated, respectively, the period from the 1950s to the 1960s and the period of the 1970s. The second debate revolved around a more scientific approach based on behavioralism (holding that political actions can be explained in an objective manner based on quantitative techniques), which competed against the more traditional IR found in the first debate. The third debate pitted pluralism (positing that international relations is influenced by a growing body of institutions and actors) against realism (asserting that the state remains all important, as does the free market) and also against Marxism (viewing the state as important but as an instrument with which to control the economy). Such debates continued to display a trait that is pertinent to IR and sport—namely, that despite very important contributions from other parts of the world, IR essentially continued to be dominated by Anglo-Saxon institutions that focused on the primacy of the state.

All three of these debates continue to shape contemporary IR. However, the fourth debate (from the 1980s onward) is arguably the most influential in shaping current IR. This debate involves those who see IR from a positivist perspective (holding that IR can be used to accurately analyze the international political system) and postpositivists (asserting that IR needs to dramatically widen its scope and question how far it has supported the status quo, which has resulted in exploitation of the majority of the world's population).

Therefore, the focus of IR has largely been dominated by "high" politics—the behavior and actions of states and state leaders—rather than the "lower" levels of politics, such as the role that sport played in international society (e.g., in diplomacy). This tendency is evident in the dearth, during the eras of the first three debates, of literature reflecting on the ways in which sport affects—and is affected by—international relations. Indeed, up to the postpositivist era, only a handful of publications addressed sport and international relations. Very few fell in what can be termed IR; most emanated instead from other branches of the social sciences (see, for example, Lowe, 1978; Galtung, 1982) or sat on the edge of IR (e.g., Mtodzikowski, 1973; Szczepaniak, 1981; Kyröläinen & Varis, 1981). Two exceptions came in the form of articles published in a leading IR journal—*Foreign Affairs*—in which Tunis (1936) and Washburn (1956) highlighted the exploitation of sport by dictatorships (especially the Soviet Union) as a tool of control, unification, and nationalism. Even these studies, however, further demonstrated the focus on high politics; sport is mentioned in them only as a tool of the state, a means to govern and marshal community.

Latterly, those from other disciplines—principally historians (e.g., Beck, 2003; Hobsbawm, 1983; C. Hill, 1996; Riordan & Krüger, 1999)—have reflected on the role of sport (especially soccer and the Olympic Games) in shaping international relations in the era of the first great debate, particularly in the creation of nation-states and nationalism, institutions that were often in the embryonic stages of their development.

During the fourth debate, some authors linked to postpositivism in IR have considered the importance of sport, largely in negative terms, as a way of distracting society from the realities of international relations (e.g., Shapiro, 1989; Baudrillard, cited in Redhead, 1997, p. 42). And even this debate has sidelined a wider discussion about the increasing avenues by which the study of sport relates to IR and has something to say about international society. It was for this reason that Levermore and Budd's (2004) edited collection *Sport and International Relations* was published. It argued that key areas in which sport interacts with international relations include the following:

- The continued role of sport in reaffirming nationalism and regional identities
- Sport in relation to inclusion and exclusion, such as the use of sport in social and economic development programs (including those addressing sport and gender)
- Sport and conflict, such as the use of sport in international political protest (including protests against nations and nationalism)
- Formal and informal uses of sport in diplomacy between states and international institutions and organizations, including the importance of sport federations, sport clubs, and sport stars in international society, as well as the dissemination of messages across communities around the world
- Sport and propaganda (by states and commercial organizations)
- Sport and the international political economy

Nonetheless, sport has remained largely ignored by IR, despite the demonstrable increase in the interaction between sport and international relations highlighted by the media. For example, the shift in the global distribution of power, particularly the increasing economic and political influence wielded by the so-called Global South (Gilpin, 2003), has been mirrored, to some extent, by a shifting center of power in international sport, as for instance, Dubai has become a center of sport governance and China has risen as an international sporting power (Allison, 2005; Grohmann, 2008).

The general lack of reflection on the relationship between sport and international relations was highlighted by a recent review of leading IR textbooks and journals. Books consulted include Brown & Ainley (2009), R. Jackson & Sørensen (2010), Griffiths, O'Callaghan, & Roach (2007), Baylis, Smith, & Owens (2007), T. Dunne, Kurki, & Smith (2010), and Calvocoressi (2010); journals consulted included the most-cited IR journals (*European Journal of International Relations, Foreign Affairs, International Affairs, International Organisation, International Security, International Studies Quarterly, Journal of Conflict Resolution, Journal of Peace Research, Journal of Common Market Studies, Review of International Political Economy,* and *World Politics*). Many fail to even include an entry for sport in their index or database, though some do consider (in passing) the economic power of sport merchandising companies and the growing importance of sporting arenas to international relations (e.g., Baylis et al., 2007, p. 422; Pigman, 2010). Some reference has been made, for example, to the role of sport in diplomatic relations between Paraguay and Russia (Karchagin, 2007), to the ways in which sport provides a useful window on the economic benefits and problems inherent in globalization (Milanovic, 2005), and to the 2008 Olympic Games as a means of enhancing China's status internationally (Nye, 2011). Less well-cited journals linked to IR have also provided some insight into the role of sport and international relations. For example, *Global Society* has considered the postcolonial politics of international cricket (Holden, 2008) and global capitalism (Smart, 2007), and *Politikon*—with its focus on Africa—has published articles on the impact of the 2010 World Cup (Black, 2007; Kersting, 2007).

At the same time, a growing number of articles have considered both the staple IR topics and these changes, but they are written by those on the fringes of IR—or outside of IR altogether. This is reflected in the *International Journal of the History of Sport* (Special Issue 2009, *Soft and hard power politics: China after the Olympics*) and *Global Networks* (Special Issue 2007, *Globalization and sport*), which have provided space for discussion of sport and international relations. Here are some examples of topics addressed by authors working on the margins of IR:

- The development of transnational institutions and networks Armstrong (2007), the growing importance of sport in global governance, and the continued use of sport as a tool for nations, foreign policy, and nationalism (S. Jackson & Haigh, 2008)

- The rise of sport stars, clubs, and federations as political actors in helping stimulate diplomacy (Stoddart, 2006)

- The allowing and limiting of political protest (Levermore, 2008c)

- The use of sport as a vehicle to promote social and economic development (Coalter, 2008; Levermore & Beacom, 2009; Levermore 2008a, 2008b) and human rights (Giulianotti & McArdle, 2007)

- The role of sport in fueling the process of globalization (Foer, 2004; Majumdar & Hong, 2005)

- The engagement of the Olympic Movement with international diplomacy (Beacom, 2012)

Critical Findings and Key Debates

In this section, we explore how IR can contribute to a better understanding of the dynamics of international sport and its relationship to global society. We do this by considering literature that addresses sport in the context of the four core theories of the book: governance, community, capital, and identity.

Governance

A significant increase in scholarly activity regarding sport governance has been stimulated by interest in relations between the state and civil society as articulated through sport, as well as concern with regulation of the international sport-industrial complex. For instance, conferences and workshops offered by the Sport and Politics Study Group of the United Kingdom's Political Studies Association at times reflect interest in the governance of sport (e.g., the regulation of sport federations) and the efficacy of sport-based programs as a conduit for international development. Furthermore, these processes are evidence that international relations is articulated through the pluralism of sport actors involved in negotiation in order to establish international protocols across a number of issues, such as anti-doping, media coverage, and international migration of players (Maguire, 1999). Governance and IR issues have also been articulated in the context of a number of recent international sport events. One particularly visible example was the intriguing dynamic that unfolded in Ukraine, whose government faced pressure from the Union of European Football Associations (UEFA) to ensure that its infrastructure was ready to host the 2012 UEFA European Football Championship. However, it was also being instructed by the International Monetary Fund (IMF) to limit public funding of infrastructure projects if it wanted to receive IMF funding needed to address considerable economic difficulties.

In the context of IR, the focus on governance is related to increasing interest in the politics of interdependence and transnational relations. Commenting on changing trends in global governance, Barnett and Duvall (2005, p. 1) noted that in less than 10 years the concept had "gone from the ranks of the unknown to one of the central orienting themes in the practice and study of international affairs of the post Cold War period." Developing this theme, Mundy (2007, p. 341) argued that after 1990, IR began an important movement away from the traditional (realist, neoliberal, and neo-Marxist) "tripartite inter-paradigm debate about world order, towards a newly reconstructed debate about global governance." Its roots in modern intellectual endeavor, however, can be traced back further than that. Kooiman (1993) identified interest in the idea of governance—as opposed to government—during the 1970s as a result of the perceived failure of state institutions in Western liberal democracies to deliver in key areas of societal regulation, social welfare, and development. In response, the idea of governance was perceived as achieving the regulation of society through a process of coordinating the activities of a range of public and private stakeholders.

Almost all IR perspectives (especially away from postpositivism) typically focus on regulation of international society, and their concerns include the process of consensus building, negotiation of trade agreements, and other international regulatory frameworks. From this perspective, diplomatic discourse provides the medium through which international and global governance take place (Cooper, English, & Thakur, 2002; Betsill & Corell, 2007; Cooper, Hocking, & Maley, 2008). Central to IR (and to the subgenre of diplomatic theory) is concern with the relative influence of actors in the international system and the ways in which authority relating to governance has been redistributed. Cooper, English, and colleagues (2002) argued—from a realist perspective—that in the post–Cold War global environment the hierarchical state system continued to act as a brake on the evolution of international organizations and subsequent shifts in global governance.

For some, the "primacy of the state" argument remains convincing when viewing certain ways in which sport is governed by states or multistate institutions. The so-called Bosman ruling of 1995, for example, would appear to have demonstrated the capacity and willingness of the European Union to act to ensure that the regulations of sporting bodies remain subservient to its wider regulatory framework (Parrish, 2003). In that case, the focus was on protecting the freedom of movement of individuals—a cornerstone of the single-market principles—in the face of attempts by clubs to impose limits on movement through transfer regulations. In 2007, the European Commission's White Paper on Sport developed this point further, attempting to achieve a balance between the desire of sport organizations to retain a degree of control over the governance of their sports while at the same time ensuring that their actions remain in the spirit of European Union legislation. For detailed analysis of the impact of the White Paper on Sport, please see the special edition of the *International Journal of Sport Policy and Politics* ("Implementing," 2009), in particular the articles by García and J. Hill.

The continuing rationale for state intervention as a mode of governance is also articulated in other ways. For example, increasing concern over the secretive nature of sport organizations and questions about their "capacity to act simultaneously as regulatory institutions and as commercial entities in the negotiation of sponsorship and broadcasting rights" (Lee, 2004, p. 114) would appear to provide a rationale for state and regional government organizations to intervene. Such an argument appears to gain support by a number of developments on the ground. In one case, pressure from state actors was brought to bear on the International Olympic Committee (IOC) to reconstitute itself in the face of widespread evidence of corrupt practices used to secure the Salt Lake City bid for the 2002 Winter Games (Beacom, 2000). A further example is the continued importance placed on state leaders in bidding for mega sport events. Since 2004, Vladimir Putin and Barack Obama have both strenuously lobbied (with mixed success) for the Winter and Summer Olympics to be held in their countries.

The counterbalance to the realist perspective is evidenced, for example, in the significant change in the diplomatic process (Melissen, 2007) wherein a wide array of national, transnational, and international actors have increasingly engaged in diplomatic discourse. From this viewpoint, governance has typically involved "leadership from below," as in the following examples:

- Clusters of small states have often worked through the United Nations (UN) to influence international policy and governance.
- Nongovernmental organizations (NGOs) have increasingly expanded into diplomatic roles since (good) governance depends on nongovernmental input. Cooper, English, et al. (2002, p. 6) refer to Kofi Annan as arguing that NGOs are "essentially partners of the UN, developing a role not only in mobilizing public opinion, but also in the process of deliberation and policy formation and . . . in the execution of policy on the ground."

In that context, NGOs with a sport focus (sport NGOs) do have a role to play, for example, in relation to debate concerning the efficacy of development interventions aimed at contributing to the UN Millennium Development Goals (MDGs) (see Levermore & Beacom, 2009, for a discussion of sport-in-development as an alternative strategy for addressing the MDGs). This role is also reflected in the development of bilateral relations between the IOC and the UN in relation to a range of issues, including human rights, the status of refugees, and the so-called Olympic Truce (Beacom, 2012). This relationship is at times complex; for example, in 1992, the IOC proposal that athletes from Yugoslavia be allowed to compete as independent individuals in the Barcelona Olympics required special dispensation from the UN Security Council, since it ran contrary to the council's Resolution 757, which included sport as an element of UN sanctions policy (Beacom, 2000).

The relationship between diplomacy and governance is further articulated in interlinking discourses referred to as "multistakeholder diplomacy." Introducing this idea, Hocking (2006, p. 14) commented on diplomacy as increasingly concerned with the development of networks involving a range of state and nonstate actors, focusing on the "management of issues demanding the application of recourses in which no single participant possesses a monopoly." Beacom (2012) has explored multistakeholder diplomacy in the context of developments in diplomatic discourse relating to the Olympic and Paralympic Games. In this sense of actors working together to address common (often complex) problems (e.g., transnational environmental issues), the boundaries between diplomacy and global governance have become increasingly blurred (Cooper, Hocking, et al., 2008).

Lee (2004, p. 113) notes that the general trend toward fragmented authority outside the reach of the state, which characterizes modern governance,

> is especially applicable to the governance of sport, where the administration of both professional and amateur sports has traditionally remained predominantly private, founded upon a system of national and interna-

tional federations, which have zealously guarded their autonomy from the public sphere while simultaneously lobbying for public funding of their physical and human infrastructures.

The governance of sport cannot, then, be considered in isolation from wider shifts in international governance. In the 1980s and into the 1990s, literature on the government and politics of sport focused on forms of state intervention—particularly, in terms of international relations, on the institution of sporting boycotts (Allison, 1988; C. Hill 1996). The IR perspective on the international governance of sport provides a point of reference from which we can consider the redistribution of power and authority in the international system. Furthermore, the efforts by sport organizations themselves to influence international governance on a broader front is evidenced in a number of ways—for example the IOC's attempts to promote reconciliation through the Olympic Truce and other initiatives, often in conjunction with the UN, as well as the granting of observer status to the IOC in the UN General Assembly in October 2009. At the same time, the continued influence of states on the governance of sport reflects their continued pivotal role in every aspect of international relations.

Community

The concept of community has long held significance from an IR perspective. In one sense, Kantian ideas of the emergence of a universal ethical community as the basis for a just society (Wood, 2004) have provided the terms of reference for a wide range of radical arguments concerning the reordering of international society. In another sense, the idea of political community, explored by writers such as Deutsch, concerns itself with what holds national and international political communities together and what can lead to their disintegration (Der Derian, 1995). In yet another sense (associated with pluralism, from the third debate discussed earlier), the focus has been on the emergence of a range of new (transnational) civil society actors rooted in ideas of community and mutualism that have shifted the dynamics of international society (Colas, 2002). For context, note that Deutsch (1954) reflected, in his discussion of the political community, on the elements that enabled collectives with distinctly different characteristics to operate as discrete political units able to deliver effective governance over extended periods of time. His reflections ranged from the Greek city-states, comparing scale and political institutions with those of the Roman Empire, on through to the factors that contribute to the operation of the United States as a political community, and ultimately to debate concerning the possible emergence of a global political community. He was concerned, in particular, with the role of shared interests, the right to share benefits, and belief in the legitimacy of the institutions underpinning the community.

There is a long tradition of linkage between community development (taken here to mean strategies aimed at cultivating mutual aid, local networks, and communal coherence) and sport. This connection is rooted in the notion that sport has agency in facilitating a range of social objectives (Elias & Dunning, 1986; Holt, 1989; MacAloon, 2006). Sport has indeed frequently been used by a range of practitioners to address community issues. The UK Action Sport initiatives of the early 1980s adopted sport, in the aftermath of the inner-city riots of 1981, as a conduit for responding to concerns about community cohesion and inclusion (Hylton & Bramham, 2008). The idea that sport can contribute to community development has been widely embraced by public policy makers in, for example, the United Kingdom (CCPA, 2002), Australia (Social Inclusion Unit, 2005), and Canada (Clark, 2008). The establishment of this domestic policy perspective has, to some extent, prepared the way, contributing to a "moral imperative" (Beacom, 2009, p. 98) for the international community to respond to wider development needs through sport.

As table 10.1 details, many examples exist of development agendas being addressed internationally through community-based sport and physical activity programs. This is particularly so for wider social and health initiatives. Draper, Kolbe-Alexander, and Lambert (2009) carried out a detailed investigation of a community-based physical-activity program designed to promote health in disadvantaged communities in the Western Cape area of South Africa. The community-based approach depends on effective engagement with a range of stakeholders and empowerment of local community members. While many questions remain concerning the production of an evidence base that illustrates the efficacy of such activity, anecdotal and case study evidence is accumulating and appears to lend support to the contention that sport has, on a number of levels, something tangible to offer in the community development process. For case study evidence of impact on community development, see Beacom and Read (2011); for a more general discussion of the challenge of evaluating the efficacy of sport-based development programs, see Coalter (2009).

Many categories of actors are involved in the support and delivery of what is termed "sport for development." They include the state, multilateral institutions, multinational companies, sport clubs, sport stars, sport federations, and community-based and nongovernmental organizations. State leaders, too, can be added to this list, as illustrated by Beyond Sport (under the patronage of Tony Blair) and the Peres Center for Peace, both of which use sport in attempting to meet development objectives. This role of sport in the social and economic development process is a further example of the diffusion of actors currently involved in governance. The range of actors and institutions involved in the sport-for-development process is illustrated in table 10.1.

Table 10.1 Selected Sport-for-Development Programs Highlighting Diversity of Actors

Name of program	Details of program	Contributing institutions and actors
A Ganar/ Vencer	This US$3.6 million program (funded largely by the Inter-American Development Bank) is used to train 3,200 young people in work and entrepreneurial skills. It operates in Quito, Montevideo, Rio de Janeiro, and other cities in Latin America.	The program is run by an NGO, Partners of the Americas, and funded by the Inter-American Development Bank with contributions from Nike Foundation and Microsoft.
Alive & Kicking	Aims include the employment of those without jobs to stitch leather balls for sport (especially soccer) that are donated to children in disadvantaged communities in sub-Saharan Africa. The balls contain health awareness messages warning children about the dangers of HIV/AIDS, malaria, and tuberculosis.	Partners include soccer federations (e.g., the English Football Association and UEFA), governmental bodies (UK Sport), private companies (e.g., Fair Trade Sports), awareness campaigns and NGOs (e.g., EduSport, Tackle Africa).
Bayer Cares Foundation	Since 1990, it has devoted €2.6 million (nearly US$3.5 million) to social projects in Brazil, including a soccer academy designed to get disadvantaged children into school. In 1993, the American Chamber of Commerce awarded Bayer the ECO Prize in recognition of this project.	Bayer (Brazil) and soccer coaches
Coaching for Hope	Uses soccer in South Africa, Burkina Faso, and Mali to "create better futures" (Coaching for Hope, n.d.) for young people. Coaching courses are organized by professional coaches from the UK to train local youth workers; simultaneously, local coaches learn how to deliver HIV/AIDS awareness sessions to young people in their communities.	The program is part of the international volunteering and development charity Skillshare International. Partners include Adidas, the English FA, and English soccer clubs.
Diambars de Saly	Diambars is a football academy in Senegal that educates and trains 48 street children annually. This program also opened in South Africa in 2010.	Co-established by two international football players, it is sponsored by Adidas. The International Federation of Association Football (FIFA) has funded, through its Football for Hope scheme, the building of a cultural center.
Football For Hope	FIFA partners with NGOs that promote the use of soccer (no other sport) to enhance education, social integration, and empowerment of young people. One element of this initiative is the establishment of 20 Football for Hope centers across Africa as part of the 2010 World Cup initiatives. The first five centers delegated to run the Football for Hope program (announced in 2007) were Mathare Youth Sports Association, Play Soccer Ghana, the Association des Jeunes Sportifs de Kigali Espérance (Rwanda), Grassroot Soccer (South Africa), and the Association Malienne pour la Promotion de la Jeune Fille et de la Femme (Mali).	Spearheaded by FIFA and funded by official partners (Adidas, Emirates, Sony, Coca-Cola, Hyundai, and Visa). Financial support is also provided to 39 NGOs that run discrete development-through-soccer projects in locations ranging from Mali to Tahiti. *(continued)*

Table 10.1 *(continued)*

Name of program	Details of program	Contributing institutions and actors
Football 4 Peace International	Initiated in the Palestine/Israel border area in 2001 and then extended to the border of Northern Ireland and the Republic of Ireland, this initiative uses sport to bring communities in conflict together through sport. Currently, 24 mixed communities with more than 1,000 children participate in the program.	It is supported by the English FA, the University of Brighton, British Council Israel, Israel Sports Administration, and German Sport University Cologne.
Mathare Youth Sports Association (MYSA)	Based in the Mathare township in Nairobi and in operation since 1987, this group organizes sport teams and matches with a strict code of behavior and prescribed duties for all participants. Stated benefits include HIV/AIDS awareness, leadership training, and community service work (e.g., environmental cleanup).	Supporting partners include 9 domestic and international development agencies, 9 companies in the private sector, 12 governmental departments (local and national, as well as support from Norwegian government ministries), and 9 sport institutions. Partial funding is received through FIFA's Football for Hope program.
NBA Cares	This corporate social responsibility program of the U.S.-based National Basketball Association (NBA) addresses a range of social and developmental issues within the US and internationally through basketball-based integrations (NBA, 2013). This includes a series of international initiatives under its Basketball Without Borders programs. The 2012-2013 community report records that to date, leagues, players, and teams have contributed more than US$20 million to charity and more than 2.3 million hours to community and program development initiatives.	The National Basketball Association and UNICEF
Peres Center for Peace	Established by Israeli politician and diplomat Shimon Peres to "build an infrastructure of peace and reconciliation by and for the people of the Middle East that promotes socioeconomic development, while advancing cooperation and mutual understanding" (Press Center Mission, n.d.). Sport is used in one of five pillars of the program (Nurturing a Culture of Peace in the Region's Youth). For example, the Twinned Peace Sport Schools "encourage reconciliation between young Palestinian and Israeli boys and girls from disadvantaged and peripheral communities by providing an extracurricular program of sport training, Peace Education instruction, auxiliary educational support, and joint Palestinian–Israeli sporting and social activities" (Pores Center Sport, n.d.).	Specific partners are not publicly declared, but the group's website indicates contributions from governments, corporations, foundations, organizations, and private individuals.

Name of program	Details of program	Contributing institutions and actors
Right to Play	Styled as the largest sport-for-development NGO, this is an "international humanitarian organization that uses sport and play programs to improve health, develop life skills, and foster peace among children and communities in some of the most disadvantaged areas of the world. This includes girls, the disabled, child combatants and refugees" (Right to Play, 2010). Specifically, it supports the building of community infrastructures through training of local community leaders to deliver its programs. It is located in regions marked by war, poverty, and disease in Africa, Asia, the Middle East, and South America.	Contributors include various UN agencies (e.g., UN Refugee Agency, UNICEF, UNESCO, the World Health Organization, the International Labour Organization, the CORE Initiative, CARE), celebrated athletes (who act as role models), the Olympic and Paralympic Movements, local NGOs, and Adidas.
United for UNICEF	In this scheme started in 1999, Manchester United Football Club supports vulnerable children (e.g., those affected by emergencies such as the 2004 Indian Ocean tsunami) by collecting donations at soccer matches, highlighting UNICEF policy campaigns, and using Manchester United staff and players as ambassadors. For example, during the 2007 preseason tour of South Africa, prominent players visited UNICEF-supported projects in Cape Town and Johannesburg.	Contributors are UNICEF and Manchester United; local NGOs benefit.
International Inspiration	This international sport-for-development initiative was part of the international engagement efforts conducted by the London Organising Committee of the Olympic and Paralympic Games in the lead-up to the 2012 London Games. It has touched the lives of 12 million children across 20 countries through a series of sport-based interventions often involving sport leadership programs developed in conjunction with in-country organizations.	Delivery commenced in August 2007 and involved a range of stakeholders including UK Sport and the key delivery partners UNICEF and the British Council. Contributions totaling about £9 million (about US$14 million) came from the UK's Department for International Development; the UK's Department of Culture, Media, and Sport; the UK's Foreign and Commonwealth Office; UNICEF; the British Council; and the English Premier League.

As demonstrated in a number of these examples, international multilateral institutions (e.g., the UN) were largely responsible for the considerable increase in sport-for-development programs. Since the United Nations declared 2005 to be its Year of Peace and Development through sport and physical exercise (United Nations, 2005), there has been a rapid rise in the number of sport-for-development initiatives and an increasing range of stakeholders engaged in the process (e.g., sports equipment manufacturers, international sport federations). Even before that, official attempts by multilateral institutions to use sport have been ongoing for some time. For example, in 1978, UNESCO (the United Nations Educational, Scientific, and Cultural Organization) General Conference adopted the International Charter of Physical Education and Sport; for a summary of milestones in sport and development, see "Timeline" (n.d.) in this chapter's reference list. The UN is particularly important in this process for the following reasons:

1. It has driven a moral imperative for action through sport to enhance community development, especially in its attempt to promote the MDGs through sport-based programs.

2. As a particularly significant power broker, it has gone some way toward setting the terms of reference for international development through sport (e.g., United Nations, 2003). Its focus on the concept of partnership, replacing the traditional donor–recipient relationship, gives community-based organizations in a number of contexts the opportunity to have a voice in the wider development process.

Linking sport for development with the 2012 Olympic and Paralympic Games, the initiative named International Inspiration engaged a number of stakeholders, including the London Organising Committee of the Olympic and Paralympic Games, the British Council, UNICEF, and the English Premier League, as well as UK government departments (with development, sport, and foreign policy briefs) in support of sport-based interventions aimed at promoting community development. Launched in 2007, the initial objective, to "transform" the lives of 12 million children across 20 countries through sport-based initiatives, was in many respects the international face of London 2012 (the verb "transform" was amended to "enrich" in 2009, perhaps reflecting concern that expectations regarding the capacity of sport to deliver a range of benefits could be overinflated, ultimately having a negative impact on such initiatives). This objective was to be achieved by working through local schools and community organizations. Program delivery (in particular, sport leadership initiatives) was dependent on the expertise and support of a number of partners, including the Youth Sport Trust and, crucially, in-country community-based organizations. The program's objective, in line with a growing body of sport-for-development initiatives, was to use sport and physical activity to address a range of quality-of-life issues (Levermore and Beacom, 2012), including concerns about social exclusion, the development of life skills, leadership training, and healthy living. Notwithstanding questions that remain concerning the efficacy of this intervention, the initiative did demonstrate the need to engage with a multiplicity of actors (grassroots as well as national and transnational) in order to initiate, resource, and deliver such programs.

An understanding of IR can, it is argued, provide valuable insights into shifting power relations concerning sport in the wider community development frame. For example, more critical IR perspectives—especially from a postcolonial or radical feminist perspective as found in the fourth debate discussed earlier—highlight the dynamics of unequal power relations through the discourses of imperialism inherent in sport-for-development programs. For instance, some programs are criticized as being focused mainly on young males living in urban centers and mainly on sports that are "Western." FIFA, in particular, is criticized for stipulating that no sport other than soccer can be used in its sport-for-development program. A further example derives from followers of the south Asian sport of kabaddi, who have protested that this sport is rarely used in sport for development and is excluded from mega sport events such as the Commonwealth Games and the Olympics ("India," 2006). IR can contribute to this debate insofar as it comments on the developing role of civil society groups in international society and on the extent to which opportunities exist for such bodies to transcend their local settings and influence the wider development process.

Identity: Globalization and Localization

A core question underpinning this edited collection concerns the extent to which the processes of globalization and localization have affected global sport. Levermore (2004, pp. 16–30) related sport to a core area of IR—the representation of the "inter-state worldview"—by exploring how sport is wittingly and unwittingly used to bolster the impression the that "we" live "naturally" in neatly drawn bounded territories (nations or states). He went on to consider how this perception of nationalism and national stereotypes was built up through media representation and action by sport federations and governments. One example (not addressed in Levermore's 2004 publication) involves actions taken by FIFA and the English Football Association that prevented the world-famous soccer player Puskás from playing in England because he refused to play for his national team, Hungary, following the 1956 Soviet invasion ("Ferenc Puskás," 2006).

Thisinter-state worldview stands in direct contrast to the ethnonationalist viewpoint associated with Anthony D. Smith, who argues that nationalism remains a very strong and natural feature of international society:

> *Nations are self-aware ethnic groups; they are the largest groups based on a conviction of ancestral relatedness, and come into being when the majority of their members feel they belong to, and participate in, the nation.* (2006, pp. 169–170)

A third perspective posits that forces of localism and globalization are weakening national identities. This approach is associated with Fukuyama

(2004, p. 161), who suggests that the system of interlinking states—and identification with an individual state—is being undermined from below by people's protests against the tyranny of the state and from above by the power of the global economy (resulting in increased mobility of labor, capital, and information). He goes on to argue that a strong state system is needed in the 21st century, one made up of smaller but stronger states. Sen (2006) and Maloouf (2000) add to this debate by noting that the notion of national identity has been widened to recognize that equally important identities (e.g., related to territory, faith, and family) coexist with national identity. Moreover, "national" identity might also incorporate a cosmopolitanism that engages and revels in global citizenship.

These well-defined debates have been taken up in the last decade by a range of scholars across the social sciences who are interested in the relationship between sport and nationalism. Many take a view that sport and fandom assist in the construction of an imagined belief in the nation—far removed from the concept of ethnonationalism. For example, King (2006) highlights how nationalism is plotted through soccer fandom and argues that nationalism is being altered through the processes of the global economy, transnationalism, and localism. So, too, does Lechner (2007, p. 215), who, considering a case study of the Dutch national soccer team, notes that media coverage associated with the team's involvement in national competitions assists the "myth of national football distinction." Similarly, Black (2007) and Kersting (2007) illustrate how sporting mega events are enveloped by a discourse that highlights the inclusive nation-building elements associated with it.

However, though many events have taken place since 2004 that in practice highlight both sides of this debate, the one-dimensional "immutable worldview" picture has in many ways grown stronger. Examples include the ability of sport to cement the immutability of the dominance of nation-states, partly through the unifying effects that sport is supposed to portray (noted in the community section of this chapter) and also in projecting the competition of nation against nation in sporting contests. Instances that echo A.D. Smith's ethnonationalist perspective are evident in academic approaches to nationalism. For instance, Schrag (2009) considers how the 2006 World Cup in Germany and the 2008 Olympics in Beijing were demonstrations of an accurate national expression. Many more examples are evident in everyday mass media discourse; here are selected examples since 2004:

• The way sport has been used in an effort to unify populations and reduce hostility to occupying military forces in Iraq and Afghanistan. Sports used in this manner include cricket (Leicester, 2010) and boxing ("Boxing," 2008), and soccer has been the favored tool of the British government, which invited the English Football Association to organize matches between local residents and occupying forces shortly after occupation began. Furthermore, in 2006, the media spotlight focused on a series of successes for the Iraqi national soccer team, which, commentators claimed, helped increase cohesion in the country (see, for example, Parker & Kubacy, 2006; Philp & Haynes, 2007).

• The "peace match" between Turkey and Armenia, a football World Cup qualifying match in September 2008, which the Armenian president invited his Turkish equivalent to attend. This event started a process that resulted in the establishment of diplomatic ties between the two nations for the first time; no diplomatic ties had been previously established due to the genocide of 1.5 million Armenians in the First World War (Halpin, 2009).

• The Peace Games, organized with the assistance of the International Olympic Committee in 2006 to provide an opportunity for communities across the Democratic Republic of the Congo to integrate, with the specified aim of developing trust and confidence. This effort was one of the highlighted topics at a conference held in South Africa in 2009 (the International Association for Physical Education and Sport for Girls and Women World Congress at Stellenbosch University) that considered identity and sport.

Similarly, sport events—especially those held between competing national teams—continue to highlight tensions along ethnic, national, and civilizational lines. Examples include the following:

• A Dutch company's selling of more than 100,000 replica Nazi war helmets to soccer fans (especially Dutch and English) for the 2006 World Cup held in Germany. The company claimed that the helmets were intended to tease Germans; they were banned by police. In response to the helmets, German toilet tissue manufacturers produced orange (the color of the Dutch national team) toilet rolls, which sold well throughout Germany (Graham, 2006).

• Controversy over Pakistani cricketers not selected to play in the Indian Premier League (IPL) in 2010. When Bollywood stars objected, their films were boycotted (Miglani, 2010).

• Considerable unrest in Egypt and Algeria as a result of two World Cup 2010 qualifying matches ("Egypt-Algeria," 2009).

• The demonizing of Islam through sport. Since 2004, growing mass media attention has highlighted threats attributed to Islam, either for potential terrorism or as a religion with traits that are harsh and undemocratic, disadvantage women, and are basically "backward." Examples include the German newspaper *Der Tagesspiegel* printing a cartoon before the 2006 World Cup depicting Iranian players as suicide bombers (this just after the uproar over a Danish newspaper's publication of a cartoon depicting Muhammad); regular headlines highlighting the threat of Islamic terror at sport events, such as "Olympics Threatened by Islamic Separatists" (Branigan, 2008); and the continual depiction of the British boxer Amir Khan by reference to his

Muslim identity—for example, "Bolton Wanderer on Pilgrimage From Mecca to Muhammad" (Syed, 2006).

The danger with such representation is that it leads to exclusionary practices. Sport events tend to have only a fleeting effect on unifying communities. For example, analysis by Hussey (2006) noted that racial problems were as much of a problem in France a few years after its success in the 1998 World Cup as they had been before it. Mignon (cited in Kuper, 2005, p. 6) argues that "this idea of integration by football was an illusion," as ethnic groups continue to experience high levels of poverty and racism. Furthermore, sport events have continued to highlight negative stereotypes of low-income countries. Soon after the announcement that the World Cup was to be held in South Africa in 2010, a series of images (relating, for example, to a ramshackle transportation system, lack of restaurants, tourist facilities, and technology) was sent around the world via e-mails expressing incredulity that such a "backward" country would host such a tournament.

Yet there is an argument from critical perspectives of IR that sport—in particular, sport events—also allow for contestation of the dominant interstate worldview representation. Historically, this has meant that sport events have allowed parallel—revolutionary or alternative—ideologies to be disseminated alongside dominant discourses. For some, this protest also involves challenging the exclusionary aspects of nationalism. One instance involves the international soccer competitions ("World Cups" from 2005 to 2010 organized by subnational entities not affiliated with FIFA in the Turkish Republic of Northern Cyprus, Occitania, Sápmi, and Malta) that have arisen for unrepresented nations—that is, nations that do not currently have official state recognition. Although this approach can be viewed as further evidence of cementing the inter-state worldview (due to the desire to join the community of states), some see such tournaments as recognizing the inherent problem of the inter-state system, supporting as it does entities that are artificially premised upon false notions of ethnicity.

Such evidence, though, is heavily outweighed by examples that contribute to the immutable picture of nations and states in the inter-state worldview. Likewise, soccer victories for Iraq and the playing of cricket in Afghanistan have made no recognizable impact on the ethnic confrontations in either country.

Exploitation for Capital

The link between capital and international relations is fundamental and has attracted a number of sharply dissenting IR perspectives, including a variety of Marxist interpretations that focus on the exploitative nature of world markets (Waever 1996) and neoliberal approaches that explore the role of the marketplace as a mechanism central to enhancing economic welfare (Elliot, 2002). The emergence and expansion of modern sport itself have been linked to the development of capitalism. Budd (2004, p. 31) argues that "sport has followed capitalism in becoming global and expresses ever more clearly the competitive, exploitative relations of capitalist society." Recent evidence supports this assertion through increasing reports of the plundering of talented African soccer players, who either get traded to make profit for people smugglers without any chance of success or, for the lucky few who make it, gain considerable wealth for the soccer clubs they play for ("Neo-imperialism," 2007). Others take a less normative position, focusing on the processes by which modern sport has engaged with—and been engaged by—the commercial environment (Andrews, 2004). Although these processes can be appreciated from sociological, economic, and political perspectives, IR again provides an alternative frame of reference through which this key aspect of modern sport can be understood.

An important contribution from IR is the subdiscipline known as international political economy (IPE). Much like IR (as discussed in this chapter's introduction), IPE, as it has been adopted by scholars seeking an alternative perspective on the dynamics of international relations, has become part of the debate on the boundaries and connections between so-called academic disciplines. For example, is IPE, in its concern with the governance of international institutions, anything more than the investigation of "political aspects of economic decision making" (Burnham, 2003, p. 415), and should it attract recognition as a distinct academic discipline?

When considering issues of sport and capital in the context of IR, IPE provides a valuable conceptual framework because it facilitates an understanding of the interface between private corporate interests and public bodies who would traditionally seek to influence the governance of sport. This framework is significant not just in the investigation of various modern sporting forms but also in the context of specific international sporting events, such as the Olympic Games. IPE provides a route to understanding the interaction between the multiplicity of stakeholders involved in, for example, the bidding process for the Games. It provides a tool for unpacking the political, social, and economic interests in such processes and the increasingly global dimension of the Games (Askew, Close, & Xu, 2007). When considering the impact of sporting events on the changing global economy, IPE provides a perspective on the characteristics of the "global Games" in what Nauright (2004) and Nauright and Schimmel (2005) describe as "event-driven" economies, where states without the advanced infrastructure and systems of governance necessary to promote and host such events are increasingly disadvantaged.

Lee (2004) provides an example of the application of IPE to sport. His assessment of the governance of world soccer identified the increasing contribution of IPE to IR discourse. In particular, he noted that the shifting away of political authority from the core executive and other traditional state entities—and toward a more complex governance driven by a web of interdependencies between organizations at subnational, national, international, and transnational levels—has necessitated rethinking how we investigate the dynamics of international relations. This rethinking, he argues, is particularly appropriate in relation to sport, where governance through a range of autonomous and semiautonomous organizations takes place alongside appeals to the public sphere for funding and other forms of resourcing. It also links directly to a central concern of IPE: the evolving relationship between sources of political authority and the activities of those actors (e.g., in international trade and international finance) leading the emerging (global) markets. In this sense, then, IPE, as an aspect of IR, provides a framework for analyzing contemporary developments in international sport (Forster & Pope, 2005).

Much of the literature relating to sport and IPE tends toward the perspective that focuses on the increasing effect of private sport interests on the economics of sport. For example, Ben-Porat (2002), assessing the political economy of the Israeli football league (from 1989-1990, during which time 500 foreign players were employed in the first, second, and third divisions of the league), argues that commercial realities and the impact of globalization on sport (in particular, the pressure to import "cheap" foreign players) have supplanted a league structure that had been dominated by political patronage and a parochial mentality with rigid public control of governance of the game.

Other examples of the effect of private commercial interests include the following:

• The effect of the development process on the evolution of baseball in the Dominican Republic. Klein (2007) adopts a critical dependency IPE perspective, which focuses on the effect of private North American–based sporting interests on the game. He argues that pursuant to relaxation of racial segregationist policies in North America, players from Latin America were increasingly "poached" for North American teams, which gradually eroded the Latin American player base and undermined the economic strength of the Latin American leagues.

• What commentators consider an unhealthy competition between Adidas and Nike in soccer in order to gain a competitive advantage, especially during World Cup events (Gregory, 2006). Adidas is an official sponsor of FIFA and the World Cup; Nike sponsors individual players and teams. Both spend in excess of €200 million (about US$260 million annually) in sponsorship and advertising (H. Dunne, 2006). *The Times* (Marcotti, 2010) highlighted how these tensions are manifested, noting complaints by the French player Emmanuel Petit that FIFA favors players contracted to Adidas; after the final of the 1998 World Cup in France, official photos of the winning team highlighted only Adidas players. This struggle extends even to competing for the patronage of sport-for-development schemes (Levermore, 2009).

Summary

In discussing what he considered to be a knowledge gap in the understanding of international sport in the context of the social sciences, MacAloon (1981, preface, xvii) registered his surprise and concern as follows: "I took this scholarly vacancy as further evidence of the contempt of 'serious culture' for the ludic side of life; a contempt from which those of us who are having our most important experiences in sport, felt ourselves daily to suffer." Thirty years later, sport has moved up the political agenda nationally and internationally, and awareness has grown of the role of sport in cultural and social life. Yet from the traditional perspectives of IR, little has changed in relation to the study of sport. For many in the discipline, it continues to be of marginal interest and unworthy of serious scholarly activity. Only when sport engages with "high politics" does it gain a mention from them—and even then often a cursory one. At the same time, many engaged in the study and practice of sport are reticent about moving beyond the comfort zone of a limited range of theoretical constructs. This chapter, therefore, seeks to draw attention to the opportunities inherent in the study of international sport from the perspectives of IR by providing an overview of the discipline, including core concepts and theoretical perspectives and debates. These debates are applied to four areas—governance, community, capital, and identity.

There are limitations, of course, to what can be achieved by such endeavor. Though we are fully engaged with the IR debates, we sit on the margins of that academic community; therefore, our application of IR to sport is rarely critiqued and contested by those who are at the center of IR. Yet no academic discipline facilitates wholly objective analysis of the phenomena at the center of its investigations. S. Smith (2003, p. 234), commenting on the development of the discipline of IR, has noted that "all knowledge is partial; theory is not the mirror of nature and thus all knowledge claims about the world are made in the context of power . . . [and] all our theories reflect and support specific social forces." Nevertheless, theoretical constructs that have evolved in and between academic disciplines do provide useful conceptual tools for going beyond explanations and help move us toward understanding the characteristics of social phenomena. It is in this context that we suggest IR has the potential to contribute to an understanding of the dynamics of sport in international society.

References

Allison, L. (Ed.). (1988). *Politics of sport*. New York: St. Martin's Press.

Allison, L. (Ed.). (2005). *The global politics of sport: The role of global institutions in sport*. London: Routledge.

Andrews, D. (2004). Sport in the late capitalist moment. In T. Slack (Ed.), *The commercialisation of sport* (pp. 5-28). London: Routledge.

Armstrong, G. (2007). The global footballer and the local war-zone: George Weah and transnational networks in Liberia, West Africa. *Global Networks, 7*(2), 230–247.

Askew, D., Close, P., & Xu, X. (2007). *The Beijing Olympiad: The political economy of a sporting mega event.* London: Routledge.

Barnett, M., & Duvall, R. (2005). Power in global governance. In M. Barnett & R. Duvall (Eds.), *Power in global governance* (pp. 1–33). Cambridge, UK: Cambridge University Press.

Baylis, J., Smith, S., & Owens, P. (2007). *The globalization of world politics.* Oxford, UK: Oxford University Press.

Beacom, A. (2000). Sport and International Relations: The case for cross-disciplinary investigation. *The Sports Historian, 20*(2), 1–23.

Beacom A. (2009). Disability sport and the politics of development. In R. Levermore & A. Beacom (Eds.), *Sport and international development* (pp. 98–123). Basingstoke, UK: Palgrave.

Beacom, A. (2012). *International diplomacy and the Olympic movement: The new mediators.* Basingstoke, UK: Palgrave.

Beacom A., & Read, L. (2011). Sustaining development through sport. In B. Houlihan & M. Green (Eds.), *The Routledge handbook of sport development* (pp. 337-352). London: Routledge. Beck, P.J. (2003). The relevance of the "irrelevant": Football as a missing dimension in the study of British relations with Germany. *International Affairs, 79*(2), 389–411.

Ben-Porat, A. (2002). The political economy of soccer: The importation of foreign soccer players to the Israeli league. *Soccer and Society, 3*(1), 54–68.

Betsill, M., & Corell E. (Eds.). (2007). *NGO diplomacy: The influence of non-governmental organizations in environmental negotiation.* Cambridge, MA: MIT Press.

Black, D. (2007). The symbolic politics of sport mega-events: 2010 in comparative perspective. *Politikon, 34*(3), 261–276.

Boxing is good for reconciliation. (2008, March 27). *The Economist.* www.economist.com/node/10926023.

Branigan, T. (2008, July 26). Olympics threatened by Islamic separatists. *The Observer.*

Brown, C., & Ainley, K. (2009). *Understanding International Relations* (4th ed.). London: Palgrave MacMillan.

Budd, A. (2004). Sport and capitalism. In R. Levermore & A. Budd (Eds.), *Sport and International Relations—An emerging relationship* (pp. 31–47). London: Routledge.

Burnham, P. (2003). Political economy. In I. McLean & A. McMillan (Eds.), *Concise Oxford dictionary of politics* (pp. 381-384). Oxford, UK: Oxford University Press.

Calvocoressi, P. (2010). *World politics since 1945.* London: Longman.

CCPR. (2002). Everybody wins: Sport and social inclusion. www.cfds.co.uk./assets/0000/1696/00027.pdf.

Clark, W. (2008). *Kids' sports.* Component of Statistics Canada catalogue no. 11-008-X: Canadian Social Trends. www.statcan.gc.ca/pub/11-008-x/2008001/article/10573-eng.pdf.

Coaching for Hope. (n.d.). About us. www.coachingforhope.org/about_us.php.

Coalter, F. (2008). *A wider social role for sport*. London: Routledge.

Coalter, F. (2009). Sport-in-development: Accountability or development? In R. Levermore & A. Beacom (Eds.), *Sport and international* development (pp. 55–75). Basingstoke, UK: Palgrave.

Colas, A. (2002). *International civil society*. Cambridge, UK: Polity Press.

Cooper, A., English, J., & Thakur, R. (Eds.). (2002). *Enhancing global governance: Towards a new diplomacy?* New York: United Nations University Press.

Cooper, A., Hocking, B., & Maley, W. (Eds.). (2008). *Global governance and diplomacy: Worlds apart?* Basingstoke, UK: Palgrave Macmillan.

Der Derian, J. (Ed.). (1995). International theory: Critical investigations. New York, NY: NY University Press.

Deutsch, K. (1954). *Political community at the international level*. Cambridge, MA: MIT Press.

Draper, C.E., Kolbe-Alexander, T.L., & Lambert, E.V. (2009). A retrospective evaluation of a community-based physical activity health promotion program . *Journal of Physical Activity and Health, 6*(5), 578–588.

Dunne, H. (2006). Everything to play for. *Corp Comms, 36.* www.corpcommsmagazine.co.uk/features/209-everything-to-play-for.

Dunne, T., Kurki, M., & Smith, S. (2010). *International relations theories: Discipline and diversity*. Oxford, UK: Oxford University Press.

Egypt-Algeria World Cup anger turns violent in Cairo. (2009, November 20). BBC. http://news.bbc.co.uk/1/hi/8369983.stm.

Elias, N., & Dunning, E. (1986). *Quest for excitement: Sport and leisure in the civilizing process*. Oxford, UK: Blackwell.

Elliot, L. (2002). The global politics of the environment. In S. Lawson (Ed.), *The new agenda for International Relations* (pp. 109-127). Cambridge, UK: Polity Press.

Ferenc Puskás. (2006, November 17). *The Times* [of London].

Foer, F. (2004). Soccer vs. McWorld. *Foreign Policy, 140*, 32.

Forster, J., & Pope, N. (2005). *The political economy of global sporting organisations*. London: Routledge.

Fukuyama, F. (2004). *State building—Governance and world order in the twenty-first century*. London: Profile Books.

Galtung, J. (1982). Sport as a carrier of deep culture and structure. *Current Research on Peace and Violence, 2*(2/3), 133–143.

García, B. (2009). Sport governance after the White Paper: The demise of the European model? *International Journal of Sport Policy, 1*(3), 267–284.

Gilpin, R. (2003). *Global political economy: Understanding the international economic order*. Princeton, NJ: Princeton University Press.

Giulianotti, R., & McArdle, D. (2007). *Sport, civil liberties, and human rights*. London: Taylor & Francis.

Graham, B. (2006, January 23). Fans face cup ban over "Nazi" helmets. Daily Telegraph. www.telegraph.co.uk/news/worldnews/europe/germany/1508580/Fans-face-cup-ban-over-Nazi-helmets.html.

Gregory, S. (2006, May 22). Competition: Global game. *Time Magazine*.

Griffiths, M., O'Callaghan, T., & Roach, S.C. (2007). *International relations: The key concepts*. London: Routledge.

Grohmann, K. (2008, August 21). China is the new sports superpower: Rogge. *Reuters*. www.reuters.com/article/newsOne/idUSPEK22518020080821.

Halpin, T. (2009, October 10). Football diplomacy seals the deal between Armenia and Turkey. *The Times* [of London].

Hill, C. (1996). *Olympic politics: Athens to Atlanta*. Manchester, UK: Manchester University Press.

Hill, J. (2009). The European Commission's White Paper On Sport: A step backwards for specificity? *International Journal of Sport Policy and Politics, 1*(3), 253–266

Hobsbawm, E.J. (1983). *The invention of tradition*. Cambridge, UK: Cambridge University Press.

Hocking, B. (2006). Multistakeholder diplomacy: Foundations, forms, functions, and frustrations. In J. Kurbalija & V. Katrandjiev (Eds.), *Multistakeholder diplomacy: Challenges and opportunities* (pp. 13–29). Malta/Geneva: DiploFoundation.

Holden, G. (2008). World cricket as a postcolonial international society: IR meets the history of sport. *Global Society, 22*(3), 337–368.

Holt, R. (1989). *Sport and the British*. Oxford, UK: Clarendon Press.

Hussey, A. (2006, April 2). Special report: French football: Le temps modernes. *Observer Sport Monthly*.

Hulton, R. & Bramham, P. (Eds.). (2008). Sports development: Policy process and practice. London: Routledge.

Implementing the European Commission White Paper on Sport [Special issue]. (2009). *International Journal of Sport Policy and Politics, 1*(3).

India wants kabaddi at Olympics. (2006, December 23). *The Times of India*. http://timesofindia.indiatimes.com/articleshow/910987.cms.

Jackson, R., & Sørensen, G. (2010). *Introduction to IR: Theory and approaches* (4th ed.). Oxford, UK: Oxford University Press.

Jackson, S., & Haigh, S. (2008). Between and beyond politics: Sport and foreign policy in a globalizing world. *Sport in Society, 11*(4), 349–358.

Karchagin, Y. (2007). Russia, Paraguay advance co-operation. *International Affairs, 53*, 113–121.

Kersting, N. (2007). Sport and national identity: A comparison of the 2006 and 2010 FIFA World Cups. *Politikon, 34*(3), 277–293.

King, A. (2006). Sport and nationalism. In G. Delanty & K. Kumar (Eds.), *The SAGE handbook of nations and nationalism* (pp. 249-259). London: Sage.

Klein, A. (2007). Latinizing the national pastime. *International Journal of the History of Sport, 17*(4) , 403–429.

Kooiman, J. (1993). *Modern governance: New government—Society interactions*. London: Sage

Kuper, S. (2005, November 12). Racism lives on in France as World Cup win fades. *Financial Times*.

Kyröläinen, H., & Varis, T. (1981). Approaches to the study of sports in International Relations. *Current Research on Peace and Violence, 4*(1), 55–88.

Lechner, F.J. (2007). Imagined communities in the global game: Soccer and the development of Dutch national identity. *Global Networks, 7*(2), 193–229.

Lee, S. (2004). Moving the goalposts: The governance and political economy of world football. In R. Levermore & A. Budd (Eds.), *Sport and International Relations: An emerging relationship* (pp. 112–128). Basingstoke, UK: Palgrave.

Leicester, J. (2010, January 27). Cricket helps Afghans beat their war miseries. NBC Sports. http://nbcsports.msnbc.com/id/35101598/ns/sports-other_sports/.

Levermore, C. (1924). *League of Nations.* New York: Brooklyn Daily Eagle.

Levermore, R. (2004). Sport and International Relations: Continued neglect? In R. Levermore & A. Budd (Eds.), *Sport and International Relations—An emerging relationship* (pp. 16–30). London: Routledge.

Levermore, R. (2008a). Sport: A new engine of development? *Progress in Development, 8*(2), 183–190.

Levermore, R. (2008b). Sport-in-international development: Time to treat it seriously? *Brown Journal of World Affairs, 14*(2), 55–66.

Levermore, R. (2008c, August 6). The double-edged sword of sport and political protest. *Foreign Policy in Focus.* www.fpif.org/articles/the_double-edged_sword_of_sport_and_political_protest.

Levermore, R. (2009). Sport-in-international development: Theoretical frameworks. In R. Levermore & A. Beacom (Eds.), *Sport and international development* (pp. 26–54). Basingstoke, UK: Palgrave.

Levermore, R., & Beacom, A. (Eds.). (2009). *Sport and international development.* Basingstoke, UK: Palgrave.

Levermore, R., & Beacom, A. (Eds.). (2012). Sport and international development Basingstove: Palgrave.

Levermore, R., & Budd, A. (Eds.). (2004). *Sport and International Relations—An emerging relationship.* London: Routledge.

Lowe, B. (1978). *Sport and International Relations.* Champaign, IL: Stipes.

MacAloon, J. (1981). *This great symbol: Pierre de Coubertin and the origins of the modern Olympic Games.* Chicago: University of Chicago Press.

MacAloon, J. (2006). Muscular Christianity after 150 years. *The International Journal of the History of Sport, 23*(5), 687–700.

Maguire, J. (1999). *Global sport: Identities, societies, civilizations.* Chichester, UK: Wiley.

Majumdar, B., & Hong, F. (2005). *Modern sport—The global obsession.* London: Routledge.

Maloouf, A. (2000). *On identity.* London: Harvill.

Marcotti, G. (2010, March 1). Wider view of France '98 gives Emmanuel Petit opportunity to look back in anger. *The Times* [of London].

Melissen, J. (2007). *The new diplomacy: Soft power in international relations.* London: Palgrave.

Miglani, S. (2010, January 21). Shunning Pakistani players is not cricket. Reuters. http://blogs.reuters.com/pakistan/2010/01/21/shunning-pakistani-players-is-not-cricket/.

Milanovic, B. (2005). Globalization and goals: Does soccer show the way? *Review of International Political Economy, 12*(5), 829–850.

Mtodzikowski, G. (1973). Sport we wepolczesnych stosunkach miedzynarodowych [Sport in contemporary international relations]. *Sprawy miedzynarodowe, 26*(4), pp. 1-8.

Mundy, K. (2007). Global governance educational change: Comparative education, (43)3, 321-323.

Nauright, J. (2004). Global games: Culture, political economy, and sport in the globalised world of the 21st century. *Third World Quarterly, 25*(7), 1325–1336.

Nauright, J., & Schimmel, S. (Eds.). (2005). *The political economy of sport.* Basingstoke, UK: Palgrave.

Neo-imperialism at the point of a boot. (2007, November 1). *The Economist.* www.economist.com/node/10064522.

Nye, J. (2011) *The future of power.* New York: PublicAffairs Books.

Parker, N., & Kubacy, M. (2006, December 16). For 63 minutes Iraqis were united in a dream of glory. Then Qatar scored. *The Times* [of London].

Parrish, R. (2003). *Sports law and policy in the European Union.* Manchester, UK: Manchester University Press.

Peres Center for Peace. (n.d.). Mission. www.peres-center.org/our_mission.

Peres Center for Peace. (n.d.). Sport. www.peres-center.org/sport_current.

Peres Center for Peace. (2013). Community report. www.nba.com/media/cares/NBA_carescommunityreport_v1.pdf.

Philp, C., & Haynes, D. (2007, July 28). United in hope as game kicks off—and fear when final whistle blows. *The Times* [of London].

Pigman, G. (2010). *Contemporary diplomacy.* Cambridge, UK: Polity Press.

Redhead, S. (1997). *Post-fandom and the millennial blues—The transformation of soccer culture.* London: Routledge.

Right to Play. (2010). Government of Canada announces funds for Right to Play. www.righttoplay.com/internationalnews-and-media/pages/pressreleases/CIDAFunding.aspx.

Riordan, J., & Krüger, A. (1999). *The international politics of sport in the twentieth century.* New York: Spon.

Schmidt, B. (2002). On the history and historiography of International Relations. In W. Carlsnaes, T. Risse, & B. Simmons (Eds.), *Handbook of International Relations* (pp. 3–23). London: Sage.

Schrag, D. (2009). "Flagging the nation" in international sport: A Chinese Olympics and a German World Cup. *International Journal of the History of Sport, 26*(8), 1084–1104.

Sen, A. (2006). *Identity and violence.* London: Penguin.

Shapiro, M. (1989). Representing world politics: The sport/war intertext. In M. Shapiro & J. Der Derian (Eds.), *International/intertextual relations—Postmodern Readings of World Politics* (pp. 69-96). Lexington, MA: Heath.

Smart, B. (2007). Not playing around: Global capitalism, modern sport, and consumer culture. *Global Networks*, 7(2), 113–134.

Smith, A.D. (2006). Ethnicity and nationalism. In G. Delanty & K. Kumar (Eds.), *The SAGE handbook of nations and nationalism* (pp. 169-181). London: Sage.

Smith, S. (2003). International Relations and international relations: The links between theory and practice. *Journal of International Relations and Development*, 6(3), 233–239.

Social Inclusion Unit. (2005, May). Social Inclusion Board: Overview of the Social Inclusion Agenda. Adelaide: Social Inclusion Unit, Government of South Australia.

Stoddart, B. (2006). Sport, cultural politics, and International Relations: England versus Germany, 1935. *Soccer and Society*, 7(1), 29–50.

Syed, M. (2006, September 23). Boxing: Bolton wanderer on Pilgrimage from Mecca to Muhammad. *The Times* [of London].

Szczepaniak, M. (1981). The role of sports in International Relations. *Indian Journal of Politics*, 15(1–2), 48–60.

Tharoor, S. (2008, June 8). Shashi on Sunday. *Sunday Times of India, Chennai.*

Tiessen, R. (2010, May 20–21). Global subjects or objects of globalization? The promotion of global citizenship in Sport for Peace and Development programs. Sport and International Development workshop, Dalhousie University.

Timeline of major developments in sport & development. (n.d.). Sport and Development.org. http://www.sportanddev.org/learnmore/history_of_sport_and_development/timeline/.

Tunis, J.R. 1936. The Dictators Discover Sport. *Foreign Affairs* 14 (4), 606–616.

United Nations. (2003). *Sport for Development and Peace: Towards achieving the Millennium Development Goals.* Report from the UN Inter-Agency Task Force on Sport for Development and Peace.

United Nations. (2005). *Sport 2005: International Year of Sport and Physical Education.* www.un.org/sport2005/.

Waever, O. (1996). The rise and fall of the inter-paradigm debate. In S. Smith, K. Booth, & M. Zalewski (Eds.), *International theory: Positivism and beyond* (pp. 149-185). Cambridge, UK: Cambridge University Press.

Washburn, J.N. (1956). Sport as a Soviet tool. *Foreign Affairs*, 34(3), 490–499.

Wood, A. (2004). *Kant*. Chichester, UK: Wiley.

IV

Governance: Regulation, Organization, and Implementation

Questions about the governance of sport that surfaced in part III are also dealt with extensively here. Individuals and communities, in sport and in society more generally, are faced with what has been described as a runaway world that induces a sense of future shock. In such a context, questions of governance arise. How can individuals and communities order their lives, regulate wider sporting and societal processes, and organize and implement more effective policies regarding sport and physical activity that enhance well-being, human performance, and social development? This section addresses these concerns by drawing on expertise in the study of sport law, social policy, management, and education.

For Deborah Healey, author of chapter 11 on sport and the law, the importance of understanding matters of law as they pertain to sport has increased significantly over the past 20 years. This importance stems from both a heightened understanding of legal rights and responsibilities and the commercialization of sport across the globe. With regard to the latter, disputes have intensified concerning sponsorship, marketing, and broadcasting in both the private and the public sectors. In terms of rights and responsibilities, Healey notes that athletes now expect to perform in a safe and well-organized work space and to be treated with procedural fairness. This increased sensitivity applies in both elite and non-elite contexts and involves broad questions of governance and regulation. Thus, as Healey astutely observes, a more sophisticated approach to legal risk management is required in the sport world, and, despite (and because) of societal variation, an understanding of law is vital.

Issues of governance and regulation also surface when examining sport and social policy. In chapter 12, Ramón Spaaij expertly explores these issues and notes that social policy as an academic discipline is thus concerned with analysis, explanation, and evaluation. For Spaaij, the term "social policy" is used to describe policies and practices aimed at promoting social welfare and well-being—that is, with both addressing and ameliorating social problems and analyzing the appropriateness and effectiveness of policies and programs. Involving governments as well as the voluntary, informal, and commercial sectors, attention in social policy currently focuses on how social resources and provisions can be delivered to people in need. In this connection, greater attention is now given, at least in some advanced industrial societies, to the role that sport can and does (and does not) play in areas such as social exclusion, unhealthy lifestyles, crime, community cohesion, intercultural dialogue, and urban regeneration.

In assessing the appropriateness and effectiveness of social policies, questions of management also surface, and chapter 13, by Lucie Thibault, provides a comprehensive account of how a knowledge of management studies can play a crucial role in relation to sport. In similar fashion to that of Spaaij, Thibault highlights various sectors' involvement with sport, but her focus is on the role of management, organizations, and business practices. Thibault ably describes the variety of organizations typically responsible for managing sport participation programs for all, as well as those targeted for elite athletes. She also attends to the management of teams, leagues, tournaments, events, and facilities. Another aspect of management studies and sport involves the production and distribution of sporting goods, equipment, and sportswear and the delivery of sport services, programs, and products—from the state and the private and voluntary sectors—at local, national, and global levels. Here, then, questions of management interweave with matters of law, social policy, and political science. An understanding of each is vital to understanding sport in the contemporary world.

Whereas the provision of sport at elite and leisure levels involves a variety of groups and social actors, the education of children more usually involves the state. In chapter 14, Dawn Penney examines the position and role of sport in educational structures and institutions, with particular reference to health and the physical education curricula, as well as cocurricular and extracurricular school sport settings. In addition, Penney perceptively points to the importance of tertiary institutions and physical education teacher education programs in studying the connections between sport and education. Taken as a whole, these various contexts provide opportunities to investigate wider questions of governance and matters of politics, sport policy, identity, equity, inclusion, and social capital. These matters not only lie at the heart of this chapter on sport and education but also serve as overriding themes in part IV of this collection on social science and sport and physical activity.

CHAPTER 11

Sport and the Law

Deborah Healey, LLB, LLM (Hons)

The focus of the law on the sport industry has dramatically increased over the last 20 years in response to heightened understanding of legal rights and responsibilities and the global explosion in sport commercialization. Worldwide consumer interest has created additional commercial opportunities for sport, and the size of the sporting economy has grown markedly, thanks to increased sponsorship, marketing, and broadcasting of sport, as well as more consistent government funding. All of this means that more is at risk when a sport dispute occurs. Athletes who devote much of their energy to their sport expect to have a safe and well-organized environment in which to participate; they also expect to be treated with procedural fairness. This greater awareness among athletes of their rights and of the significant commercial impact of illegal or negligent acts on their livelihood means legal risk for sport. From the opposite perspective, sports themselves strive to enforce both their rules and regulations and the lucrative arrangements to which they are parties. As a result, many areas of law once considered to be irrelevant to sport now apply in this new commercial environment.

All of these features result in increased involvement of the law in a wide variety of sporting situations. Thus sports need to engage in more sophisticated legal risk management at the same time as they seek out commercial opportunities to increase participation and exposure. While the position differs from country to country, the law has become an important feature of the environment of sport worldwide.

In exploring the involvement of law in this new era for the sport industry, this chapter focuses on the governance of sporting bodies and contextualizes governance in sport from a number of perspectives against the background of the changing nature of sport. National legal systems vary, but the legal issues raised in this chapter are common to most jurisdictions. The legal *solutions*, however, differ, and examples are presented here from a number of jurisdictions, particularly Australian law. The chapter considers the landscape of sport, the difficulties arising from its organization, ways in which the law applies to it, and limitations of court involvement. Governance, which at its simplest refers to the way in which an organization is controlled, is then considered in the context of sport, and the chapter surveys, in general terms, the legal governance obligations placed on organizations and their officers. Finally, it outlines self-regulatory mechanisms, based in contract law, developed by sport both internationally and in Australia to ensure compliance with the law and resolution of legal issues. Thus the material goes beyond the governance requirements of the legal system and surveys important developments in self-regulation aimed at ensuring effective governance in the sport environment in a practical, cost-effective way. This self-regulation works effectively and provides sport with tailored, cost-effective options that aid governance at all levels of the sport hierarchy.

The Global Organization and Regulation of Sport

Sport can be characterized globally by significant similarities and distinctions. A real dichotomy exists in most countries between the most popular sports and sport at the community level. Sports that are most popular in a particular country often employ structural and governance arrangements similar to those of major corporations. Other sports with very large participation numbers, which can be characterized as community sports, usually use simpler governance structures. Both groups carry significant responsibilities across a range of complex legal areas. The community sports, however, often do not have the organizational structure or funds to support officials, employees, and volunteers to govern effectively and to comply with relevant laws. These sports find it difficult to win sponsors and are dependent on government funding, which often requires compliance with conditions imposed by funders and thus may come at the expense of other strategic objectives of that sport. Community sports may also lack appropriate comprehensive risk management strategies and the funds or ability to seek proper advice on the discharge of their general legal obligations.

Commercialism is the key to much of the application of the law to sport worldwide. Sport is organized and regulated in different ways in different jurisdictions, and the most popular sports in a given jurisdiction are usually the most commercially successful. The way in which the law applies can be influenced by a sport's status—amateur or professional—and by the links between the two groups. For this reason, it is useful to consider the ways in which sports are differently organized in different countries or regions.

In Europe, for example, professional sport and amateur sport are generally merged into a sporting hierarchy managed by a single sporting organization. The sports themselves have tried to minimize the impact of the law on the capacity of sport to organize itself independently; indeed, they have argued that sport and commerce are separate. This has, however, become increasingly difficult to justify in relation to some sports. Developments in the European Union have recognized the importance of sport to communities even as the Treaty for the Functioning of the European Union and its predecessors have been applied to aspects of sport (more on this later).

In the United States, amateur sport and professional sport are separate. Amateur sports consist of community leagues, school athletic associations, state and national regulatory boards, the National Collegiate Athletic Association, the Amateur Sports Act of 1978, the U.S. Olympic Committee, and Olympic rules and processes; the roles of schools and colleges are a fundamental feature. Professional sports are controlled by their own rules and by collective bargaining agreements with their athletes, and professional leagues are joint ventures made up of their teams. Given this structure, there is less connection between the amateur and the professional than is the case in Europe and Australia (Nafziger, 2008).

The federal nature of Australia means that sport is played there at the local, state, and national levels. The more popular professional sports—such as the football codes (rugby, rugby league, Australian football, cricket, and soccer), golf, and tennis—provide lucrative careers for professionals but are closely integrated with their nonprofessional cohorts. Broadcast rights and healthy sponsorships provide substantial funds to these sports for developing and organizing at all levels. The sports also receive government funding to support athlete development and grassroots participation.

Many other Australian sports, both professional and amateur, such as netball, basketball, hockey, and baseball, fall into a different category. They have difficulty negotiating lucrative sponsorship and broadcast contracts, and they are often dependent on government funds at the federal and state levels, through state departments of sport and recreation, to support an organization and its objectives (e.g., increased participation).

The whole system of sport organization and funding in Australia was recently reviewed (Independent Sport Panel, 2009), and the government response included sport funding of A$1.2 billion (about US$1.25 billion) over four years. It emphasized participation at all levels and greater cooperation between the Commonwealth, the states and territories, and the various institutes and academies of sport in the development of athletes (Commonwealth of Australia, 2010). In the 2011–2012 financial year, the Australian Sports Commission (ASC) provided more than A$135 million (about US$139 million) of government funding to National Sporting Organizations, and additional funds were awarded to organizations for athletes with disabilities (Australian Sports Commission, 2012a). Funds awarded by the ASC are subject to compliance with principles of good governance and implementation of specified policies (Australian Sports Commission, 2009).

The organization of sport is unlike that of most other areas of commerce or endeavor in that it involves an unusual mix of commercial and non-commercial objectives and outcomes. Government funding recognizes that participation and involvement in sport bring significant ongoing benefits to the health and well-being of the community. Particularly in Australia, a hierarchy of stakeholders at national, state, and local levels grapple with governance issues. The issues include development of strategic objectives, compliance with the law, protection of athletes' rights, sport development, growth of participation numbers in an increasingly sedentary society, training of coaches and officials, management of volunteers, and protection of the reputation of sport—all of which are essential to sport's continued prosperity.

Overview: The Place of Law in Sport

This chapter addresses the role of law in the world of sport. The law is "the system of rules which a particular country or community recognizes as regulating the actions of its members" (Oxford, n.d.). Until relatively recently, those involved in sport often expressed surprise that the law was interested in sporting activity, but the changing nature of sport has mandated a new approach to this issue. In the words of one commentator (Grayson, 1993, p. 1), the "rule of law in sport is as essential for civilisation as the rule of law in society generally. Without it generally, anarchy reigns. Without it in sport, chaos exists."

Following the growing commerciality of sport, the trend worldwide has been for courts to be more receptive to sport-related disputes, though (as will be discussed later) this is not without limits. Unlike most other areas, sport at all levels also has its own class of self-regulation, which means that in addition to the application of the law of the land (or the particular jurisdiction), sport is governed by normative rules, codes, and conventions. This self-governance takes place at the local level. In addition, the international nature of sport, particularly at the elite level, creates a need for consistency of rules and decision making in the international arena, where athletes from more than one country are involved. This need ranges from the obvious call for consistent rules of the game to more complex areas of international controversy. In some sporting disputes—regarding doping, for example—the laws of a given jurisdiction may be simply unhelpful; it seems only fair that athletes from different jurisdictions, particularly those competing at the international level, should be subject to the same rules and penalties about performance-enhancing substances and methods. In such circumstances, it is necessary to rely on international law or to establish an overarching system of self-regulation in order to achieve desired outcomes. As a result, in some areas of dispute, sport law involves applying the general law of the land to the problem, but others are addressed by an emerging body of law that lies outside of national courts and is specifically related to sport disputes (Gardiner, 2012). One example is the Court of Arbitration for Sport, which is discussed later in the chapter.

Aside from the international aspects, the way in which the law applies to sport in particular jurisdictions is also a matter of interest. The European Union, for example, promotes an internal economic market among member countries, which means, in simple terms, that commercial obstacles to trade and commerce and territorial cohesion in Europe are in breach of what is currently known as the Treaty on the Functioning of the European Union (article 2). The key determinant of application of the treaty is economic activity, and the regulations of sporting organizations and their commercial contracts are areas of potential application of the treaty's provisions.

Traditionally, there had been no express mention of sport in the treaty, and sporting organizations argued that it did not generally apply to sport because of sport's special features. Thus the application to sport has been contentious, and a number of investigations have addressed this issue, including the *Helsinki Report on Sport* (Commission of the European Communities, 1999), the *Nice Declaration* (European Council, 2000), and the *White Paper on Sport* (Commission of the European Communities, 2007). The traditional view of sporting associations has, of course, been challenged by commercialization, which has increased the potential for commercial sport-related activities to be subject to the treaty, particularly in areas such as competition law, though there has been some recognition of sport as special (Nafziger, 2008).

Cases such as the famous Bosman ruling (*Union Royale Belge des Sociétés des Football Association v. Bosman*, 1995) confirmed the applicability of the treaty provisions regarding freedom of movement for workers among member states to professional soccer player transfers. Later decisions applied the treaty provisions to other situations, such as limitations on the number of team members hailing from other member states. The application of the treaty generally to sport issues was confirmed in *Meca-Medina & Majcen v. Commission of the European Communities* (2006), which took a narrower view of areas of sport that were excluded. The European Court of Justice noted there that regulatory restrictions in sport that might be subject to the treaty should be judged as to their inherency and proportionality. In the context of doping in *Meca-Medina*, the rules were inherently necessary, and penalties were a necessary consequence of applying the system, so they were not in breach of the treaty's competition law provisions. Since the *Meca-Medina* decision, the provisions of the treaty have been applied in sporting situations as diverse as sport regulation, team selection, rules governing player agents, and broadcast rights.

More recently, the enactment of amendments by the Lisbon Treaty (2007), which gave the Treaty on the Functioning of the European Union (TFEU) its current name, changed the position in some respects. For the first time, the TFEU now incorporates specific reference to sport, in article 106, which, though limited by its express terms to the promotion and fostering of cooperation in sport, "gives legal status to the idea that the specificity of sport is to be respected and its wider nature and functions" (Gardiner, et al., 2012, p. 204). Commentators believe that article 106 will not significantly change the effect of the TFEU on sport but will clarify the position and allow development of a more comprehensive sport policy in the European Union (Parrish, García, Miettinen, & Siekmann, 2010, pp. 61–62).

By way of contrast, in the United States, most areas of sport are subject to the usual legal rules, with some exceptions. For example, U.S. antitrust law, which encompasses the Sherman Antitrust Act (1890) and a number of other laws, applies to all sports except baseball, thanks to a Supreme Court decision exempting that sport almost 100 years ago (*Federal Baseball Club of Baltimore, Inc., v. National League of Professional Baseball Clubs*, 1922). Major League Baseball is not, therefore, subject to antitrust law despite the extent of its commercial activities. In addition, though joint ventures potentially attract competition law sanctions for collusive activity, some professional sport leagues have successfully argued that they constitute a single entity and therefore cannot collude (e.g., *Copperweld v. Independence Tube Corp*, 1984; *American Needle, Inc., v. National Football League*, 2010). Sport broadcast rights would ordinarily be subject to antitrust law, and collective selling would be scrutinized, but the Sports Broadcasting Act of 1961 created an exemption for the collective sale of rights to broadcast the major professional leagues. This exemption means that arrangements made in relation to broadcasting differ between sports. The National Football League sells collective exclusive rights to every game, but other sporting leagues sell exclusive rights to some games while individual teams sell the remainder (Kaburakis, 2008).

In Australia, the law applies to sport as to any other undertaking, and we can find ample evidence of this reality by taking a short survey of various legal areas. As in other countries, legal problems in Australia have resulted in almost routine court proceedings concerning commercial contracts of all kinds, including sponsorship, broadcasting, and employment disputes. In fact, complex commercial legal tools such as competition law have been used in a number of very significant Australian sport cases (e.g., *News Limited v. Australian Rugby Football League* 1996; *News Limited v. South Sydney District Rugby League Football Club Limited* 2003; *Hospitality Group Pty. Ltd. v. Australian Rugby Union* 2001). The C7 case, involving the demise of a pay television sport channel, is among the largest pieces of litigation and is the largest broadcasting and competition law litigation ever conducted in Australia (*Seven Network Limited v. News Limited* 2009). The case underscored the important role that sport plays in broadcasting. The claims in the case were based on allegations of collusive behavior and misuse of market power resulting in the loss by the applicant, Channel 7, of important sport broadcast rights and the subsequent commercial failure of its C7 pay television sport channel.

When the case started, Channel 7 claimed some A$1.1 billion (US$1.13 billion) in damages for loss, including the loss of its opportunity to become an integrated media company. Following a number of legal setbacks for the applicant, including the rejection of a key expert's report on loss, the claim was reduced to between A$195 million (US$201 million) and A$213 million (US$219 million) in damages by the end of the hearing; meanwhile, the cost of running the case reportedly exceeded A$200 million. The proceedings were dismissed both at first instance and on appeal, and the judge was extremely critical of the cost of running the case—86,000 documents were discovered, and 9,000 were admitted into evidence (Healey, 2008). More recently, the court considered the racing industry's refusal to include horses produced by artificial insemination in thoroughbred stud books, leaving them unable to compete in horse races; the court found that this practice was not in breach of competition laws (*McHugh v. Australian Jockey Club Limited*, 2012).

Another area of interest is the practice known as ambush marketing, in which an advertiser associates itself with an event or entity without their agreement and therefore benefits without paying for the positive association. This practice may involve illegality but generally consists of conduct that can be prevented by tighter contractual and other controls. Stringent laws have been put in place to prevent ambush marketing of major events (e.g., Australia's Commonwealth Games Arrangements Act 2001, and the London Olympic Games and Paralympic Games Act 2006), and some instances of ambush marketing have infringed intellectual property laws or constituted misleading conduct (*Talmax v. Telstra Corporation* 1996).

In another area, laws regarding compensation for personal injury were changed throughout Australia in the early 2000s (Healey, 2006). This change was motivated in part by an increase in personal injury litigation in sport and recreation, as well as the perceived unfairness of large awards of compensation to persons who had chosen to engage in activities deemed risky.

Professional athletes in Australia are often employed under collective bargaining agreements. Some are subject to industrial awards. The general law of employment applies to the arrangements of many other athletes and officials. Laws prohibiting discrimination exist in Australia at both the commonwealth and state levels, but issues of discrimination, racism, and vilification are often initially dealt with internally by sport itself through self-regulation in the form of policies (discussed later in the chapter).

Other legal areas relevant to sport in Australia include privacy law, due to the importance of member lists as a form of potential commercial intellectual property, and child protection, which demands proactive attention in order to ensure that children are protected in the context of relationships with participants, coaches, and officials. Both of these areas involve potential legal issues that can affect the reputation of a sporting organization.

In addition, sport faces the ordinary range of commercial issues that affect all businesses, such as contract law, employment law, leases and licenses, occupational health and safety, and insurance law. In many areas in Australia, the treatment of sport by the law and the court system is identical to that of any other business.

The complexity and substantial costs of the court system, however, mean that for many less commercial or less wealthy sports and athletes, recourse to the courts is not a real option for resolving their legal issues or disputes.

Are the Courts Always Interested in Sport?

In Australia, courts will not always intervene in legal disputes involving members of sporting organizations. For example, courts will not necessarily intervene in cases involving sport tribunals, though they are likely to do so when an issue affects the livelihood of participants or involves a flagrant breach of procedural fairness principles. Procedural fairness demands that a person being disciplined knows in sufficient detail the nature of the accusation made, that the person has the opportunity to state a case, and that the tribunal acts in good faith. In *Carter v. NSW Netball Association* (2004), for example, such a breach in an internal tribunal hearing about the treatment of junior athletes led to a result that threatened the livelihood of a coach who was also a schoolteacher; in these circumstances, the court was prepared to intervene.

In cases not involving a professional athlete or employment, courts may decline to become involved, instead regarding the dispute as something that should be addressed internally. In other situations, courts may take a fairly limited approach to intervention—for example, finding a breach of procedural fairness principles but referring the matter back to the original tribunal for a rehearing with regard to those principles. One well-known instance of this approach came in the Williams case (*Australian Football League v. Carlton Football Club Limited*, 1998, and *Carlton Football Club v. Australian Football League*, 1997), wherein a professional player felt dissatisfied with the disciplinary decision of the Australian Football League (AFL) Tribunal and appealed to the court. The tribunal had suspended him for nine weeks for on-field contact with a referee in breach of the rules of the game. The first judge overruled the AFL Tribunal's finding despite the fact that both the AFL rules and the player's contract stated that findings of the AFL Tribunal were final and binding. The Court of Appeal found that the parties had agreed for such matters to be finalized in the AFL Tribunal, that doing so would ordinarily be effective, and that it was effective in this case. The court refused to intervene.

In another case, involving a criminal charge relating to violence on the Australian rules football field, a judge queried why a matter of "everyday" sporting violence was in court at all. The judge stated that matters such as a punch to the face of an opponent were handled weekly in disciplinary tribunals set up in sport (*Watherston v. Woolven*, 1987). It is quite clear that the formal court system could not handle the large number of such on-field disciplinary matters that are dealt with regularly by sport tribunals in a timely, efficient, and cost-effective way.

Perhaps the most striking example of this trend of judicial nonintervention occurred in 2000. In *Raguz v. Sullivan* (2000), the New South Wales Supreme Court upheld both the jurisdiction of the Court of Arbitration for Sport (CAS) in Australia and the terms of the Australian Olympic Athlete Agreement giving CAS exclusive jurisdiction over disputes relating to athlete selection. The court declined to hear a dispute in relation to selection of a particular athlete because of the agreement signed by the athlete, who had consented to this exclusion in a participation agreement, albeit in standard form. The courts have thus determined that in some situations another forum may be appropriate for hearing a sport claim and that the parties may contract to use that forum. (The development of systems of self-regulation for resolving disputes and dealing with legal risk is discussed later in the chapter.) The value of self-regulatory alternatives also rests in part on the fact that the parties to sport disputes often need to continue to work together in order to achieve good outcomes in sport, where good relationships and cooperation can be key to success.

Governance

As noted earlier, governance refers to the way an organization is controlled. Directors who control a corporation do not own the assets—they control them on behalf of the corporation. A more comprehensive legal definition of corporate governance is that of Owen J., contained in the Report of the HIH Royal Commission (2003), set up to investigate the collapse of Australian insurance company HIH, which coincidentally affected many sports who were insured with the company when it collapsed. The report describes governance as

> *the framework of rules, relationships, systems and processes in and by which authority is exercised and controlled in corporations. It includes the practices by which that exercise and control of authority is in fact effected. . . . [T]he key to good corporate governance lies in substance, not form. It is about the way the directors of a company create and develop a model to fit the circumstances of that company and then test it periodically for its practical effectiveness. (Report, 2003, sections 6.1, 6.6)*

The Report of the HIH Royal Commission is thoroughly considered in du Plessis, Hargovan, & Bagaric (2011). Directors play the central role in the process of governance. Corporate theory also recognizes the importance of managing internal stakeholders for the benefit of the organization and its stakeholders. Sport involves a substantial number of internal and external stakeholders (e.g., participants, fans, funders) and the usual commercial stakeholders (e.g., sponsors). The type of corporate governance arrangements developed by a board depends on the place of the particular organization in the sport hierarchy, its size and structure, and the extent of its commercialization.

Even before the global financial crisis of 2008, corporate governance in Australia had been brought sharply into focus by issues including the solvency of companies such as One.Tel, HIH Insurance, and James Hardie, and steps had been taken to revisit existing assumptions and practices focused on corporate governance. The ASX Corporate Governance Council (2010, p. 10) identifies the following essential corporate governance principles:

1. Lay solid foundations for management and oversight.
2. Structure the board to add value.
3. Promote ethical and responsible decision making.
4. Safeguard integrity in financial reporting.
5. Make timely and balanced disclosure.
6. Respect the rights of shareholders.
7. Recognise and manage risk.
8. Remunerate fairly and responsibly.

These principles exhibit common sense and practicality, and it would be difficult to find anyone who disagreed, but implementing them would prove difficult for many in sport without further detailed guidance. In the context of sporting organizations, the Australian Sports Commission (2012c, p. 2) has described corporate governance in sport as involving the following elements:

- How an organisation develops strategic goals and direction
- How the board/committee of an organisation monitors the performance of the organisation to ensure it achieves these strategic goals, has effective systems in place and complies with its legal and regulatory obligations
- Ensuring that the board/committee acts in the best interests of the members

Beyond this, the ASC has drafted a number of documents containing both principles and more practical advice to help sport organizations improve their governance processes; some of these are mentioned in the following discussion.

Regulation

This section discusses basic legal governance obligations imposed on organizations and their officers in Australia, where, as has been noted, individual sports involve a hierarchy of organizations at various levels, all of which are charged with running various aspects of the relevant sport, game, or contest. These complex organizational structures complicate governance. Sporting organizations differ from most other commercial organizations in that many of them are not for profit—they pursue a primary purpose of furthering the development of their sport or code rather than that of making profit to return it to shareholders. This does not mean that they cannot make a profit; it does mean that they do not distribute any surplus funds to members. Not-for-profit organizations are generally incorporated in Australia as companies limited by guarantee under the Corporations Act (2001) or state-based associations law, both of which are discussed here.

There are, of course, organizations involved in sport that are for-profit organizations with shareholders; in Australia, for example, some professional teams are owned by shareholders or individuals. In fact, some of the teams playing in the most important sport leagues in Australia are privately owned, such as the Brisbane Broncos and the Melbourne Storm in the National Rugby League (NRL). However, most teams in the NRL competition, and all teams in the Australian Football League, are community-based clubs owned by members who are sport fans. Clubs in the A-League, the premier soccer competition, are generally privately owned, as are teams in the National Basketball League (NBL). Solvency has been a significant issue for many of the community clubs, particularly those in the A-League and the NBL. Other sports, such as V8 Supercars, are privately owned. Privately owned organizations have more direct accountability to shareholders in the form of return of profits.

Regardless of whether sporting organizations are community based or privately owned, certain common features accrue once they become incorporated. Their individual members or shareholders are protected from liability for the activities of the corporation or association in most situations, because the process of incorporation creates the organization as a legal person separate from its members. The organization, however, takes on obligations imposed by the incorporating law, and its directors and officers assume legal obligations designed to protect the position of the corporation or association and improve its governance.

Where sporting organizations are truly commercial in nature and not community based, they are generally incorporated by shares. However, as stated, in Australia most sports are not for profit and have members who are either individuals or are themselves organizations. If they are commercially substantial, they are incorporated as companies limited by guarantee under the Corporations Act. The regulatory framework imposed on corporations in Australia "comprises a complex ecosystem of hard and soft law" that includes "the Corporations Act and its mix of mandatory and replaceable rules and other non-binding codes of practice and guidelines" (Hill, 2010, p. 75).

Smaller organizations with lower turnover are incorporated as associations under the associations laws of the states and territories (Associations Incorporation Act 1964, 1981, 1985, 1987, 1990, 1991, 2009). In all cases, the incorporation document, which serves as the constitution or rules of the organization, forms a contract between the members.

Whether or not an organization has a commercial nature, the law imposes minimum obligations on officeholders and members in order to enforce basic standards and to ensure that the organization is governed properly. The extent to which directors are responsible at law for governing the company is important. Legal duties are imposed by the common law generally, which is the judge-made law of the courts, by the Corporations Act, and by the associations' laws.

At common law, directors have always had a duty to exercise reasonable skill and care, and they owe a fiduciary duty of good faith to the company. Directors exist to benefit the company, so the powers of directors must be used in the company's interests. Put simply, these obligations mean that directors must become familiar with the company and how it is run (*Daniels t/as Deloitte, Haskins, & Sells v. AWA Ltd.*, 1995). They must not allow their own or any other person's interests to come before the interests of the company, and they must not make use of their position as a director to gain an advantage for themselves or anyone other than the company. It is no answer for a director to say that dishonesty was not involved in the particular situation or that the company has not suffered any loss because of the director's actions in breach of these rules. These basic duties apply to all organizations and are particularly important if the governing law of a particular organization contains no specific duties. These commonlaw rules apply to corporations and associations.

The duties imposed on corporations under the Corporations Act are in addition to those imposed by common law; they are similar but not identical to them. Substantial civil and criminal penalties apply to contraventions. Criminal penalties involve fines of up to A\$220,000 (about US\$226,000) per offense and possible imprisonment for up to five years. Officers of the company can also be disqualified from managing a company in the future. For these purposes, an officer may be a director, secretary, or executive officer (Corporations Act 2001, section 9). Officers must exercise a degree of care and diligence that a reasonable person would exercise in the circumstances and act for a proper purpose and always in the best interest of the company. An officer who is reckless or intentionally dishonest may be held criminally liable. Insolvent trading is prohibited, and the test involves whether the company can pay its debts as they fall due. Directors may be personally liable for debts incurred through insolvent trading, though some defenses exist (Corporations Act 2001, sections 95A, 181, 182, 183, 184[1], 588G, 588H).

For constitutional reasons, the laws that apply to incorporated associations in Australia are state laws, which differ greatly between the states and territories. Where the association laws impose no specific obligations on directors and officers, the common-law rules discussed earlier are applied. New South Wales, for example, has no comprehensive provisions dealing with directors' responsibilities but does have provisions addressing insolvent trading in some situations (Associations Incorporation Act 2009, sections 67–71). New South Wales also has provisions relating to disclosure of interests and dishonest use of position and information (Associations Incorporation Act 2009, sections 31–33). South Australia provides that officers of particular categories of associations must act with reasonable care and diligence, and insolvent trading is an offense (Associations Incorporation Act 1985, sections 3, 49AD). Other states and territories do not specify duties, but Western Australia, Victoria, and South Australia require disclosure of pecuniary interests.

Governance Systems

Thus we know what directors and officers must not do. But what must they do to ensure effective governance of their sporting organizations? The Australian Sports Commission (2012c, p. 12) identifies six major areas of corporate governance that are the domain of board members:

- Board composition, roles, and powers
- Board processes
- Governance systems
- Board reporting and performance
- Member relationships and reporting
- Ethical and responsible decision making

Governing an organization means putting in place mechanisms to determine its objectives and implementing strategies, at both the big-picture and administration levels, to ensure that they are attained. Depending upon its place in the sporting hierarchy, a sporting organization may have obligations to its international, national, state, or local body, as well as to other umbrella bodies, such as the Australian Olympic Committee or the Commonwealth Games Federation. All organizations, of course, are obliged to comply with the law. They also have obligations to their stakeholders, such as funding bodies and other contractual partners. The organization's members, be they individuals or organizations, are also key stakeholders. If organizations are national or peak bodies, they generally play an important role in assisting with compliance by their fraternal bodies and protecting the interests of their individual members at all levels. This work involves providing key advice and assistance regarding common issues, setting up overarching solutions such as national tribunals, assisting with documentation, and helping with grassroots issues. They may even provide whole-of-sport advice and guidance on individual issues and areas of concern. All of these tasks must be factored into objectives.

The ASC (2012c, p. 12) identifies the following essential governance systems for an effective organization:

- A strategic planning framework identifying core organizational values, goals, and performance management indicators
- Clearly documented board–management interaction, including appropriate delegations and authority of all parties
- A thorough process for identifying and monitoring legal, compliance, and risk management requirements
- A thorough system of audit, including internal and external processes
- A performance management system to provide evidence and ensure monitoring of legal compliance and performance against plans

The ASC emphasizes consultation with all stakeholders during the strategic planning phase, clarity in setting measurable performance indicators, risk management systems that comply with Australian Standard AS/NZS 4360:2004, and compliance systems that meet Australian Standard AS 3806-2006, including effective internal controls, effective reporting, and focus on financial security.

For sport organizations operating at a national level, proper governance is important to individual members and participants who rely on the organization to enhance their experience of the sport and to ensure protection of their rights. In the long term, this broader national governance role helps the sport enhance its reputation in the community and build its membership and participation rate, thus increasing its marketability with sponsors and enhancing its reputation with funders.

In assessing what is required of an organization and its board and officers in light of ASC's guidance, it is clear that the task of governing a sport body is not a simple one, particularly when most sport boards are voluntary and many of the downstream functions are necessarily carried out by volunteers. Thus the question of whether too much is expected of company directors is raised regularly in Australia. Commentators recognize that the position of a director is demanding if performed properly and that expanding expectations may ultimately render the task impossible, particularly in relation to nonexecutive directors operating on a part-time basis. At the same time, regulators and the public demand even higher standards (Clarke, 2007, p. 36). These issues are particularly acute for sporting organizations.

Conclusions on Governance in Sport

It should be apparent by now that sporting organizations are diverse. For some organizations, corporate governance is approached in a relatively standard way—that is, in the manner of other commercial organizations—to the extent that there is a standard way. For others, governance continues to be particularly challenging due to a lack of resources and skills and to the unique challenges of the sporting area. Most nonsporting commercial bodies, for example, do not have to deal with child protection issues unless they operate in areas like education or child care, and then they are likely to be specialists and to have access to significant resources to deal with compliance. They do not need detailed tribunal systems to resolve disciplinary and other disputes. Nor do they have hundreds of participants engaged in risky activities as part of their primary objective. Without the guidance of bodies like the Australian Sports Commission, it is doubtful that many sports would have the resources to strike a balance between adequate governance and effective sport development and operation.

Aspects of Industry Self-Regulation in Sport

While the traditional view in most countries, and particularly in Australia, has been that courts should not involve themselves in sport and that sporting disputes should be "left on the field," the last 30 years or so have shown that courts will in many situations treat sport in the same way in which they treat other areas of activity. On the other hand, as described earlier, courts will not always intervene to resolve sporting disputes. Resort to the courts and the legal system may also be out of the financial reach of—or even do damage to—many sports. A major case affects the financial health of any organization, and the following discussion addresses some recurring controversies for sport. Individual athletes are also often unable to afford to pursue disputes through the court system.

Alongside the greater acceptance of the application of law to sport, the unusual nature of sport has spurred the development of more inventive methodologies and schemes of self-regulation for resolving important issues. These measures stand in addition to the more established codes, conventions, and disciplinary systems that have been developed by particular sports. Some self-regulation has been developed to resolve issues that courts would not address, whereas other issues have arisen in areas that are legal or quasi-legal but do not require the formal attention of a court. In addition, some elements of sport are international and operate across multiple jurisdictions, requiring global uniformity of decision making for proper functioning and resolution of disputes. Governance requirements and issues management may mean that a different approach yields a better outcome for all involved; for example, one factor that can argue in favor of non-court-based solutions is the possibility of cost-effective resolution by decision makers who are attuned to the special needs of sport.

In this context, a number of schemes, some of them quite complex, have been developed and operated effectively to resolve issues in sport by means of sport industry self-regulation, or private regulation. They are generally established under a range of contracts and incorporated into the workings of international and national federations and their downstream cohort of organizations, or in a national sport not operated by a federation per se and its downstream organizations, binding them and their individual members as a condition of membership or participation. These schemes often give considerable attention and weight to issues of procedural fairness that are particularly important to athletes.

A number of these schemes appear to work extremely well, though no mechanism is universally successful. The fact that sport was traditionally seen as something outside the ambit of the law, even in Australia, may be part of the reason that these initiatives have been embraced by the sporting community, which has contributed to their success. Indeed, sport has effectively taken itself out of the legal system proper in developing these self-regulatory initiatives, several of which are discussed in the following sections.

The Court of Arbitration for Sport

The Court of Arbitration for Sport (CAS) is an international system of dispute resolution that continues to grow in importance. It plays a particularly important role in resolving disputes that involve the Olympics—a vast commercial sporting spectacle involving large numbers of athletes and officials from many countries, most of whom compete under extremely pressurizing conditions in a foreign land. Peak opportunities for Olympic athletes arise only once every four years, which makes it highly likely that disputes will regularly arise in, around, and at the Olympics themselves.

The Court of Arbitration for Sport was set up by the International Olympic Committee in 1984 to settle disputes in Olympic sports, both at the time of the Olympics and at other times. It is in fact not a court but a forum set up under rule 59 of the Olympic Charter. It offers a degree of certainty for all involved because it is cross-jurisdictional and stays the same, in terms of procedures and approach, regardless of where the Olympics take place. To ensure that it is independent of the IOC, it is administered by an independent body, the International Council of Arbitration for Sport. CAS is based in Switzerland, and its jurisdiction is based on Swiss law, though other law can be nominated as the law of contract. An Oceania Registry of CAS is based in Sydney, Australia.

In simple terms, CAS provides contract-based dispute resolution and arbitration. The regulations and bylaws of many international and national federations affiliated with the IOC nominate CAS as the forum for resolution of disputes in their sport or nominate CAS as an appeals forum for disputes that the sport itself may handle at first instance. Other sports can also nominate CAS as the forum for resolution of their disputes. CAS has both an ordinary jurisdiction and an appellate jurisdiction. Ordinary jurisdiction proceedings usually relate to contracts and civil disputes, and appellate jurisdiction proceedings include resolving disputes about tribunal decisions of sporting organizations where their rules provide for it. Athletes competing in the Olympics are required to agree that all disputes arising during the course of the Games will be heard by CAS and that hearings of the CAS appeal tribunal are final, nonappealable, and nonreversible. CAS establishes a special panel, the ad hoc division, to hear disputes at that time. Advisory opinions may also be provided by CAS at the request of bodies such as the IOC, international federations, national Olympic committees, and the World Anti-Doping Agency. CAS hears most international doping disputes under the World Anti-Doping Code.

CAS hearings are conducted in accordance with the CAS Code, and panel members are eminent lawyers from a range of countries who are involved or interested in sport issues. CAS has heard matters involving a wide range of issues, including eligibility, doping, discipline, and commercial contracts. CAS decisions are generally published on the CAS website.

CAS, then, is a global specialist tribunal that provides effective resolution of disputes and arbitration in sport. Doping cases account for a significant proportion of its cases and have significantly influenced the development of its jurisprudence (Gardiner et al. 2012). While CAS is not appropriate for all sport disputes, and is often criticized for being a relatively expensive forum, there is no doubt that it effectively resolves a significant number of high-profile sporting disputes in a timely and effective manner.

Anti-Doping as a Global System: The WADA Code

Another area where sport has established a specialized international system of self-regulation is that of anti-doping efforts. The issue of doping is problematic from a legal perspective because sporting organizations, to put it simply, wish to prohibit the use not just of illegal substances but of all substances that they identify as performance enhancing. Some performance-enhancing drugs are illegal, and possession or ingestion of them would constitute a criminal offense, whereas others are completely legal and thus fall outside the scope of criminal law. In addition, a substance may be deemed performance enhancing by one sport but not another. International sport takes place, of course, across jurisdictions that have different laws and norms, and nothing less than a common approach to the issue of anti-doping would be successful. Earlier attempts at dealing with doping on a jurisdictional basis were fraught with difficulties, including gaps in coverage, dissimilar penalties of enforcement, and many lengthy challenges raised through the court system. Public opinion has been galvanized by the death of more than one sport participant associated with performance-enhancing drugs the lack of uniform rules and sanctions, and the sometimes arbitrary approach taken to the issue by some individuals and sporting organizations, as well as ongoing controversies in a number of sports and the very public revocation of a number of Olympic medals due to issues of performance enhancement. Sport authorities have accepted that the public believes that doping is fundamentally contrary to the spirit of sport and that inaction is unacceptable; as a result, sports and governments have taken a more holistic approach to the problem.

The combination of statute and contract and the adoption of the World Anti-Doping Agency (WADA) Code in 2003 by all Olympic (and many non-Olympic) sports worldwide created an international system of doping regulation and discipline under the auspices of WADA. The WADA Code is the foundational document of the World Anti-Doping Program, which includes standards for technical and operational areas, models of best practice, and nonmandatory guidelines. States commit to the code by ratifying the United Nations Educational, Scientific, and Cultural Organization's International Convention Against Doping in Sport. Other signatories include WADA, the IOC, international sport federations, the International Paralympic Committee, national Olympic and Paralympic committees, major event organizations, and national anti-doping organizations, such as the Australian Sports Anti-Doping Authority. The WADA Code is binding on signatories and their members. Core provisions of the WADA Code must be included in signatories' anti-doping policies, whereas other provisions are more flexible. The scheme operates as a network of contracts wherein the WADA Code outlines the responsibilities of all relevant organizations.

In Australia, all organizations and athletes funded by the Australian Sports Commission, be they in Olympic or non-Olympic sports, are part of and subject to this system. Organizations funded by the ASC need to have WADA Code–compliant anti-doping policies as a condition of funding. The WADA Code provides for in-competition and out-of-competition testing of athletes, standardized penalties for positive results, and referral of most doping-related proceedings to the CAS as arbiter and appeal court. To facilitate out-of-competition testing, athletes who are part of relevant, nominated national and international testing pools must maintain and supply onerous information about their whereabouts. The WADA Code contains penalties for others involved in doping by an athlete, such as trainers and officials. It also provides for therapeutic use exemptions, but these must be implemented in a very strict fashion to prevent abuse of the system. The WADA Code leaves many issues outside of the basic common ground to the discretion of national authorities.

The Australian Sports Doping Agency was established by legislation in 1991, then superseded, under the Australian Sports Anti-Doping Authority Act (2006), by the Australian Sports Anti-Doping Authority (ASADA). The act also established the National Anti-Doping Scheme, which addresses many issues left to national authorities by the WADA Code and lays out details of doping control, whereabouts reporting by athletes, and the full investigative powers of ASADA. ASADA holds the power to investigate allegations of doping violations, present cases before sport tribunals, publish findings, and undertake monitoring in relation to doping. The ASADA Act built on the earlier system by implementing uniform investigation, prosecution, and enforcement processes. It operates outside the ambit of the court system in CAS, which the parties—members of organizations bound by their Olympic membership, by opting into the system, or by their funding source—have agreed to use. These parties include sports, athletes, referees, trainers, coaches, doctors, and other officials. It is unlikely that the courts will become involved except in a very limited range of circumstances.

In this case, then, the international governing bodies of sport, along with world governments, have implemented a uniform system of global anti-doping control and discipline that supersedes the laws of individual jurisdictions in order to create a universal code. The code provides common goals, treatment of athletes, and penalties, along with standardized testing protocols and mechanisms. It means that all athletes are treated under a common rule in the fight to eliminate the use of performance-enhancing drugs in sport.

Australian Selection Disputes

The Australian selection system for the Olympics is another good example of workable and effective industry self-regulation in sport. Following a number of high-profile challenges to the selection processes for the Olympic and Commonwealth Games teams during the late 1990s (e.g., *Forbes v. Australian Yachting Federation, Inc.*, 1996), the Australian Olympic Committee (AOC) implemented an alternative system for challenging selections to the Australian Olympic team prior to the 2000 Olympics in Sydney. The system was set up to create a fair appeal mechanism for athletes that was cost effective and speedy. At the outset, the AOC assisted organizers of all Olympic sports with a compulsory template for setting out selection criteria relevant to their particular sport. The AOC held briefing sessions to help organizers determine criteria acceptable to their sport and to help officials and athletes understand the way in which the system would work. The system contained an internal appeal process to be managed by the sport itself, followed by appeal to CAS if either the athlete or the sport was dissatisfied with the outcome. This system was implemented through a standard Olympic Athlete Agreement and related agreements. Athletes who were likely to be selected or involved in the selection process were bound by terms under which they agreed to the process, which meant that for all intents and purposes the jurisdiction of the ordinary courts was negated by the substituted appeal process.

Despite much negative comment from the media, and from some in sport, to the effect that lawyers were now selecting the Olympic team, the CAS heard only 12 appeals on selection issues for the 2000 Olympics, and only 3 of them were ultimately upheld. As previously noted, the jurisdiction of CAS as final arbiter under the Olympic Athlete Agreement was challenged and ultimately upheld in *Raguz v. Sullivan* (2000). Raguz had signed the Olympic team membership form, which stated that all selection disputes would be referred solely and exclusively to CAS and expressly surrendered other appeal rights. The New South Wales Supreme Court found that its jurisdiction was effectively excluded, based on its analysis of the agreement and the relevant CAS rules. The arbitration agreement constituted by the documents was not a domestic agreement because, under CAS rules, the seat or legal place of arbitration by CAS and its panel of arbitrators was Lausanne, Switzerland. Thus a carefully drafted system of contracts, coupled with a recognized and fair alternative forum, precluded intervention by the Australian courts. After the Sydney Olympics, the AOC commissioned a review and further refined these processes, and few selection disputes or appeals have been reported in relation to subsequent Olympic and Commonwealth Games (Australian Sports Commission, 2006). In terms of governance, this approach provides a predictable, fair, and equitable system for athletes and a more predictable course of action for the sports if athletes are unhappy with the outcome of elite selections.

Systems of Discipline

As discussed earlier in the chapter, the courts in Australia have generally been reluctant to take over the role of sporting tribunals in areas such as the disciplining of participants, except in limited circumstances. Almost without exception, Australian sports at all levels of participation have internal systems in place for dealing with day-to-day disciplinary issues, whether they arise out of on-field conduct, failure to comply with rules or codes, or other issues relating to membership or participation. Provision for these tribunals is contained in the rules of the organizations at the relevant level and may involve appeal rights to some higher or more authoritative tribunal in the sport.

Professional sports generally maintain detailed systems, some of which are contained in collective bargaining arrangements. Proceedings are generally quite formal at the professional or elite level, and participants are routinely represented by legal counsel. Proceedings typically involve detailed formal documentation, including written submissions of parties, prehearing conferences, detailed written tribunal determinations, and formal appeal processes. At the other end of the scale, local sporting tribunals mainly hear issues related to on-field conduct, with no legal representation of the parties or even lawyers on the tribunal, little formality (though appropriate rules of procedural fairness still apply), and oral determinations handed out at the time of hearing. At a minimum, these tribunals provide a place where disputes may be resolved and where parties can be heard on contentious issues that result in an outcome and allow the issue to be finalized. In many cases, they are examples of very long-standing schemes of self-regulation that work effectively in the interests of the parties.

Member Protection Policies

In an attempt to provide guidance to Australian National Sporting Organizations (NSOs) on day-to-day issues of member protection, the Australian Sports Commission developed a member protection policy (MPP) template for use in addressing important yet sometimes delicate issues of harassment, discrimination, and child protection. The template includes position statements declaring that the identified conduct will not be tolerated by the organization, as well as steps that the organization will take to deal with complaints in relation to that conduct. Member protection officers appointed by the sport deal with complaints made under the MPP, and complaint escalations may culminate in disciplinary proceedings before a tribunal set up for that purpose. Some of the conduct would potentially constitute breach of law and must also be reported to police. For example, discrimination and racial vilification may be prohibited by state or federal law, such as the Racial Discrimination Act (1975) and the Sex Discrimination Act (1984), and child protection issues may involve a breach of criminal law. Organizations might seek to resolve some noncriminal complaints internally by means of warnings followed by discipline if the matter is not resolved satisfactorily. The MPP template also contains policies regarding issues such as reference check procedures (which may be required by state laws) for people dealing with children, position statements on otherwise legal sexual relationships between coaches and athletes, and the use of images of children.

The MPP template is amended by the NSO and incorporated into its constituent documentation. It is quite important that this be done properly in order for it to be effective, and doing so can present a challenge given the complex hierarchies of individual sports.

The MPP system has been implemented by NSOs and has been subject to periodic review by the ASC with input from the sports. It is another example of whole-of-sport management of important legal areas that makes governance far simpler for sporting organizations. The MPP plays an important role in helping sport organizations deal with important issues, often at the grassroots level, without needing to obtain comprehensive and expensive legal advice on every occasion. Of course, legal advice will be required from time to time on these issues, but in many cases diligent organizations can use the MPP to resolve their internal issues effectively.

Summary

This chapter looks at how the law is involved in sport and particularly at legal issues relevant to the governance of sport. It shows that there is really no such thing as a standard sporting organization and that governance obligations have a significant effect on sporting organizations, regardless of whether they are large and commercial or smaller with local participants. The chapter underscores the onerous nature of the legal obligations placed on directors and officers in sport. It also describes the approach to governance advocated by legal experts and explores sport governance in Australia by the Australian Sports Commission. Finally, it describes and analyzes some examples of industry self-regulation, both international and Australian, which have grown out of the particular nature of sport. This self-regulation covers a number of areas in standard ways outside of the judicial system, based on contract law. These schemes provide innovative, cost-effective solutions to disputes between sporting organizations and their members. They are conducted by sport for sport, and they work equally well for commercial and community sports. More such systems are likely to emerge in order to resolve other contentious issues in sport in the future.

References

Amateur Sports Act of 1978, 36 USC § 220501 (1978).

American Needle, Inc., v. National Football League (2010) 500 U.S.

Associations Incorporation Act 1964 (Tasmania), 1981 (Queensland), 1981 (Victoria), 1985 (South Australia), 1987 (Western Australia), 1990 (Northern Territory), 1991 (Australian Capital Territory), 2009 (New South Wales).

ASX Corporate Governance Council. (2010). *Corporate governance principles and recommendations with 2010 amendments* (2nd ed.). Sydney: Author. www.asx.com.au.

Australian Football League v. Carlton Football Club Limited (1998) 2 VR 546.

Australian Sports Anti-Doping Authority Act 2006 (Commonwealth of Australia).

Australian Sports Commission. (2006). Getting it right: Guidelines for selection www.ausport.gov.au/_data/assets/pdf_file/0016/11540/9_Selection_Policy_guidelines.pdf.

Australian Sports Commission. (2009). *Eligibility criteria for the recognition of National Sporting Organizations by the Australian Sports Commission 2009–2013*. Belconnen, Australian Capital Territory: Author. http://www.ausport.gov.au/__data/assets/pdf_file/0003/336432/2009-13_NSO_Recognition_Eligibility_Criteria.pdf.

Australian Sports Commission. (2012a). *Australian Sports Commission annual report 2011–2012*. Bruce, Australian Capital Territory: Author. www.ausport.gov.au/about/publications/annual_reports/annual_report_2011-2012.

Australian Sports Commission. (2012b). *Governing sport*. Bruce, Australian Capital Territory: Author.

Australian Sports Commission. (2012c). *Sports governance principles*. Bruce, Australian Capital Territory: Author. www.ausport.gov.au/supporting/governance/governance_principles.

Carlton Football Club v. Australian Football League (1997) 71 ALJR 1546.

Carter v. NSW Netball Association [2004] NSWSC 737 (17 August 2004).

Clarke, T. (2007). *International corporate governance: A comparative approach*. New York: Routledge.

Commission of the European Communities. (1999). *Helsinki report on sport*. Brussels: Author.

Commission of the European Communities. (2007). *White paper on sport*. Brussels: Author.

Commonwealth Games Arrangements Act 2001.

Commonwealth of Australia. (2010). Australian sport: The pathway to success. Barton, Australian Capital Territory: Author. http://ausport.gov.au/about/pathway_to_success.

Copperweld v. Independence Tube Corp (1984), 104 S Ct 2731.

Corporations Act 2001 (Commonwealth).

Daniels t/as Deloitte Haskins & Sells v. AWA Ltd. (1995) 13 ACLC 614.

Du Plessis, J.J., Hargovan, A., & Bagaric, M. (2011). *Principles of contemporary corporate governance* (2nd ed.). New York: Cambridge University Press.

European Council. (2000). *Nice declaration: Declaration on the specific characteristics of sport and its social function in Europe*. Nice: Author.

Federal Baseball Club of Baltimore, Inc., v. National League of Professional Baseball Clubs (1922), 259 US 200.

Forbes v. Australian Yachting Federation Inc. (1996) 131 FLR 241.

Gardiner, S., O'Leary, J., Welch, R., Boyes, S., & Naidoo, U. (2012). *Sports law* (4th ed.). London: Routledge.

Grayson, E. (1993). Sport and the Law Journal. Cited in Gardiner, S., James, M., O'Leary, J., & Welch, R. *Sports Law* (3rd ed.), London: Cavendish.

Healey, D. (2006). Warnings and exclusions post personal responsibility. *Australian and New Zealand Sports Law Journal*, 1(1), 7–41.

Healey, D. (2008). Seven loses the football: Why all the fuss? In T. Hickie, D. Healey, J. Scutt, & A. Hughes (Eds.), *Essays in sport and Law*. Melbourne: Australian Society of Sports History.

Hill, J.G. (2010). The architecture of corporate governance in Australia. Sydney Law School Research Paper 10/75. http://papers.ssrn.com/sol3/papers.cfm?abstract_id=1657810.

Hospitality Group Pty. Ltd. v. Australian Rugby Union (2001) 110 FCR 157; (2001) ATPR 41-831.

Independent Sport Panel. (2009). *The future of sport in Australia*. Barton, Australian Capital Territory: Commonwealth of Australia. www.health.gov.au/internet/main/publishing.nsf/Content/1DDA76A44E5F4DD4CA257671000E4C45/$File/Crawford_Report.pdf.

Kaburakis, A. (2008). The US and EU systems of sport governance: Commercialized v. socio-cultural model: Competition and labor law. *The International Sports Law Journal*, (3/4), 108–129.

Lisbon Treaty. (2007, December 13). European Union. http://eur-lex.europa.eu/LexUriServ/LexUriServ.do?uri=OJ:C:2007:306:FULL:EN:PDF.

London Olympic Games and Paralympic Games Act 2006. UK Public General Acts, 2006, c. 12.

McHugh v. Australian Jockey Club Limited (2012) 13 FCA 1441.

Meca-Medina & Majcen v. Commission of the European Communities, Case C0519/04 P (2006, July 18).

Nafziger, J. (2008). A comparison of the European and North American models of sports organisation. *The International Sports Law Journal*, (3/4), 100–107.

News Limited v. Australian Rugby Football League (1996) 58 FCR 447; (1996) ATPR 41-521.

News Limited v. South Sydney District Rugby League Football Club Limited (2003) 215 CLR 563.

Oxford Dictionaries. (n.d.) Law. http://oxforddictionaries.com/definition/english/law.

Parrish, R., García, B.G., Miettinen, S., & Siekmann, R. (2010). *The Lisbon Treaty and EU sports policy*. Brussels: European Parliament. www.europarl.europa.eu/committees/en/studiesdownload.html?languageDocument=EN&file=32471.

Racial Discrimination Act 1975 (Commonwealth of Australia).

Raguz v. Sullivan (2000) 50 NSWLR 237.

Seven Network Limited v. News Limited (2009) FCAFC 166.

Sex Discrimination Act 1984 (Commonwealth of Australia).

Sherman Antitrust Act (1890), 15 U.S.C. §§ 1–7.

Sports Broadcasting Act of 1961. 15 U.S.C. § 1291.

Talmax v. Telstra Corporation (1996) ATPR 41-535.

Treaty on the Functioning of the European Union. European Union.

Union Royale Belge des Sociétés de Football Association v. Bosman (1995), Case C-415/93.

Watherston v. Woolven [1987] SCSA 226.

CHAPTER 12

Sport and Social Policy

Ramón Spaaij, PhD

The term "social policy" is used to describe policies and practices aimed at promoting social welfare and well-being. Social policy also denotes an academic discipline concerned with the analysis, explanation, and evaluation of such initiatives—that is, the study of the social relations necessary for human well-being and the systems by which well-being may be promoted (Dean, 2006; Midgley, 2009). Social policy is fundamentally concerned with how to address and ameliorate social problems and with the analysis of the appropriateness and effectiveness of policies and programs designed to improve welfare and well-being (C. Alcock, Payne, & Sullivan, 2004).

Traditionally, the term "social policy" was used predominantly to define the role of the state in relation to the social welfare of its citizens (Hill, 2003), focusing on policy areas such as social security, education, health, and housing. More recently, increased emphasis in social policy analysis has been placed on the mixed economy of welfare, composed of four sectors—government, voluntary, informal, and commercial—through which social provisions can be delivered to people in need (Gilbert, 2009). This relative shift, discussed at length in this chapter, has heightened the political prominence of sport as a domain for the amelioration of a range of social problems, including social exclusion, unhealthy lifestyles, crime, and urban decay. A key development in this regard has been the widespread adoption of sport, notably its community-based and volunteer-driven forms, as a vehicle for social policies promoting social inclusion, community cohesion, intercultural dialogue, and urban regeneration.

This chapter does not aim to provide an exhaustive overview of the discipline of social policy. Rather, it seeks to examine key concepts, perspectives, and developments in social policy that are relevant and have been applied to the study of sport. The chapter commences with a concise overview of the discipline's emergence and development, as well as its relationship to other social science disciplines. This is followed by an overview of the main theoretical perspectives on social policy and their interpretation of sport. I then address some key concepts and examine their relevance to sport governance. The final part of the chapter discusses major contemporary debates surrounding sport and social policy and the remaining gaps in the knowledge base.

The key concepts and theoretical perspectives discussed in this chapter are presented from a primarily European perspective, along with some examples and insights from the United States and other areas of the world. One reason for taking this approach is that the discipline of social policy has been developed particularly in relation to the welfare state, against standards considered the norm in developed countries such as the United Kingdom at particular points in time. Many developing and transitional countries are characterized by qualitatively different social security arrangements, with people relying on alternative types of welfare provision, most notably informal care or security, in the absence of entitlement to social protection from the state (e.g., Wood & Gough, 2006). It is difficult to discern any established and distinctive social policy discipline in these settings, nor has there been a comparable long-standing focus on sport as a vehicle of social policy. An important exception is the social development perspective, which is discussed at length in this chapter.

Discipline of Social Policy: A Historical Overview

The discipline of social policy is relatively new. At the beginning of the 20th century, elements of what we would now consider social policy were taught in social work training courses. Later, the separately taught subject of "social administration" was developed at a number of British universities. Social administration determined the early content and direction of social policy. It was only during the second half of the 20th century that the subject's name was changed to social policy and that it began to be more widely recognized as a distinct field of academic inquiry (C. Alcock et al., 2004). However, concern about questions of social policy grew throughout the 19th century. The early development of social administration and social policy as an academic subject was significantly influenced by the idea that scientific principles should be adopted to study welfare issues (Midgley, 2009). Pioneers of this approach, such as one of sociology's founding fathers, Auguste Comte, believed that scientific methods could be applied not only to explain natural phenomena but also to analyze and improve social conditions.

The use of scientific methods in social welfare research was fostered by the widespread employment of the census in Europe in the 19th century. The census permitted the collection of a large amount of statistical data on social conditions and provided information on which to base proposals for social reform. The surveys of poverty undertaken by Charles Booth (1892) and Seebohm Rowntree (1902) in England and by Paul Kellogg (1914) in the United States contributed to the debate about how society might attempt to measure and explain poverty objectively and how minimum standards of living might be defined and achieved. Their findings were used by social reformers to pressure governments to take ameliorative action.

These developments were both co-constitutive and reflective of something of a political watershed in the development of the role of the state in welfare provision, especially in the United Kingdom (C. Alcock et al., 2004). The economic doctrine of laissez-faire gradually gave way to "New Liberalism," which envisaged a positive role for the state in ameliorating social problems, and the rapid expansion of government provision of social services played a major role in creating social policy as an academic subject. Although social policies had previously been studied at universities, the massive growth of government intervention in social welfare facilitated a more systematic examination of government social policies and their effects on people's well-being (Midgley, 2009). The period immediately following the Second World War can be characterized as the golden age of the welfare state. During this period, many Western countries took steps to further extend or consolidate public social welfare provision. In the UK, postwar reforms were based largely on a report by Sir William Beveridge (1942), a former civil servant and academic. The social policy designs recommended by Beveridge were intended to defeat the five key social challenges on the road to postwar reconstruction: want, disease, ignorance, squalor, and idleness. He argued that it was the duty of the state, as the representative body of all citizens, to act to remove these social evils. Beveridge presented his policies as ways of defending capitalism, of securing its continued existence; he was what George and Wilding (1976) termed a reluctant collectivist.

The first department of social policy opened at the London School of Economics in 1950 and was headed by Richard Titmuss. The department was concerned primarily with training welfare professionals during a period of rapid expansion of the welfare state. Academic concern focused on the role of the state as the primary provider of welfare (Ackers & Abbott, 1996). Titmuss' work was ideologically aligned with Fabianism and social democratic thinking (discussed later in this section). He contended that the circumstances of the Second World War created an unprecedented sense of social solidarity among the British people, which made them more willing to accept the expansion of egalitarian policies and collective state action (McBeth, 2004). He argued that governments should assume responsibility for social welfare and formulate and implement substantive social policies to address the problems of poverty, social deprivation, and inequality (Titmuss, 1968, 1974).

Titmuss had a major influence on the subsequent development of social policy as an academic subject (P. Alcock, Glennerster, Oakley, & Sinfield,

2001). His publications were widely read, and he initiated a research agenda that drew international attention. He also recruited new faculty whose academic work further enhanced the subject's reputation. Titmuss and his colleagues played a major role in shaping the Labour government's social policy agenda in the mid-1960s (Reisman, 2001). In the 1960s and 1970s, several other British universities also established interdisciplinary departments of social policy or social administration, and many of Titmuss' former students were recruited to staff these departments (Midgley, 2009).

For much of the postwar period, the idea that social welfare can best be achieved through substantive government intervention has been highly prominent. The initially dominant social democratic perspective viewed the state as a benign force with a unique potential for enhancing the welfare of all (Kearns, 1997). In the mid-1970s, however, this view came under serious attack, indicating the breakdown of the postwar welfare consensus in which a basic commitment to public welfare was sustained by all the major political parties (though there were dissenting voices). From a range of political and ideological directions, the social democratic and Fabian assumptions that had underpinned the postwar consensus came under fierce criticism (Clarke, Cochrane, & Smart, 1987).

In accounts of the "welfare crisis," a number of economic and political arguments recur. First, there was strong evidence that the demand for welfare provision outstripped available financial resources. Critics argued that public welfare programs were overly expensive and damaged the economy by creating high levels of personal taxation, which in turn not only destroyed incentives but also caused inflation (C. Alcock et al., 2004). Social expenditures had experienced a period of rapid growth during the postwar years in virtually all industrialized nations, consistently outstripping the growth in GDP (Organisation for Economic Co-Operation and Development, 1980). The ability of governments to continue funding expansive welfare programs was increasingly questioned as rates of growth slowed, rapidly in some cases, as during the economic crises of the 1970s and 1980s. On both sides of the Atlantic, the advent of stagflation (the combination of inflation and recession) appears to have enabled neoconservative ideas to be more vocally expressed and more widely supported (Mishra, 1990; P. Alcock, 2008). Critics of Keynesian economics and the Beveridgean welfare state further argued that demographic changes (i.e., the aging population) would place social expenditures under even greater pressure, which would inevitably lead to the collapse of the public welfare system.

Commentators on the political right also charged that public welfare programs were inefficiently administered and even harmful (Hayek, 1959; Friedman, 1962). They questioned whether a welfare state was desirable any longer since it had failed to provide what it promised and instead had damaged notions of individual responsibility. These critics asserted that public social welfare systems actually created new social problems or worsened those already in existence by promoting unnecessary public dependence among large numbers of people for whom greater self-sufficiency was both possible and desirable (Murray, 1982; Mead, 1986). This argument has inspired conservative political leaders in several industrialized nations (Hill, 2003; Stoesz, 2009).As shown in this chapter, sections of the political left have also sought to address these criticisms, for example the Third Way approach.

This brief overview of the emergence and early development of social policy highlights its interdisciplinary nature. It is an academic discipline that draws upon the theories, concepts, and research techniques of several other disciplines, including sociology, economics, psychology, political science, philosophy, public administration, and history. The boundaries between social policy and other social science subjects are porous and fuzzy at best. As P. Alcock (2008) notes,

> *although on the one hand we can see social policy as a discrete academic discipline, which is studied and developed in its own right, on the other we can recognize that it is also an inter-disciplinary field, drawing on and developing links with other cognate disciplines at every stage and overlapping at times with these in terms of both empirical foci and methods of analysis. (p. 3)*

Contemporary social policy is characterized by ideological conflict about the nature of social welfare and the role of the state in welfare provision. In this field, we have seen the rise to prominence of several competing perspectives that challenge social democratic thinking about social policy and welfare. These perspectives are discussed in the following sections.

Main Theoretical Perspectives

Seven influential perspectives on social policy can be distinguished, and the aim of this section is to identify and succinctly outline the core features and arguments of each perspective and its interpretation of sport. The plurality and internal heterogeneity of each perspective remain underexplored here. The seven perspectives are summarized in table 12.1. Some of them are also discussed in chapters 5 and 9 (on the sociology of sport and on political science and sport, respectively), which further indicates the interdisciplinary nature of social policy.

Social Democracy and Fabianism

The social democratic perspective on social policy is intimately linked to the emergence of the modern welfare state in Western Europe. It is commonly

Table 12.1 Theoretical Perspectives on Social Policy and Sport

Perspective	Values	Means	Interpretation of welfare	Interpretation of sport
Social democracy and Fabianism	Equality, collectivism	State domination over civil society, confined role for markets	Pervasive state involvement in social and economic life	Sport has many positive benefits and acts as a form of social and cultural glue; it is desirable to reduce barriers to sport participation in order to spread the benefits of sport.
Neo-Marxism	Equality, collectivism	Organized labor movement	Pervasive involvement of state and labor unions in social and economic life	Sport can liberate or constrain. It largely serves the interests of dominant groups and institutions, but it can also act as a site for resistance or change by subordinated groups.
Neoliberalism	Acceptance of inequality; individualism	Market fundamentalism, autonomous civil society	Minimal government, residual welfare	The commercial and voluntary sectors are the optimal deliverers of (diversity in) sporting opportunities.
Feminism	Rights of women as individuals (liberal feminism); women's ability to live and act autonomously (radical feminism).	Social movements, radical democracy, power from below	Anti-statist or limited state intervention; self-directed, nonhierarchical provision	Sport is characterized by hegemonic masculinity, and sport development reproduces sport as a patriarchal institution. Sport can also act, in more limited ways, as a site for challenging traditional masculine and feminine values.
Third way	Equality of opportunity, conservative individualism	Civil society, market and state, pragmatism	Welfare pluralism, social investment state	Sport is a means for promoting social cohesion and social inclusion, mainly through public–private partnerships.
Postmodernism	Identity, lifestyle, recognition, and social justice	New social movements, identity politics, radical democracy	Participative inclusion, decentered power in an increasingly disorganized world	Sport is a paradox—significant to individual and collective self-image and lifestyle, but often reflecting institutional anxiety to exercise control and impose order.
Social development	Economic and social participation	Enhancing people's capabilities (i.e., human and social capital)	Pluralistic investment strategies	Sport can act as a site of economic and social advancement. Sport development can serve as a basis for creating positive social and economic outcomes.

associated with Keynesian forms of economic interventionism designed to secure full employment and economic growth, as well as redistributive forms of state welfare. Social democratic theorists explain the expansion of public welfare programs in terms of the response of the state to a range of economic, political, and social processes, notably industrialization, democratization, and the formation of the class system. The term "social democracy" is not as widely used in the UK, where the development of social policy was linked to the influence of the Fabian Society. Led by Beatrice and Sidney Webb, the Fabian Society argued that the state could be harnessed to promote the collective good and act as a neutral umpire for the demands of differing interests. This view of the state was to form the backbone of social policy. Fabianism promised a new society based on a philosophy of gradualism and collectivist solutions organized through the state and guided by detailed empirical analysis of social problems (Clarke et al., 1987).

From a social democratic or Fabian perspective, sport holds enormous extrinsic value in relation to the promotion of the collective good. In this view, sport offers many actual or potential benefits and acts as a form of social and cultural glue. Sport policies that emanate from this perspective are driven mainly by the state and seek to distribute social justice in the face of market trends. Their aim is to reduce gaps in sport provision and to alleviate barriers to sport participation in order to spread the benefits of sport to all segments of the population (Hylton & Totten, 2008).

Neo-Marxist Perspectives on Social Policy and Sport

One of the strongest critiques of the social democratic and Fabian perspective has come from the socialist and anti-capitalist tradition. These critics regard the welfare state as an ambiguous phenomenon that brings real benefits to subordinate groups while also subjecting them to social control in the interest of capitalism (Lavalette, 1997). They view the welfare state as "a device to stabilise rather than a step in the transformation of capitalist society" (Offe, 1982, p. 12). They also point out that the stabilizing influence that the welfare state brought to capitalism would be fiscally and politically unsustainable (O'Connor, 1973); capitalism could neither survive without having a welfare state nor endure the costs and implications of having one (Dean, 2008).

Neo-Marxist analyses of social policy portray the welfare state as a weapon in the hands of the capitalist class that serves two functions: first, to "buy off" the working class and ensure that their potentially revolutionary spirit is undermined; and second, to police and discipline the working class through the careful direction of funds and supervision by officials and professionals such as social workers (Clarke et al., 1987). They argue that welfare services have not replaced the exploitative relationships of the labor market and that these services have also helped support capitalist development by providing a secure base for the market economy. For neo-Marxists, state welfare is in a constant state of contradiction between the pressure to meet people's welfare and the pressure to support the growth of economic markets (P. Alcock, 2008).

Neo-Marxists tend to argue that sport largely serves the interests of dominant groups and institutions. They contend, for example, that state intervention in sport reproduces class divisions and social inequalities and induces subordinate groups to identify with the greater good of the nation (Hargreaves, 1985). However, neo-Marxists acknowledge that sport can also act as a site for resistance and change by subordinate groups or individuals (Hylton & Totten, 2008).

Neoliberal Perspectives on Social Policy and Sport

As noted earlier, the social democratic perspective has also come under concerted attack from the New Right. One major strand of New Right thinking, neoliberalism, has its roots in classical liberal thinking, particularly in the writings of the Scottish economist and philosopher Adam Smith. Neoliberal ideals are underpinned by belief in individual freedom and the free market (Hayek, 1959). Neoliberals argue that comprehensive welfare states have the effect of "squeezing out" commercial and voluntary alternatives, thus limiting both consumer choice and the freedom of individuals to supply welfare goods and services; public welfare systems thus need to be sharply cut back to allow greater choice through the private provision of goods and services. The emphasis is upon privatization, deregulation, and the introduction of quasi markets in the public sector.

For neoliberals, public provision of social welfare should be residual, that is, provide a minimal safety net only for those who are not able to compete or operate effectively in the market (Pratt, 1997). Friedman (1962), for example, has argued that individuals' natural initiative and drive can be released only if they are allowed to compete freely in the marketplace. Neoliberals also reject the idea that people possess welfare rights as a constitutive element of citizenship. Mead (1986) has stressed the importance of "the common obligations of citizenship" to go along with limited welfare benefits. For Mead, the main problem with the welfare state "is not its size but its permissiveness" (p. 3). Some parallels exist between Mead's analysis and the Third Way motto of "rights and responsibilities," as discussed in a following section.

Neoliberalism's rise to prominence suggests something of a paradigm shift, wherein many intellectuals, politicians, policy makers, and the general public now view social policy and welfare in a different way than they did three decades ago. Evidence of this sea change includes "the acceptance by left-of-centre political parties of the market as an allocative instrument with much to recommend it, indeed in many cases one to be preferred over non-market mechanisms" (Pratt, 1997, p. 48). At a theoretical level, neoliberalism has been successful in recasting the ways in which we think about the respective responsibilities of the individual and the state (Gilbert, 2002).

Neoliberalism's interpretation of sport focuses on fostering the commercial and voluntary sectors as the optimal deliverers of (diversity in) sporting opportunities and views the market as the guardian of individual rights and natural justice. The role of the state in the provision of sport is thus to be kept to a minimum. This ideology is reflected in new forms of corporate governance in sport, for instance the exponential growth of external revenue sources such as television and corporate sponsorship (Giulianotti & Robertson, 2009).

Feminist Perspectives on Social Policy and Sport

Feminist scholars have developed a profound critique of social policy, emphasizing the patriarchal nature of the postwar welfare state (Pateman, 1989; Finch, 1991), which is seen as upholding and reinforcing traditional assumptions about the roles of men and women in the family and the workplace. McIntosh (1981) argued that "all women suffer from the stereotype of the woman as properly dependent upon a man. But all women suffer in quite practical terms from the fact that there are few viable alternatives to such dependence" (p. 33). In addition to seeing the welfare state as an instrument of bourgeois control, as neo-Marxists claim, feminists view it as "especially oppressive to women, in that it harnesses them into the team that pulls the whole welfare charabanc along" (McIntosh, p. 34). Wilson's (1977) pioneering study of women and welfare contended that public welfare policies "amount to no less than the state organization of domestic life" (p. 9). Women had become the employees of the welfare state on a massive scale but found themselves for the most part doing the same kind of work they had traditionally done at home. These jobs remained low paid and low in status in the public sector; hence the charge that state patriarchy had replaced private patriarchy.

For feminists, sport tends to reinforce patriarchy and gender divisions. They argue that despite challenges to male hegemony, women are still institutionally excluded from the governance of sport. Anderson (2009) found that sport and its ancillary organizations and occupations have managed to reproduce its masculinized nature. He suggests that, because orthodox notions of masculinity are institutionally codified in sport, it will take more than affirmative action programs to bring gender equality off the field; it will also require gender integration on the field, that is, women and men competing against each other.

Social Policy and the Third Way

The term "Third Way" is generally associated with the writings of the British sociologist Anthony Giddens and the social policies of the Clinton administration in the United States (1992–2000) and the New Labour government in the UK (1997–2007). The Third Way is concerned with restructuring traditional social democratic doctrines to respond to globalization and the knowledge economy. The Third Way perspective emphasizes individual obligations and social responsibilities in addition to social rights, particularly in the area of paid work obligations (Lister, 1998). Giddens (1998) argues that while government has a whole cluster of responsibilities for its citizens and others, "old-style" social democracy was inclined to treat rights as unconditional claims. The main obligations are connected with work, but others are concerned with housing or looking after the welfare of young children with the help of health professionals (Powell, 2008).

The Third Way perspective advocates a welfare mix in which private and public welfare are combined in a synergetic way. The approach is much more receptive than traditional social democracy to solutions based on the market and civil society. Social investment is to be generated and distributed not wholly through the state but by the state working in conjunction with commercial, voluntary, and informal agencies. This welfare pluralism focuses on coordination and collaboration through public–private partnerships. Indeed, "partnership" has become a buzzword of the Third Way perspective, and the practice is seen as a way to bring all interests together and solve implementation problems (Hill, 2003).

Few European countries remain untouched by the Third Way perspective, and it has also influenced political leaders in several Latin American and Asian countries. This development has led Powell (2008) to argue that it is "likely that elements such as 'active' and 'positive' welfare, consumerism, obligations and a more pluralistic welfare state are here to stay, and it is very doubtful that there will be a return to the traditional social democratic welfare state" (p. 97). However, the Third Way perspective remains controversial. Critics have pointed out that, at least in practice, the Third Way is another form of New Right thinking and that it is merely a kinder, gentler variant of neoliberalism (Mishra, 1999; Hill, 2003). In sport policy, the Third Way perspective has become particularly influential in the promotion of sport as a means of enhancing social inclusion and community cohesion, particularly through its emphasis on "active citizenship" and public–private partnerships (Spaaij, 2013). These issues are discussed in a later part of the chapter.

Postmodernist Perspectives on Social Policy and Sport

Social policy scholars were initially reluctant to engage with postmodernist perspectives, which for many researchers offered insufficiently usable concepts in what was a highly empirical field. In the mid-1990s, however, some contributors began to promote a postmodernist take on social policy, showing that global restructuring undermined traditional beliefs in the state and its role in social amelioration (Carter, 1998). Postmodernists propose a shift in analytical focus from a statist perspective toward an approach that sees the governance of social welfare as constituted by a dispersed and decentered network of power relations (Carlson, 2004). They also challenge social policy analysts' concern with class, arguing that class is of declining political and social significance in postindustrial societies and emphasizing instead the importance of new social movements (Melucci, 1996; Touraine, 2000). The rise of these movements has significant implications for social policy, offering a new perspective on what it means to be a citizen and a client of the welfare state. For example, Fitzpatrick (2008) asserts that "as well as providing for basic needs and aiming at the goal of social justice, perhaps social policy should also try to fulfill other needs, ones that are less material in nature and related more to quality of life" (p. 119).

The influence of postmodernism also extends to the delivery of welfare services. Postmodernists criticize the emphasis placed on universality in Fabian and social democratic approaches, and postmodernist approaches tend to be underpinned by a politics of difference, which, instead of seeking to reconcile differences into a single consensus, would use differences as a resource for multiplying sources of resistance to existing normative categories and classifications (Carlson, 2004). Difference could be protected if diversity and equity (based on need and empowerment) were to replace sameness and equality as the principles underlying universalism (Mouffe, 1993). This project would entail a bottom-up approach "in which needs would no longer be defined by experts but would be negotiated from below and delivered in a manner which would empower users of social policy, and be accountable to them" (Carlson, 2004, p. 142).

In the context of sport policy, postmodernists argue that although sport can be highly significant to individual identity and lifestyle, it is ultimately superficial. State intervention in sport reflects an institutional anxiety to exercise control and impose order in an increasingly disorganized world (Hylton & Totten, 2008).

Social Development Perspectives on Social Policy and Sport

The social development perspective, which originated in the Global South, seeks to integrate social welfare and economic development. By advocating the integration of economic and social policy, the effective use of economic policy to achieve social goals, and the promotion of social investment strategies that encourage participation in the productive economy, social development analysts argue that social welfare is not antithetical to economic progress but that the two are interdependent (Midgley, 2009). Proponents of this perspective believe that economic participation is the primary means by which most people meet their social needs (Sherraden, 1991) and that adequate investments should be made to ensure that people have the skills, knowledge, resources, and opportunities to participate effectively in the productive economy. Investments should be directed in particular to enhancing the social and human capital of individuals and communities (Woolcock & Narayan, 2000).

Social development theorists reject the argument that the free market will create wealth and prosperity for all. They contend that governments have a key role to play in ensuring that people have the capabilities to participate effectively in the economy, in removing barriers to economic participation, and in protecting those who are vulnerable to economic exploitation (Sen, 1999). They recognize that these goals can be achieved through the agency of the state, community, and market and that an appropriate balance between these agents should be found (Midgley, 2009). Like Third Way and neoliberal scholars, social development theorists propose a pluralistic approach to social welfare provision. They draw attention to the role of international development and financial agencies and transnational nongovernmental organizations (NGOs) in the integration of economic and social policy (Hall & Midgley, 2004).

In relation to sport, the social development perspective is increasingly prominent in the "sport-in-development" movement, which focuses on delivering social and health benefits to impoverished communities in the Global South through sport programs (e.g., Levermore & Beacom, 2009). This trend is examined further in the remainder of this chapter.

Key Concepts

The discipline of social policy may be relatively new, but the idea that sport might be directed toward wider social objectives is central to the history of modern sport, as is also shown in this book in chapter 1 (the history of sport) and chapter 10 (international relations and sport). Many aspirations currently voiced in relation to sport and social policy can be traced, in one form or another, throughout the history of modern sport. In the 19th century, several European states were concerned with the physicality of their agents and the general population, not only in preparation for war, but also for the purposes of hygiene and health. Sport has also been central to social movements such muscular Christianity (MacAloon, 2006), the rational recreation interventions of the late 19th century (Kidd, 2008), and the establishment of organizations such as the YMCA (Saavedra, 2009). For the present purpose, the focus is on key concepts that emanate from the contemporary social policy literature and that can be usefully applied to the study of modern sport. Three concepts are discussed here: equality, social inclusion, and partnerships (welfare mix).

Equality: Sport for All?

The principle of equality occupies a central place in debates about social policy (Blakemore & Griggs, 2007). There are, however, differing interpretations of equality. Bagilhole (1997) distinguishes three views of equality. The notion of *equality of condition* acknowledges that even where access is open to all, there may be material and cultural disparities that need to be considered. *Equality of outcome* considers the effect and amelioration of historical disadvantages; such policies may privilege marginalized groups (this is sometimes referred to as affirmative action). *Equality of opportunity* involves the recognition that all social groups need equal access to facilities and services. This concept is reflected in equal opportunity policies aimed at improving access to jobs, education, health, and sport and recreation. One renowned example of such policies is the enactment of Title IX in 1972 in the United States. Title IX requires, among other things, that women be provided with an equitable opportunity to participate in sport and that female athletes receive equal treatment, for example in the provision of equipment and supplies, the scheduling of games and practice times, coaching, practice and competitive facilities, and access to tutoring and scholarships.

In social policy, the main contrast in relation to equality is found between the traditional left conception of equality of outcome and the center-left and Third Way ideology of equality of opportunity (Taylor-Gooby, 2008). How does this contrast play out in sport policy? Sport is sometimes portrayed as a "level playing field" where we can play unfettered by wider social inequalities. The reality of a level playing field has, however, never been achieved, and successes remain incomplete and partial (Hylton & Totten, 2008). Neo-Marxist and feminist perspectives sensitize us to the continuing significance of class, gender, and racial inequalities in sport. They suggest that "sport for all" is unlikely to happen against the backdrop of a capitalist and patriarchal society. Social influences such as class, gender, ethnicity, and age affect patterns of sport participation and can act as barriers to participation (Collins & Kay, 2003); this issue is discussed in more detail in chapter 5 (the sociology of sport). From a social democratic perspective, tackling inequality by reducing barriers to participation is a central premise and aim of sport development. However, "sport for all" will not just happen naturally: Inclusive, low-threshold sporting opportunities must be delivered at local sport facilities before individual access and participation can be achieved. Unless there is recognition of the needs and aspirations of diverse people in society and in client groups, sport providers will continue to reproduce social inequalities in society (Hylton & Totten, 2008).

Social Inclusion

There has been something of a paradigm shift from a concern with equality of outcome to a focus on social inclusion and equality of opportunity, most notably in countries where Third Way and neoliberal thinking has been dominant. A key aspect of this shift is the growing use of the language of social inclusion and exclusion rather than that of poverty—the emphasis being on paid work and education as *the* mechanisms of inclusion (Lister, 1998). Recent policy and political focus on social inclusion have been underpinned by a concern with inadequate civic participation and a lack of social integration and community cohesion (Bloyce & Smith, 2010). In social policy, the notion of social inclusion is reflective of an "active" welfare state that promotes personal responsibility for public issues. It emphasizes active citizenship and people's responsibility to make active contributions to their communities, for example through civic participation and associational life in sport clubs (Coalter, 2007; Spaaij, 2013).

In several respects, social inclusion emerges as more dynamic, multifaceted, and methodologically plural than a poverty-based approach (Rodgers, 1995; Percy-Smith, 2000). It is a dynamic process or set of processes rather than a static, all-or-nothing condition. It is also understood in a global–local context—that is, in relation to transnational, national, and local influences as they affect and co-shape inclusionary and exclusionary processes. Further, as a condition, social inclusion is multidimensional. The notion of social exclusion encompasses not only the lack of access to goods and services that underlies poverty and economic disadvantage but also inequalities in other dimensions of social, political, and cultural life (Vobruba, 2000). Indicators of social exclusion include lack of access to the labor market and education, as well as poverty, poor health, lack of access to social supports and networks, exclusion from services, and discrimination (Percy-Smith, 2000).

The growing popularity of the term "social inclusion" in sport policy signifies a relative shift from sport *as* welfare to sport *for* welfare. Sport is now commonly thought of and used in an instrumental fashion, as a vehicle for social policies targeted at promoting social inclusion (Coalter, 2007; Bloyce & Smith, 2010). Sport is seen as potentially contributing to efforts to address a wide array of social issues that have been linked to social inclusion, such as civic participation, neighborhood renewal, community safety, and integration. In the Netherlands, for example, sport has become embedded across a range of social policies. The Dutch Ministry of Health, Welfare, and Sport (2005) views sport as "a highly desirable and effective way of achieving key government objectives." In its policy statement *Tijd voor Sport* ("Time for Sport"), the national government expresses concern about increasing vandalism in inner-city areas, unhealthy lifestyles, segregation between groups, and diminishing community cohesion. The Dutch government has recently taken several initiatives as part of its Large Cities Policy (*Grotestedenbeleid*), in which sport and leisure play an important role. In the UK, there has arguably been an even stronger association between sport and the promotion of social inclusion (e.g., Department for Culture, Media, and Sport, 2000; Coalter, 2007; Tacon, 2007). One example is the development of the Policy Action Team 10, which was tasked with developing an action plan to maximize the impact of arts, sport, and leisure in the context of neighborhood renewal, while simultaneously raising civic participation.

At the level of the European Union (EU), sport has only recently become a genuine social and cultural concern as part of EU policy on social inclusion (Gasparini, 2010). The EU has funded and promoted several sport-focused projects and events for enhancing social inclusion and intercultural dialogue. The year 2004, designated as the European Year of Education through Sport, witnessed the establishment and funding of a range of projects and partnerships across the continent. Among the objectives was that of encouraging the exchange of good practice concerning the role that sport can play in education to promote the social inclusion of disadvantaged groups. The *White Paper on Sport*, adopted by the European Commission in 2007, also expresses a belief in sport's contribution to social inclusion at the EU level, noting, for instance, that sport "makes an important contribution to economic and social cohesion and more integrated societies" (p. 7).

The concept of social inclusion does have its critics. First of all, when it is associated with a wide variety of social objectives, ranging from unemployment to social integration and civic participation, the concept is very vague. Furthermore, postmodernists argue that the concept is outdated, as global processes lead to the redundancy of traditional boundaries and social inequalities, and lifestyle and identity are increasingly individualized and self-determined through consumption. For postmodernists, as noted earlier, policy attempts to promote social inclusion through sport reflect an institutional anxiety to exercise social control and impose social order (Hylton & Totten, 2008). Others have stressed that, in the ways in which social inclusion has been applied to sport, the concept fails to recognize that poverty and socioeconomic status (together with other sources of social division) lie at the core of social exclusion (Collins & Kay, 2003; Bloyce & Smith, 2010). Bloyce and Smith contend that there is "a clear need to think far more clearly and analytically" about the potential of sport for helping to achieve desired social outcomes associated with social inclusion (p. 106). They found that one of the major weaknesses of many sport-focused social inclusion schemes has been "the failure to change the habitus, that is, the deeply seated values and beliefs, of participants towards their propensity for engaging in what are regarded as undesirable behaviours" (p. 106).

Partnerships in Sport

The increased emphasis on nonstate forms of welfare provision through the private and nonprofit sectors has shifted the boundaries between state and individual responsibility (Lister, 1998; Gilbert, 2002). In sport policy, this shift is reflected in a focus on partnerships. There is a recognition that sport can rarely yield economic, environmental, health, or social benefits when acting alone; rather, "it needs to be a partner, often a minor one, with those promoting other policies" (Collins & Kay, 2003, p. 4). In the context of sport, a partnership can be defined as any cooperation between organizations or individuals to further sport experiences and opportunities. Partnerships in sport can take on myriad forms, and they tend to vary according to factors such as time scale (temporary or permanent), types of partner (public, voluntary, or commercial), power distribution, and scale (transnational, national, local) (Robson, 2008). Many examples exist of partnerships in sport, some of which are discussed in chapters 10 (international relations and sport) and 13 (management studies and sport).

In the context of social policy, the varying scale of partnerships in sport is of particular import. Partnerships in sport can be focused locally or nationally or can extend beyond national boundaries. While no global social policy exists as such, social policy analysts are increasingly concerned with transnational cooperation in social policy and with "globalizing" social policy concepts, such as supranational or global citizenship. It is now widely accepted among social policy analysts that there is a need to address the global contexts and dimensions of social policy (Yeates, 2007). The governance of sport is also characterized by complex webs of global–local interdependence, which require a rethinking of the concepts and analytical categories we use (Maguire, 2005). For example, professional soccer clubs are tied into transnational business and competitive configurations that extend beyond the nation-state. Giulianotti and Robertson (2009) have found that soccer's transnational governance harbors significant problems associated with intensified multipolar complexity, governmental probity, political representation, and social exclusion. These issues are discussed further in chapters 8 (Economics and Sport) and 9 (Political Science and Sport). They are also examined in the discussion that follows here in relation to sport in international development contexts.

Key Debates

We can distinguish at least four major areas of contemporary debate on social policy aspects of sport: social integration and intercultural dialogue through sport, health benefits of sport, sport as social control, and sport in international development. In this section, each of these debates is addressed in relation to recent sport research.

Social Integration and Intercultural Dialogue Through Sport

Social inclusion policies associated with sport take on myriad forms; there is no single approach that applies across all countries. In Europe, one of the key debates in regard to sport and social policy involves the role that sport can play in promoting social integration of minority ethnic groups. In 2003, the European Commission prompted a comparative study examining the contribution of sport as a means of fostering intercultural dialogue among young people from different ethnic backgrounds (Amara, Aquilina, Henry, & PMP Consultants, 2004). The study classified five policy approaches to sport in respect to minority ethnic groups; three of these approaches focus on cultural diversity and pluralism:

• *Interculturalism* refers to the promotion of intercultural exchange by placing equal valuation on cultures that are brought together to produce a new "cultural mix." This position values diversity as a cultural and political resource. Policies associated with such thinking include the promotion of intercultural encounters between minority ethnic groups in the context of sport.

• The philosophy of *separate but equal development* is evident in political terms in the protection of political minorities. In sport, this approach is reflected in a policy of funding minority ethnic sport associations.

• *Market pluralism* is associated with the classical liberal individualism of the Anglo-Saxon model of the state. The focus is on fostering the commercial and voluntary sectors as the optimal deliverers of diversity in sporting opportunity and experience (Henry, 2010).

The remaining two policy approaches emphasize cohesion rather than diversity and take unitary views of national culture:

• *Assimilation* refers to inclusion policies seeking to integrate minority ethnic groups into the national culture. This approach addresses generalist problems, such as the use of sport in combating social exclusion, rather than focusing on specific target groups.

• *Nonintervention* occurs when populations are deemed homogeneous and there is little perceived need for targeted sport policy initiatives (Henry, 2010).

This classification shows the diversity in the ways that social inclusion is conceptualized and promoted in the realm of sport. It enables us to identify different national and supranational models of sport policy in relation to social integration and intercultural dialogue. Different models of integration and assimilation result from "the processes of nation-building, democratisation, and the experience of international relations, particularly colonial and post-colonial relations" (Henry, 2010, p. 59). According to Gasparini (2010), countries such as Germany, the Netherlands, and the UK have observable (yet shifting) multicultural policies in the area of sport and physical activity, which involve multicultural education and endeavors to instill intercultural skills in sport teachers and instructors. In France, on the other hand, these forms of official policy are substituted for by the generic terms "urban policy" and "combating exclusion." French sport policies tend to be directed at specific districts or populations facing social "problems," not at constituted groups or at ethnic minorities (Gasparini). Arnaud (1999) has found that the spatial or social concentration of minority ethnic groups in particular contexts (i.e., impoverished urban areas, at-risk youth) means that services may be, de facto, delivered largely to minority ethnic groups by virtue of this concentration.

Research in this area has also examined the community impact of intercultural encounters in sport, reflecting the issues of community addressed in part II of this book. Research by Krouwel, Boonstra, Duyvendak, and Veldboer (2006) in the Netherlands found that sport activities "seem to perform a strong function in the reinforcement of existing (ethnic) identities, rather than in new identity formation" (p. 176). Tensions and discrimination in other societal spheres can cause members of marginalized minority ethnic groups to prefer to be part of ethnically homogeneous sport teams. For these groups, sport activities are particularly useful as a way to temporarily get away from social spheres marked by tense relations and to seek refuge among others with similar ethnic and cultural backgrounds; in other words, during leisure time, there is a clear wish to be among those with whom social interaction is uncomplicated, symmetrical, and meaningful.

Walseth (2006) has found that sport can also function as a refuge from difficult life and family situations. Sport activities, she argues, provide a "free space" in which some young Muslim women can construct individual identity and alternative forms of femininity. This body of research also shows that intercultural encounters in sport are not necessarily peaceful and meaningful. Cultural "mixing" in sport does not automatically lead to social cohesion or integration. If minority ethnic groups are forced into playing sport with majority ethnic groups, they may well be less inclined to participate in sport or report more negative sport experiences, which would further reduce the potential for intercultural dialogue. In this regard, Krouwel and colleagues (2006) conclude that it is doubtful that sport is an ideal social sphere or vehicle for increasing intercultural interaction and meaningful exchange.

Sport for Welfare: Health Benefits

We have seen how sport is often adopted in an instrumental fashion as a vehicle for social policy intended to promote social inclusion. It is widely recognized among medical professionals, health researchers, and sport providers that sport can also have beneficial health outcomes on a range of indicators (World Health Organization, 2003). The health costs of physical inactivity and sedentary lifestyles have been addressed with regard to several major chronic diseases, notably cardiovascular disease, diabetes, and colon cancer. Scientific evidence that supports these claims is used not only to develop intervention programs aimed at improving health among selected population groups but also to start integrating the work and approaches of various fields of policy development relating to sport and health (Westerbeek, 2009; King, 2009). The World Health Organization has noted that regular physical activity "can be a practical means to achieving numerous health gains, either directly or indirectly through its positive impact on other major risks, in particular high blood pressure, high cholesterol, obesity, tobacco use and stress" (p. 2). To this end, several governments have introduced national physical activity guidelines; for example, the National Physical Activity Guidelines for Australia recommend physical exercise of at least a moderate level on most days of the week for a total of 30 minutes or more on each of those days. The guidelines for children and adolescents recommend at least 60 minutes of moderate to vigorous physical activity every day (Department of Health and Ageing, 2004). Similar physical activity guidelines have been promoted in other countries, including Canada, the UK, the Netherlands, and the United States.

The "sport for health" discourse remains controversial, and three important criticisms have been raised. At the level of policy implementation, there is often a disconnection between sport organizations and health providers. King (2009) notes that policy where the health and sport sectors overlap "appears to be made in a fog of disagreements about goals, causes and means" (p. 190). The disconnection between the two policy sectors seems to emanate from the historically differential reasons for which sport and health organizations were established. Others have argued that, in order to make more adequate sense of the complex relationship between sport participation and health, "we need to pay particular attention to the ways in which health inequalities are socially patterned and to the differential health outcomes that are to be found amongst various social groups" (Bloyce & Smith, 2010, p. 130). Finally, some scholars question the assumed objectivity of and consensus in the epidemiological science in regard to interpreting issues such as overweight and obesity and their relationship to sport and physical activity. Gard and Wright (2005) argue that the "obesity epidemic" is not so much a natural phenomenon as it is "a social idea (ideology) constructed at the intersection of scientific knowledge and a complex of culturally-based beliefs, values, and ideals" (p. 168). This argument points to another important dimension of social policy and sport: sport as a form of social control.

Sport as Social Control

Contemporary perspectives on social policy tend to emphasize the need for an "active" welfare state that promotes personal responsibility and individual opportunity, as opposed to what is characterized in a pejorative way as a "passive" welfare state that encourages dependence and lack of initiative (Lister 1998, p. 224). As noted earlier, this paradigm shift is reflected in sport policies that emphasize active citizenship and civic participation (Coalter, 2007). This development raises the important question of the extent to which social policy plays a political-ideological function in terms of maintaining social order and regulating the behavior of citizens. Neo-Marxist and postmodernist perspectives on social policy sensitize us to the idea of social policy as a form of social control. Social policy is not unequivocally "a good thing." At times, the welfare system becomes more concerned with controlling people than with meeting their needs or respecting their rights as independent citizens (Blakemore & Griggs, 2007). Social control can be directly coercive, such that an individual's autonomy or freedom is deliberately and obviously suppressed, but it can also be subtly oppressive by encouraging people to fit into accepted social roles or suppressing their individuality in less obvious ways, as noted in relation to the social construction of obesity and overweight. Blakemore and Griggs argue that, in the context of social policy, "the prospects for 'benign' social control and for greater openness, freedom and democratic participation in providing and running welfare services are mixed" (p. 129): On the one hand, we are witnessing a tendency toward more control and paternalism, especially in the areas of employment and social security; on the other, there are important countervailing influences to the enormous growth of the power of public and quasi-public bodies over the lives of individuals, such as human rights and equity legislation.

In sport policy, the issue of social control remains underexplored and undertheorized despite the attention that historians and sociologists of sport have drawn to it (see chapters 1 and 5). However, in relation to the aforementioned concepts of social inclusion and integration, the significance of this theme is readily visible. Gasparini (2010) rightly notes that the terms "integration" and "cohesion" as applied to sport invite critical questions, particularly when used as political injunctions. Integration may at the same time signify both a normative program and a social process. Imposed by the state, integration as a normative program is the desired outcome of an official policy and becomes an injunction to adapt to the host society. This normative program is strongly criticized by neo-Marxists, feminists, and postmodernists alike, albeit on different grounds.

Little research has explored the idea of sport as social control in depth (but see chapter 9 of this volume for a general discussion of the political uses of sport). Research by Spaaij (2009) shows that sport policies aimed at enhancing the social inclusion of disadvantaged young people tend to operate in a broader political-ideological context that focuses on generating order in impoverished urban neighborhoods and normalizing the behavior of those who reside in them, particularly "at-risk" youth and ethnic minorities. It could be argued, then, that in the wider context of political concern about social cohesion, immigration, and crime, serving disadvantaged youth is not the ultimate goal of such sport programs. Ultimately, they are a means through which government agencies and their partners seek to civilize and regulate particular social groups in order to normalize their behavior (i.e., toward choosing not to drop out or refraining from criminal or antisocial behavior), to make them meet their social responsibilities, and to integrate them into society. Thus, Spaaij argues, sport-focused interventions also tend to serve as a form of social control and regulation.

Spaaij's research suggests that sport is increasingly becoming a substantial aspect of the neoliberal policy repertoire aimed at generating social order in disadvantaged inner-city neighborhoods. This argument is certainly not new, and it is not limited to Western Europe. One of the earliest sport-focused interventions designed to promote social inclusion is the creation of midnight basketball programs in the United States during the 1980s. These programs sought to reduce crime by young African American males in impoverished urban neighborhoods with high levels of recorded youth crime and delinquency (Hartmann, 2001). The programs offered supervised basketball games during the so-called high-crime" hours (between 10 p.m. and 2 a.m.). Since the 1990s, several similar sport-focused programs have been introduced with the aim of reducing crime and delinquency (e.g., Nichols, 2007).

Sport in International Development

In recent years, sport has come to be viewed increasingly as an effective tool for international development. This view is closely aligned with the social development perspective on social policy and also resonates with the more domestically focused Third Way perspective on social inclusion. The potential of sport as a tool for international development is being harnessed by an ever-expanding range of organizations at the local, national, and transnational levels. Programs that use sport as a vehicle for community development take myriad forms. Partnerships may include transnational NGOs, multinational corporations, international aid organizations, national and supranational governing bodies and sport organizations, individual sport clubs, and elite athletes. For example, UNICEF has developed partnership agreements with major sport federations—such as CONCACAF (the governing body for soccer in North America), CONMEBOL (the governing body for soccer in South America), the West Indies Cricket Board, and the International Olympic Committee—mobilizing these organizations not only to highlight UNICEF messages and activities at sporting events but also to build durable, program-driven partnerships in a range of countries in the Global South (UNICEF, 2006). Statements representing the aspirations of this type of partnership tend to stress the idea that through "sport and physical education, individuals can experience equality, freedom and a dignifying means for empowerment, particularly for girls and women, for people with a disability, for those living in conflict areas and for people recovering from trauma" (Beutler, 2008, p. 365). The United Nations Inter-Agency Task Force on Sport for Development and Peace (2003) has been a major proponent of this vision, arguing that sport can play a pivotal role in achieving the UN's Millennium Development Goals through the use of innovative global partnerships.

Some sport-in-development partnerships closely follow the argument put forward by proponents of the social development perspective that adequate investments should be made to ensure that people have the skills, knowledge, resources, and opportunities to participate effectively in the productive economy. The A Ganar Alliance is a prominent example of a social development approach to community development through sport (Spaaij, 2010). A Ganar is a team sport partnership model for youth employability in Latin America and the Caribbean that is coordinated by the transnational NGO Partners of the Americas. The original funding for A Ganar came from the Multilateral Investment Fund of the Inter-American Development Bank, and it is now funded in part by the U.S. Department of State. The program currently operates in 13 countries in Latin America and the Caribbean. A Ganar is built on the belief that team sport offers an effective tool (or "hook") for motivating youth to participate in vocational training and for teaching employment skills. Other prominent initiatives in the field of sport for development, such as the renowned Mathare Youth Sports Association in Kenya, are discussed at length in chapter 10 (International Relations and Sport) (see also Levermore & Beacom, 2009). That chapter also examines some of the important criticisms aimed at advocates of the power of sport ideology.

Summary

This chapter examines some of the key perspectives, concepts, and debates in social policy and their applications to sport. Social policy is a profoundly interdisciplinary field, and much of the thinking about social policy draws upon insights from sociology, economics, philosophy, and many other disciplines. Moreover, social policy perspectives and their applications to sport are not limited to issues of governance but also address issues of community, identity, and capital (redistribution), and community has become particularly dominant in discussions of active citizenship, social inclusion, and community cohesion. The chapter shows that, in addition to sport *as* welfare, which is reflected in debates on enhancing mass participation in sport and reducing barriers to participation, there has been—both historically and at present—a discourse focused on sport *for* welfare. In this discourse, sport is viewed in a rather instrumental fashion as a vehicle for social policy aimed at promoting social inclusion, community cohesion, intercultural dialogue, positive health outcomes, and other social objectives. This discourse has been challenged from a range of theoretical and ideological perspectives but nevertheless remains highly prominent in both policy making and academic research.

Social policy invites us to critically examine not only the pros and cons of the sport-for-welfare debate but also its political-ideological underpinnings, as well as its implications for welfare provision in and through sport. On the one hand, social policy offers a toolkit for analyzing shifts in thinking about welfare provision, particularly in terms of the retreat of public welfare systems and the emergence of new forms of welfare pluralism and partnerships, in which informal systems of care, professionally administered nongovernmental organizations, and commercial welfare services play a prominent role, and in which citizens are urged to work toward the improvement of welfare in their communities. On the other hand, the notion of social control, which emanates primarily from neo-Marxist, feminist, and postmodernist perspectives on social policy, allows us to penetrate the often romanticized and overgeneralized assumptions surrounding the wider social benefits of sport and to achieve a more critical, reflexive engagement with the subject. Thus, despite its status as a relatively new academic discipline, social policy thus has much to offer in the analysis of social, political, economic, and moral dimensions of modern sport.

References

Ackers, L., & Abbott, P. (1996). *Social policy for nurses and the caring professions*. Buckingham, UK: Open University Press.

Alcock, C., Payne, S., & Sullivan, M. (2004). *Introducing social policy*. Harlow, UK: Pearson.

Alcock, P. (2008). The subject of social policy. In P. Alcock, M. May, & K. Rowlingson (Eds.), *The student's companion to social policy* (3rd ed.) (pp. 3-10). Malden, MA: Blackwell.

Alcock, P., Glennerster, H., Oakley, A., & Sinfield, A. (Eds.) (2001). *Welfare and well-being: Richard Titmuss's contribution to social policy.* Bristol: Policy Press.

Amara, M., Aquilina, D., Henry, I., & PMP Consultants. (2004). *Sport and multiculturalism.* Brussels: European Commission.

Anderson, E. (2009). The maintenance of masculinity among the stakeholders of sport. *Sport Management Review, 12,* 3–14.

Arnaud, L. (1999). *Politiques sportives et minorités ethniques.* Paris: L'Harmattan.

Bagilhole, B. (1997). *Equal opportunities and social policy.* London: Longman.

Beutler, I. (2008). Sport serving development and peace: Achieving the goals of the United Nations through sport. *Sport in Society, 11,* 359–369.

Beveridge, W. (1942). *Social insurance and allied services* (Cmnd 6404). London: HMSO.

Blakemore, K., & Griggs, E. (2007). *Social policy: An introduction* (3rd ed.). Buckingham, UK: Open University Press.

Bloyce, D., & Smith, A. (2010). *Sport policy and development.* London: Routledge.

Booth, C. (1892). *Life and labour of the people in London* (Vol. I). London: Macmillan.

Carlson, J. (2004). Contemporary theoretical perspectives. In C. Alcock, S. Payne, & M. Sullivan (Eds.), *Introducing social policy* (pp. 124-148). Harlow, UK: Pearson.

Carter, J. (1998). Postmodernity and welfare: When worlds collide. *Social Policy & Administration, 32,* 101–115.

Clarke, J., Cochrane, A., & Smart, C. (1987). *Ideologies of welfare.* London: Hutchinson.

Coalter, F. (2007). *A wider social role for sport.* London: Routledge.

Collins, M., & Kay, T. (2003). *Sport and social exclusion.* London: Routledge.

Dean, H. (2006). *Social policy.* Cambridge, UK: Polity.

Dean, H. (2008). The socialist perspective. In P. Alcock, M. May, & K. Rowlingson (Eds.), *The student's companion to social policy* (3rd ed.) (pp. 84-90). Malden, MA: Blackwell.

Department for Culture, Media, and Sport (DCMS). (2000). *A sporting future for all.* London: Author.

Department of Health and Ageing. (2004). *Get out and get active: Australia's physical activity recommendations.* Canberra: Commonwealth of Australia.

European Commission. (2007). *White paper on sport.* Brussels: European Commission.

Finch, J. (1991). Feminist research and social policy. In D. Groves & M. MacLean (Eds.), *Women's issues in social policy* (pp. 194-212). London: Macmillan.

Fitzpatrick, T. (2008). Postmodernist perspectives. In P. Alcock, M. May, & K. Rowlingson (Eds.), *The student's companion to social policy* (3rd ed.) (pp. 113-120). Malden, MA: Blackwell.

Friedman, M. (1962). *Capitalism and freedom.* Chicago: University of Chicago Press.

Gard, M., & Wright, J. (Eds.). (2005). *The obesity epidemic: Science and ideology.* London: Routledge.

Gasparini, W. (2010). Intercultural dialogue or integration through sport? European models under scrutiny. In W. Gasparini & A. Cometti (Eds.), *Sport facing the test of cultural diversity* (pp. 9-20). Strasbourg: Council of Europe Publishing.

George, V., & Wilding, P. (1976). *Ideology and social welfare.* London: Routledge & Kegan Paul.

Giddens, A. (1998). *The third way: The renewal of social democracy.* Cambridge, UK: Polity.

Gilbert, N. (2002). *Transformation of the welfare state.* Oxford, UK: Oxford University Press.

Gilbert, N. (2009). Welfare pluralism and social policy. In J. Midgley & M. Livermore (Eds.), *The handbook of social policy* (pp. 411-420). London: Sage.

Giulianotti, R., & Robertson, R. (2009). *Globalization and football.* London: Sage.

Hall, A., & Midgley, J. (2004). *Social policy for development.* London: Sage.

Hargreaves, J. (1985). From social democracy to authoritarian populism: State intervention in sport and physical recreation in contemporary Britain. *Leisure Studies, 4,* 219–226.

Hartmann, D. (2001). Notes on midnight basketball and the cultural politics of recreation, race, and at-risk urban youth. *Journal of Sport and Social Issues, 25,* 39–71.

Hayek, F. von. (1959). *The constitution of liberty.* Chicago: University of Chicago Press.

Henry, I. (2010). Concepts of multiculturalism, interculturalism, and their relationship to sports policy. In W. Gasparini & A. Cometti (Eds.), *Sport facing the test of cultural diversity* (pp. 59-64). Strasbourg: Council of Europe Publishing.

Hill, M. (2003). *Understanding social policy* (7th ed.). Oxford, UK: Blackwell.

Hylton, K., & Totten, M. (2008). Developing "sport for all"? Addressing inequality in sport. In K. Hylton & P. Bramham (Eds.), *Sports development* (pp. 37-79). London: Routledge.

Kearns, K. (1997). Social democratic perspectives. In M. Lavalette & A. Pratt (Eds.), *Social policy: A conceptual and theoretical introduction* (pp. 11-30). London: Sage.

Kellogg, P. (1914). *Wage-earning Pittsburgh.* New York: Russell Sage Foundation.

Kidd, B. (2008). A new social movement: Sport for development and peace. *Sport in Society, 11,* 370–380.

King, N. (2009). *Sport policy and governance: Local perspectives.* Oxford, UK: Elsevier Butterworth-Heinemann.

Krouwel, A., Boonstra, N., Duyvendak, J.W., & Veldboer, L. (2006). A good sport? Research into the capacity of recreational sport to integrate Dutch minorities. *International Review for the Sociology of Sport, 41,* 165–180.

Lavalette, M. (1997). Marx and the Marxist critique of the welfare state. In M. Lavalette & A. Pratt (Eds.), *Social policy: A conceptual and theoretical introduction* (pp. 50-79). London: Sage.

Levermore, R., & Beacom, A. (Eds.). (2009). *Sport and international development.* Houndmills, UK: Palgrave Macmillan.

Lister, R. (1998). From equality to social inclusion: New Labour and the welfare state. *Critical Social Policy, 18,* 215–225.

MacAloon, J. (2006). Muscular Christianity after 150 years. *International Journal of the History of Sport, 23,* 687–700.

Maguire, J. (2005). *Power and global sport: Zones of prestige, emulation, and resistance.* London: Routledge.

McBeth, M. (2004). Traditional theories of welfare. In C. Alcock, S. Payne, & M. Sullivan (Eds.), *Introducing social policy* (pp. 105-123). Harlow, UK: Pearson.

McIntosh, M. (1981). Feminism and social policy. *Critical Social Policy, 1,* 32–42.

Mead, L.M. (1986). *Beyond entitlement.* New York: Free Press.

Melucci, A. (1996). *Challenging codes.* Cambridge, UK: Cambridge University Press.

Midgley, J. (2009). The definition of social policy. In J. Midgley & M. Livermore (Eds.), *The handbook of social policy* (pp. 3-10). London: Sage.

Midgley, J., & Sherraden, M. (2009). The social development perspective in social policy. In J. Ministry of Health, Welfare, and Sport. (2005). *Tijd voor sport* [Time for sport]. The Hague, Netherlands: Author.

Mishra, R. (1990). *The welfare state in capitalist society.* New York: Harvester Wheatsheaf.

Mishra, R. (1999). *Globalization and the welfare state.* Cheltenham, UK: Elgar.

Mouffe, C. (1993). *The return of the political.* London: Verso.

Murray, C. (1982, Winter). The two wars against poverty. *The Public Interest, 69,* 4–16.

Nichols, G. (2007). *Sport and crime reduction.* London: Routledge.

O'Connor, J. (1973). *The fiscal crisis of the state.* New Brunswick, NJ: Transaction Books.

Offe, C. (1982). Some contradictions of the modern welfare state. *Critical Social Policy, 2,* 7–16.

Organisation for Economic Co-Operation and Development. (1980). *The welfare state in crisis.* Paris: Author.

Pateman, C. (1989). *The disorder of women.* Cambridge, London: Polity.

Percy-Smith, J. (Ed.). (2000). *Policy responses to social exclusion: Towards inclusion?* Buckingham, UK: Open University Press.

Powell, M. (2008). Third way perspectives. In P. Alcock, M. May, & K. Rowlingson (Eds.), *The student's companion to social policy* (3rd ed.). (pp. 90-98). Malden, MA: Blackwell.

Pratt, A. (1997). Neo-liberalism and social policy. In M. Lavalette & A. Pratt (Eds.), *Social policy: A conceptual and theoretical introduction* (pp. 31-49). London: Sage.

Reisman, D. (2001). *Richard Titmuss: Welfare and Society* (2nd ed.). Basingstoke, UK: Palgrave.

Robson, S. (2008). Partnerships in sport. In K. Hylton & P. Bramham (Eds.), *Sports development* (pp. 99-125). London: Routledge.

Rodgers, G. (1995). What is special about a "social exclusion" approach? In G. Rodgers, C. Gore, & J. Figueiredo (Eds.), *Social exclusion: Rhetoric, reality, responses* (pp. 43-55). Geneva: International Labour Organisation.

Rowntree, B.S. (1902). *Poverty: A study of town life.* London: Macmillan.

Saavedra, M. (2009). Dilemmas and opportunities in gender and sport-in-development. In R. Levermore & A. Beacom (Eds.), *Sport and international development* (pp. 124-155). Houndmills, UK: Palgrave Macmillan.

Sen, A. (1999). *Development as freedom*. New York: Knopf.

Sherraden, M. (1991). *Assets and the poor: A new American welfare policy*. New York: Sharpe.

Spaaij, R. (2009). Sport as a vehicle for social mobility and regulation of disadvantaged urban youth: Lessons from Rotterdam. *International Review for the Sociology of Sport, 44*, 247–264.

Spaaij, R. (2010). Using recreational sport for social mobility of urban youth: Practices, challenges, and dilemmas. *Sociétés et Jeunesses en Difficulté, 9*, 1–26.

Spaaij, R. (2013). Sport, social cohesion, and community building: Managing the nexus. In P. Leisink, P. Boselie, M. van Bottenburg, & D.M. Hosking (Eds.). (In press). *Managing social issues: A public values perspective*. Cheltenham, UK: Elgar.

Stoesz, D. (2009). Reagan and beyond. In J. Midgley & M. Livermore (Eds.), *The handbook of social policy* (pp. 169-178). London: Sage.

Tacon, R. (2007). Football and social inclusion: Evaluating social policy. *Managing Leisure, 12*, 1–23.

Taylor-Gooby, P. (2008). Equality, rights, and social justice. In P. Alcock, M. May, & K. Rowlingson (Eds.), *The student's companion to social policy* (3rd ed.) (pp. 34-41). Malden, MA: Blackwell.

Titmuss, R. (1968). *Commitment to welfare*. London: Allen and Unwin.

Titmuss, R. (1974). *Social policy: An introduction*. London: Allen and Unwin.

Touraine, A. (2000). *Can we live together?* Cambridge, UK: Polity.

UNICEF. (2006). *Sport for development in Latin America and the Caribbean*. Panama: UNICEF Regional Office for Latin America and the Caribbean.

United Nations Inter-Agency Task Force on Sport for Development and Peace. (2003). *Sport as a tool for development and peace*. New York: United Nations.

Vobruba, G. (2000). Actors in processes of inclusion and exclusion: Towards a dynamic approach. *Social Policy and Administration, 34*, 601–613.

Walseth, K. (2006). Sport and belonging. *International Review for the Sociology of Sport, 41*, 447–464.

Westerbeek, H. (Ed.). (2009). *Using sport to advance community health: An international perspective*. Nieuwegein, Netherlands: Arko Sports Media.

Wilson, E. (1977). *Women and the welfare state*. London: Tavistock.

Wood, G., & Gough, I. (2006). A comparative welfare regime approach to global social policy. *World Development, 34*(10), 1696–1712.

Woolcock, M., & Narayan, D. (2000). Social capital: Implications for development theory, research, and policy. *The World Bank Research Observer, 15*, 225–249.

World Health Organization. (2003). *Health and development through physical activity and sport*. Geneva: Author.

Yeates, N. (2007). Globalization and social policy. In J. Baldcock, N. Manning, & S. Vickerstaff (Eds.), *Social policy* (3rd ed.) (pp. 627-653). Oxford, UK: Oxford University Press.

CHAPTER 13

Sport and Management Studies

Lucie Thibault, PhD

As is evident in other chapters of this book, sport permeates all areas of life: politics, economics, business, law, health, education, media, culture, and tourism, to name a few. This chapter focuses on one of these areas—management—and the roles that organizations and business practices play in sport. The academic discipline of sport management has gained prominence with the growing global importance of the sport industry. In the European Union, for example, it is estimated that sport "generates a value-added effect of €407 billion [roughly US$500 billion]" (EU Sport Directors, 2006, p. 1); in the United States, the size of the sport industry was estimated to be US$435 billion in 2012 (Plunkett Research, 2012). Furthermore, with an estimated 2 percent of the global GDP being generated by sport (EurActiv, 2009; Lapper & Landa, 2012; World Economic Forum, 2009), it is clear that sport is an important industry in many parts of the world (PricewaterhouseCoopers, 2010).

Business activities related to sport occur in all three organizational sectors: public (government units and agencies), nonprofit (voluntary organizations), and commercial (for-profit organizations). A variety of organizations in these sectors, both large and small, are typically responsible for managing sport participation programs for all and sport programs for elite and professional athletes; managing teams, leagues, tournaments, events, and facilities; and producing and distributing sporting goods, equipment, and sportswear. Sport management also considers the diversity of organizations involved in delivering sport services, programs, and products—sporting goods manufacturers and retailers, professional sport leagues and franchises, nonprofit local sport clubs, governments, and organizations responsible for delivering large-scale events at the international level.

The increasing scope and importance of sport in society make sport management a crucial function to consider. Management is "the process of working with and through individuals and groups and other resources (such as equipment, capital, and technology) to accomplish organizational goals" (Hersey, Blanchard, & Johnson, 2008, p. 7). In sport management, the focus is placed on accomplishing organizational goals to promote and enhance sport and sport-related activities for individuals acting as participants, athletes, consumers, fans, coaches, officials, volunteers, leaders, members of the media, or sponsors, or playing other roles as sport stakeholders. The management of sport has become a significant area of interest in both practice and research. On sport as an industry worthy of more attention, legitimacy, and focus for research, Chadwick (2009, p. 202) noted that

> *sport has now emerged as an industrial sector in its own, with a number of studies and estimates that it makes a major contribution to economic and commercial activity both within and across national boundaries. At the same time, sport continues to have a profound influence on the social, cultural, health and psychological spheres of human existence. The prevailing appeal of sport is such that a wide range of institutions, organizations, bodies, clubs, teams and individuals are both affected by and involved in sport.*

Sport as a Unique Industry

Chadwick (2009) is one among a number scholars who have discussed sport's distinctiveness from other industries. For example, Smith and Stewart (2010), Babiak and Wolfe (2009), and Wakefield (2007) have noted the unique features of sport and how they highlight the need for a specific field of study in sport management and sport marketing. Smith and Stewart's list of unique sport features is very similar to Babiak and Wolfe's list, and the two groups agreed on three common attributes: passion, economics (or anti-competitive business practices), and transparency or level of scrutiny. The fourth attribute is stakeholder management for Babiak and Wolfe; it is sport's fixed supply schedule for Smith and Stewart. From a sport marketing perspective, Wakefield identified a list of 10 attributes that distinguish sport from other products and services, and some of these items are congruent with Babiak and Wolfe's and Smith and Stewart's. The following paragraphs explore these unique attributes of sport management and sport marketing.

The first attribute of sport is *passion*. For Babiak and Wolfe (2009), Smith and Stewart (2010), and Wakefield (2007), passion relates to the intensity and devotion that individuals and consumers feel toward sport products and services (e.g., programs, competitions, events). The intensity and devotion go beyond the passion that consumers typically feel for traditional products, such as laundry detergent, a box of crackers, or a vacuum cleaner. This passion for sport is evident, for example, in the degree to which fans identify with athletes, teams, leagues, and even sportswear and equipment. Passion in sport is particularly evident in the level of global support generated for World Cup events in soccer. Fans' strong identification with sport brands (whether a team, a league, or certain sporting goods) speaks to their loyalty, affiliation, and commitment to sport products. Smith and Stewart (p. 4) focused predominantly on the passion of fans and what they called "sport's ability to arouse strong passionate attachments, unstinting loyalty, vicarious identification, and blind optimism."

With respect to the second dimension, *economics*, Babiak and Wolfe (2009) discussed the unique benefits that the sport industry (referring generally to professional sport leagues and franchises) receives from regulatory agencies—for example, monopoly, special protection from antitrust laws, and financial resources from public sources for sport infrastructures and franchises. Along similar lines, Smith and Stewart (2010) focused their arguments on the anti-competitive business practices that professional sport organizations enjoy; specifically, they argued that professional sports engage

> *in cartel-like behaviour because they rely on the cooperation of teams and collective agreements on areas like salary ceilings, player recruitment and drafting, admission pricing, game scheduling, income-redistributions, and broadcasting arrangements to maintain an equitable competition and to maximise marketing and licensing opportunities. (p. 7)*

Wakefield (2007) noted professional sports' monopoly power and antitrust exemptions, as well as the use of public funds to subsidize facilities (e.g., stadiums) used by professional sport teams. He also addressed how fans, sponsors, and media members contribute financial resources to support the activities of professional sport—a situation that does not typically occur in relation to most products and services. Wakefield discussed exchanges between stakeholders in sport as being predominantly social in nature, as opposed to economic, and argued that contractual power for general goods and services favors owners, whereas contractual power for professional sport favors employees (i.e., athletes).

Professional sport organizations are not the only sport organizations that enjoy some of these economic and competitive advantages. Sport organizations in the nonprofit sector also receive benefits from public and other nonprofit organizations. For example, in most countries, governments fund nonprofit sport organizations to help them achieve their goals. Public lotteries are also widely used in developed countries as an important source of funds for nonprofit sport organizations and sport initiatives. As well, national governments and nonprofit organizations (e.g., the International Olympic and Paralympic Committees and international sport federations) recognize national sport organizations as carrying exclusive responsibility for a sport within a country. This status allows organizations to access and share resources and to involve their sport in exclusive, high-profile, competitive sport events (e.g., the Winter and Summer Olympic Games and Paralympic Games, as well as continental games such as the Asian Games, Pan American Games, and All-Africa Games).

The third dimension, *transparency* or *level of scrutiny*, addresses the very public nature of sport in the social sphere. Most activities in high-profile sports (e.g., professional sports, Olympic sports, World Cups, and other international sport competitions) are covered extensively and intimately by the media. Consequently, widespread scrutiny is applied to decisions made by leaders of sport organizations and to actions undertaken (on or off the field) by coaches, officials, and athletes (e.g., cutting athletes from the team, addressing a win–loss record, hiring and firing coaches, personal behavior). As an example, Tiger Woods' behavior off the golf course made world news headlines for several months in late 2009 and early 2010 (e.g., Briggs, 2010; Lampert-Stokes, 2010). Another example can be found in the child sex abuse scandal involving assistant football coach Jerry Sandusky and Penn State University's "culture of reverence" that concealed this abuse over a 14-year period (Chappell, 2012; Shade, 2012; Wolverton, 2012). Such coverage of sport organizations' activities differs greatly from the coverage received by organizations operating outside of the sport sector (Babiak & Wolfe, 2009; Smith & Stewart, 2010), though it is true that some sport organizations receive little or no media coverage, particularly those operating in the nonprofit sector and those responsible for sports that are less well established.

Finally, with respect to the fourth dimension, *stakeholder management*, Babiak and Wolfe (2009) discussed the extensive and complex network of stakeholders with which sport organizations must interact—for example, media, government, sponsors, fans, consumers, local communities, shareholders, coaches, officials, athletes, and participants. The number and diversity of these stakeholders, along with their divergent interests, add to the complex nature of managing sport organizations. Building on the work of other sport scholars, Smith and Stewart (2010) argued that key sport stakeholders (e.g., spectators, club officials, organizing bodies, clubs, and media) often disagree about the best way to govern sport.

Smith and Stewart (2010), for their fourth unique attribute, addressed the fixed supply schedule of sport. Specifically, they noted that sport organizations' main product—on-field performance—"cannot be increased in the same way that a manufactured good like a motor car or a generic service like dental work can" (p. 8). Sport organizations face limitations that cannot be surmounted, such as the fixed number of games in a season, the fixed number of athletes on a team, and the maximum seating capacity of a sport venue. Whereas other industries can increase their output by hiring more employees, acquiring more raw materials, or increasing the production schedule, sport organizations operate within limitations imposed on them by the nature of their industry.

Collectively, these attributes of sport contribute to the industry's distinctiveness. However, not all scholars agree that sport management is unique or distinct from its parent discipline of management in general. In fact, in the late 1990s, Slack (1998, p. 21) believed that "there [was] very little if anything about [sport management] literature or our field that could not be provided by a business school." Building on his previous work, Slack argued that sport organizations are not much different from organizations operating in other industries, and, consequently, that sport management scholars needed to consider the research being published in management journals and apply and build upon theoretical and conceptual frameworks developed in the broader field of management—a field that is more established and enjoys a longer history (Slack, 1996, 1998).

In another view, Chadwick (2009) acknowledged sport as a unique context (e.g., in the uncertainty of outcome of a sporting contest) yet believed that sport management should not isolate itself from management. He expressed concern that in isolation "sport will never be more than a management outpost, a ghetto in which highly specific work is undertaken by academics and researchers working outside the mainstream management literature" (p. 202). As a result, he believed that a "consensual relationship between the generic and sport management literatures" is necessary for the sake of the quality of research in sport management (p. 202). The relationship between sport management and management studies is discussed further in a later part of this chapter. For now, let us turn to a historical overview of sport management, which is followed by analysis of sport management's core concepts, main theoretical perspectives, critical findings, and key debates.

Historical Overview

The origins of the organization, management, and business of sport can be traced back to the very beginning of sport. The hosting and organizing of tournaments, competitions, and other sport events have required the use of leadership and management skills by numerous individuals. In comparing contemporary sport management with the organization of ancient sport events, Parks and Olafson (1987) cautioned that, "lest we be deluded by the notion that contemporary sport management is markedly different from the ancient art of staging athletic spectacles, let us consider for a moment the following description of the Games sponsored in 11 B.C. by Herod the Great, King of Judea and Honorary President of the Olympics" (p. 1). Parks and Olafson invoked the following description by Frank (1984, p. 158):

> [T]he games began with a magnificent dedication ceremony. Then there were athletic and musical competitions, in which large prizes were given not only to the winners but also—an unusual feature—to those who

took second and third place. Bloody spectacles were also presented, with gladiators and wild beasts fighting in various combinations, and there were also horse races. Large prizes attracted contenders from all areas and this in turn drew great numbers of spectators. Cities favored by Herod sent delegations, and these he entertained and lodged at his own expense. What comes through most clearly . . . is that gigantic sums of money were spent.

The development of sport management as an academic discipline, however, is much more recent. It is not my intention here to provide a complete history of sport management scholarship; other researchers have presented overviews of this history (e.g., Crosset & Hums, 2012; Parks, Quarterman, & Thibault, 2011; Paton, 1987; Shilbury & Rentschler, 2007; Zeigler, 1987, 1992), and are all in agreement that sport management is a very young academic discipline. The origin of sport management can be traced back to the organization of sport competition in the school setting (mostly at the high school and college levels). In fact, the early textbooks dealing with the management and organization of sport were published in the 1940s and 1950s (e.g., Hughes & French, 1954; L.B. Means, 1949; Zeigler, 1959) and focused on physical education programs and intramural and inter-school sports (Slack, 1996, 1998). As Slack noted,

these topics reflect the domain of sport management as it was in the field's formative years. Nike and ESPN [Entertainment and Sports Programming Network] were not yet created, the NHL [National Hockey League] only had six teams, merchandising and licensing agreements were virtually unheard of, and the only connection between McDonalds and the Olympics was if you stopped for a hamburger on the way to or from one of the events. (1996, p. 97)

It is widely accepted that James Mason from Ohio University was the founder of the first academic program in sport management, a graduate degree program that originated from written correspondence between Mason and Walter O'Malley in 1957 (see Crosset & Hums, 2012; Parks et al., 2011). At the time, O'Malley was president of Major League Baseball's Brooklyn Dodgers, and he believed that academic programs were desperately needed to prepare students for leadership positions in the growing sector of sport organizations (J.G. Mason, Higgins, & Wilkinson, 1981; Parks et al.). Following the development of Ohio University's sport management program in 1966, two other universities (Biscayne College, now St. Thomas University, and St. John's University) launched undergraduate programs specializing in sport management (Crosset & Hums).

Since 1966, the field has experienced unprecedented growth in academic circles, and by 2012 more than 400 colleges and universities worldwide were offering academic sport management programs at the undergraduate or graduate level or both (North American Society for Sport Management, 2012). Thus the academic growth of the field in less than 50 years has been remarkable, though perhaps it is not surprising in light of the size and scope of the global sport industry and the economic activity generated through community sport, sport events, sporting goods, sport facilities, and sport teams and leagues. As Shilbury and Rentschler (2007, p. 33) noted, "there are a growing number of academics 'branded' as sport management scholars whose focus is solely dedicated to sport management teaching and to research related to the management of sport." Furthermore, they explained, these programs were "originally housed in physical education and/or sport studies" (p. 33), but, as the field has grown, sport management programs have increasingly been located in business schools (e.g., Coventry University, Deakin University, Griffith University, Massey University, Temple University, and the University of Massachusetts).

There has also been a parallel growth in the number of professional and academic associations and publications diffusing research and information about sport management. A number of regional and continental sport management associations have been established to bring together scholars and students interested in academic and professional issues affecting sport management (see table 13.1).

The creation of sport management associations has been accompanied by a proliferation of professional and academic publications on sport management. Professional publications include *Athletic Business, SportsBusiness Journal, SportsBusiness Daily, Sports Business Exchange*, and *SportBusiness International*. For scholarly publications, Thibault (2007) compiled a list of journals dealing with sport management and related issues; an updated version is provided in table 13.2.

There is also a trend in recent years toward specialization of disciplines related to sport management. As table 13.2 makes evident, journals now exist to exclusively address some of sport management's subdisciplines—for example, sport marketing and sponsorship, sport finance, sport economics, and sport communication.

Sport management scholars are also publishing their research in journals of the parent disciplines of management and marketing (e.g., Amis, Slack, & Hinings, 2004; Babiak & Thibault, 2009; Pritchard, Funk, & Alexandris, 2009; Sherry, Shilbury, & Wood, 2007). In fact, in an article in the *Journal of Management Inquiry*, Wolfe and his colleagues called for greater attention by organizational theorists to the topic of sport as a rich setting for building upon management theories. They argued that "the context of sport can contribute to an understanding of management and of organizations" and explained that sport is "an effective setting for studying a number of organizational phenomena," such as loyalty, pay equity and structure, motivation,

Table 13.1 Regional and Continental Academic Associations in Sport Management

Academic association	Year created
North American Society for Sport Management www.nassm.com	1986
European Association for Sport Management www.easm.net	1993
Sport Management Association of Australia and New Zealand www.smaanz.org	1995
International Sport Management Alliance This alliance led to the development of the World Association for Sport Management	1999
Asian Association for Sport Management http://aasmasia.com	2002
Sport Marketing Association www.sportmarketingassociation.net	2002
Asociación Latinoamericana de Gerencia Deportiva www.algede.com	2009
African Sport Management Association www.asma-online.org	2010
World Association for Sport Management' www.worldsportmanagement.com	2012

In addition to these regional and continental associations, there are several national sport management associations (e.g., the Federation for Sport Economics and Sport Management of Germany; the Hellenic Association of Sports Management; the Korean Society for Sport Management; the Sport Management Society of China; and the Taiwan Association for Sport Management).

commitment, performance, product development, human resources, strategy, and resources (Wolfe et al., 2005, p. 185). Some management and marketing journals have published special issues addressing sport and sport-related topics (e.g., the *European Journal of Marketing* in 1999, the *Journal of Management and Organization* in 2010, *Management Decision* in 2009 and *Public Management Review* in 2009).

Professional and academic journal publications have been complemented by numerous books published on the topic of sport management throughout the world (e.g., Beech & Chadwick, 2004; Chelladurai, 2009; Gillentine, Baker, & Cuneen, 2012; Hoye, Smith, Nicholson, Stewart, & Westerbeek, 2009; Masteralexis, Barr, & Hums, 2012; Pedersen, Parks, Quarterman, & Thibault, 2011; Slack & Parent, 2006; Taylor, Doherty, & McGraw, 2008; Trenberth & Hassan, 2012). Based on Slack's (2003, p. 118) premise that "one of the indicators of the strength of an academic discipline, or sub-discipline, is the quantity and quality of the literature by which it is underpinned," sport management now occupies a strong position.

As a function of its evolution, the field of sport management has progressively become more specialized. Topics covered in journals and in undergraduate and graduate courses now include, for example, organizational theory, organizational behavior and human resource management, sport economics, sport finance, sport events and facilities, sport marketing and sponsorship,

Table 13.2 English-Language Journals Relevant to Sport Management

Journal	Year of first volume
SPORT MANAGEMENT	
Journal of Sport Management	1987
European Sport Management Quarterly (formerly *European Journal for Sport Management*)	1994
Sport Management Review	1998
International Journal of Sport Management	2000
The SMART Journal (on hiatus as of 2009)	2005
Journal of Applied Sport Management (formerly *Journal of Sport Administration and Supervision*	2009
Journal of Physical Education and Sport Management	2010
Sport, Business and Management: An International Journal	2011
SPORT MARKETING AND SPONSORSHIP	
Sport Marketing Quarterly	1992
International Journal of Sports Marketing and Sponsorship	1999
International Journal of Sport Management and Marketing	2005
SPORT ECONOMICS AND FINANCE	
Journal of Sports Economics	2000
International Journal of Sport Finance	2006
EVENT MANAGEMENT	
Event Management: An International Journal (formerly *Festival Management & Event Tourism*)	1993
International Journal of Event Management Research	2005
Journal of Venue and Event Management	2009
SPORT MEDIA AND COMMUNICATION	
Journal of Sports Media	2006
International Journal of Sport Communication	2008
Sport and Communication	2013
SPORT POLICY AND POLITICS	
International Journal of Sport Policy and Politics (formerly *International Journal of Sport Policy*)	2009
PEDAGOGY OF SPORT MANAGEMENT	
Sport Management Education Journal	2007
INTERCOLLEGIATE SPORTS	
Journal of Intercollegiate Sport	2008
Journal of Issues in Intercollegiate Athletics	2008
OTHER	
Case Studies in Sport Management	2012

A version of this table was presented at the 2007 International Sport Science Congress held in Seoul, Korea, and published in its proceedings (Thibault, 2007). This list includes *only* journals published in English; additional academic journals in sport management are published in other languages (e.g., French, Japanese, and Korean). In addition, newly created sport management organizations (e.g., in Iran and Africa) are planning new journals. The list does not include journals from related disciplines (e.g., recreation and leisure management, sport tourism) or general sport journals that may publish sport management articles (e.g., the *Journal of Sports Sciences*, *Quest*, *Research Quarterly for Exercise and Sport*).

consumer behavior, sport media and communication, sport law, and sport policy. Other chapters of this book cover some of these topics—for example, sport media (chapter 7), sport economics (chapter 8), sport law (chapter 11), and sport policy (chapter 12). Although these fields may be distinct from sport management, they are related to the organization and governance of sport, and sport leaders need to understand a range of issues in the social sciences, the media, economics, and social policy, to name a few, in order to be effective in their work.

Core Concepts

Because sport management is a relatively new discipline, its scholars rely extensively on theoretical and conceptual progress achieved in the parent disciplines of management and marketing. These disciplines possess long histories, proven legitimacy, and credibility, both in academia and in practice. As a result, the core concepts of the field of sport management are no different from the foundational concepts of management and marketing (Amis & O'Brien, 2005; Mullin, Hardy, & Sutton, 2007; Slack, 1998; Slack & Parent, 2006).

Slack (1998, p. 22) argued that "management is actually made up of a number of sub-disciplinary areas: organizational theory, organizational behaviour, strategy, operations management, finance, accounting, marketing, human resources management, economics, industrial relations, etc." For the purposes of this section, the focus is on three main subdisciplinary areas as core concepts in sport management: organizational theory, organizational behavior, and marketing. The topic of marketing is covered under the more general field of sport management, but, given the volume of research and interest in this area, sport marketing could stand on its own, just as marketing is typically distinct from management studies in the parent disciplines. In fact, the distinction between sport management and sport marketing was underscored when academicians specializing in sport marketing created their own organization—the Sport Marketing Association—in 2002. At the same time, members of other academic associations related to sport management (see table 13.1) consider the topics of organizational theory, organizational behavior, and marketing as key elements of their mandates, along with the topics of sport economics and finance, sport law, media, social policy, governance, and sport tourism.

Organizational Theory

Organizational theory is defined as "the study of how organizations function and how they affect and are affected by the environment in which they operate" (Jones, 2010, p. 7). According to Slack and Parent (2006), students of sport management programs need to be introduced to organizational theory because it will help them better understand the organizations for which they will work and with which they will interact in the future. This understanding will also help students address problems and challenges they face in the course of their work; for example, it can help them design appropriate structures based on the organizational environment, manage changes, provide appropriate leadership, and adopt appropriate technologies and strategies to achieve the goals of the organization.

Some of the topics addressed by organizational theory are effectiveness, organizational structure and design, change and innovation, strategy, and organizational culture. For more details about how these topics have been applied to sport organizations, consult Amis and O'Brien (2005), Slack and Parent (2006), and Thibault and Quarterman (2011). Some topics covered in organizational theory are explained briefly in the following bullet points:

- *Effectiveness* is the degree to which an organization reaches its goals (Daft, 2010; Jones, 2010).

- *Organizational design* is the collective juxtaposition of structure and context. Structure refers to the internal characteristics of organizations, whereas context characterizes the whole organization. Structure includes the dimensions of specialization, formalization, and centralization; contextual dimensions include the size of the organization, technology, goals, strategy, and the environment (Daft, 2010; Jones, 2010).

- *Environment* refers to all elements considered "outside the boundary of the organization . . . [that] have the potential to affect all or part of the organization" (Daft, 2010, p. 140). The overall environment includes both task environments and the general environment. Task environments are sectors with which the organization must interact directly on an ongoing basis; elements include, for example, suppliers, customers, competitors, labor markets, stock markets, governments and their regulations, economic conditions (e.g., recession, inflation, unemployment), and technology in the production .

- *Organizational change* refers to the adoption of a new system, procedure, or behavior to enhance the organization's operations, whereas *innovation* refers to the adoption of a new system, procedure, or behavior that is novel to the industry in which the organization operates (Daft, 2010).

- *Strategy* is the development of plans that help an organization address the challenges it faces from the environment.

- *Organizational culture* involves the values, norms, and expectations that are shared by members of the organization and guide their behaviors in the workplace (Daft, 2010). Given the importance of individuals to the culture of an organization, this topic is also closely related to the concept of organizational behavior.

Organizational Behavior

Whereas organizational theory addresses the structure and design of organizations, organizational behavior deals with the people in organizations. Most scholars and leaders agree that people are the most valuable resource in an organization (Heery & Noon, 2008; Hersey et al., 2008; Mathis & Jackson, 2008) and that, as a result, it is critical to understand and effectively manage people in organizations. Organizational behavior is defined as "a multidisciplinary field devoted to understanding individual and group behavior, interpersonal processes, and organization dynamics with the goal of improving the performance of organizations and the people in them" (Schermerhorn, Hunt, & Osborn, 2008, p. 5). Topics related to organizational behavior include (to name a few) decision making, power, politics, leadership, motivation, teamwork and group dynamics, conflict, communication, and human resources management. For more details about how organizational behavior has been applied in sport organizations, consult Chelladurai (2006), Cuskelly, Hoye, and Auld (2006), and Taylor et al. (2008). Some topics covered in the study of organizational behavior are explained briefly in the following bullet points:

- *Decision making* involves several steps: specifically defining the problem, identifying the criteria for the decision, developing and evaluating alternatives, selecting one of the alternatives, implementing it, and, finally, evaluating the decision (Schermerhorn et al., 2008).

- *Power* can be interpreted as control over resources or as the ability to influence. For individuals, sources of power can originate from the organization or from personal characteristics. Organizational power can consist of what is called legitimate power (based on the position one holds in the organization), reward power (based on one's ability to reward employees—e.g., through promotion, a bonus, or a pay raise), and coercive power (based on one's ability to punish employees—e.g., through firing, demotion, or withholding a pay raise). Personal sources of power include expert power (based on an individual's knowledge, experience, or judgment), referent power (based on personal characteristics—e.g., charisma, charm, and appeal), and power based on information (i.e., an individual's access to valuable information, as distinct from expertise). Any of these sources of power can be effective in influencing employees. With power and influence, of course, comes politics, and organizations are of course not immune to political behavior by their employees (Schermerhorn et al., 2008).

- *Organizational politics* refers to "the management of influence to obtain ends not sanctioned by the organization or to obtain sanctioned ends through nonsanctioned influence means" (Schermerhorn et al., 2008, p. 227).

- *Leadership* is the process of influencing people to work individually or collectively toward achieving a goal (Hersey et al., 2008). Good leadership is an important element in managing people in an organization.

- *Motivation* refers to "individual forces that account for the direction, level, and persistence of a person's effort expended at work" (Schermerhorn et al., 2008, p. 102).

- *Teamwork* and *group dynamics* are central in organizations, since most tasks accomplished are achieved by groups of people. Teams in organizations make recommendations, run activities, make products, and deliver services (Schermerhorn et al., 2008). Given the importance of teams in organizations, it is vital to ensure favorable dynamics between members of groups in order to maximize the chance of achieving effective outcomes. In any situation where individuals work together, however, conflict is bound to occur.

- *Conflict* is disagreement between individuals over personal issues or ways to achieve organizational goals. Conflict resolution strategies and negotiations are thus valuable in addressing organizational issues (Schermerhorn et al., 2008).

- *Communication* is an important process through which organizations receive and disseminate information. Communication can be formal or informal and can take place through various channels (e.g., face-to-face meetings, written communications, electronic communications) (Schermerhorn et al., 2008).

- *Human resources management* refers to understanding and managing people in an organization, and it is an important responsibility for organizational leaders. Human resources management involves several steps, including recruitment, selection, training, job analysis, evaluation, performance appraisal, compensation, and termination (Heery & Noon, 2008; Mathis & Jackson, 2008). All of these steps are central to the selection of the best employees for an organization and to the process of ensuring that they are properly supported to enable attainment of organization goals.

Marketing

Marketing is defined as "the art and science of creating and managing successful exchanges" (Chernev, 2009, p. 1). Furthermore, Chernev explained that "the core activity of a market is the exchange of goods and services among market participants" (p. 1). In the context of sport, Mullin et al. (2007) defined sport marketing as "all activities designed to meet the needs and wants of sport consumers through exchange processes" (p. 12). They further explained that sport marketing has two central elements: the marketing *of* sport and the marketing done *through* sport. Marketing of sport involves marketing sport products and services to consumers, whereas marketing through sport involves marketing non-sport-related products and services through the use of sport-related entities (e.g., athletes, teams) and events. Scholars in sport marketing rely on the parent discipline through the application of its core elements.

One core element in the operationalization of marketing is the marketing mix, which includes products and services, brands, price, incentives, communication, and distribution. Additional topics addressed under the umbrella of marketing and the marketing mix include branding, promotion, advertising, sponsorship, and consumer behavior. For more details about how these topics have been applied in sport organizations, consult Amis and Cornwell (2005), Mullin et al. (2007), Shank (2008), and Wakefield (2007). Some topics covered in marketing are explained briefly in the following bullet points:

- *Branding* refers to the name of the brand and the marks associated with an organization, which provide points of differentiation from other products and organizations in the marketplace (Mullin et al., 2007; Shank, 2008).

- *Promotion* represents all activities undertaken to publicize an organization, product, or service. It may include advertising, as well as reduced price, rebates, coupons, and contests. These strategies are all focused on convincing consumers to purchase the product or service (Mullin et al., 2007; Shank, 2008).

- *Advertising* is a communication process that highlights features of a product or service in the hope of convincing consumers to purchase it. Advertising is an element of promotion (Mullin et al., 2007; Shank, 2008).

- *Sponsorship* is a promotional strategy in which an organization's brand, product, or service is affiliated with another entity, such as an event, product, or service. Sport events, teams, leagues, and facilities are often sponsored to provide organizations and their products or services with enhanced visibility in the market. Sport sponsorship is often coveted because it allows an organization to target a specific group of individuals—fans—who may represent the target market for the product or service (Amis & Cornwell, 2005; Shank, 2008).

- *Consumer behavior* is the "processes involved when individuals or groups select, purchase, use, or dispose of products, services, ideas, or experiences to satisfy needs and desires" (Solomon, 2009, p. ix).

These core concepts (organizational theory, organizational behavior, and marketing)—as applied to the context of sport organizations—have been addressed in several textbooks and in numerous scholarly publications.

Accreditation of Sport Management Programs

Recent years have seen a trend toward accreditation of sport management programs offered by colleges and universities, a process that includes the establishment of curriculum requirements. With the rapid growth of academic programs in the field, concerns emerged over the quality and standardization of content areas covered in courses, as well as increased pressure for more rigor in these programs (Gladden & Williams, 2012). As a result, in 1989, members of the North American Society for Sport Management and the National Association for Sport and Physical Education initiated discussions to address quality in the provision of sport management programs in colleges and universities (Commission on Sport Management Accreditation, 2009). These discussions eventually turned to accreditation, and, in 2008, accreditation for sport management academic programs was launched (Commission on Sport Management Accreditation, 2009; Gladden & Williams). As part of the process, the Commission on Sport Management Accreditation (COSMA) identified what it called "common professional components" required for academic programs (2008, p. 11):

- Social, psychological, and international foundations of sport
- Management (including sport management principles, sport leadership, sport operations management, event and venue management, and sport governance)
- Ethics in sport management
- Sport marketing and communication
- Finance, accounting, economics (including principles of sport finance, accounting, and the economics of sport)
- Legal aspects of sport
- Integrative experience (such as strategic management, internship, and capstone experiences [an experience that enables a student to demonstrate the capacity to synthesize and apply knowledge, such as a thesis, project, or comprehensive examination]) internships; and capstone experiences enabling students to demonstrate capacity to synthesize and apply knowledge, such as a thesis, project, comprehensive examination, or course)

As these components make clear, the preparation of future sport leaders includes content areas that go beyond organizational theory, organizational behavior, and marketing. COSMA executives felt that students in undergraduate sport management programs need to be exposed to other areas both for the purposes of a well-rounded education and for better preparation to work successfully in the field. These other areas include, for example, sport sociology, sport psychology, finance, economics, accounting, and sport law.

Main Theoretical Perspectives

Although the main theoretical perspectives found today in sport management and sport marketing originate from the parent disciplines (i.e., management, organizational theory, organizational behavior, and marketing), this was not always the case in the early development of sport management research. In the late 1990s, Slack (1996, 1998) felt that much of the research in sport management was devoid of sound theory. He argued that sport management scholars did not typically use the theoretical developments and strides made in organizational studies to frame their research. Slack (1996, p. 99) acknowledged the increasing research being undertaken in sport management but argued that sport management "studies that are not based on sound and current theories are limited in their relevance and generalizability. As such, they gain us little credibility with practicing sport managers or with scholars in the broader academic community." Furthermore, Slack (1996) maintained that "we need to provide a strong theoretical base to our research" (p. 104), and he believed the first step would necessarily involve becoming familiar "with current concepts and theories from the area of management" (p. 99). The call for sound sport management research has, for the most part, been answered. More work may still need to be done to promote greater adoption of theories from organizational, management, and marketing studies, but progress has been made in enhancing the quality, credibility, and legitimacy of scholarship and research in sport management and sport marketing. Sport management scholars have increasingly based their research on theoretical and conceptual frameworks from the parent discipline.

The array of theoretical approaches used in sport management research is too extensive to cover fully in this chapter. Many theories have arisen in management and marketing to address the field's many core concepts and their subconcepts. For example, the study of each subconcept identified in the preceding section of this chapter (e.g., organizational effectiveness, change, human resources management, consumer behavior) could be undertaken through various theoretical approaches and epistemologies. Some emerging theoretical and conceptual approaches being used in sport management are discussed in the sections on critical findings and key debates. Fundamentally, all of the theories are centered on addressing organizational issues and challenges; analyzing successes and failures in sport organizations; increasing our understanding of the people involved in, affecting, or affected by organizations; and generally enhancing the effectiveness of sport organizations.

A number of scholars have offered directions to help researchers in sport management enhance the quality and credibility of research. Slack (1996, 1998), Frisby (2005), Costa (2005), Chalip (2006), Zeigler (2007), and Chadwick (2009) have all argued for greater scrutiny in research in sport organizations and sport management. Frisby's (2005, p. 3) concerns about sport management research dealt predominantly with the need to consider the "ugly sides of sport" and the need for critical theory in sport management research and practice. She believed that critical theory could address some of the negative aspects of sport in society, such as corruption, bribery, greed, abuse, environmental destruction in the building of sport facilities, exclusion of women and minorities from sport and from leadership positions, and impoverished conditions of sport workers and participants in developing countries—issues that have been inadequately examined in our discipline. Drawing from the work of Alvesson and Deetz (2000), Frisby argued that "criticalists view management as an activity that is messy, ambiguous, political, and fragmented, and they believe that conceptualizing it as a technical function involving planning, organizing, coordinating, and controlling fails to capture the essence of what managers actually do" (p. 5). She noted that critical theory "can be best understood as a way of empowering individuals by confronting injustices in order to promote social change," and she believed that it "is a very relevant lens for understanding and reflecting on organizational practices and how we teach, research, and theorize about sport management" (Frisby, p. 2).

Along similar lines, Zeigler (2007) argued for greater attention to social issues affecting sport management. His concerns focused predominantly on the increasing commercialization of sport and the use of athletes as commodities. He argued that

> *sport, like all other social institutions, is inevitably being confronted by the need to become truly responsible. Many troubling and difficult decisions, often ethical in nature, will have to be made by professors of sport management who continue the development of this profession/ discipline as it seeks to prepare those who will guide sport in the years ahead.* (2007, p. 316)

Chalip (2006) presented what he termed the "malaise" of sport management as an academic discipline, which should be perceived not as a sign of weakness but as a healthy and "necessary process for our maturation"; this malaise involves "the field's status, direction, and future" (pp. 2, 1). According to Chalip, one of the most important debates has centered on the relevance of academic research for sport management practitioners. To address the malaise, he believed that sport management required two complementary streams of research: the derivative model and the sport-focused model. In the derivative model, the inspiration originates from theoretical and conceptual frameworks in the parent disciplines (e.g., management, marketing, finance, accounting, and economics). In the sport-focused model, the inspiration is to identify a theory that is grounded in sport. Chalip (p. 15) argued that if we are to "build a discipline that can stand on its own," we need to develop a sound sport-focused research agenda that creates new theory or finds relevance in existing theories, and the outcome must include building sound sport management practice. He identified and discussed five legitimations for sport that are most commonly used internationally to warrant public funding and attention: sport's contribution to health, to positive socialization, to economic development, to community development, and to national identity. In developing a sport-focused research agenda, Chalip demonstrated how these five legitimations were connected to other important sectors beyond sport, such as public health, education, social services, tourism, public management, technology, and law.

In a Delphi study on the status of sport management research, Costa (2005) surveyed the perspectives of leading sport management scholars. Her data analysis revealed that the most important successes of sport management research were the use of theory originating from parent disciplines, the development of sport management theory, the increase of high-quality research outlets in the field, and the overall generation of sport management knowledge. Regarding strategies for enhancing sport management research, Costa's findings revealed the need to improve faculty members' access to resources and professional development opportunities for research, the need to increase research training of doctoral students, and the need to increase the interdisciplinary nature of research by encouraging collaborative endeavors among researchers. Research participants also raised the dichotomy between quantitative and qualitative research. Even though the use of both methods was deemed important for broadening research in sport management, some research participants felt that qualitative research was underappreciated. Others felt that the issue of research methods had more to do with rigor than with pluralism. Costa (pp. 132–133) noted that the debate among research participants regarding the distinction between qualitative and quantitative methods "reflects a more subtle paradigmatic difference between those who feel that sport management research can be conducted in a strictly objective (i.e., positivist) manner and those who feel that the management of sport is socially constructed." Ultimately, the key point is that to ensure rigor in sport management research (or any other research, for that matter), the use of sound theoretical and conceptual frameworks must be supported with appropriate research methods strategies. Increasingly, researchers in sport management have applied theoretical and conceptual frameworks to their studies and have adopted quantitative, qualitative, and mixed methods to collect empirical data on a diverse range of organizational phenomena.

Critical Findings

Knowledge about sport organizations, sport management, and sport marketing has increased in the past 20 years. The research undertaken since the late

1980s and early 1990s has covered the role that sport organizations play in sport systems around the world and the issues and challenges that leaders face as they work to provide sport programs, events, products, and services. This research has contributed greatly to the credibility and legitimacy of the field in academic circles.

In a discussion of research in sport management, Zeigler (2007, p. 309) called for the creation of an "inventory of scholarly and research findings about sport management theory" in order to assist students, practitioners, and scholars involved in sport management. Zeigler's rationale for this inventory was based on the fact "that the profession simply does not know where it stands in regard to the steadily developing body of knowledge in the many sub-disciplinary and professional aspects of sport management (e.g., sport ethics, sport law, sport economics, sport marketing)" (p. 314). It would be very challenging, however, to answer this call, given the volume of research produced in sport management, the number of scholarly publications in the field, and the limited access to research published in other languages (Thibault, 2007; Zeigler, 2007).

Even though the quantity and quality of sport management research have increased as the discipline has become more established, there is still much work to be done, and a number of topics related to sport management are emerging as important areas for further research. They include the globalization and internationalization of research, teaching, and practice in sport management; the role of sport management in promoting access, equity, and social inclusion in sport; the use of technology, social media, and social marketing in sport; and ethical practices, social responsibility, and environmental sustainability in sport management.

Globalization and Internationalization

Global issues affecting sport are addressed in other chapters of this book, particularly chapter 10, which explores international relations and sport. The increasingly global nature of sport, along with related issues of sport governance, have also been addressed elsewhere—for example by Maguire, Jarvie, Mansfield, and Bradley (2002), J. Means and Nauright (2007), Thibault (2009), and Wheeler and Nauright (2006). Maguire et al. (p. 4) summarized some of the global issues as follows:

> [S]port is bound up in a global network of interdependency chains that are marked by uneven power relations. . . . People across the globe regularly view satellite broadcasts of English Premier League and European Champions League matches. The best players from Europe, South America and Africa perform in these games. The players use equipment . . . that is designed in the West, financed by multinational corporations such as Adidas and Nike and hand-stitched, in

the case of soccer balls, in Asia using child labour. This equipment is sold, at significant profit, to a mass market in the towns and cities of North America and Europe. Several transnational corporations are involved in the production and consumption phases of global soccer. Some of these corporations own the media companies and also have, as in the case of Sky TV, shareholdings in the soccer clubs they screen.

As this quotation makes clear, numerous organizations and structures are involved in the globalization of sport—including transnational corporations, professional sport leagues and teams, and media conglomerates—all of which play a role in creating both the promise and the peril of the globalization of sport. Scholars and leaders of sport organizations need to understand the interaction between these organizations; the power they hold over other organizations, governments, and populations of developing countries; and their interests in, and effects on, the global sport system. Toward this end, organizational theory, organizational behavior research, and marketing research can enhance our understanding of sport management.

In addition to much-needed research on the governance of international sport, calls have been made for greater internationalization of academic programs in sport management in order to better prepare future leaders to address global issues affecting, and affected by, sport. Thibault (2009, p. 2) explained that "sport management students should be sensitized to issues of multilingualism, multiculturalism, and multidisciplinarity in the delivery of sport in a global context," and Danylchuk (2011) argued that "as leaders in the field of sport management, we must ensure that we teach, research, and advocate from an international perspective" (p. 6). Given the importance of globalization in all facets of society, sport management scholars and practitioners must be exposed not only to the advantages of globalization but also to its challenges. It is imperative for leaders of sport organizations to be at the forefront of international business practices. As C.W.L. Hill (2011) noted, the shift in the world economy, wherein national economies are no longer isolated from each other, requires leaders and managers to consider the opportunities, challenges, and threats of international business. As sport organizations operate increasingly in the global marketplace, leaders of these organizations must respond effectively to differences in government regulations, business strategies, language and cultural practices, and policies regarding human resources (to name just a few challenges). For example, sport leaders must be ready to meet the challenges posed by the growing mobility of coaches and athletes across national and continental boundaries, as well as the negotiation of international sponsorship deals and broadcast rights for various sport endeavors.

Access, Equity, and Inclusion

Even though sport may bring people together through increased social interaction, it has also served to exclude (Coalter, 2007, 2008; M.F. Collins & Kay, 2003; Frisby, Crawford, & Dorer, 1997; Frisby, Reid, & Ponic, 2007; B. Hill & Green, 2008; Kidd, 1995; Paraschak, 2007). Globally, several groups have traditionally been underserved and marginalized in sport—for example, immigrants, girls and women, older adults, Aboriginal people, individuals with low income, youth at risk, people with disabilities, rural populations, and people from poorer countries. Sport systems in many nations focus largely on elite sport, while marginalized populations' access to sport remains limited. As Frisby, Crawford, et al. (1997, p. 9) explained,

> *instead of examining how the sport system, particularly at the local level, can be changed to provide marginalized groups and individuals with greater access to the health and other benefits of involvement [in sport], sport management researchers have largely focused on organizations catering to elite athletes who already have access to the system.*

Sport organizations are often plagued by issues of inequity and limited access. For example, on the topic of gender in sport, Shaw and Hoeber (2007, p. 194) explained that some gender-inclusive research has focused on the "management, coaching, and administration of sport, where women often remain in low level, less valued positions and are less able than men to influence decision-making processes including those regarding gender equity." The fact that marginalized populations (M.F. Collins & Kay, 2003; Frisby, Crawford, et al., 1997; Frisby, Reid, et al., 2007; Paraschak, 2007) are often excluded from governance, decision making, and policy making in sport organizations severely limits their ability to influence or offer input into decisions that could help them gain increased access to sport programs and services. Greater research into access, equity, and inclusion may help identify barriers to participation and lead to the development of strategies for increasing participation by underserved and marginalized populations in sport and in sport management.

In discussions of access, equity, and social inclusion, one could raise the issue of resources invested in high-performance sport relative to resources invested in sport for all. In many countries, the support of high-performance sport appears to come at the expense of sport-for-all initiatives. Considerable financial resources are invested in developing athletes to achieve podium results in international high-profile competitions. Training facilities and competition stadiums are built, and coaches and other staff members are hired, while sport-for-all programs typically receive less attention and fewer resources. Although success in high-performance sport may enhance national pride, unity, and identity, the majority of the population does not directly benefit from investments made (often by governments) in high-performance sport (e.g., health and well-being, social, and skill development). This imbalance between the investment in professional sport (e.g., through subsidized or free use of training and competition facilities) and the investment in nonprofessional sport—that is, between high-performance sport and sport for all—is another issue that requires attention from sport management scholars and leaders.

Technology, Social Media, and Social Marketing

Recent technological changes have dramatically increased the ease with which people can communicate. Along the way, technological advancements have affected the coverage of sport in traditional media, the marketing of sport in society, and the ways in which information is shared within and between organizations. With respect to marketing, technology and social networking (i.e., social media) strategies have led to important developments in how organizations advertise and promote their products and services. Viral marketing, word-of-mouth marketing, and buzz marketing have all been greatly facilitated by new technology and opportunities for social networking. According to Marsden (2006, p. xvii), viral marketing, word-of-mouth marketing, and buzz marketing "include all promotional activity that uses word of mouth connections between people, whether digital or traditional, as communications media to stimulate demand." The speed of information sharing between individuals and organizations has been greatly increased by satellite technology, fiber optics, broadband service, mobile devices (e.g., personal digital assistants, mobile telephones), the Internet, electronic mail, instant messaging, webcasts, podcasts, webinars, and blogs, along with social media platforms such as Facebook, Twitter, LinkedIn, Pinterest, and YouTube. In sport, these new means of communication and marketing have led many organizations (e.g., the International Olympic Committee, the English Premier League, Major League Baseball, the National Collegiate Athletic Association) to develop new policies regarding the use of social media intended to regulate the behavior of leaders, coaches, officials, and athletes (Burns Ortiz, 2011; Waldie, 2012).

These new technologies and social networking strategies have also changed the nature of consumers' (e.g., fans') experiences with sport products (e.g., sport competitions) and with athletes, coaches, and officials; moreover, they have encouraged increased consumption of sport products (e.g., fantasy sport leagues, online video games). Chapter 7 of this book, which covers media and sport, addresses the influence of some of these new technologies on the quality, quantity, and flow of sport information being shared in the public sphere. The appropriation of these technologies by sport leaders is believed to be critical in reaching target markets (e.g., consumers, fans) as well as other stakeholders (e.g., athletes, coaches, officials, sponsors, governments). As noted by Mullin et al. (2007, p. 467),

> *as on-demand connectivity and real-time access continue to move past the buzz word stage and become reality, it means a decline in the role and impact of newspapers, magazines and other traditional forms of the printed word. Not only will they no longer be timely, they will also become inefficient due to cost and ROI [return on investment] for sponsors and advertisers alike. Why wait for the six o'clock news when instant news can be downloaded to your cell [mobile telephone] or PDA whenever you want it?*

However, technology can also serve to exclude people. Specifically, access to technology is often reserved for individuals who have certain resources (e.g., money, expertise and skills, infrastructure). The same applies to organizations and to certain countries and regions of the world. Therefore, research is needed in order to examine technology's effect on sport generally (i.e., from various perspectives—such as those of athletes, coaches, officials, fans, and spectators) and on sport organizations. We also need to understand the effect that limited (or lack of) access to technology can have on sport, sport organizations, and sport systems.

Social marketing is "about influencing behaviors, . . . [it] utilizes a systematic planning process and applies traditional marketing principles and techniques, and . . . [its] intent is to deliver a positive benefit for society" (Kotler & Lee, 2008, p. 8). It has been applied to the context of sport in order to incite social change and to address important social issues—for example, to encourage physical activity among inactive populations, to educate athletes about the harms and consequences of using performance-enhancing drugs and unethical strategies to win, and to promote girls' and women's access to sport.

Even though social marketing typically uses traditional marketing principles and techniques, it can be more effective when it makes use of new social networking strategies enabled by new technologies (Andreasen, 2006; Kotler & Lee, 2008). Technology can be used to facilitate the creation and maintenance of important communities in society. As Andreasen (p. 129) noted, "there are communities in cyberspace chat rooms. Bloggers send emails to like-minded readers. Many communities are really matters of self-identification." Thus, promoting social change in sport and reaching a target audience can often be achieved by using a given community's preferred modes of communication (e.g., television, radio, social media, e-mail, instant messaging, blogs). Sport leaders need to be informed by further research into new media in order to better understand how social marketing can be achieved.

Ethical Practices, Social Responsibility, and Environmental Sustainability

In recent years, sport management has placed greater importance on considerations of ethical practice, social responsibility, and environmental sustainability. Indeed, greater focus on ethical practices in sport and in sport management is imperative in light of incidents of corruption, bribery, and questionable practices in international sport organizations (e.g., the International Olympic Committee, the International Federation of Association Football), drug use in high-performance competitions, and exploitative behavior by leaders (e.g., unfair labor practices in developing countries, incidents of sexual abuse of athletes by coaches) (Forster, 2006; D. Hill, 2008; Jennings & Sambrook, 2000; Maennig, 2005; D. Mason, Thibault, & Misener, 2006; Thibault, 2009). Ethics in sport management has been addressed in previous research (DeSensi & Rosenberg, 2010; Milton-Smith, 2002; Zakus, Malloy, & Edwards, 2007), but further examination is needed of ethical issues and dilemmas facing managers. DeSensi and Rosenberg captured this sentiment well in noting that, "for the most part, there is a lack of understanding or appreciation for ethical theories and their relevance to sport" and that "there are relatively few available works that specifically address these subjects [ethics and morality] in relation to sport management" (pp. 4, 5).

Sport management has also seen the emergence of increased focus on corporate social responsibility (CSR) in sport and sport-related organizations (Babiak & Wolfe, 2009; Godfrey, 2009). CSR is defined as a set of actions undertaken by organizations "that appear to further some social good, extend beyond the explicit pecuniary interests of the firm, and are not required by law" (Godfrey, p. 704). Godfrey noted that "as sport becomes an increasingly prominent economic and social institution across the globe, the question of what social responsibilities athletes, coaches, team owners, league officials, and global sport organizations' personnel have should constantly be asked" (p. 712).

CSR practices are increasingly evident in sport organizations—for example, charitable fundraising initiatives tied to local sport events (Filo, Funk, & O'Brien, 2009) and partnerships between professional sport leagues and community outreach initiatives, as in the National Basketball Association's Read to Achieve literacy program and Major League Baseball's partnership with the Boys and Girls Clubs of America (Babiak & Wolfe, 2009; Sheth & Babiak, 2010). As noted by Babiak and Wolfe (p. 738), "given the emphasis on social responsibility in other industries as well as its dramatic growth over the past two decades in sport, we are confident that this will remain an important issue facing professional sport organizations for years to come."

The concept of CSR is related to that of environmental sustainability, and some sport management theorists have called for closer examination of the impact that sport, sport organizations, and sport events have on the natural environment (Chalip, 2006; Frisby, 2005; Zeigler, 1992, 2007). For example, Trendafilova and Chalip (2003, p. 84) argued that "although there is world-wide recognition that environmental problems are increasingly associated with outdoor recreational sports, and despite efforts to control and manage those problems, progress to date has been minimal." Other scholars have pointed out that sport's impact on the natural environment goes well beyond outdoor recreational sports; in fact, they note that all forms of sport practice (e.g., sport facilities, large-scale sport events, and professional sport teams and leagues) have an important ecological footprint (Babiak and Trendafilova, 2011; Babiak & Wolfe, 2009; A. Collins, Flynn, Munday, & Roberts, 2007; Mallen & Chard, 2011). The growing concern over the environmental damage caused by sport and our consumption of sport means that more research is needed on this topic. As noted by A. Collins et al. (2007, pp. 459–460), "whilst studies have succeeded in investigating selected social and welfare effects connected to sporting events, fewer studies have investigated their local and global environmental impacts." One could argue that the need for additional research goes beyond sporting events, since all forms of sport participation have an environmental impact, and this reality has rarely been addressed or measured.

Key Debates

Sport management has seen a variety of debates in recent years. Those addressed here are the growth of academic programs in sport management; job market challenges for graduates of sport management programs; the location of sport management programs in academic institutions; and the themes of community, capital, and governance.

Growth of Academic Programs in Sport Management

Sport management's rapid growth has led to some issues and concerns in college and university programs. This growth, along with perhaps limited control over quality, may have put sport management in a highly vulnerable position; although one can recognize success in the discipline, it is important to discuss its vulnerabilities as well. A number of sport management academic programs throughout the world may have been created because of their appeal to a large pool of students. As leaders of universities and colleges become more sensitive to market pressures, they are increasingly concerned about their ability to draw students to their institutions, and sport management programs help them attract students. As reported by Helyar (2006, p. R5), the managing director of the University of Oregon's MBA program, Paul Swangard, noted that "an awful lot of these [sport management programs] are driven by the tuition revenue model; it's a real easy way to fill classrooms." Crosset and Hums (2012) also noted student recruitment as an important motive for university administrators' development of academic programs in sport management, even as they raised the issue of quality in some sport management programs.

The creation of numerous sport management programs (North American Society for Sport Management, 2012) in a relatively short time and the accompanying concerns about quality have led to the establishment of standards to ensure the proper professional preparation of students. As mentioned in the Core Concepts section of this chapter, the Commission on Sport Management Accreditation was established and standards were developed to ensure the quality and rigor of sport management programs in postsecondary institutions (Commission on Sport Management Accreditation, 2008, 2009). Given the voluntary nature of accreditation and the resources (time and money) needed, however, it is reasonable to think that administrators of many sport management programs may not seek accreditation for their programs.

Job Market Challenges for Sport Management Graduates

Although there is no shortage of students interested in and admitted to undergraduate and graduate sport management programs, questions have been raised about the work opportunities available for graduating students. Helyar (2006, p. R5) noted that graduates' access to entry-level positions in sport management was limited: "The competition for entry-level positions in this field is brutal. The pay is low and the hours are long, but there's a patina of glamour and a lot of sport junkies." Along similar lines, Belson (2009) reported on how the economic recession had affected the number and quality of positions available in the U.S. sport industry. The poor job market appears to be leading students to stay in school, though applying for graduate school programs in sport management may add to the problem of having too many qualified students entering a poor job market. As Belson (paragraph 12) wrote,

> *every year, they [colleges and universities offering sport management programs] churn out thousands of graduates who, even in good times, are willing to work for low pay in return for the chance to work around athletes and arenas. The teams, leagues and others in the sports industry have taken advantage of their willingness to make financial sacrifices, and may continue to do so.*

Thus the plethora of academic programs in sport management, and their many students and graduates, means that too many individuals are competing for too few jobs. In addition, they must also compete with graduates from other programs (e.g., business, management, communication, sport studies) who also seek work in sport management, making it very difficult for graduates to gain employment, particularly in the highly sought-after professional sport industry (e.g., teams, leagues, players associations, corporations that sponsor sport, sport media). Graduates also compete for jobs in other sectors of sport management (e.g., various levels of government, sport facility management, sport event management, nonprofit sport organizations, local sport clubs, and athletics in schools, colleges, and universities). In order to help graduates meet the challenges involved in finding work in sport management, websites have been created to regularly advertise positions and internship opportunities—mainly, but not exclusively, in professional sport (e.g., TeamWorkOnline.com, WorkInSports.com).

Location of Sport Management Academic Programs

As mentioned in the historical overview section of this chapter, Shilbury and Rentschler (2007) have noted the increasing trend of locating sport management programs in business schools rather than in schools of physical education or kinesiology. Chalip (2006, p. 2) has also addressed the ongoing debate over "whether the appropriate home for sport management should be a business school or a department specializing in sport studies (e.g., kinesiology). As a hybrid discipline, we are about sport and about management." As a result, Chalip argued, it does not matter in which department sport management is housed; What does matter is the quality of our research, our scholarship, and our students.

Some may believe that business schools offer more legitimacy and credibility than do schools of physical education or kinesiology, since the focus in business schools is on management (and other related subdisciplines, such as marketing, finance, economics, accounting, and strategy). Sport management programs located in business schools may also have access to greater resources (for course development, course delivery, and research) than their counterparts in schools of physical education or kinesiology (Fink & Barr, 2012). Nevertheless, the location of sport management programs in academia is not an indication of quality, and quality is fundamentally the most important consideration. Scholars specializing in areas such as sport management, sport marketing, sport finance, sport economics, sport law, and sport communication can be hired in business schools or in schools of physical education or kinesiology. University administrators play an important role in hiring decisions and in the location of sport management programs. Regardless of the location of sport management programs, scholars in the field must advocate for quality and rigor in sport management academic programs as a higher priority than location in the institution (Chalip, 2006; Fink & Barr, 2012).

Community, Capital, and Governance

The themes of community, capital, and governance have been used to help form the structure of this book. They are discussed in this section in relation to their applicability to sport management. Governance may be the most relevant of the three, but community and capital are meaningful as well.

In the context of sport management, *community* refers to a collective of organizations and stakeholders with which organizations interact on an ongoing basis in order to achieve their goals. For example, the International Olympic Committee must work closely with national Olympic committees, international sport federations, and the organizing committee of a given Olympic Games. On a smaller scale, a local nonprofit sport organization responsible for a sport (e.g., a triathlon club) must interact with other clubs in its region, with a regional organization (provincial or state nonprofit triathlon organization), and its national and international organizations. In addition, the club may have to negotiate with local governments or private clubs for access to facilities and other important resources (e.g., funding, equipment, technology, competition locations). In the professional realm, a sport team must interact with many organizations—for example, the league, the players association, sponsors, media, and governments. Thus sport organizations of all types are part of elaborate communities and networks of organizations with which they collaborate in their day-to-day operations.

On the topic of *capital*, sport organizations are structures where capital is constantly generated, expended, and invested. The major sources of capital are financial and human resources. Professional sport organizations (i.e., teams and leagues) generate important financial resources from fans and consumers through ticket and merchandise sales, from sponsors that pay teams and leagues to be affiliated with their sport product, from media that pay for the rights to broadcast sport events, and from governments that often subsidize teams' use of publically owned facilities. These financial resources are needed to cover the salaries of athletes and other employees of the organization and to pay for its operations. With respect to *social capital*, sport organizations are central structures for the training and employment of paid individuals and volunteers. In addition, sport leaders are responsible for providing a diverse range of sport skills, opportunities, and experiences to the population as active participants. Whether for active participants in high-performance sport, for sport-for-all participants, or for passive participants (e.g., fans and spectators), sport organizations are important instruments through which social relations are developed, promoted, and perpetuated (cf. Nicholson & Hoye, 2008).

With respect to *governance*, sport organizations are the very structures that make sport happen—schools, local community centers, clubs, sport facilities, commercial operators, and sporting goods manufacturers and retailers, to name a few. These organizations represent structures where rules, regulations, policies, and procedures are developed, enforced, and perpetuated for the effective production and delivery of programs, services, and goods. As a result, leaders of sport organizations have a responsibility to ensure that sport is delivered to the population. They also have a responsibility to ensure that sport is fair and ethical, that sport is inclusive and accessible to all members of society, and that sport organizations achieve their goals. Sport management research and practice prepare sport leaders, employees, and volunteers to assume these responsibilities. In essence, sport, sport organizations, and sport management as an academic discipline are important actors in relation to community, capital, and governance.

Summary

The field of sport management has made great strides in the last 20 years (Chadwick, 2009; Chalip, 2006; Costa, 2005; Slack, 1996; Zeigler, 1992, 2007). The theoretical and conceptual frameworks underpinning studies of organizational and marketing phenomena, as well as sound research methods (whether qualitative, quantitative, or mixed), have contributed to the legitimacy and credibility of the field. In addition, studies in sport management and marketing have contributed to greater understanding of the roles that organizations and governance play in sport, as well as the issues and challenges facing all types of sport organizations. Research in sport management has also clarified the roles that people play in sport organizations—whether as consumers, fans, participants, athletes, coaches, officials, volunteers, or leaders—and the ways in which they interact. Sport marketing research has allowed leaders to better understand the strategies used to enhance the exchange of products and services in sport and their effect among consumers and fans. Through sport marketing, we have also developed understanding of how and why fans and consumers behave in certain ways.

Sport management cannot be isolated from other disciplines covered in this book, such as psychology, sociology, media, economics, political science, international relations, law, social policy, and education. It also cannot be isolated from its parent disciplines: organizational theory, organizational behavior, and marketing. By interacting with scholars from these disciplines, sport management leaders and students can become better prepared to address the challenges and opportunities of the field.

On a concluding note about research in sport management, Chadwick (2009, p. 202) explained that "while the literature stock already displays signs of health and diversity, scholars will have a major role in moving sport management research and the literature from the margins to the mainstream: from the outside lane to the inside track." Along similar lines, Slack (1996, p. 97) called for a shift among sport management scholars from "the locker room to the board room." Given the recent developments and specialization in sport management scholarship, the future is promising. As the field of sport management continues in its establishment as an academic discipline, the quality of its scholarship will grow.

References

Alvesson, M., & Deetz, S. (2000). *Doing critical management research*. London: Sage.

Amis, J., & Cornwell, T.B. (Eds.). (2005). *Global sport sponsorship*. Oxford, UK: Berg.

Amis, J., & O'Brien, D. (2005). Organizational theory and the study of sport. In B. Parkhouse (Ed.), *The management of sport: Its foundation and application* (4th ed., pp. 76–95). New York: McGraw-Hill.

Amis, J., Slack, T., & Hinings, C.R. (2004). The pace, sequence, and linearity of radical change. *Academy of Management Journal, 47*, 15–39.

Andreasen, A.R. (2006). *Social marketing in the 21st century*. Thousand Oaks, CA: Sage.

Babiak, K., & Thibault, L. (2009). Challenges in multiple cross-sector partnerships. *Nonprofit and Voluntary Sector Quarterly, 28*, 117–143.

Babiak, K., & Trendafilova, S. (2011). CSR and environmental responsibility: Motives and pressures to adopt green management practices. *Corporate Social Responsibility and Environmental Management, 18*, 275–302.

Babiak, K., & Wolfe, R. (2009). Determinants of corporate social responsibility in professional sport: Internal and external factors. *Journal of Sport Management, 23*, 717–742.

Beech, J., & Chadwick, S. (2004). *The business of sport management*. Essex, UK: Pearson Education.

Belson, K. (2009, May 26). In sports business, too many hopefuls for too few positions. *New York Times*. www.nytimes.com/2009/05/27/sports/27class.html.

Briggs, B. (2010, March 16). Price tag for Tiger's transgressions? $50 million. *Sports biz on NBCNews.com*. www.msnbc.msn.com/id/35767087/.

Burns Ortiz, M. (2011, September 27). Commentary: Guide to leagues' social media policies. *ESPN Page 2*. http://espn.go.com/espn/page2/story/_/id/7026246/examining-sports-leagues-social-media-policies-offenders.

Chadwick, S. (2009). From outside lane to inside track: Sport management research in the twenty-first century. *Management Decision, 47*, 191–203.

Chalip, L. (2006). Toward a distinctive sport management discipline. *Journal of Sport Management, 20*, 1–21.

Chappell, B. (2012, June 21). Penn State abuse scandal: A guide and timelines. *National Public Radio*. www.npr.org/2011/11/08/142111804/penn-state-abuse-scandal-a-guide-and-timeline.

Chelladurai, P. (2006). *Human resource management in sport and recreation* (2nd ed.). Champaign, IL: Human Kinetics.

Chelladurai, P. (2009). *Managing organizations for sport and physical activity: A systems perspective* (3rd ed.). Scottsdale, AZ: Holcomb Hathaway.

Chernev, A. (2009). *Strategic marketing management* (5th ed.). Chicago: Brightstar Media.

Coalter, F. (2007). *A wider social role for sport: Who's keeping the score?* London: Routledge.

Coalter, F. (2008). Sport-in-development: Development for and through sport? In M. Nicholson & R. Hoye (Eds.), *Sport and social capital* (pp. 39–67). Oxford, UK: Butterworth-Heinemann.

Collins, A., Flynn, A., Munday, M., & Roberts, A. (2007). Assessing the environmental consequences of major sporting events: The 2003/04 FA Cup Final. *Urban Studies, 44*, 457–476.

Collins, M.F., & Kay, T. (2003). *Sport and social exclusion*. London: Routledge.

Commission on Sport Management Accreditation. (2008). *Accreditation principles and self study preparation*. www.cosmaweb.org/sites/all/pdf_files/accrPrinciples.pdf.

Commission on Sport Management Accreditation. (2009). Commission on Sport Management Accreditation: History. www.cosmaweb.org/history.

Costa, C.A. (2005). The status and future of sport management: A Delphi study. *Journal of Sport Management, 19*, 117–142.

Crosset, T.W., & Hums, M.A. (2012). History of sport management. In L. Pike Masteralexis, C.A. Barr, & M.A. Hums (Eds.), *Principles and practice of sport management* (4th ed., pp. 3–25). Sudbury, MA: Jones & Bartlett.

Cuskelly, G., Hoye, R., & Auld, C. (2006). *Working with volunteers in sport: Theory and practice*. London: Routledge.

Daft, R.L. (2010). *Organization theory and design* (10th ed.). Mason, OH: South-Western Cengage Learning.

Danylchuk, K. (2011). Internationalizing ourselves: Realities, opportunities, and challenges. *Journal of Sport Management, 25*, 1–16.

DeSensi, J.T., & Rosenberg, D. (2010). *Ethics and morality in sport management* (3rd ed.). Morgantown, WV: Fitness Information Technology.

EurActiv. (2009, February 10). Davos underlines economic value of sport. www.euractiv.com/sports/davos-underlines-economic-value-news-221098.

EU Sport Directors. (2006). EU-Sport Directors meeting 29/30 March 2006 in the Vienna Hofburg: Conclusions of the Austrian EU-Presidency. http://ec.europa.eu/sport/library/doc/b22/doc468_en.pdf.

Filo, K., Funk, D.C., & O'Brien, D. (2009). The meaning behind attachment: Exploring camaraderie, cause, and competency at a charity sport event. *Journal of Sport Management, 23*, 361–387.

Fink, J.S., & Barr, C.A. (2012). Where is the best "home" for sport management? In A. Gillentine, R.E. Baker, & J. Cuneen (Eds.), *Critical essays in sport management: Exploring and achieving a paradigm shift* (pp. 17–25). Scottsdale, AZ: Holcomb Hathaway.

Forster, J. (2006). Global sports organisations and their governance. *Corporate Governance, 6*, 72–83.

Frank, R. (1984). Olympic myths and realities. *Arete: The Journal of Sport Literature, 1*, 155–161.

Frisby, W. (2005). The good, the bad, and the ugly: Critical sport management research. *Journal of Sport Management, 19*, 1–12.

Frisby, W., Crawford, S., & Dorer, T. (1997). Reflections on participatory action research: The case of low-income women accessing local physical activity services. *Journal of Sport Management, 11*, 8–28.

Frisby, W., Reid, C., & Ponic, P. (2007). Levelling the playing field: Promoting the health of poor women through a community development approach to recreation. In K. Young & P. White (Eds.), *Sport and gender in Canada* (2nd ed., pp. 120–136). Don Mills, ON: Oxford University Press.

Gillentine, A., Baker, R.E., & Cuneen, J. (2012). *Critical essays in sport management: Exploring and achieving a paradigm shift.* Scottsdale, AZ: Holcomb Hathaway.

Gladden, J.M., & Williams, J. (2012). Sport management accreditation: Why it is an imperative step forward. In A. Gillentine, R.E. Baker, & J. Cuneen (Eds.), *Critical essays in sport management: Exploring and achieving a paradigm shift* (pp. 27–40). Scottsdale, AZ: Holcomb Hathaway.

Godfrey, P.C. (2009). Corporate social responsibility in sport: An overview and key issues. *Journal of Sport Management, 23*, 698–716.

Heery, E., & Noon, M. (2008). *A dictionary of human resource management* (2nd ed.). Oxford, UK: Oxford University Press.

Helyar, J. (2006, September 16). Failing efforts: Are universities' sports-management programs a ticket to a great job? Not likely. *The Wall Street Journal*, p. R5.

Hersey, P., Blanchard, K.H., & Johnson, D.E. (2008). *Management of organizational behavior: Leading human resources* (9th ed.). Upper Saddle River, NJ: Prentice Hall.

Hill, B., & Green, B.C. (2008). Give the bench the boot! Using Manning theory to design youth-sport programs. *Journal of Sport Management, 22*, 184–204.

Hill, C.W.L. (2011). *International business: Competing in the global marketplace* (8th ed.). New York: McGraw-Hill/Irwin.

Hill, D. (2008). *The fix: Soccer and organized crime.* Toronto: McClelland & Stewart.

Hoye, R., Smith, A., Nicholson, M., Stewart, B., & Westerbeek, H. (2009). *Sport management: Principles and applications.* Oxford, UK: Butterworth-Heinemann.

Hughes, W.L., & French, E. (1954). *The administration of physical education: For schools and colleges.* New York: Ronald Press.

Jennings, A., & Sambrook, C. (2000). *The great Olympic swindle: When the world wanted its games back.* London: Simon & Schuster.

Jones, G.R. (2010). *Organizational theory, design, and change* (6th ed.). Upper Saddle River, NJ: Pearson Education.

Kidd, B. (1995). Confronting inequality in sport and physical activity. *Avante, 1*, 1–19.

Kotler, P., & Lee, N.R. (2008). *Social marketing: Influencing behaviors for good* (3rd ed.). Thousand Oaks, CA: Sage.

Lampert-Stokes, M. (2010, April 5). Tiger Woods admits he lied and deceived. Reuters. www.reuters.com/article/idUSTRE6331BI20100405.

Lapper, J., & Landa, S. (2012, January 6). Androulla Vassiliou: "Supporting sport at the grassroots level is one of my priorities." Interview with Androulla Vassiliou for Toute l'Europe. www.touteleurope.eu/index.php?id=2778&cmd=FICHE&uid=5650&no_cache=1&display%5Bfiche%5D=5650.

Maennig, W. (2005). Corruption in international sports and sport management: Forms, tendencies, extent, and countermeasures. *European Sport Management Quarterly, 5*, 187–225.

Maguire, J., Jarvie, G., Mansfield, L., & Bradley, J. (2002). *Sport worlds: A sociological perspective.* Champaign, IL: Human Kinetics.

Mallen, C., & Chard, C. (2011). A framework for debating the future of environmental sustainability in the sport academy. *Sport Management Review, 15,* 230–242.

Marsden, P. (2006). Introduction and summary. In J. Kirby & P. Marsden (Eds.), *Connected marketing: The viral, buzz, and word of mouth revolution* (pp. xv–xxxv). Oxford, UK: Butterworth-Heinemann.

Mason, D., Thibault, L., & Misener, L. (2006). An agency theory perspective on corruption in sport: The case of the International Olympic Committee. *Journal of Sport Management, 20*, 52–73.

Mason, J.G., Higgins, C.R., & Wilkinson, O.J. (1981). Sports administration education 15 years later. *Athletic Purchasing and Facilities, 5*(1), 44–45.

Masteralexis, L.P., Barr, C.A., & Hums, M.A. (2012). *Principles and practices of sport management* (4th ed.). Sudbury, MA: Jones & Bartlett.

Mathis, R.L., & Jackson, J.H. (2008). *Human resource management* (12th ed.). Mason, OH: Thomson South-Western.

Means, J., & Nauright, J. (2007). Going global: The NBA sets its sights on Africa. *International Journal of Sports Marketing and Sponsorship, 9*, 40–50.

Means, L.B. (1949). *The organization and administration of intramural sports.* St. Louis: Mosby.

Milton-Smith, J. (2002). Ethics, the Olympics, and the search for global values. *Journal of Business Ethics, 35*, 131–142.

Mullin, B.J., Hardy, S., & Sutton, W.A. (2007). *Sport marketing* (3rd ed.). Champaign, IL: Human Kinetics.

Nicholson, M., & Hoye, R. (Eds.). (2008). *Sport and social capital.* Oxford, UK: Butterworth-Heinemann.

North American Society for Sport Management. (2012). Sport management programs. www.nassm.com/InfoAbout/SportMgmtPrograms.

Paraschak, V. (2007). Doing race, doing gender: First Nations, "sport," and gender relations. In K. Young & P. White (Eds.), *Sport and gender in Canada* (2nd ed., pp. 137–154). Don Mills, ON: Oxford University Press.

Parks, J.B., & Olafson, G.A. (1987). Sport management and a new journal. *Journal of Sport Management, 1*, 1–3.

Parks, J.B., Quarterman, J., & Thibault, L. (2011). Managing sport in the 21st century. In P.M. Pedersen, J.B. Parks, J. Quarterman, & L. Thibault (Eds.), *Contemporary sport management* (4th ed., pp. 4–27). Champaign, IL: Human Kinetics.

Paton, G. (1987). Sport management research—What progress has been made? *Journal of Sport Management, 1,* 25–31.

Pedersen, P.M., Parks, J.B., Quarterman, J., & Thibault, L. (2011). *Contemporary sport management* (4th ed.). Champaign, IL: Human Kinetics.

Plunkett Research. (2012). Sports industry overview. www.plunkettresearch.com/sports-recreation-leisure-market-research/industry-statistics.

PricewaterhouseCoopers. (2010). Back on track? The outlook for the global sports market to 2013. www.pwc.com/gx/en/entertainment-media/pdf/Global-Sports-Outlook.pdf.

Pritchard, M.P., Funk, D.C., & Alexandris, K. (2009). Barriers to repeat patronage: The impact of spectator constraints. *European Journal of Marketing, 43,* 169–187.

Schermerhorn, J.R., Hunt, J.G., & Osborn, R.N. (2008). *Organizational behavior* (10th ed.). Hoboken, NJ: Wiley.

Shade, M. (2012, November 1). Ex-Penn State president charged with perjury in Sandusky case. Reuters. www.reuters.com/article/2012/11/01/us-usa-pennstate-idUSBRE8A00YS20121101

Shank, M.D. (2008). Sports marketing: A strategic perspective (4th ed.). Upper Saddle River, NJ: Prentice Hall

Shaw, S., & Hoeber, L. (2007). Gender relations in Canadian amateur sport organizations: An organizational culture perspective. In K. Young & P. White (Eds.), *Sport and gender in Canada* (2nd ed., pp. 194–211). Don Mills, ON: Oxford University Press.

Sherry, E., Shilbury, D., & Wood, G. (2007). Wrestling with "conflict of interest" in sport management. *Corporate Governance: The International Journal of Business in Society, 7,* 267–277.

Sheth, H., & Babiak, K. (2010). Beyond the game: Perceptions and practices of corporate social responsibility in the professional sport industry. *Journal of Business Ethics, 91,* 433–450.

Shilbury, D., & Rentschler, R. (2007). Assessing sport management journals: A multidimensional examination. *Sport Management Review, 10,* 31–44.

Slack, T. (1996). From the locker room to the board room: Changing the domain of sport management. *Journal of Sport Management, 10,* 97–105.

Slack, T. (1998). Is there anything unique about sport management? *European Journal for Sport Management, 5,* 21–29.

Slack, T. (2003). Sport in the global society: Shaping the domain of sport studies. *International Journal of the History of Sport, 20,* 118–129.

Slack, T., & Parent, M.M. (2006). *Understanding sport organizations: The application of organization theory.* Champaign, IL: Human Kinetics.

Smith, A.C.T., & Stewart, B. (2010). The special features of sport: A critical revisit. *Sport Management Review, 13,* 1–13.

Solomon, M. (2009). *The truth about what customers want ". . . and why they buy. . . ."* Upper Saddle River, NJ: Financial Times Press.

Taylor, T., Doherty, A., & McGraw, P. (2008). *Managing people in sport organizations: A strategic human resource management perspective.* Oxford, UK: Butterworth-Heinemann.

Thibault, L. (2007). Present issues in sport management and future research. *Proceedings of the 2007 International Sport Science Congress: Pursuing happiness through sport and leisure* (pp. 285–293). Seoul, Korea: Korean Alliance for Health, Physical Education, Recreation and Dance.

Thibault, L. (2009). Globalization of sport: An inconvenient truth. *Journal of Sport Management, 23,* 1–20.

Thibault, L., & Quarterman, J. (2011). Management concepts and practice in sport organizations. In P.M. Pedersen, J.B. Parks, J. Quarterman, & L. Thibault (Eds.), *Contemporary sport management* (4th ed., pp. 71–93). Champaign, IL: Human Kinetics.

Trenberth, L., & Hassan, D. (2012). *Managing sport business: An introduction.* Abingdon, UK: Routledge.

Trendafilova, S., & Chalip, L. (2003). The political economy of managing outdoor sport environments. In M.M. Parent & T. Slack (Eds.), *International perspectives on the management of sport* (pp. 81–97). Burlington, MA: Butterworth-Heinemann.

Wakefield, K.L. (2007). *Team sports marketing.* Burlington, MA: Butterworth-Heinemann.

Waldie, P. (2012, July 20). An Olympian struggle: IOC vs. social media. *The Globe and Mail.* http://m.theglobeandmail.com/sports/olympics/an-olympian-struggle-ioc-vs-social-media/article4432121/?service=mobile.

Wheeler, K., & Nauright, J. (2006). A global perspective on the environmental impact of golf. *Sport in Society, 9,* 427–443.

Wolfe, R., Weick, K.E., Usher, J.M., Terbord, J.R., Poppo, L., Murrell, A.J., et al. (2005). Sport and organizational studies. *Journal of Management Inquiry, 14,* 182–210.

Wolverton, B. (2012, July 12). Penn State's culture of reverence led to "total disregard" for children's safety. *The Chronicle of Higher Education.* http://chronicle.com/article/Penn-States-Culture-of/132853/.

World Economic Forum. (2009, January 31). Sport: An untapped asset. Davos, CH: Author. www.weforum.org/sessions/summary/sport-untapped-asset.

Zakus, D.H., Malloy, D.C., & Edwards, A. (2007). Critical and ethical thinking in sport management. *Sport Management Review, 10,* 133–158.

Zeigler, E.F. (1959). *Administration of physical education and athletics: The case method approach.* Englewood Cliffs, NJ: Prentice Hall.

Zeigler, E.F. (1987). Sport management: Past, present, future. *Journal of Sport Management, 1,* 4–24.

Zeigler, E.F. (1992). Using the rays from history's shining lantern as we face an uncertain future. *Journal of Sport Management, 6,* 206–214.

Zeigler, E.F. (2007). Sport management must show social concern as it develops tenable theory. *Journal of Sport Management, 21,* 297–318.

CHAPTER 14

Sport and Education

Dawn Penney, PhD

This chapter centers on a relationship that has long been recognized internationally as holding considerable national and social significance for governments—and one that remains highly contested. The contestation associated with sport and education encompasses the position and role of sport in educational structures and institutions, particularly in physical education (and health and physical education) curriculum programs and in cocurricular and extracurricular school sport. The chapter reaffirms that schools and schooling remain prime focuses for research directed toward sport and education, and it identifies tertiary institutions—specifically, physical education teacher education programs—as important sites of research intended to engage critically with current and prospective representations of sport in education. Furthermore, the chapter draws attention to fact that the relationship between sport and education is not bounded by formal educational settings, nor does it relate only to the experiences, lives, and interests of children and young people. Rather, the relationship between sport and education presents opportunities for research that can generate important insights relating to governance and present opportunities other issues foregrounded in this collection. It connects particularly with interests in politics, social policy, identity, and capital, as well as equity and inclusion.

Core Concepts

This discussion aligns with contemporary thinking in the sociology of education—specifically, education policy sociology—in acknowledging governance as involving far more than formal organizational structures and rules. Here governance is conceptualized and approached as a complex political and social process involving government and policy networks with wide-reaching influences. From this perspective, governance is dynamic and operates both in and through education and sport policy, policy structures, and networks (Ball, 2009) that are acknowledged to be always changing and, arguably, increasingly complex, as established policy and network boundaries (between education and sport and between government and nongovernment sectors) are blurred and reconfigured. The contemporary global context is acknowledged as one in which "new forms of state steering and regulation" have emerged and whereby the "rules of engagement" (Ball, 1998, p. 120) in policy arenas have been both rewritten and reframed amid changed (but not entirely deconstructed) policy structures and relations (Ball & Junemann, 2012). Governance, then, is itself shaped by historical, social, and political contexts (see Ranson, 2008). It "*constitutes* a system of rule and power in relation to the diverse and competing social interests within society" (Ranson, p. 208, original emphasis) and in so doing constitutes and *mediates* the "public sphere" (and inherent relations) in which collective action occurs and by which it is framed (pp. 208–209).

Against this backdrop, regulation is similarly associated with complex and changing social and political processes, such that acts and mechanisms of regulation are often far from overt. It is fundamentally linked with notions of control—of knowledge, meanings, ways of knowing, and ways of being in sport and education—and, as such, it is identified as a key concept for research in the field. In this chapter, regulation is considered specifically in relation to the concepts of the "schooling of bodies" and embodied learning in policy, curriculum, and pedagogy in sport and physical education. This approach directs attention to research that has revealed and explored the relationship between sport and education as a mechanism of social (and political) control via both overt and subtler means of influence on the content and form of physical education and sport, particularly in schools. Embedded in this view is the recognition that sport in education represents a context and a means of expression, legitimation, or, conversely, suppression of particular understandings and identities—with the latter needing to be understood as socially, culturally, and historically located and embodied by individuals and reflected in institutional practices and government policies. It is a context in which links between social and physical capital are similarly embodied and institutionalized.

Yet, while prompting enhanced awareness of the mechanisms of control that operate amid everyday normalized practices of sport and education, regulation is emphasized as never being absolute or assured. Rather, it is conceptualized as necessitating simultaneous consideration of agency and of control, with attention drawn to the complexities inherent in the sustained maintenance of particular structures, relations, ways of thinking, and ways of being in sport and education. In this regard, research informed by education policy sociology, and policy studies more broadly, is identified as an important point of reference. Insights are also offered from the field of curriculum studies, and research in physical education reveals the significance of curriculum as a structure and mechanism that shape (and inherently limit) thinking about sport in education.

Curriculum, pedagogy, and assessment are acknowledged as embedded features of the educational landscape. Here, the conceptual emphasis is that they are institutional tools and interrelated fields of social, political, and pedagogic control. They are simultaneously presented as avenues that ultimately offer opportunities for the expression of (some) agency. Hence, notions of regulation, control, and agency in relation to sport and in education are further explored in considering the interpretation and pedagogic enactment of curricula and the expression of policy in the lived experience of teaching, coaching, and learning. Teachers and coaches are identified as having a critical role to play in shaping experiences and their outcomes in sport and education. Research highlights the fact that in many respects, they exert a defining influence in relation to what individuals learn in and through sport and education and in the identities deemed legitimate and accorded status in sport within and beyond schools. This information reaffirms that the processes of governance and regulation are always contested in many policy sites and that, conceptually, they need to be recognized as inseparable from the interpretations and actions of individuals. It also prompts acknowledgment that, alongside regulation, there is a need to engage with the self-regulation of values, meanings, identities, and practices in the fields of sport and education.

Theoretical Perspectives

This section addresses theoretical perspectives in three areas of concern: schooling bodies and embodied learning, body pedagogies in sport and education, and policy positions and processes. The first perspective establishes that physical education and sport need to be acknowledged as value laden, such that they shape our bodies and minds to align with dominant social and cultural values and hierarchies. Attention is thereby directed to the social and political significance of both the specific content of physical education and the act of teaching. The term body pedagogies reflects that instructional actions in physical education and sport influence our understandings of our bodies. In this sense, the educative role of teaching and coaching encompasses a social and cultural role, conveying meanings about the value and potential of different bodies. Finally, a policy perspective reveals that education and sport are complex arenas, influenced by many agencies and organizations with interests in various political and social agendas.

Schooling Bodies and Embodied Learning

Historical studies have arguably best served to convey that sport *in* education, particularly in the context of physical education, plays an integral part in schooling bodies. Kirk's (1992, 1993, 2002) research, in particular, has provided an invaluable analysis of the historical development of physical education in Britain and Australia with specific focus on ways in which that development has directly reflected social, political, and economic agendas at particular points in time in specific national contexts. Kirk's work firmly establishes physical education as a mechanism for schooling bodies and shaping minds to align with dominant social and cultural values and hierarchies. Sport, *in a particular form*, plays a central role in this process, simultaneously symbolizing and embodying those values and hierarchies. Kirk's analysis thus reveals the social and political significance of both particular curriculum content (skills, knowledge, and understandings embedded in selected activities incorporated into physical education) and of the mode of its transmission in terms of pedagogy. Highly pertinent, then, from a theoretical standpoint, are Bernstein's (1971, 1990) concepts of classification and framing, as well as the dynamic relationship between them. For example, the adoption of the Ling system of Swedish gymnastics in the early part of the 19th century in Britain and Australia highlighted that while the activity per se was undeniably important, so too was the associated pedagogy. It was the combination of specific content (in relation to movement) and a particular mode of instruction (militaristic in style) that generated the "formality and functionality" (Kirk, 1992, p. 57) and the sense of discipline and purpose. As Kirk (1993, p. 45) explains, "[d]iscipline, regulation, order, control: these were the key elements of a scheme aimed, above all else, at schooling the docile body." Decades on, and irrespective of the international context, the lack of neutrality and the combined influence of form and content in physical education are fundamentally important in the consideration of the core concepts introduced here.

The notion of embodied learning captures the centrality of the body in physical education and acknowledges the inherent ties between bodily and social regulation. Shilling's work (1993a, 1993b, 2005) has been invaluable in extending the theoretical tools that researchers in sport and physical education have to draw on in exploring issues associated with embodied learning from sociocritical perspectives. His early work directed research attention to the significance of physical education and sport in schools in relation to both physical capital and social capital. As discussed further a bit later in the chapter, Shilling and a growing number of researchers since (Evans, Davies, & Wright, 2004; Evans, Rich, Davies, & Allwood, 2008; Hay & lisahunter, 2006; Hay & Macdonald, 2010) have highlighted the fact that the embodied learning occurring in and through sport in education serves to accord differential status to particular bodies and bodily knowledge (as expressed in movement skills and abilities in physical education, health and physical education, and sport) and that, furthermore, physical capital is inherently tied to social capital. This linkage is fundamental to the recognition that learning in these contexts is firmly associated with the social regulation of bodies, social hierarchies, and values.

Here, social class and cultural values very clearly come into play, and once again Kirk's (1992) historical perspective is illuminating. After the Second World War, different social, political, and economic contexts are shown to give rise to a different orientation in physical education, embedded in which were new forms of corporeal regulation of "the masses." Thus *sport* was "portrayed as a 'language' that all people of all social classes and nationalities could 'speak' [and *embody*], as a 'common denominator' between political and cultural divisions" (Kirk, 1992, p. 50, emphasis added). In this context, the inclusion of competitive team games and other sports in physical education in Britain became inherently linked to the production of "a conflict-free society" (Kirk, 1992, p. 50) and national identity. Kirk's (1992) research also served to reveal, however, the ways in which sport in education (and the form and content of physical education) function to legitimate and reproduce established social class structures and dominant values. The focus on team games and competitive sport in physical education in Britain that has come to be established as "traditional physical education . . . had until the 1950s only been 'traditional' to the private schools in Britain" (Kirk, 1992, p. 84). As Kirk (1992) explains, the form and focus of the so-called "new physical education" (see also Evans, 1990) that was promoted as being "for everyone" celebrated bourgeois class values that were inherently gendered, promoting stereotypical images and understandings of masculinity and (through different sports) patriarchal images of femininity. Sport, as it existed and was experienced in the curriculum of the elite private schools, was presented as "a unifying medium in society" (Evans, 2004, p. 99) and a means by which to promote social order.

Body Pedagogies in Sport and Education

Recent research in the fields of health and physical education and coaching studies reflects efforts to extend both the theoretical sophistication of inquiry and the depth of understanding of pedagogy. The concept of body pedagogies has proved to be a valuable point of reference for research variously aligned with the sociology of education, the body, and health. An emerging body of research has extended understanding of the means by which socially and culturally laden messages about bodies and health are conveyed in and through sport, physical education, and education more broadly. Evans and colleagues (2008, p. 17) explain that the term "body pedagogies"

> *refers to any conscious activity taken by people, organisations or the state . . . designed to enhance individuals' understandings of their own and others' corporality. Occurring over multiple sites of practice . . . they define the significance, value and potential of the body in time, place and space.*

The concept of body pedagogies thus encourages new lines of pedagogical research linked to sport and education. It highlights the fact that embodied learning in and through participation in sport is by no means confined to formal schooling and that other contexts of participation and performance similarly represent sites of learning and, prospectively, regulation.

Policy Positions and Processes

From a structural perspective, the phrase that gives this chapter its title ("sport and education") is arguably symbolic, reflecting the fact that while the *connections* between sport and education continue to attract political and research attention, relations remain invariably framed by a context that simultaneously emphasizes a clear *distinction* between sport and education. Moreover, sport and education are often positioned as distinct policy arenas and as the responsibility of different government ministers and agencies. Houlihan's (1997) comparative research reaffirmed this as a reoccurring feature internationally and also highlighted the tensions surrounding the relationship between sport and education. The policy relations between sport and education have been recognized as a critical issue in the governance and regulation of sport in schools, particularly in relation to physical education curriculum. As Houlihan (1997, 2000) identified, schools are sites where interests relating to sport development meet interests in curriculum and learning. What happens in the name of physical education and sport in schools is most definitely of interest to sporting organizations and to research undertaken from the perspectives of sport development and sporting excellence. Houlihan (2000) emphasized that certainly in the UK, the "boundaries of school sport are especially difficult to determine" (p. 178) and that various sectors have policy interests in school sport such that it represents a notably "crowded policy space" (p. 181). It is, then, a site characterized by policy competition and complexity:

> *Each policy sector with an interest in school sport has the capacity to initiate policy and to influence the interpretation of the policy initiatives of others. . . . New policy is introduced into a context where differing and often competing interests will view young people variously as future or potential workers and citizens, health sector clients, elite athletes, consumers of leisure services, etc. Moreover, new policies are introduced into a policy space which may not only be crowded but which already possesses a pattern of power relations established as a result of implementation of earlier policy. (Houlihan, 2000, p. 181)*

Internationally, this is a situation that many readers will relate to and that is increasingly reflected in research exploring political and policy issues in physical education and school sport (e.g., Fry & McNeil, 2011; Petrie &

lisahunter, 2011). Vivid insights have been gained into the complex and contested nature of policy development relating to "sport and education" thanks to research employing sociocritical and poststructuralist approaches in investigating policy and curriculum developments instigated by national or federal governments. This work has explored and illustrated the implications (in terms of the discourses privileged in official texts and reflected in curriculum requirements) of particular structural arrangements and power relations inherent in policy arenas and initiatives that variously determine, in Ball's (1990, p. 17) terms, "who can speak, when, where and with what authority" in policy developments (see also Evans & Penney, 1995b; Glover, 1994; Penney & Evans, 1999; Talbot, 1993b; Swabey, 2006; Swabey & Penney, 2011).

A further dimension of the blurring of boundaries (in relation to policy, discourse, and pedagogy) relates to one of the opening points of this chapter—that teaching and learning occurring in and through sport are by no means confined to formal educational institutions. Regulation is thus similarly not bounded. Sport (formal and informal) beyond the curriculum and schools is a significant site of learning for children, young people, and adults of all ages. As such, it is also a site of regulation and self-regulation of bodies and identities.

Critical Findings

This section addresses critical findings in four areas of interest: policy and curriculum; the significance of discourses, structures, and relations; sport, education, health, and well-being; and coaching. Policy and curriculum development in physical education is shown to present opportunities to challenge established inequities in education, sport and society, but invariably fail to do so by instead privileging particular discourses of sport that speak to dominant (often male, white middle-class) values. The structures associated with policies and provision of education and sport are shown to play a part in this through the control of discursive and resource relations. Discussion of sport, education, health, and well-being highlights that experiences of physical education and sport, and what we learn from these experiences, is not always supportive of health and well-being. Coaching is identified as representing a further site of social and political regulation and as having the potential to positively or negatively influence health and well-being.

Policy and Curriculum: Reproducing Dominant Discourses

Research focusing on contemporary policy and curriculum developments in physical education has revealed the political and social interests at play at the interface of sport and education; it has also enhanced our understandings of the various means by which particular interests are pursued and ultimately come to be embedded in official curriculum texts and enacted in everyday pedagogical experiences of physical education and sport in schools. The development of national or state-based curricula, particularly, brings to the fore this lack of neutrality of curriculum and reveals both subtle and overt aspects of regulation.

For example, the National Curriculum for Physical Education (NCPE) in England and Wales was shown to be a highly political policy initiative, and one of the issues at the fore of debates in the early 1990s was the association of particular curriculum content with distinct national, social, and cultural values (Evans & Penney, 1995a, 1005b; Graham & Tytler, 1993; Penney & Evans, 1998, 1999). One point repeatedly highlighted at this time was the fact that certain matters of curriculum content were nonnegotiable, which illustrated overt government regulation of curriculum with a key interest in ensuring that it expressed and promoted particular national interests. For the ministers dictating the play, sport and particular sports would serve to define the NCPE and, from their perspective, were the entirely natural focus for the curriculum design (see Evans & Penney, 1995a, 1005b; Penney & Evans, 1999). In 2010, a very similar impression of neutrality was evident in the then-coalition government's remit for a renewed focus on competitive sport in schools—specifically, traditional competitive sports—with an investment plan to match this emphasis (Department for Education, 2010).

One critical point raised amid the development of the NCPE was that physical education teaching and teacher education in the UK had long been identified with the reproduction of stereotypical gender identities, particularly through gender-differentiated curriculum and staffing arrangements in schools (Flintoff, 1996; Green & Scraton, 1998; Scraton, 1993) and a gendered tradition of teacher education (Fletcher, 1984; Flintoff, 1993; Kirk, 2002). The NCPE was thus highlighted as an opportunity to challenge established inequities, and curriculum development was seen as representing a chance to enable diverse identities (relating not merely to gender but also to class, ethnicity, ability, and sexuality) to find expression in and through physical education (see also Clarke, 2002; Dodds, 1993; Figueroa, 1993). In the main, however, research pointed to this possibility as being constrained rather than enabled by the official texts of the NCPE. Research highlighted the dominant political agenda of privileging discourses of sport and sporting discourses that simultaneously "spoke" and celebrated male, white, middle-class values as the cornerstone of the NCPE. Adopting a sociocritical stance and seeking to bring issues of equity to the fore of debates, researchers revealed that the NCPE openly expressed values and hierarchies that were simultaneously classed and gendered. Given requirements aligning with the expression of only certain traditional and stereotyped gender identities in and through sport in education (Hargreaves, 2000; Talbot, 1993a, 1996), the curriculum was seen as legitimating and being set to reaffirm rather than challenge long-standing gender inequities in sport and physical education.

From a cultural and national perspective, research by Evans and colleagues drew attention to the significance not only of the content of official texts related to the NCPE but also to the silences and absences in those texts, particularly in relation to recognition of cultural diversity in England and Wales (Evans, Davies, Bass, & Penney, 1997; Davies, Evans, Penney, & Bass, 1997). Evans and colleagues (1997) identified the mix of conservative restorationist discourses and economic rationalism within and "surrounding" (in a policy sense) the National Curriculum and NCPE as potentially constituting "a threat to the ability of the people of Wales to express and define for themselves a distinctive Welsh identity, grounded in what may be different forms of physical culture and locale" (p. 289).

Thus, one important finding, and an ongoing issue for the field, relates to the extent to which government policy associated with physical education and sport in schools needs to be acknowledged as serving to constrain or advance movement toward greater equity in sport, education, and society. The contributing mechanisms are multifaceted and complex; they are political, structural, discursive, and pedagogical in nature.

Discourses, Structures, and Relations Are Significant

Research exploring policy and curriculum with a focus on discourse has highlighted the fact that from a governance perspective the significance of structures lies in the relations that they frame, enable, and constrain and, furthermore, in the discursive strategies that can then be enacted in particular policy contexts. In the UK particularly, research throughout the 1990s emphasized that conservative restorationist discourses of competitive sport were privileged in sport policy development (see Gilroy & Clarke, 1997) and were also repeatedly taken as the prime reference point in developments relating to provision of physical education and sport in schools. As indicated earlier, very similar discourses have recently come again to the fore of government and professional debates there.

Elsewhere, tensions in developments can be similarly associated with an ongoing structural and policy divide between sport and education and with government moves to reframe, directly or indirectly, structural relations. Particular government priorities for sport and education are thus reflected in particular patterns of resourcing. For example, Houlihan (1997, p. 225) identified that the Aussie Sports program in Australia probably "best characterises the attempt by sport to subordinate the PE curriculum" and noted that, "[u]nfortunately for some schools, the attractiveness of Aussie

Sports has resided in the apparent similarity with PE which has resulted in a number of schools replacing PE with the federally funded Aussie Sports." More recently, developments in Australia and New Zealand have highlighted the significant growth in initiatives, services, and resources variously arising from sport, physical activity, and health agencies that are directed to schools and variously promoted or adopted as physical education or health and physical education (see, for example, B. Williams, Hay, & Macdonald, 2011).

Sport, Education, Health, and Well-Being: Critical Insights

Although the case made for sport or physical activity in education often stresses its potential positive effect on young people's current and prospective health and its function as a desirable regulator of health-related behaviors, research relating to school and nonschool contexts now clearly indicates that the effect will not always be positive. Furthermore, research conducted by Evans and colleagues (Evans et al., 2008; Rich & Evans, 2009), McMahon (McMahon & DinanThompson, 2008, 2011), and others internationally has highlighted the fact that the processes of regulation inherent in body pedagogies reflect wider social changes in contemporary Western and global societies, in particular the influence of dominant discourses of obesity (see, for example, Lee & Macdonald, 2010; Cliff & Wright, 2010). Schooling, and sport within and beyond schools, are shown to be not merely sites for and of the regulation of bodies, health, and identities, but also contexts that emphasize *self-regulation*—arguably one of the most significant and defining features of governance and "governmentality" (Foucault, 1991, cited in Rizvi & Lingard, 2010, p. 12) in the context of neoliberalization and globalization (see Rizvi & Lingard).

Coaching: Pedagogical and Regulatory Practice

In community or club sport settings, as in schools, individuals and their bodies are differentially positioned as they are read through the lenses of dominant social and cultural discourses; they are accorded and carry different capital value. Coaches are actors in these processes, and a growing body of literature (R.L. Jones, Armour, & Potrac, 2002; Cassidy, Jones, & Potrac, 2004; R.L. Jones, 2006, 2007; Kidman, 2005) has provided the foundation for research that approaches coaching as a fundamentally pedagogical process and points to its regulatory function. Studies conducted by Lang (2010) and McMahon (McMahon & DinanThompson, 2011; McMahon, Penney, & DinanThompson, 2011) have revealed the ways in which regulation of bodies is embedded in the pedagogical practices of coaches and in the pedagogical relations and environments that are established, maintained, and legitimated in coaching contexts. While both Lang's and McMahon's research has addressed swimming coaching and cultures, their work undoubtedly raises issues for consideration by sport coaching and sport coaches more broadly. Prominent among those issues is what athletes learn and how they feel about their bodies as a consequence of the body pedagogies that feature in coaching and team management processes and that are widely accepted as part of a particular (often celebrated) sporting culture.

The contexts that Lang (2010) and McMahon (McMahon & DinanThompson, 2008, 2011) describe are characterized by the surveillance and monitoring of swimmers' performance and of their bodies. Directly and indirectly, coaches' pedagogy and the actions of others (support staff, parents, peers) in coaching settings convey messages with regard to the behaviors that are considered legitimate, the identities that may be expressed, and the bodies (shapes, sizes, abilities) that are deemed appropriate in these settings. In bringing these issues to the fore, McMahon's research, and that conducted by R. Jones, Glintmeyer, and McKenzie (2005), has also highlighted the fact that, as in school contexts (Evans et al., 2008), there is an important dynamic in coaching situations that involves body pedagogies and health and wellbeing. Thus, there remains a need for further research critically exploring the pedagogical relations and learning environments of sport coaching and sport cultures. Similarly, there is a case for more research focusing on body pedagogies and processes of regulation inherent in participation in informal sport. For example, informed by a poststructuralist perspective, Scott's (2010) research shows behavior in swimming pools to be both ritualistic and regulatory. Though participants are not involved in organized sport or education in a formal sense, they learn and abide by particular protocols that define appropriate bodily practices in the context of the swimming pool.

Key Debates

Sport continues to attract political interest at least in part because of its perceived regulatory potential in the education of young people. Discussion here highlights that it is inappropriate to assume that physical education or sport will have any specific impact on young people. In some instances, the impact may be entirely the opposite of that desired. In considering the influence of curriculum structures or requirements upon teaching and learning in physical education, attention is drawn to the scope for varied interpretations and actions, and the critical frame for curriculum development that is set by systems for assessment. The neutrality of assessment and of judgments made about learning or performance is called into question. Debate extends to physical education teacher education as an arena that can be seen as playing a key part in a self-regulating culture, and reveals new modes of regulation inherent in changing structures of provision. Amidst curriculum reforms and innovation in physical education, questions remain about the extent to which status quo is being challenged in practice and about the capacity that various individuals have to seek to do this.

Sport—A Regulator in Education?

As discussed earlier, the presence and position that sport should have in education are matters of historical and ongoing debate, as are the related issues of the form and focus of physical education (and health and physical education) in schools. Internationally, research attention has been directed toward reaffirming that sport and physical education have an important role to play in children's development—physically, of course, but also socially, cognitively, and in relation to values and behaviors that hold lifelong significance for individual health and well-being and for the economic and social well-being of communities and nations. Studies undertaken from physiological, psychological, and psychosocial perspectives have contributed to a body of research that has provided the basis for commentaries on the benefits and outcomes of physical education and school sport (Bailey, 2006; Bailey et al., 2009). In relation to the issues central to this chapter, this body of research can also be regarded as, to some extent, a commentary on the effectiveness of "sport and education" as a regulator of young people's behaviors, attitudes, and values. In reviewing research studies internationally, Bailey and colleagues (2009) concluded that that "there is suggestive evidence of a distinctive role for . . . [physical education and school sport] in the acquisition and development of children's movement skills and physical competence" and that "[i]t can be argued that these are necessary, if not deterministic, conditions of engagement in lifelong physical activity" (p. 1). The matters invariably left unquestioned, yet of critical significance in relation to governance, are the desirability and prospective effects of such engagement.

Alongside considerations of physical activity participation, there has been increasing international political and professional interest in the prospective role that sport can play in influencing students' attitudes toward learning and school and in more directly enhancing their academic achievements. The Physical Education and School Sport (PESS) project in England—developed from case study work the Qualifications and Curriculum Authority in partnership with primary, secondary, and special schools and community sport providers—pursued affective outcomes of PESS and from case study work. The Qualifications and Curriculum Authority (2006) identified improvements in school learning environments, student attitudes, and behaviors with targeted investment in provision of high-quality PESS. Schools involved in the PESS investigation were reported as seeing improvement in pupils' confidence, self-esteem, desire to learn, concentration, and time on task—precisely the sorts of outcomes in relation to learners and school environments that the government was seeking. There remains, however, a need for considerable caution in relation to claims about psychosocial and attitudinal outcomes arising from sport in education, not least because experiences of sport and physical education in schools are destined to be highly individual. As Bailey (2006) emphasized, it would be misleading to suggest any assured impact of sport or physical education in terms of attitudes toward school or learning on the part of all children, simply because provision—particularly, inappropriate provision—can contribute to precisely the opposite outcomes of those intended, including disengagement and disillusionment. Hence, from this perspective, regulation is acknowledged as always and inevitably framed by both the interpretation and pedagogical enactment of curriculum and, furthermore, students' individual lived experience.

Curriculum: A Defining Structure?

As discussed earlier, both historical and contemporary studies have high-lighted the fact that physical education curriculum is inherently tied to the pursuit of particular political, social, and cultural interests. For several decades, research has repeatedly drawn attention to the sustained dominance of the multi-activity curriculum model in physical education, such that, in the UK and internationally, physical education curriculum is associated first and foremost with units or blocks of work focused on various physical activities (Crum, 1983; Locke, 1992; Penney & Chandler, 2000). Drawing theoretical insights from the sociology of education, research has emphasized both the stability of this structure and its significance in relation to the possibilities it generates for teaching and learning in physical education. In setting a particular frame of reference for thinking about what the essential skills, knowledge, and understandings of physical education are—and what form and focus lessons will have—the very structure of the multi-activity curriculum is central to the ongoing dominance of discourses of sport in physical education (Crum, 1983; Evans & Penney, 1995b; Penney & Chandler, 2000; Locke, 1992). This structure has been actively sustained amid curriculum "reforms" with openly political agendas at play, but it has also appeared to be happily maintained (and thus largely self-regulated) by the physical education profession (see, for example, Curtner-Smith, 1999; Thorburn 2009a, 2009b).

Thorburn's (2009a, 2009b) recent critique of the contemporary policy and curriculum context in Scotland directs attention to a situation in which the curriculum purposes that physical education is called upon to address foreground discourses of health and well-being and, at least to some extent, displace discourses of sport. In this context, ongoing research has a vital role to play in documenting and examining the factors influencing the response in terms of physical education curriculum design and pedagogy in Scottish schools. Amid multiple, and not necessarily compatible, political and professional agendas, the curriculum future of physical education is characterized by complexity, contestation, and negotiation (Jess, Atencio, & Thorburn, 2011; Thorburn & Horrell, 2011).

Pedagogy: Resistance or Regulation?

While official texts may establish specific curriculum frameworks or requirements in relation to the skills, knowledge, and understandings to be addressed in and through physical education, they invariably leave notably open the matter of *how* particular content is to be addressed. Policy and curriculum research has thus emphasized that the frames that curriculum structures or requirements set for thinking about teaching and learning in physical education are undoubtedly important but do not exert a defining influence (Ovens, 2010; Burrows, 2009; Evans & Penney, 1995b; Jess, Atencio, & Thorburn, 2011; Penney & Evans, 1999). Individual teachers are recognized as always occupying a position of some agency in their interpretation and enactment of official curriculum texts. Relative (professional) freedom thus particularly tends to be associated with the pedagogical approaches that teachers seek to employ, the learning relations they nurture and promote, and the learning environments they create. Research clearly illustrates that through each of these areas, teachers will exert a very significant influence upon who learns what both in and from sport and education. However, research focusing on physical education in senior secondary schooling in particular provides a timely reminder that decisions about pedagogy are inevitably framed by broader policy contexts, their structures, and dominant discourses. In this high-stakes arena, discourses of accountability invariably take center stage, and assessment requirements and, specifically, the focus and format of external examinations serve as key drivers of pedagogical practices. Thorburn's (2007; see also Thorburn & Collins, 2006) research in particular has highlighted the fact that there is no guarantee that the progressive intent built into new curriculum requirements will be realized. This reality is reaffirmed by Hay and colleagues' research in Australia, which also emphasizes the significance of interpretation and enactment of official texts in relation to equity and inclusion in physical education (Hay & Macdonald, 2008, 2010).

Assessment: A Regulatory Reference Point

Assessment and testing thus need to be acknowledged as having a regulatory influence and function in relation to curriculum and pedagogical practices in physical education and sport in schools and beyond. Research in education policy sociology has revealed that in many respects the key to governance in contemporary political contexts lies in the combined influence of multiple interrelated policies rather than in any single initiative. Systems for assessment thus represent a key accompaniment to curriculum developments and a critical frame of reference in interpretation and implementation (Ball, 1990). In physical education and sport, it is similarly the case that at the point of formal, summative assessment of learning and performance, the skills, knowledge, and understandings that "really matter" are overt. As Evans (2004) has emphasized, requirements and judgments about what forms of knowledge matter in physical education—and how and in what contexts these forms can legitimately be evidenced—simultaneously make statements about *whose* abilities are recognized and valued in sport and education settings. Thus, neither the content nor the pedagogy of assessment is neutral. Both carry and convey value judgments and, invariably, dominant discourses of ability in physical education and sport. Hay and Macdonald (2010) have further highlighted ways in which such judgments can reflect and reaffirm gendered (normalized, established) expectations with regard to ability in physical education. Furthermore, the questions (given in the following quotation) raised by Evans and Davies (2008) in foregrounding social class considerations in physical and health education (abbreviated to PEH in their text) highlight an ongoing need for research that acknowledges the complex ways in which regulation is embedded in notions of ability and enacted in and through schooling and sport pedagogy more broadly:

> *Does PEH connect with the physical cultures and class conditions that regulate people's lives, does it offer children and young people the "ability" in the form of confidence, competence and control of their bodies' potential to deal with them effectively; or, merely help reproduce the patterns of success and failure (whether defined in levels of participation or achievement levels), along class lines that stubbornly persist in and out of schools? (p. 210)*

Physical Education Teacher Education: Mediating Legitimate Identities and Dominant Power Relations?

Sport has long been acknowledged as an important site for the expression of identities—national, cultural, gendered, and classed identities, to name a few. From political, social, and cultural perspectives, education, and more particularly schooling, similarly represent arenas in which there is an active interest in supporting the development of particular identities and, simultaneously, suppressing others. As indicated earlier, in relation to these matters, the curriculum, pedagogy, and assessment of physical education curriculum are far from neutral. The practices routinely accepted as "normal" in physical education "are not only vehicles *for* the transmission of cultural codes, [but also] they are *in and of themselves* cultural forms" (Evans & Penney, 1995a, p. 188, emphasis added); they express and represent the social and cultural construction and mediation of identities and social relations.

Given the relative flexibility associated with curriculum, pedagogy, and assessment in physical education, teacher education would appear to have a pivotal role to play in prospective interpretations of policy and curriculum developments relating to sport and education. Internationally, research continues to point to the culture of physical education teacher education (PETE) as one in which the dominant values and power relations that Sparkes, Brown, and Partington (2010) highlight are intrinsically linked to embodied identities; thus it remains in important respects a self-regulating culture, in which and by which inequities in sport and education are perpetuated (see also Brown, 1999; Macdonald & Kirk, 1996; Sirna, Tinning, & Rossi, 2008; Skelton, 1993; Tinning, Macdonald, Wright, & Hickey, 2001). PETE has been revealed as a cultural space in which bodies are read, judged, and valued in relation to dominant sporting and social values of the "jock culture" and in which expectations to take up and position oneself in relation to dominant (exclusive) identities are particularly overt. Sparkes and colleagues explain that in this culture, embodied identities are negotiated and bodies are positioned in a network of power relations that reflects the celebrated status of "the performing jock body" (p. 342).

Informed by a relational perspective, Brown and Rich's (2002) research showed that student teachers "draw on their own identities and experiences to make sense of gendered encounters and merge them with their developing pedagogies to *take, assign and receive* gendered positions" (p. 84, original emphasis). Thus the researchers highlight physical education student teachers as simultaneously being positioned and positioning themselves in gendered terms such that their pedagogy, and students' experiences of it, legitimate particular gender and sexual identities and subordinate or deny others. This research and that of others (e.g., Azzarito & Simon, 2005; Clarke, 2002; Keyworth, 2001; Sparkes, 1994; Sparkes, Partington, & Brown, 2007; Skelton, 1993; Sparkes et al., 2010; Squires & Sparkes, 1996) demonstrate the role that research has to play in challenging sustained silences and inequities in physical education and sport in schools and in teacher education. Benn's (2002) research focusing on Muslim women's experiences of PETE revealed the significant role that institutions can play in challenging the narrowness of physical education in relation to the identities (variously relating to gender, class, race, ethnicity, culture, and sexuality) that are widely regarded as legitimate for teachers and students to express.

Meanwhile, studies such as that recently conducted by Karhus (2010) highlight the fact that regulation—specifically, regulation in the context of market-driven, neoliberal politics, economies, and governance—is very apparent in physical education teacher education. It is fundamentally a regulation of knowledge ("what physical education teachers need to know") (Karhus, p. 227) and, therefore, of what they might come to know and how they will think about physical education curriculum and teaching. Cale and Harris' (2003, 2009) work has provided vivid insights into the power of governance inherent in the combination of regulatory standards for teacher education and an accompanying system of inspection of standards, the outcomes of which are directly tied to institutional quotas for teacher education recruitment.

As Dodds (2006, p. 555) has previously identified, PETE represents a complex and always changing policy context. As she describes it,

> [t]he PE/TE policy landscape is a place where constituents, organizations, and functions are never crystal clear, where respective goals often compete, where coalitions are formed and reformed over time, and where power relations constantly shift.

More research is undoubtedly needed in order to critically examine governance working amid a landscape that encompasses standards frameworks for teacher registration, requirements for course accreditation and reaccreditation in teacher education, control of student quotas, and funding of institutions as tools of governance.

Changing Structures, Changing Relations?

In England, the past decade in particular has been characterized by notable changes in the sport and education policy landscape. Most notably, the Youth Sport Trust emerged as a highly influential organization in this domain, and Specialist Sports Colleges and School Sport Coordinator Partnerships became established key features of the changed landscape (and language) of physical education and sport in schools. The terminology of PESS, adopted and legitimated by publications emerging from the Qualifications and Curriculum Authority (2004, 2006), arguably symbolized the simultaneous structural change and discursive shift, wherein sport attained and was accorded renewed authority in matters relating to physical education specifically and to education more broadly. Commissioned evaluation studies relating to policy initiatives have inevitably been primarily concerned with generating evidence in relation to identified "measures" pertinent to stated policy objectives (e.g., Loughborough Partnership, 2008). Informed by education policy sociology and policy studies, research focusing on Specialist Sports Colleges has, however, also provided insights into the ways in which criteria associated with establishing and maintaining specialist status and, crucially, retaining funding linked to that status operate in a regulatory way, shaping development priorities and strategies in colleges and in relation to their work with partner schools and other organizations (Penney & Houlihan, 2003; Penney, 2004). From a critical perspective, the measures against which the performance of sport colleges and school sport coordinator partnerships are being judged represent a mechanism of self-regulation that may well leave dominant discourses, and therefore inherent inequities in the provision of physical education and sport, largely unchallenged. The policy arrangements and the performance measures themselves, which include attainment, attendance, and "tackling obesity, overweight and underweight" (Loughborough Partnership, p. 21), highlight the extent to which wider global discourses of accountability and performativity (see Ball, 2004; Rizvi & Lingard, 2010) are embedded systemically as pillars of governance and regulation—of bodies, identities, and the forms of participation in sport and physical activity that are deemed legitimate in education.

Flintoff's (2008) investigation of one school sport partnership reaffirms the need for more research that critically explores the extent to which new initiatives are challenging the inequities inherent in long-established discourses of competitive sport and providing an impetus for new participation opportunities for more young people:

> The research shows very little evidence of equity issues forming any significant part of the coordinators' deliberations or everyday practice. The strategy adopted by most coordinators was based on equality politics and on access. An "open door" policy to the same opportunities was seen as the fairest way to cater for all children. Very few of the planned PE and sport activities were specifically targeted at pupils that have been underrepresented in traditional extra curricular programmes, and indeed, there was some reluctance on the part of some coordinators to accept that this would constitute equitable practice. (p. 407)

Flintoff's research (2008) also brings to the fore another important issue related to policy, governance, and regulation—namely, the flexibility inherent in policy arrangements and the extent to which flexibility should be associated with the potential for agency. As Flintoff (2008) observed, while policy texts and structures may appear to enable multiple and transformative interpretations and actions, that response is far from assured. The sections that follow draw on research variously focusing on curriculum, pedagogy, and assessment in physical education to further examine matters of structure and control in relation to sport and education.

Innovations in Sport and Education: Challenging the Status Quo?

While in many instances research reaffirms the strength of established discourses and ways of thinking about sport and education, a significant body of research has also been generated focusing on curriculum and pedagogical change and innovation. There is insufficient scope here to do justice to the array of international work that has addressed changes instigated by individual teachers or departments, but three curriculum and pedagogical models, each of which has provided a focus for research spanning more than two decades, arguably stand out as particularly pertinent to the interest in governance, sport, and education. These three—Teaching Games for Understanding (TGfU), Sport Education, and Teaching for Personal and Social Responsibility (TPSR)—have all been associated with "new" or "different" pedagogy in physical education and sport. As a result, they can be seen as clear evidence that curriculum requirements can be approached and implemented in creative ways that potentially counter established practice. Even so, all of them also simultaneously point attention back to curriculum and pedagogy as inherently tied to regulation.

The development of TGfU (Thorpe, Bunker, & Almond, 1986) openly challenged assumptions about teaching and learning in sport and physical education and presented alternative ideas in relation to the structure, focus, format, and sequencing of learning activities that could best support learning. TGfU has been adopted and adapted internationally (most notably in the form of tactical games approaches) and has generated significant research interest over the years in contexts of teaching, coaching, and teacher education (for an overview, see Griffin & Butler, 2005). Yet TGfU and related approaches have arguably retained a marginal position and are still regarded as "alternative" pedagogies, seemingly leaving intact the authority of "traditional" approaches to curriculum planning and games teaching.

Sport Education (Siedentop, 1994) is a curriculum model that has similarly been adopted and adapted by physical education and sport professionals internationally and has attracted significant research interest in the field (for a comprehensive review, see Wallhead & O'Sullivan, 2005). The original development reflected Siedentop's explicit concern with the relationship between experiences of sport in physical education and the wider context of sport beyond schools. The model and pedagogical approaches advocated were presented as contrasting with traditional pedagogy-of-games teaching in particular and as promoting greater student engagement and leadership in learning. Sport Education was specifically intended to enable and encourage students' participation in sport in various capacities (including as players and performers, as coaches, as managers, and as administrators) while also prompting them to challenge aspects of sporting culture, especially in relation to fair play and equity (Siedentop, 1994).

While Sport Education and adaptations of it seek to extend opportunities for learning and participation, they can also be seen, in their focus on the development of specific values, attitudes, and behaviors, as openly concerned with regulation within and beyond schools. The model is explicitly concerned with developing particular sorts of citizens and has sought to explore the capacity of sport to serve that function in educational settings. These points have been directly reflected in some of the research studies conducted, most notably those that have sought to link with Hellison's (1995) work focusing on the development of personal and social responsibility through sporting experiences (see Hastie & Sharpe, 1999; Hastie & Buchanan, 2000). Both Sport Education and TPSR place an emphasis on the "empowerment" of students in and through the pedagogy that is promoted. More research is arguably needed that critically examines this emphasis in relation to students' lives beyond sport and education, thereby exploring the extent of and limits to empowerment and acknowledging the wider social and cultural frames of reference at play amid discourses of innovation, change, and inclusion.

Nevertheless, in foregrounding students' active role in shaping learning experiences, Sport Education and TPSR also usefully highlight the need to recognize pedagogy as always and inevitably a negotiated process and experience. Studies such as those conducted by Carlson and Hastie (1997) and Kinchin and O'Sullivan (2003) in the context of high school physical education identify the mediating role that students play in and through their participation in pedagogical encounters. As others have previously emphasized (Brooker & Macdonald, 1999), relatively few research studies have foregrounded students as co-constructors of curriculum and pedagogy and, therefore, sought to examine the processes by which and the ways in which students act to support or resist the pedagogical and regulatory intent embedded in lessons. Ultimately, in and through their participation, students in physical education and sport will actively reproduce or challenge dominant discourses embedded in established practices. Like teachers, students are always positioned to express some agency; the social construction of curriculum meanings are identified as, inherently, a collaborative process, shaped by microsocial interactions (Verscheure & Amade-Escot, 2007). Thus, more research is needed that explores the extent and nature of both teachers' and students' agency in contemporary settings of sport and education.

Individual Action: Constraint or Possibility?

Research cautions against viewing sport and physical education in schools and in wider society as definitive in relation to the positions and identities that individuals can take up. For example, Flintoff and Scraton's (2001) study of young women drew attention to the *conscious* choices that they were making in relation to their participation in physical activity. This research and other studies draw attention to agency being expressed (in selective participation); at the same time, they reaffirm structural inequity in the form of sport and physical education in schools failing to connect with body cultures, identities, and lifestyles to which many young people relate or aspire (A. Williams & Bedward, 2002) and failing to engage the fact that young people's "choices" relating to participation in sport within and beyond schools need to be acknowledged as constrained culturally, socially, and economically (Wright, Macdonald, & Groom, 2003). In this context, research such as that conducted by Oliver, Hamzeh, and McCaughtry (2009) is notable in seeking not only extended understandings of those constraints but also ways in which they might be actively challenged by approaches to provision that embrace the differing identities that young people value.

Research by Curtner-Smith (1999) and colleagues (Curtner-Smith, Todorovich, Lacon, & Kerr, 1999) focusing on implementation of the National Curriculum for Physical Education in England sought to specifically explore teachers' interpretations of and responses to the "new" curriculum. A dominant theme arising from this work and echoed by others (Penney & Evans, 1999) was that in many instances the curriculum enacted in schools and experienced by students appeared to differ very little from established practices. Resistance to reform and regulation was expressed in the accommodation of new requirements within established curriculum and pedagogical practices. Many professionals will undoubtedly relate to this scenario of externally initiated reforms. Research repeatedly reaffirms the active role that teachers play in shaping the expression of policies in practice as they interpret curriculum and other initiatives associated with sport and education. Equally, however, it clearly reveals that this interpretation is set amid individual and contextual frames of reference that inform what are recognized as appropriate and feasible responses. Individual action and agency thus need to be understood as being located amid local and institutional conditions and the discursive resources that teachers have to draw on (see, for example, DinanThompson, 2002; Kirk & Macdonald, 2001; MacPhail, 2007).

It therefore remains difficult to ascertain the extent to which maintaining status quo amid the imposition of externally driven initiatives should be associated with notions of agency—particularly when such action fails to challenge long-standing inequities in sport and education (Flintoff, 2008). An alternative reading would associate such action and outcomes with the self-regulation of established practices by the physical education and sport professional communities. As much of the preceding discussion reflects, research focused on sport or physical education in schools has highlighted the fact that, in important respects, provision and experiences in school mirror and contribute to the ongoing reproduction of wider inequities associated with sport in society. Research has clearly demonstrated that established discourses of competitive sport often remain a prime point of reference for policy initiatives, and for individual action within them, such that the opportunities offered to all are framed in relation to particular social and cultural values that privilege certain abilities and identities. In this context, equity remains essentially illusionary (Flintoff, 2008; Penney & Harris, 1997).

Summary

This chapter seeks to reflect the extensive body of research in the field of sport and education that is relevant in considering matters of governance. It highlights the significance of underpinning conceptualizations of governance and regulation in relation to the lines of inquiry pursued and the insights generated from research. In this regard, research in the field of sport and education has productively drawn on work in education policy sociology, policy studies, curriculum studies, and the sociology of the body in order to challenge potentially narrow conceptualizations of governance. In so doing, it has reaffirmed the importance of sport and education in relation to issues of identity and social capital and the need for further research that engages with the complexities of agency and control amid contemporary policy networks and organizational and institutional structures. Sport (within and beyond schools), sport coaching, and teacher education are all contexts worthy of further inquiry. Research has extended understandings of the ways in which sport and education connect with social regulation, and it continues to highlight the maintenance of long-standing inequities in sport and education settings. We arguably now possess some, but still limited, insight into the mechanisms by which regulation operates and *may be challenged* amid dynamic political and social contexts.

References

Azzario, L., & Solomon, M.A. (2005). A reconceptualization of physical education: The intersection of gender/race/social class. *Sport, Education, and Society, 10*(1), 25–48.

Bailey, R. (2006). Physical education and sport in schools: A review of benefits and outcomes. *Journal of School Health, 76*(8), 397–401.

Bailey, R., Armour, K., Kirk, D., Jess, M., Pickup, I., Sandford, R., et al. (2009). The educational benefits claimed for physical education and school sport: An academic review. *Research Papers in Education, 24*(1), 1–27.

Ball, S.J. (1990). *Politics and policy making in education: Explorations in policy sociology.* London: Routledge.

Ball, S.J. (1998). Big policies/small world: An introduction to international perspectives in education policy. *Comparative Education, 34*(2), 119–130.Ball, S.J. (2004). Performativities and fabrications in the education economy: Towards the performative society. In S.J. Ball (Ed.), *The RoutledgeFalmer reader in sociology of education* (pp. 143–155). London: RoutledgeFalmer.

Ball, S.J. (2009). Privatising education, privatising education policy, privatising educational research: Network governance and the "competition state." *Journal of Education Policy, 24*(1), 83–99.

Ball, S.J., & Junemann, C. (2012). *Networks, new governance, and education.* Bristol: Policy Press.

Benn, T. (2002). Muslim women in teacher training: Issues of gender, "race," and religion. In D. Penney (Ed.), *Gender and physical education: Contemporary issues and future directions* (pp. 57–79). London: Routledge.

Bernstein, B. (1971). On the classification and framing of educational knowledge. In M.F.D. Young (Ed.), *Knowledge and control: New directions for the sociology of education* (pp. 47-69). London: Collier Macmillan.

Bernstein, B. (1990). *The structuring of pedagogic discourse: Vol . 4. Class, codes and control.* London: Routledge.

Brooker, R., & Macdonald, D. (1999). Did we hear you? Issues of student voice in a curriculum innovation. *Journal of Curriculum Studies, 31*(1), 83–97.

Brown, D. (1999). Complicity and reproduction in teaching physical education. *Sport, Education, and Society, 34*(2), 112–130.

Brown, D., & Rich, E. (2002). Gender positioning as pedagogical practice in teaching physical education. In D. Penney (Ed.), *Gender and physical education: Contemporary issues and future directions* (pp. 80–100). London: Routledge.

Burrows, L. (2009). Discursive dilemmas in New Zealand's health and physical education curriculum. In M. DinanThompson (Ed.), *Health and physical education: Issues for curriculum in Australia and New Zealand* (pp. 147–164). South Melbourne, Victoria: Oxford University Press.

Cale, L., & Harris, J. (2003). OFSTED revisited: Re-living the experience of an Initial teacher training PE inspection. *European Physical Education Review, 9*(2), 135–161.

Cale, L., & Harris, J. (2009). OFSTED—"Brief encounters of a second kind"?! *Physical Education and Sport Pedagogy, 14*(1), 41–58.

Carlson, T., & Hastie, P. (1997). The student social system within sport education. *Journal of Teaching in Physical Education, 16*(2), 176–183.

Cassidy, T., Jones, R., & Potrac, P. (2004). *Understanding sports coaching: The social, cultural, and pedagogical foundations of coaching practice.* London: Routledge.

Clarke, G. (2002). Difference matters: Sexuality and physical education. In D. Penney (Ed.), *Gender and physical education: Contemporary issues and future directions* (pp. 41–56). London: Routledge.

Cliff, K., & Wright, J. (2010). Confusing and contradictory: Considering obesity discourse and eating disorders as they shape body pedagogies in HPE. *Sport, Education, and Society, 15*(2), 221–234.

Crum, B.J. (1983). Conventional thought and practice in physical education: Problems of teaching and implications for change. *Quest, 45*, 336–356.

Curtner-Smith, M.D. (1999). The more things change the more they stay the same: Factors influencing teachers' interpretations and delivery of National Curriculum Physical Education. *Sport, Education, and Society, 4*(1), 75–97.

Curtner-Smith, M.D., Todorovich, J.R., Lacon, S.A., & Kerr, I.G. (1999). Teachers' rules, routines, and expectations prior to and following the implementation of the National Curriculum for Physical Education. *European Journal of Physical Education, 4*(1), 17–30.

Davies, B., Evans, J., Penney, D., & Bass, D. (1997). Physical education and nationalism in Wales. *The Curriculum Journal, 8*(2), 249–270.

Department for Education. (2010). *Refocusing sport in schools to build a lasting legacy of the 2012 Games.* www.education.gov.uk/inthenews/inthenews/ a0065473/ refocusing-sport-in-schools-to-build-a-lasting-legacy-of-the-2012-games.

DinanThompson, M. (2002). *Curriculum construction and implementation: A study of Queensland health and physical education.* PhD thesis, University of Queensland, Brisbane.

Dodds, P. (1993). Removing the ugly "isms" in your gym: Thoughts for teachers on equity. In J. Evans (Ed.), *Equality, education, and physical education* (pp. 28-42). London: Falmer Press.

Dodds, P. (2006). Physical education teacher education (PE/TE) policy. In D. Kirk, D. Macdonald, S. O'Brien, & M. O'Sullivan (Eds.), *The handbook of physical education* (pp. 540–562). London: Sage.

Evans, J. (1990). Defining a subject: The rise and rise of the new PE? *British Journal of Sociology of Education, 11*(2), 155–169.

Evans, J. (2004). Making a difference? Education and "ability" in physical education. *European Journal of Physical Education, 10*(1), 95–106.

Evans, J., & Davies, B. (2008). The poverty of theory: Class configurations in the discourse of physical education and health (PEH). *Physical Education and Sport Pedagogy, 13*(2), 199–213.

Evans, J., Davies, B., Bass, D., & Penney, D. (1997). Playing for position: Education policy, physical education, and nationalism in Wales. *Journal of Education Policy, 12*(4), 285–302.

Evans, J., Davies, B., & Wright, J. (Eds.). (2004). *Body, knowledge, and control: Studies in the sociology of physical education and health.* London: Routledge.

Evans, J., & Penney, D. (1995a). Physical education, restoration, and the politics of sport. *Curriculum Studies, 3*(2), 183–196.

Evans, J., & Penney, D. (1995b). The politics of pedagogy: Making a National Curriculum physical education. *Journal of Education Policy, 10*(1), 27–44.

Evans, J., Rich, E., Davies, B., & Allwood, R. (2008). *Education, disordered eating, and obesity discourse: Fat fabrications.* London: Routledge.

Figueroa, P. (1993). Equality, multiculturalism, anti-racism, and physical education in the National Curriculum. In J. Evans (Ed.), *Equality, education, and physical education* (pp. 90-104). London: Falmer Press.

Fletcher, S. (1984). *Women first: The female tradition in English physical education, 1880–1980.* London: Althone.

Flintoff, A. (1993). Gender, physical education, and initial teacher education. In J. Evans (Ed.), *Equality, education, and physical education* (pp. 184-204). London: Falmer Press.

Flintoff, A. (1996). "We have no problems with equal opportunities here . . . We've got mixed changing rooms!" *British Journal of Physical Education, 27*(1), 21–23.

Flintoff, A. (2008). Targeting Mr Average: Participation, gender equity, and school sport partnerships. *Sport, Education, and Society, 13*(4), 393–411.

Flintoff, A., & Scraton, S. (2001). Stepping into active leisure? Young women's perceptions of active lifestyles and their experiences of school physical education. *Sport, Education, and Society, 6*(1), 5–22.

Fry, J.M., & McNeil, M.C. (2011). "In the Nation's good": Physical education and school sport in Singapore. *European Physical Education Review, 17*(3), 287–300.

Gilroy, S., & Clarke, G. (1997). "Raising the Game": Deconstructing the sporting Text—From Major to Blair. *Pedagogy in Practice, 3*(2), 19–37.

Glover, S. (1994). The national statement and profile in health and physical education: Reflections from one of the writers. *Changing Education, 1*(2), 6–7.

Graham, D., & Tytler, D. (1993). *A lesson for us all: The making of the National Curriculum.* London: Routledge.

Green, K., & Scraton, S. (1998). Gender, coeducation, and secondary physical education: A brief review. In K. Green & K. Hardman (Eds.), *Physical education: A reader* (pp. 272-289). Aachan, Germany: Meyer & Meyer.

Griffin, L.L., & Butler, J.I. (Eds.). (2005). *Teaching games for understanding: Theory, research, and practice.* Champaign, IL: Human Kinetics.

Hargreaves, J. (2000). Gender, morality, and the national physical education curriculum. In J. Hansen & N.K. Nielsen (Eds.), *Sports, body, and health* (pp. 133-148). Odense, Denmark: Odense University Press.

Hastie, P., & Buchanan, A.M. (2000). Teaching responsibility through sport education: Prospects of a coalition. *Research Quarterly for Exercise and Sport, 71*(1), 25–35.

Hastie, P., & Sharpe, T. (1999). Effects of a sport education curriculum on the positive social behaviour of at-risk rural adolescent boys. *Journal of Education for Students Placed at Risk, 4*(4), 417–430.

Hay, P.J., & lisahunter. (2006). "Please Mr Hay, what are my poss(abilities)?": Legitimation of ability through physical education practices. *Sport, Education, and Society, 11*(3), 293–310.

Hay, P.J., & Macdonald, D. (2008). (Mis)appropriations of criteria and standards referenced assessment in a performance-based subject. *Assessment in Education, 15*(2), 153–168.

Hay, P.J., & Macdonald, D. (2010). Evidence for the social construction of ability in physical education. *Sport, Education, and Society, 15*(1), 1–18.

Hellison, D. (1995). *Teaching responsibility through physical activity.* Champaign, IL: Human Kinetics.

Houlihan, B. (1997). *Sport, policy, and politics: A comparative analysis.* London: Routledge.

Houlihan, B. (2000). Sporting excellence, schools, and sports development: The politics of crowed policy spaces. *European Physical Education Review, 6*(2), 171–193.

Jess, M., Atencio, M., & Thorburn, M. (2011). Complexity theory: Supporting curriculum and pedagogy developments in Scottish physical education. *Sport, Education, and Society, 16*(2), 179–199.

Jones, R.L. (Ed.). (2006). *The sports coach as educator: Re-conceptualising sports coaching.* London: Routledge.

Jones, R.L. (2007). Coaching redefined: An everyday pedagogical endeavour. *Sport, Education, and Society, 12*(2), 159–174.

Jones, R., Armour, K.M., & Potrac, P. (2002). Understanding the sports coaching process: A framework for analysis. *Quest, 54*(1), 34–48.

Jones, R., Glintmeyer, N., & McKenzie, A. (2005). Slim bodies, eating disorders, and the coach–athlete relationship: A tale of identity creation and disruption. *International Review for the Sociology of Sport, 40*(3), 377–391.

Karhus, S. (2010). Physical education teacher education on the education market—Who's defining what physical education teachers need to know? *Sport, Education, and Society, 15*(3), 227–241.

Keyworth, S. (2001). Critical autobiography: "Straightening" out dance education. *Research in Dance Education, 2*(2), 117–137.

Kidman, L. (2005). *Athlete-centred coaching.* Christchurch, New Zealand: Innovative Print Communications.

Kinchin, G.D., & O'Sullivan, M. (2003). Incidences of student support for and resistance to a curricular innovation in high school physical education. *Journal of Teaching in Physical Education, 22*, 245–260.

Kirk, D. (1992). *Defining physical education: The social construction of a school subject in postwar Britain.* London: Falmer Press.

Kirk, D. (1993). *The body, schooling, and culture.* Geelong, Victoria: Deakin University Press.

Kirk, D. (2002). Physical education: A gendered history. In D. Penney (Ed.), *Gender and physical education: Contemporary issues and future directions* (pp. 24–38). London: Routledge.

Kirk, D., & Macdonald, D. (2001). Teacher voice and ownership of curriculum change. *Journal of Curriculum Studies, 33*(5), 551–567.

Lang, M. (2010). Surveillance and conformity in competitive youth swimming. *Sport, Education, and Society Journal, 15*(1), 19–38.

Lee, J., & Macdonald, D. (2010). "Are they just checking our obesity or what?" The healthism discourse and rural young women. *Sport, Education, and Society, 15*(2), 203–220.

Locke, F.L. (1992). Changing secondary school physical education. *Quest, 44*, 361–372.

Loughborough Partnership. (2008). *School sport partnerships: Final annual monitoring and evaluation report: School sport coordinator survey.* Leicestershire, UK: Institute of Youth Sport, Loughborough University.

Macdonald, D., & Kirk, D. (1996). Private lives, public lives: Surveillance, identity, and self in the work of beginning physical education teachers. *Sport, Education, and Society, 1*(1), 59–75.

MacPhail, A. (2007). Teachers' views on the construction, management, and delivery of an externally prescribed physical education curriculum: Higher grade physical education. *Physical Education and Sport Pedagogy, 12*(1), 43–60.

McMahon, J. & DinanThompson, M. (2008). A malleable body: Revelations from an Australian elite swimmer, *Healthy Lifestyles Journal(55)*1, 23-28.

McMahon, J., & DinanThompson, M. (2011). "Body work—Regulation of a swimmer body": An autoethnography from an Australian elite swimmer. *Sport, Education, and Society, 16*(1), 35–50.

McMahon, J., Penney, D., & DinanThompson, M. (2011). "Body practices—Exposure and effect of a sporting culture?" Stories from three Australian swimmers. *Sport, Education, and Society, 17*(2), 181–206.

Oliver, K.L., Hamzeh, M., & McCaughtry, N. (2009). Girly girls can play games/Las niñas pueden jugar tambien: Co-creating a curriculum of possibilities with fifth-grade girls. *Journal of Teaching in Physical Education, 28*(1), 90–110.

Ovens, A. (2010). The New Zealand curriculum: Emergent insights and complex renderings. *Asia Pacific Journal of Health, Sport, and Physical Education, 1*(1), 27–32.

Penney, D. (2004). Policy tensions being played out in practice: The Specialist Schools initiative in England. *Journal for Critical Education Policy Studies, 2*(1). www.jceps.com/?pageID=article&articleID=26.

Penney, D., & Chandler, T. (2000). Physical education: What future(s)? *Sport, Education, and Society, 5*(1), 71–87.

Penney, D., & Evans, J. (1998). Dictating the play: Government direction in physical education and sport policy development in England and Wales. In K. Green & K. Hardman (Eds.), *Physical education: A reader* (pp. 84-104). Aachen, Germany: Meyer & Meyer.

Penney, D., & Evans, J. (1999). *Politics, policy, and practice in physical education*. London: Spon.

Penney, D., & Harris, J. (1997). Extra-curricular physical education: More of the same for the more able? *Sport, Education, and Society, 2*(1), 41–54.

Penney, D., & Houlihan, B. (2003). Higher education institutions and Specialist Schools: Potential partnerships. *Journal of Education for Teaching, 29*(3), 235–248.

Petrie, K., & lisahunter. (2011). Primary teachers, policy, and physical education. *European Physical Education Review, 17*(3), 325–339.

Qualifications and Curriculum Authority. (2004). *High quality PE and sport for young people*. London: Department for Education and Skills.

Qualifications and Curriculum Authority. (2006). *PE and sport: Changing schools for the better*. London: Author.

Ranson, S. (2008). The changing governance of education. *Educational Management, Administration, and Leadership, 36*(2), 201–219.

Rich, E., & Evans, J. (2009). Now I am NObody, see me for who I am: The paradox of performativity. *Gender and Education, 21*(1), 1–16.

Rizvi, F., & Lingard, B. (2010). *Globalizing education policy*. London: Routledge.

Scraton, S. (1993). Equality, coeducation, and physical education in secondary schooling. In J. Evans (Ed.), *Equality, Education, and Physical Education*. London: Falmer Press.

Scott, S. (2010). How to look good (nearly) naked: The performative regulation of the swimmer's body. *Body & Society, 16*(2), 143–168.

Shilling, C. (1993a). *The body and social theory*. London: Sage.

Shilling, C. (1993b). The body, class and social inequalities. In J. Evans (Ed.), *Equality, education, and physical education* (pp. 139-153). London: Falmer Press.

Shilling, C. (2005). *The body in culture, technology, and society*. London: Sage.

Siedentop, D. (1994). *Sport education: Quality PE through positive sport experiences*. Champaign, IL: Human Kinetics.

Sirna, K., Tinning, R., & Rossi, T. (2008). The social tasks of learning to become a physical education teacher: Considering the HPE subject department as a community of practice. *Sport, Education, and Society, 13*(3), 285–300.

Skelton, A. (1993). On becoming a male physical education teacher: The informal culture of students and the construction of hegemonic masculinity. *Gender and Education, 5*(3), 289–303.

Sparkes, A. (1994). Self, silence, and invisibility as a beginning teacher: A life history of lesbian experience. *British Journal of Sociology of Education, 15*(1), 93–118.

Sparkes, A., Brown, D.H.K., & Partington, E. (2010). The "jock body" and the social construction of space: The performance and positioning of cultural identity. *Space and Culture, 13*(3), 333–347.

Sparkes, A., Partington, E., & Brown, D. (2007). Bodies as bearers of value: The transmission of jock culture via the "Twelve Commandments." *Sport, Education, and Society, 12*(3), 295–316.

Squires, S., & Sparkes, A. (1996). Circles of silence: Sexual identity in physical education and sport. *Sport, Education, and Society, 1*(1), 77–102.

Swabey, K. (2006). *The 1992 Australian Senate inquiry into physical and sport education: Representations of the field*. Unpublished doctoral dissertation, University of Queensland, Brisbane.

Swabey, K., & Penney, D. (2011). Using discursive strategies, playing policy games, and shaping the future of physical education. *Sport, Education, and Society, 16*(1), 67–87.

Talbot, M. (1993a). A gendered physical education: Equality and sexism. In J. Evans (Ed.), *Equality, education, and physical education* (pp. 74-89). London: Falmer Press.

Talbot, M. (1993b). Physical education and the National Curriculum: Some political issues. In G. McFee & A. Tomlinson (Eds.), *Education, sport, and leisure: Connections and controversies* (pp. 34-64). Brighton, UK: Chelsea School Research Centre.

Talbot, M. (1996). Gender and National Curriculum Physical Education. *British Journal of Physical Education, 27*(1), 5–7.

Thorburn, M. (2007). Achieving conceptual and curriculum coherence in high-stakes school examinations in physical education. *Physical Education and Sport Pedagogy, 12*(2), 163–184.

Thorburn, M. (2009a). Opportunities and challenges for physical education. In M. Thorburn & S. Gray (Eds.), *Physical education: Picking up the baton* (pp. 1–7). Edinburgh: Dunedin Academic Press.

Thorburn, M. (2009b). What future for physical education? In M. Thorburn & S. Gray (Eds.), *Physical education: Picking up the baton* (pp. 68–77). Edinburgh: Dunedin Academic Press.

Thorburn, M., & Collins, D. (2006). The effects of an integrated curriculum model on student learning and attainment. *European Physical Education Review, 12*(1), 31–50.

Thorburn, M., & Horrell, A. (2011). Power, control, and professional influence: The curious case of physical education in Scotland. *Scottish Educational Review, 43*(2), 71–83.

Thorpe, R., Bunker, D., & Almond, L. (Eds.). (1986). *Rethinking games teaching*. Loughborough, UK: Department of Physical Education and Sports Science, Loughborough University of Technology.

Tinning, R., Macdonald, D., Wright, J. & Hickey, C. (2001). *Becoming a physical education teacher: Contemporary and enduring issues*. Frenchs Forest, New South Wales: Prentice Hall.

Verscheure, I., & Amade-Escot, C. (2007). The gendered construction of physical education content as the result of the differentiated didactic contract. *Physical Education and Sport Pedagogy, 12*, 245–272.

Wallhead, T., & O'Sullivan, M. (2005). Sport education: Physical education for the new millennium? *Physical Education and Sport Pedagogy, 10*(2), 181–210.

Williams, A., & Bedward, J. (2002). Understanding girls' experience of physical education: Relational analysis and situated learning. In D. Penney (Ed.), *Gender and physical education: Contemporary issues and future directions* (pp. 146–160). London: Routledge.

Williams, B., Hay, P.J., & Macdonald, D. (2011). The outsourcing of health, sport, and physical education work: A state of play. *Physical Education and Sport Pedagogy, 16*(4), 399–416.

Wright, J., Macdonald, D., & Groom, L. (2003). Physical activity and young people: Beyond participation. *Sport, Education, and Society, 8*(1), 17–33.

Epilogue

The Social Sciences of Sport, Exercise, and Health: Some Final Thoughts

As I write these concluding remarks, the world of sport—locally, nationally, and globally—seems beset by a range of problems and concerns yet also contains in its subcultures people and practices that enhance our lived experiences and the communities we form. The more negative features of contemporary sport include, to name a few, betting scandals, drug use, unethical behavior, violence, and discrimination along the lines of class, gender, ethnicity, and disability. In addition, power and control of such worlds and subcultures are exercised in unaccountable, opaque, and undemocratic ways. Does this state of play reflect a broader societal context, or are these social issues and concerns derived from or exacerbated by certain aspects of sporting subcultures? For social scientists, the answer lies in probing the specific context, and the evidence suggests that sport does not just reflect society but that, in certain respects, its subcultures can compound wider dilemmas and concerns.

The insights and evidence offered in this collection make clear the benefits of taking a social science perspective on the challenges facing sport worlds, as well as the prospects for those worlds. Several strands stand out. First, things are not always what they seem. Commonsense assumptions regarding the role, function, meaning, and impact of sport do not provide a sound basis on which to assess its social worth to individuals and the communities they form. Social scientists seek to establish how things really are rather than rely on explanations offered by those in positions of power. They debunk, challenge, and critique, thus using their knowledge to question the status quo. Second, social science knowledge reveals how complex, contradictory, and unpredictable certain aspects of sport and of the sporting experience can be. There is no magic formula for explaining elite performance, no instant use of sport to solve social ills. There are no simple answers or solutions, but we can sometimes suggest what not to do as much as what we could or should do.

Third, the social science knowledge contained in this collection should empower readers to develop a healthy skepticism toward the claims made by such groups as politicians, sport officials, and media personnel regarding the effect of sport on individuals and communities. It should also engage social groups seeking social change and making sport a better place and space. The authors may differ in their disciplinary approaches and methods, but they all share an assumption that can be expressed succinctly as "show me the evidence." More specifically, social scientists of sport bring to bear a sensitivity to change and continuity over time and across space—both in the realm of individual perceptions, thoughts, and feelings and in cultural, economic, and political activity—which requires them to hold those making claims about the role and meaning of sport to account, as should readers of this book.

It is not sufficient, however, to debunk and critique, vital though that is. It is also necessary to map out the sort of sport worlds that are possible and desirable. Hence, reference is made in this book's introduction to the notion of sport and human development. As argued there, we have to become sensitive to the production, dissemination, curricular use, and application of the knowledge we provide. Social scientists enable us to ask crucial questions such as the following: How wasteful is the present system? Who are the winners and the losers in global sport—both on and off the field of play, at different levels of sport, and in different modes of movement culture? What are the costs, as well as the health benefits, of the system being constructed—for the individual, the community, and society as a whole? In addition, a social science perspective keeps open the possibility of developing the social-trustee, civic science, and professionalism approach discussed in the introduction.

Of course, each chapter varies on the type of critique offered and the vision the author provides for the future. This diversity reflects disciplinary differences and emphases, as well as each author's cultural context and background. The authors have each ably captured the "known knowns" and indicated the "known unknowns" of their areas as they relate to sport and physical activity. But there are also "unknown unknowns" about sport—things we have yet to think about and areas where we have to think outside of the box. Social science helps us do this, and the advocacy of a human development model arguably enhances this possibility because it provides us with a different way to see the use and study of sport; that is, social science equips us with different thinking tools. In pursuing this endeavor, one needs to be ever mindful of not only what knowledge we generate but also for whom and for what.

The adoption of a human development model is not easy. For students, it can be uncomfortable as it asks us to recognize that things are not as they seem to be and that our own beliefs and assumptions are open to scrutiny. In addition, social scientists who teach students in departments of physical education, exercise, and health sciences know only too well that the subject area is increasingly being (re)embedded in a sport-medical-industrial complex. That is, governments across the globe want such departments to produce bioscientific knowledge that aids in the development of elite sport performance and whose proponents claim to be able to "solve" the health problems of individuals. In this scenario, social scientists are considered useful in the production and transference of knowledge regarding the gaining or hosting and the social use of mega-events. Students quickly learn whose knowledge counts, both in sport in general and in particular departments—you have to have impact.

Yet the problems, challenges, and dilemmas facing sport worlds cannot be addressed solely from a bioscientific perspective. Indeed, in certain respects, such knowledge is part of the problem rather than the solution—consider, for example, the revelations about the toxic nature of Australian sport culture revealed in early 2013 and the disclosures regarding elite cyclist Lance Armstrong. In other aspects, bioscience is just ill equipped to deal with questions regarding, for example, ethics, perception, identity, community, politics, and economics. Accordingly, this collection identifies four broad areas of identity, community, capital, and governance to which social science can contribute. The authors have provided us with telling insights into how things really are. Our challenge is to use such knowledge to make a difference, to build sport worlds that are less wasteful of lives and resources—worlds in which a healthy habitus can be expressed and a living habitat can thrive. In this way, communities and nations could use sport to create mutual understanding of and respect for different body cultures and traditions.

Failure to do so will ensure that we continue along the trajectory we are already on. Social science knowledge shows us that this trajectory reflects past and present actions but also reminds us that it does not have to be this way. This collection points out that the future is still to be made, that alternatives exist, and that we can use a social science perspective to equip ourselves to map out a better sporting future.

Index

Note: The italicized *f* and *t* following page numbers refer to figures and tables, respectively.

About the Editor

Joseph Maguire, PhD, is a professor of sociology of sport in the School of Sport, Exercise and Health Sciences at Loughborough University in the United Kingdom. He is a past president of both the International Sociology of Sport Association (ISSA) and International Sociological Association Research Committee 27 (Sociology of Sport). He is on the executive board of the International Council of Sport Science and Physical Education and has acted as an assessor for the Association of Commonwealth Universities Scholarship Scheme. He has served on scientific committees for the World Congress of Sociology and has pre-

sented papers at the American Sociological Association, British Sociological Association, and World Congresses in Sociology and the Sociology of Sport. He is a member of the ESRC Peer Review College. His recent publications include the single-authored text *Reflections on Process Sociology and Sport*: *Walking the Line* and the coedited texts *Sport Across Asia: Politics, Cultures, and Identities* and *Sport and Migration: Borders, Boundaries and Crossings.*